LIVING NUDE STATUES

LIVE MODELS TRANSFORMED INTO STATUES

GEORGE ARTHUR LAREAU
KORINA S MITCHELL

SUFI GEORGE BOOKS
PHOENIX

ISBN 978-885570-21-X

Other photography books by George Arthur Lareau

PINHOLE BODYSCAPES:
Pinhole Camera Color Nude Photographs
pinhole.sufigeorge.net

SURREAL BODYSCAPES
Pinhole Camera Color Nude Photographs
surreal.sufigeorge.net

TABLE OF CONTENTS

FOREWORD

Living Nude Statues began as my search for great poses for models. As a specialist in photographing model portfolios, I have relied on poses that the models come up with themselves. However, this produced a lot of rather haphazard images, many of which I was too embarrassed to show. And thus began my search for great poses.

Naturally, the most admired poses are found in museums, so I copied photos of nude female statues from museums around the world to use as posing guides.

With this collection of statue poses to use with my models, I was able to create wonderful images. Then, I wondered what it would be like to turn these photographs of models in statue poses back into statues again, using photo manipulation techniques. By teaming up with Korina Mitchell, a photographer who has exceptional Photoshop skills, my wondering became wonderment at the results.

This coffee table book includes a dozen Phoenix, Arizona models who worked hard to match the poses they saw in my museum photos of nude female statues. I photographed these models in front of a green screen and later added digital backgrounds that I obtained from various sources online.

I have selected the ten best photos of each shoot, and with the additional ten for the statue versions, each model is featured on twenty pages in the book. Each set of photographs is shown on facing pages with the studio shot on the left and its transformation into a statue on the right.

George Arthur Lareau
Phoenix, Arizona
March 1, 2014

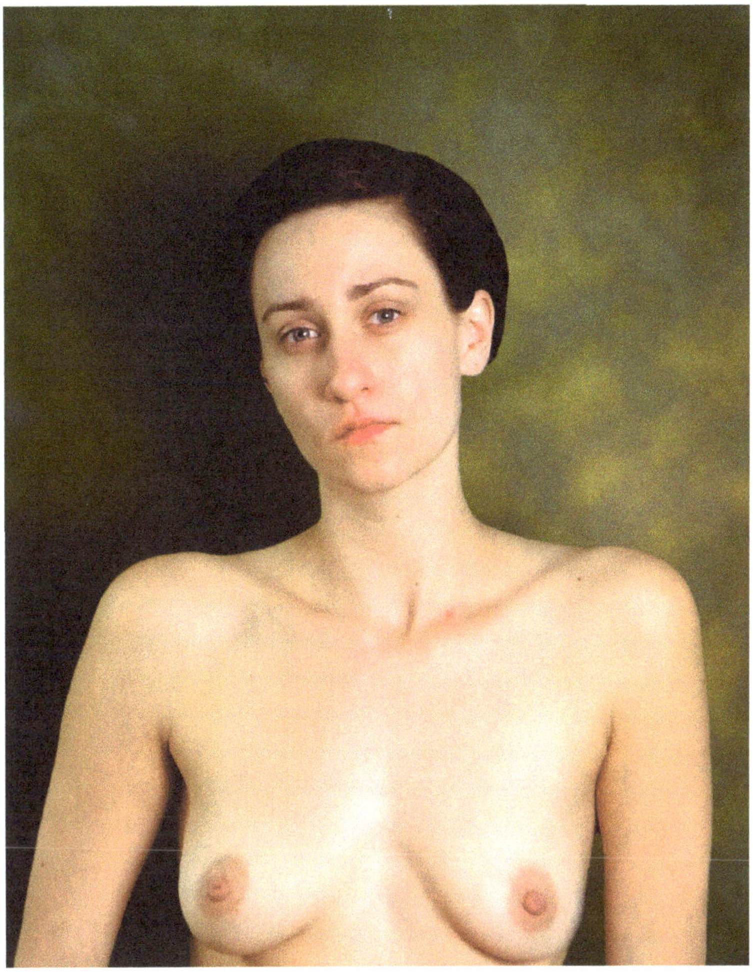

Angela Marguerite

Height 5'7" Weight 125 lbs Bust 35" Waist 26" Hips 37" Cup C

I have been modeling a few years now and it one of my favorite things to do. I am honored to be living art. I see the human form as something to be celebrated and designed to inspire. I am a bit of an artsy/hippie/peace and love type of gal.

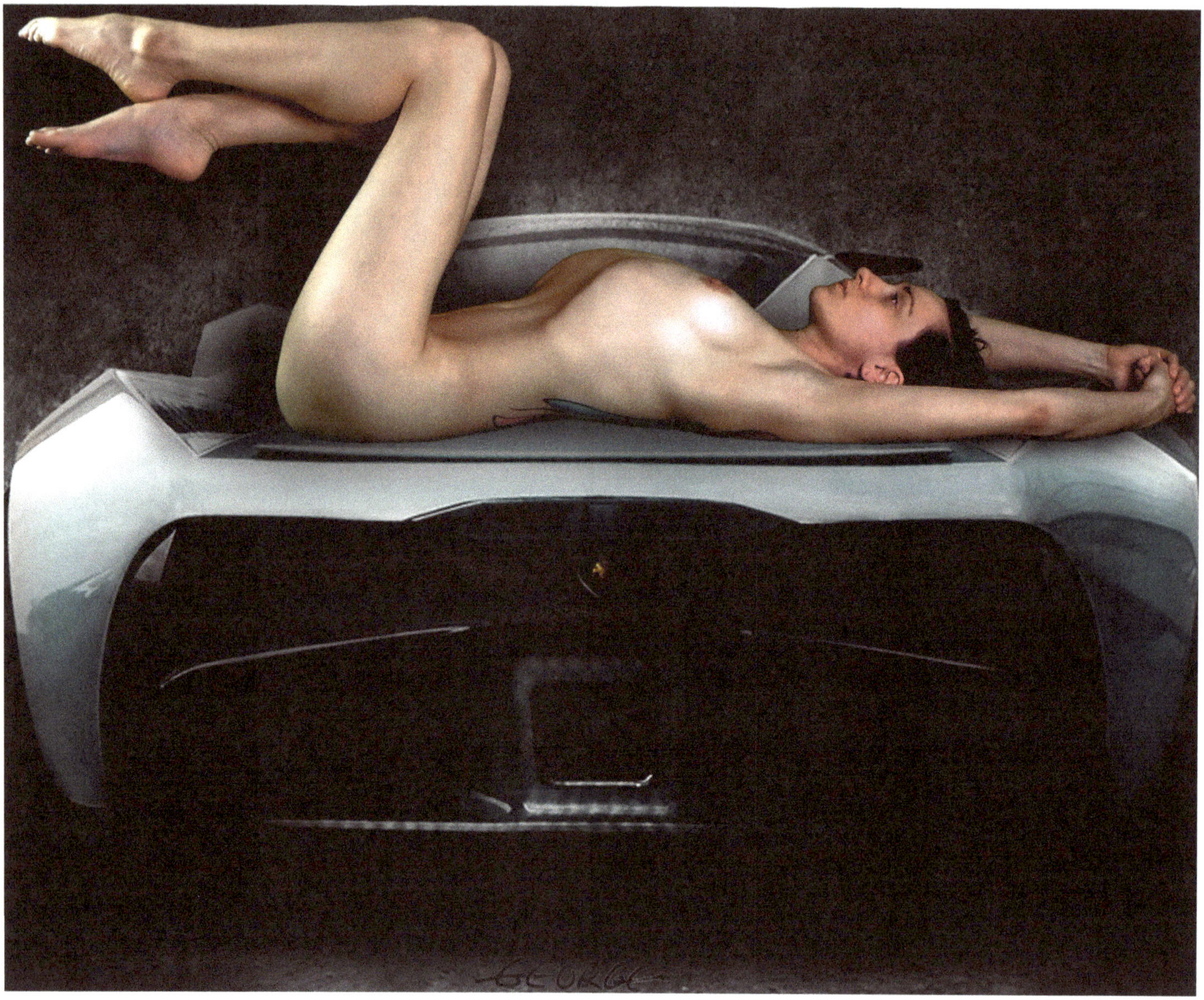
GEORGE

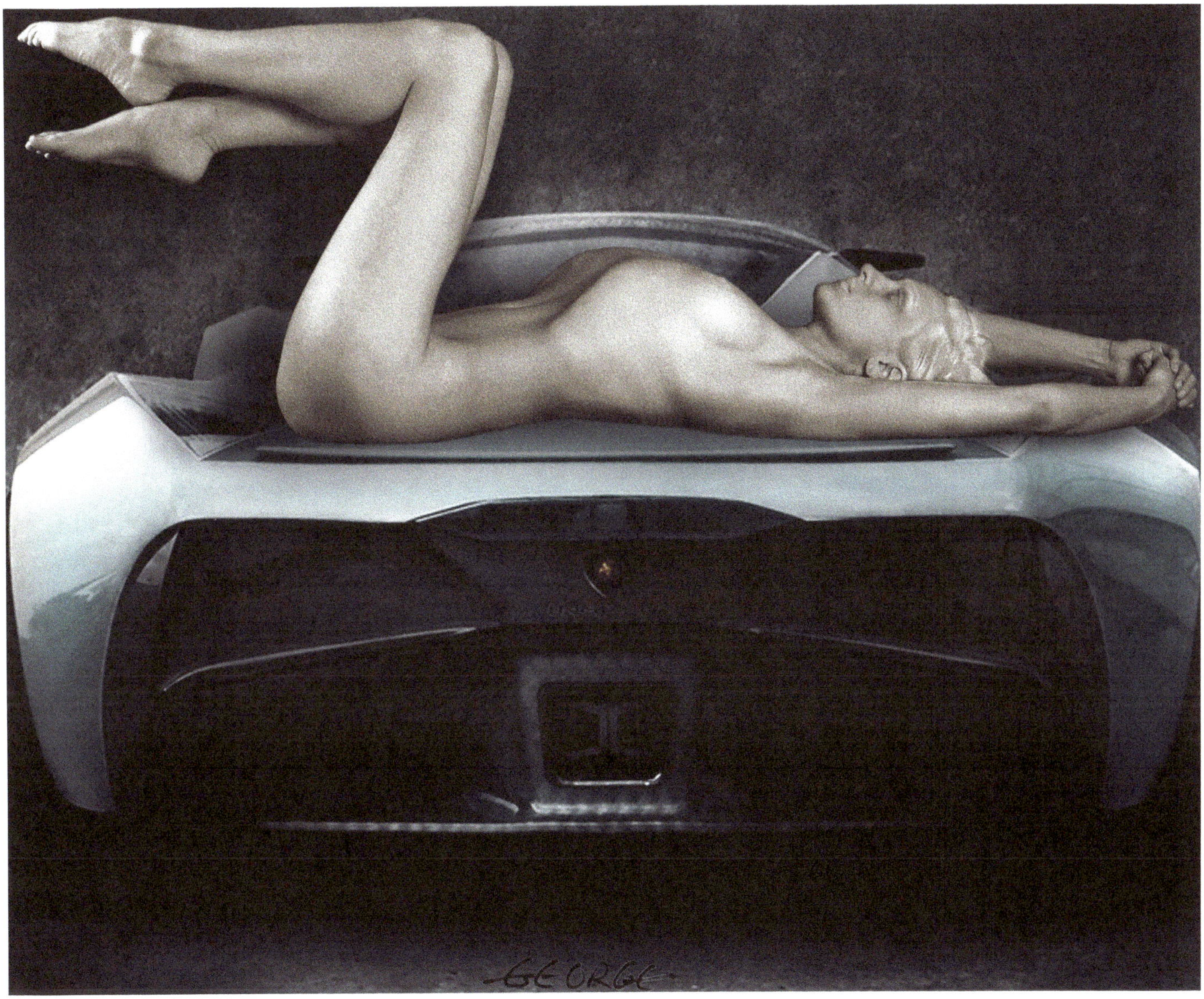
GEORGE

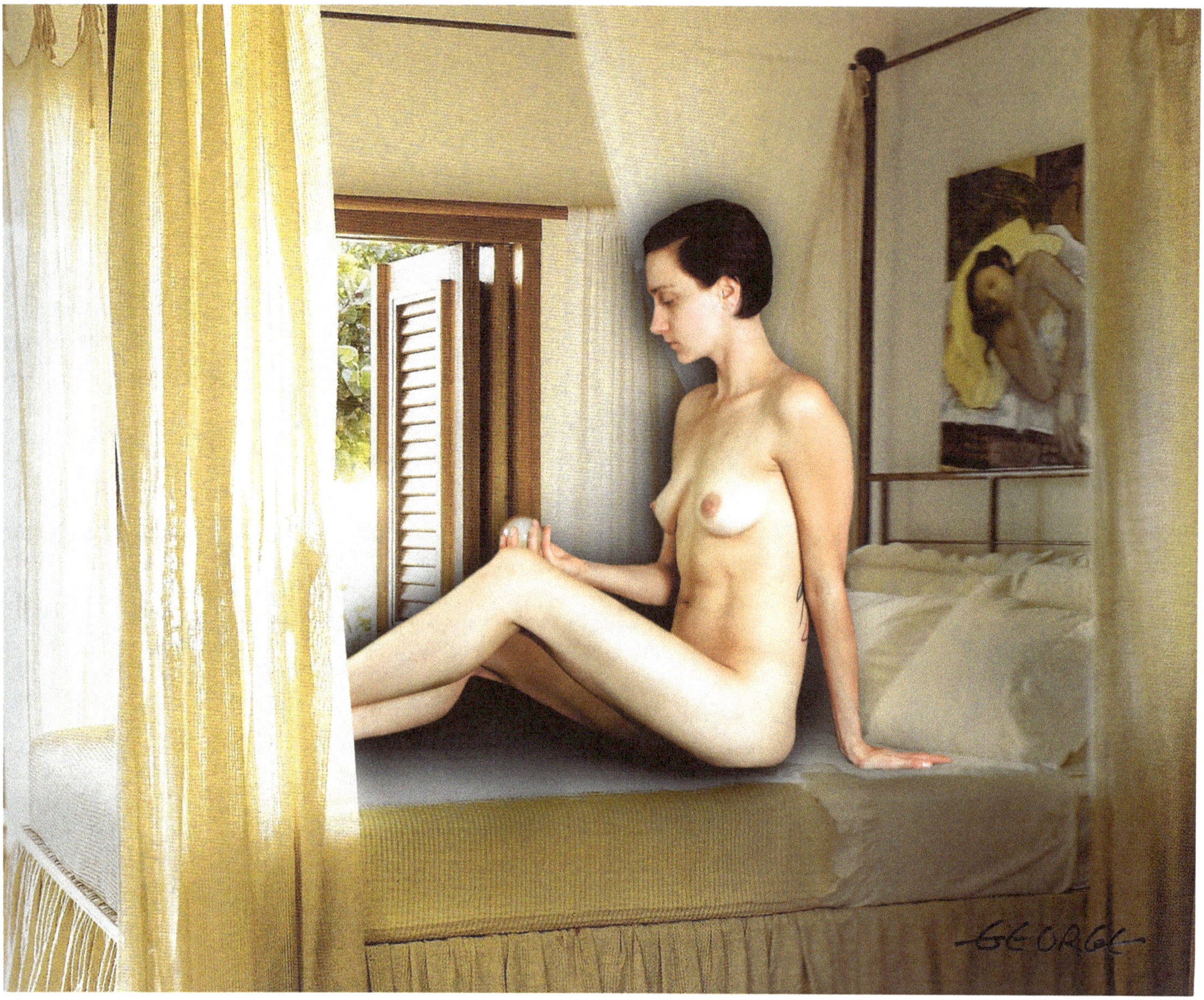
GEORGE

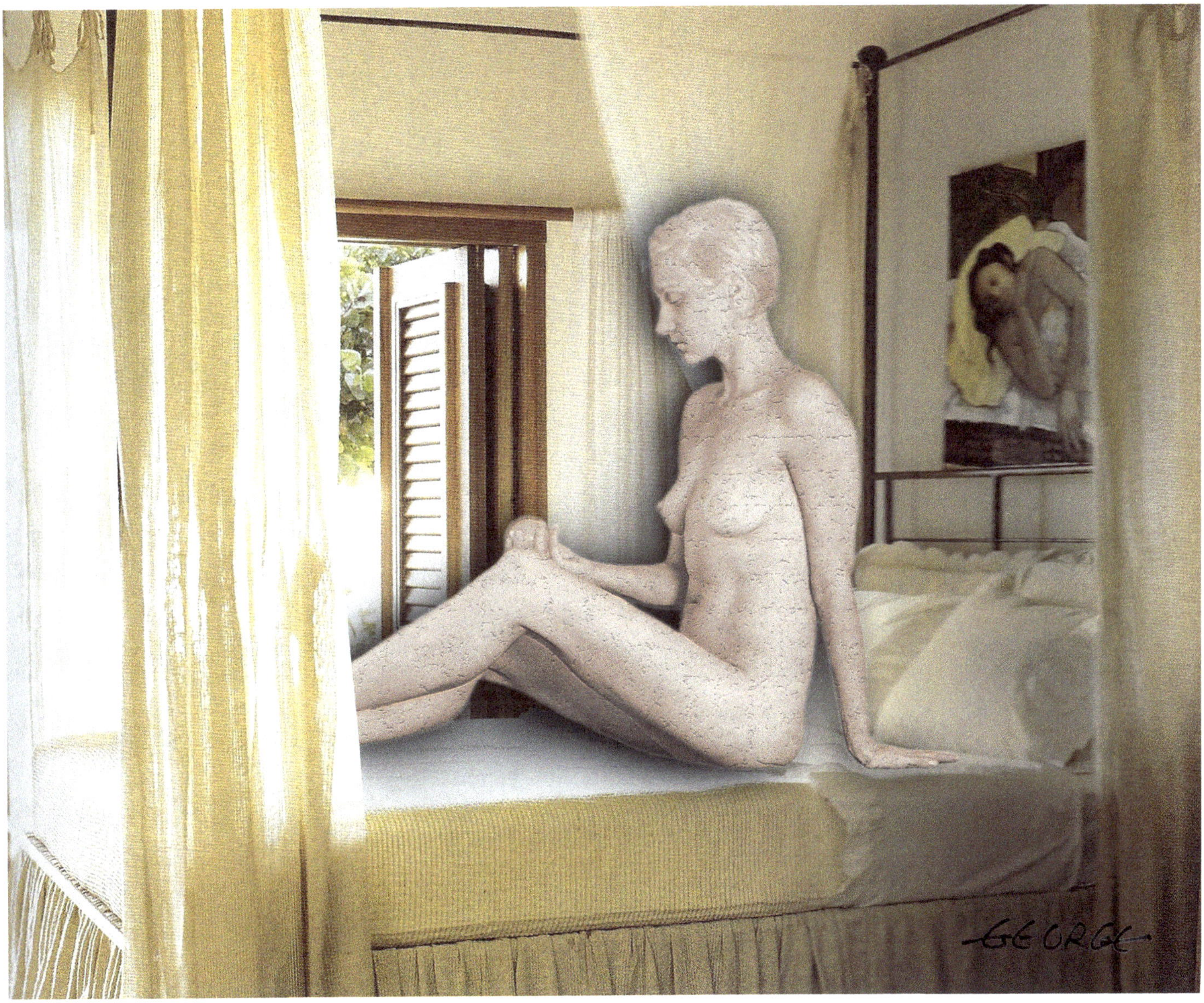
GEORGE

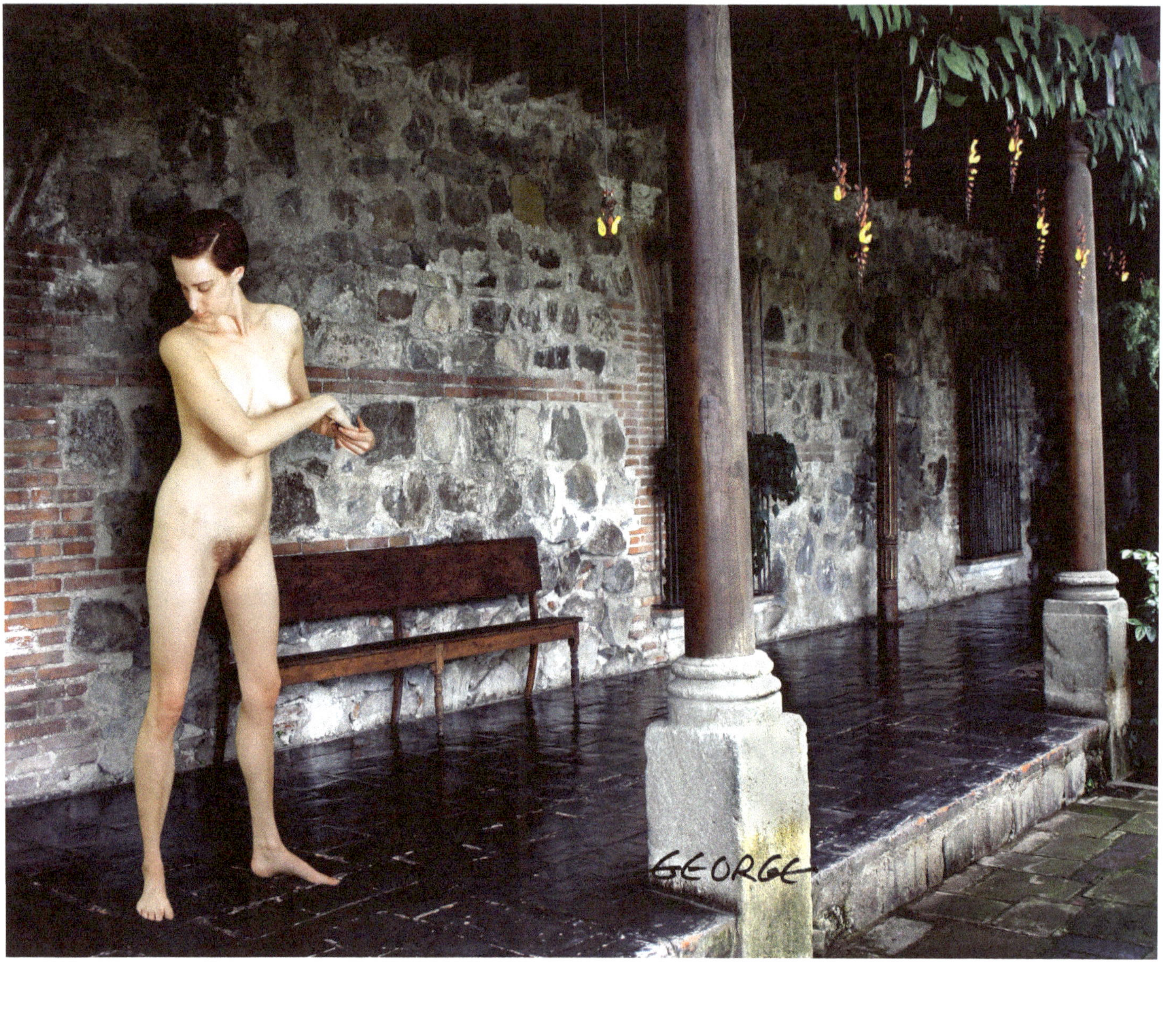
GEORGE

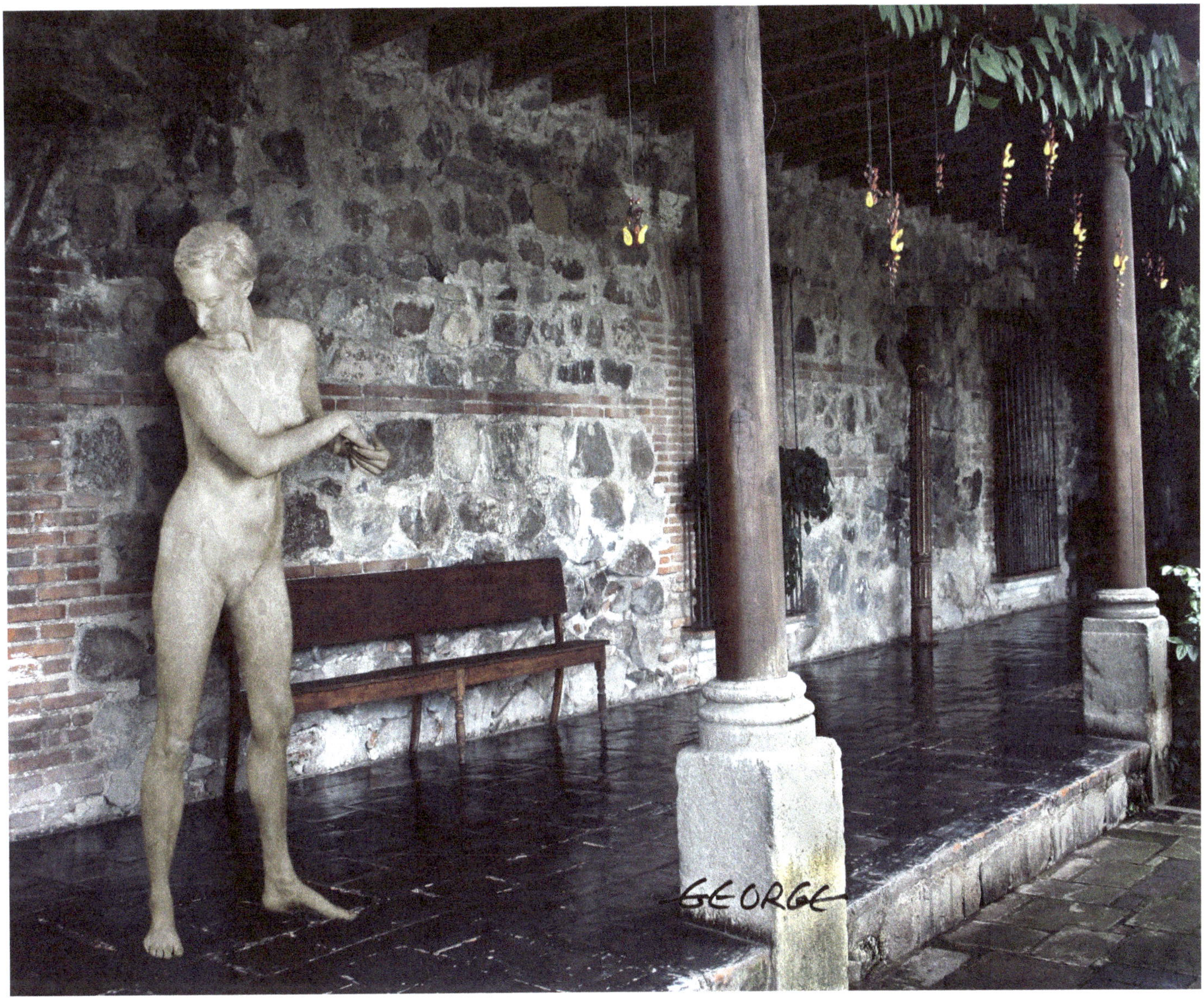
GEORGE

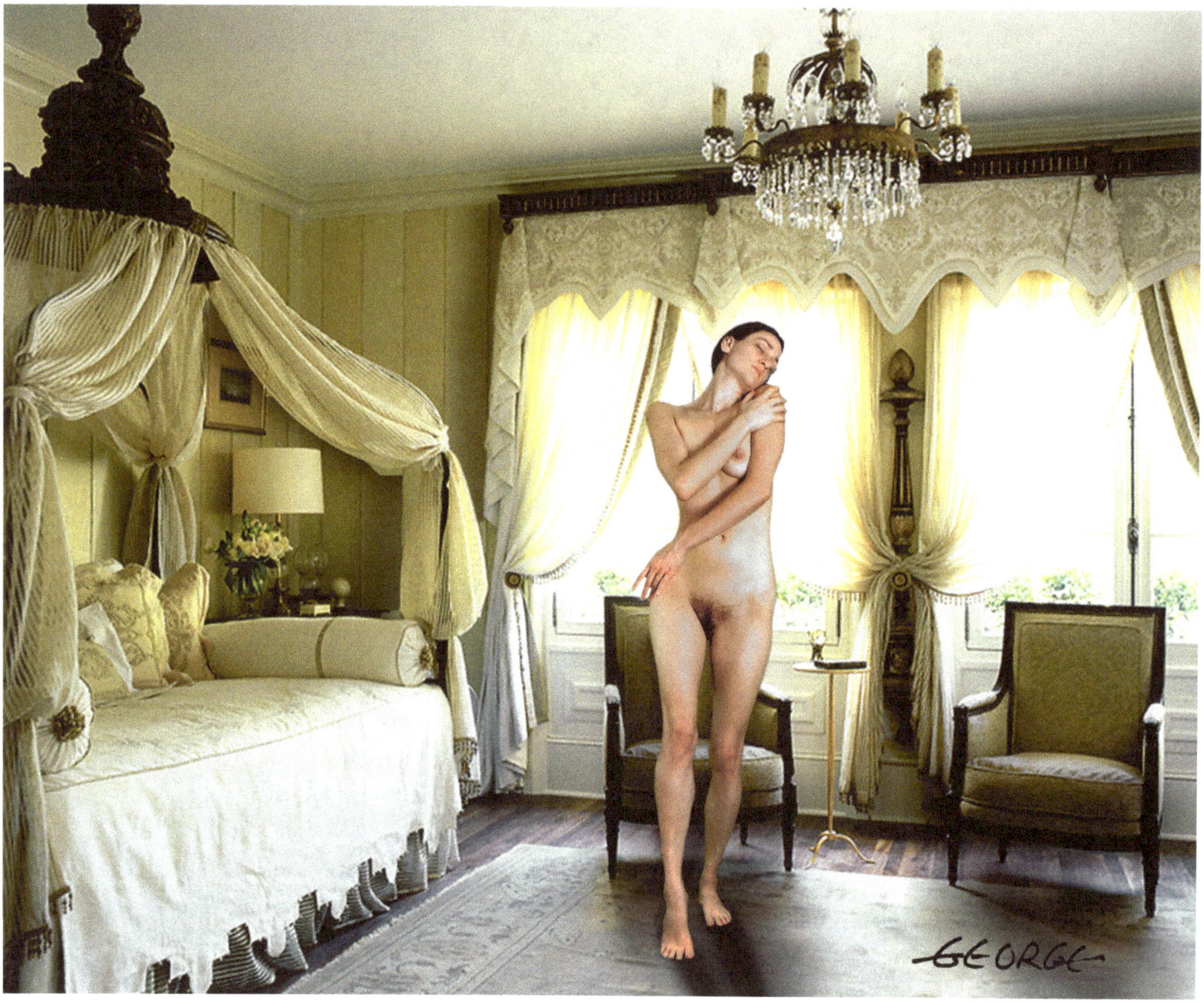
GEORGE

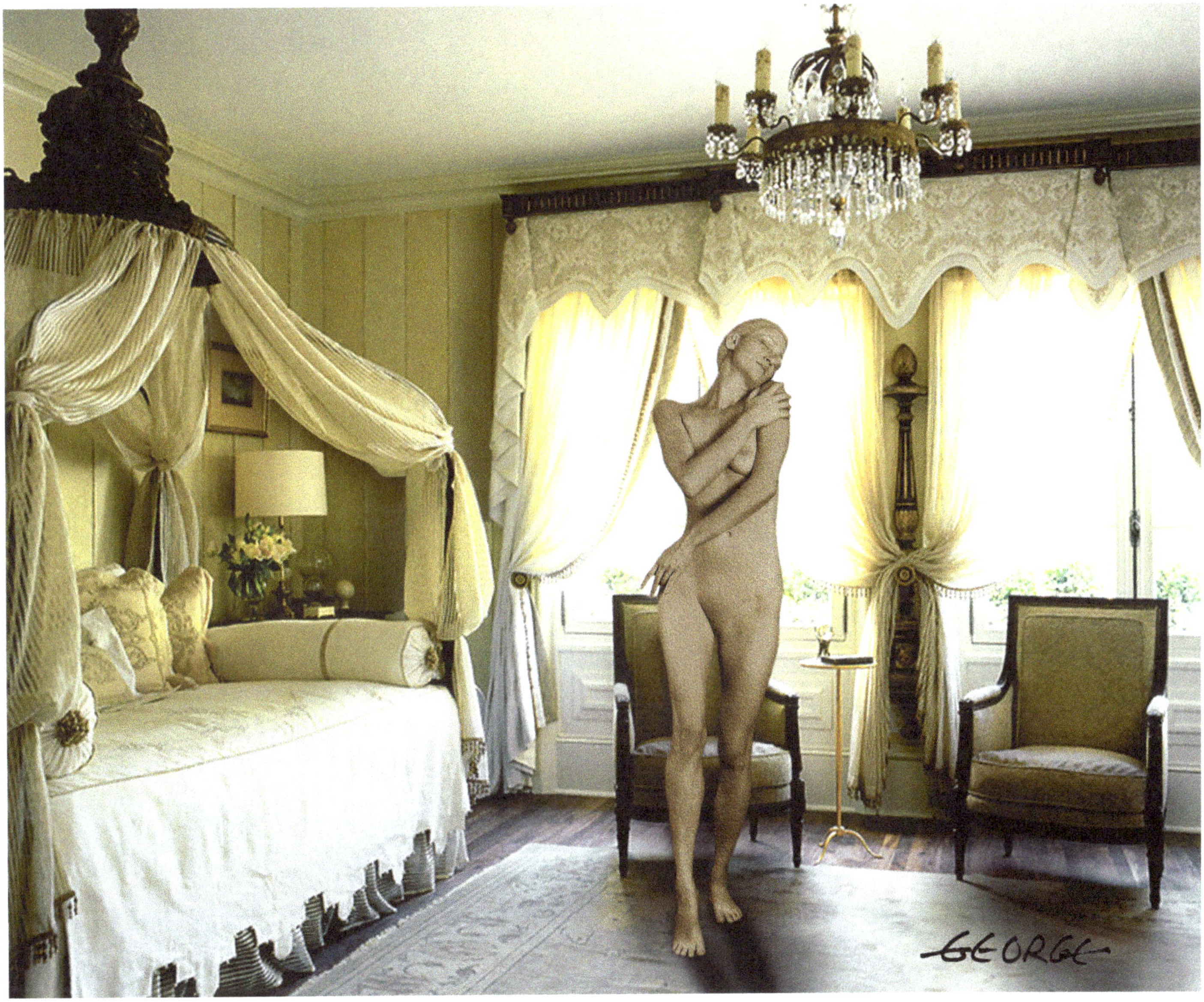
GEORGE

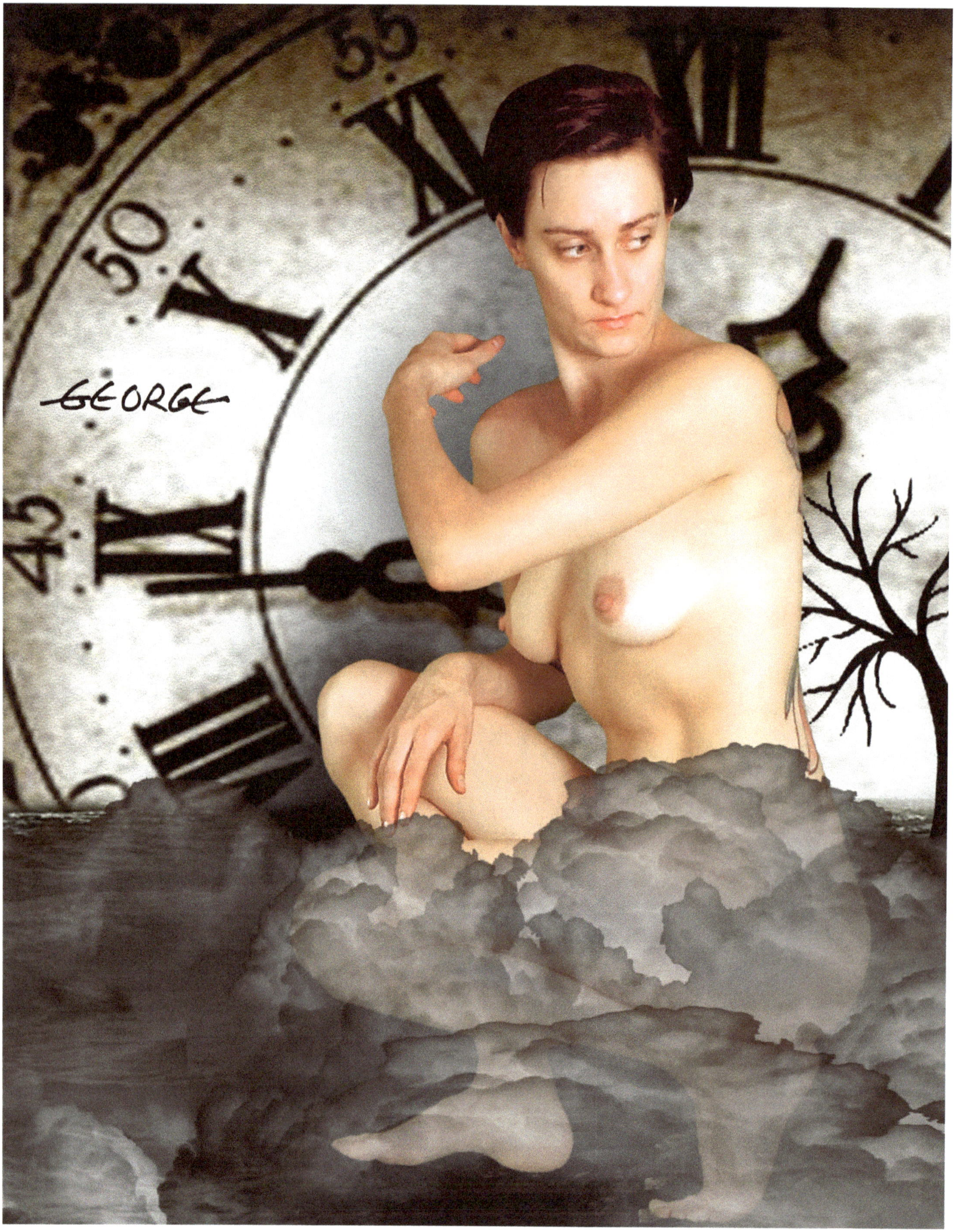
GEORGE

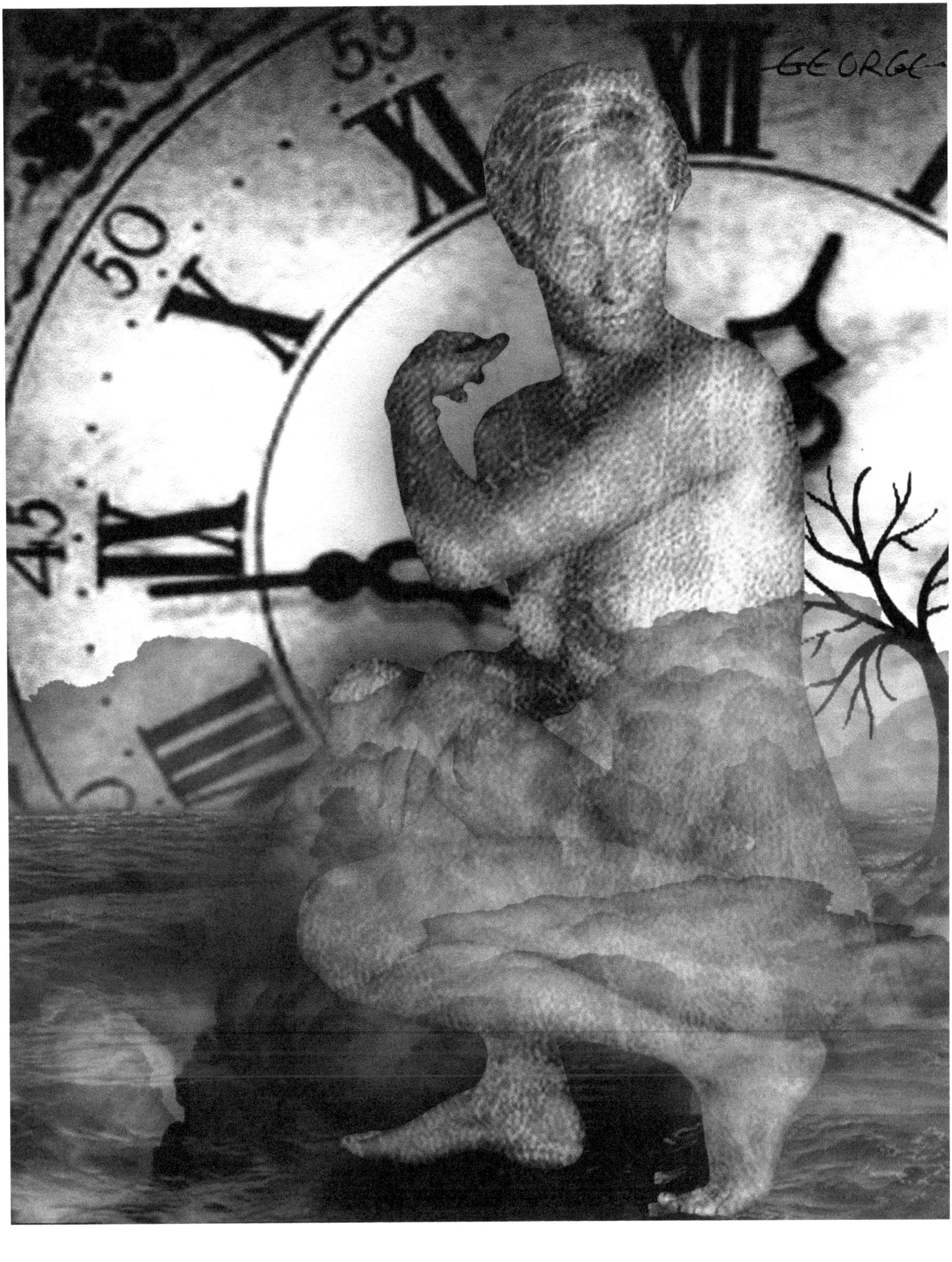
GEORGE

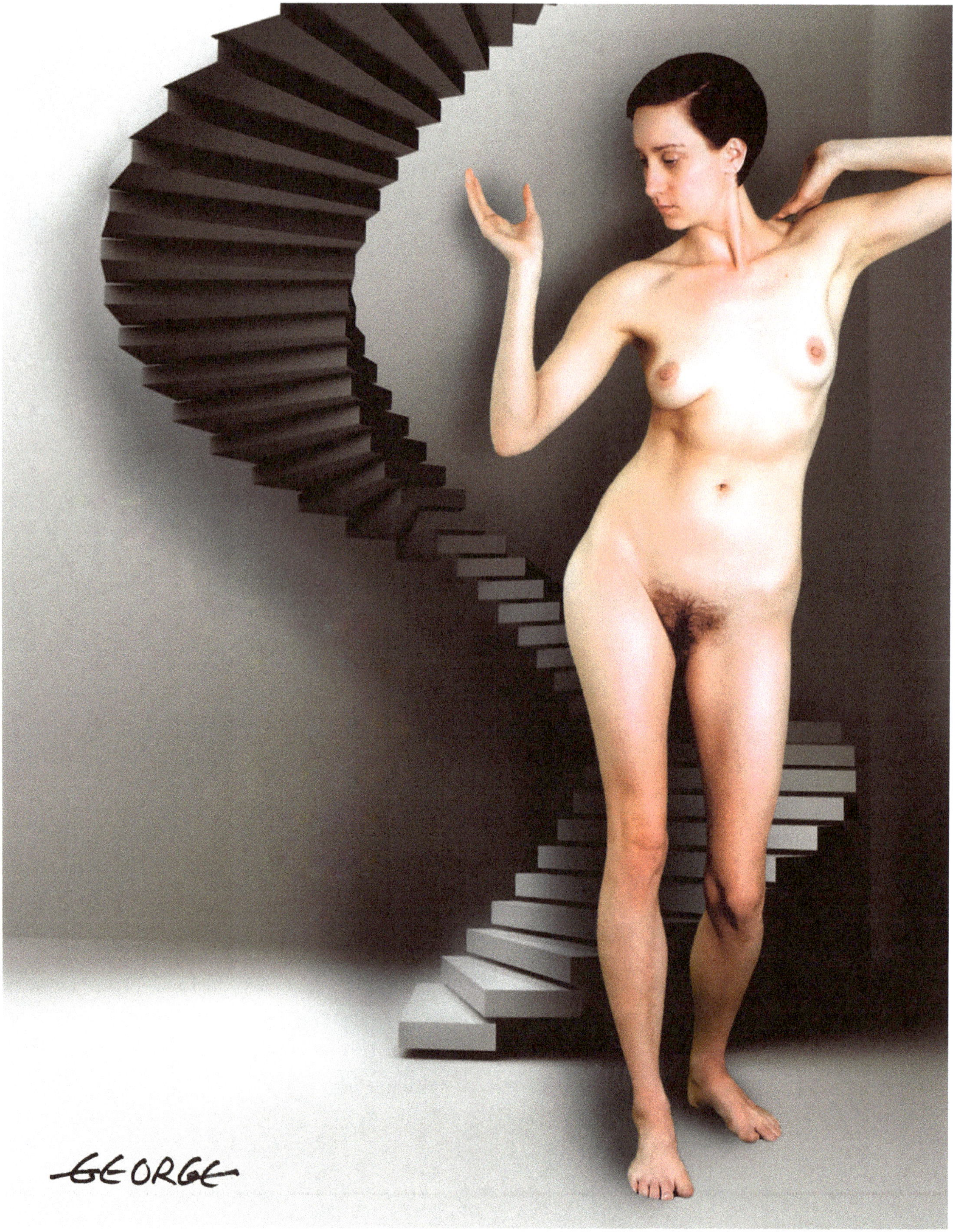
GEORGE

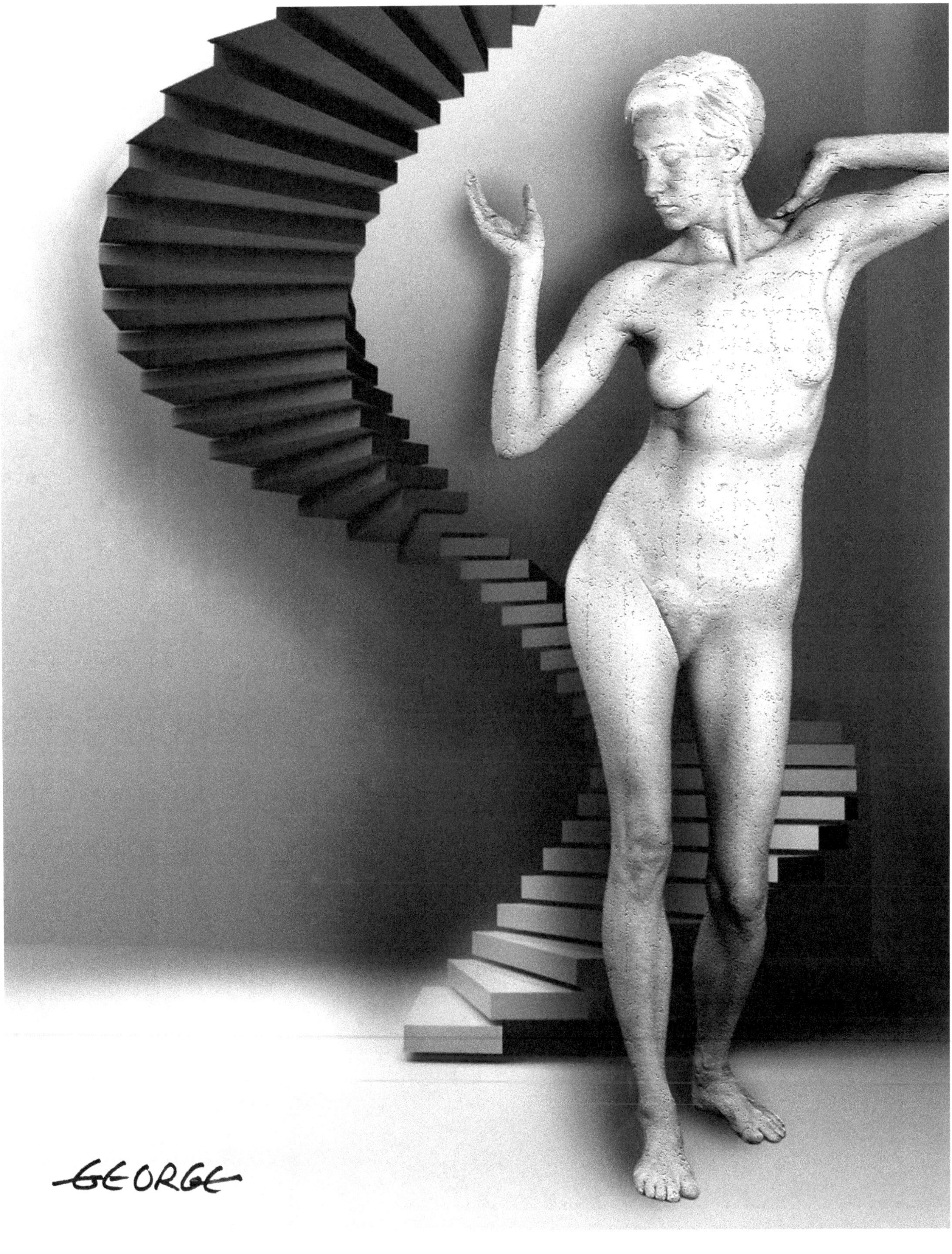

GEORGE

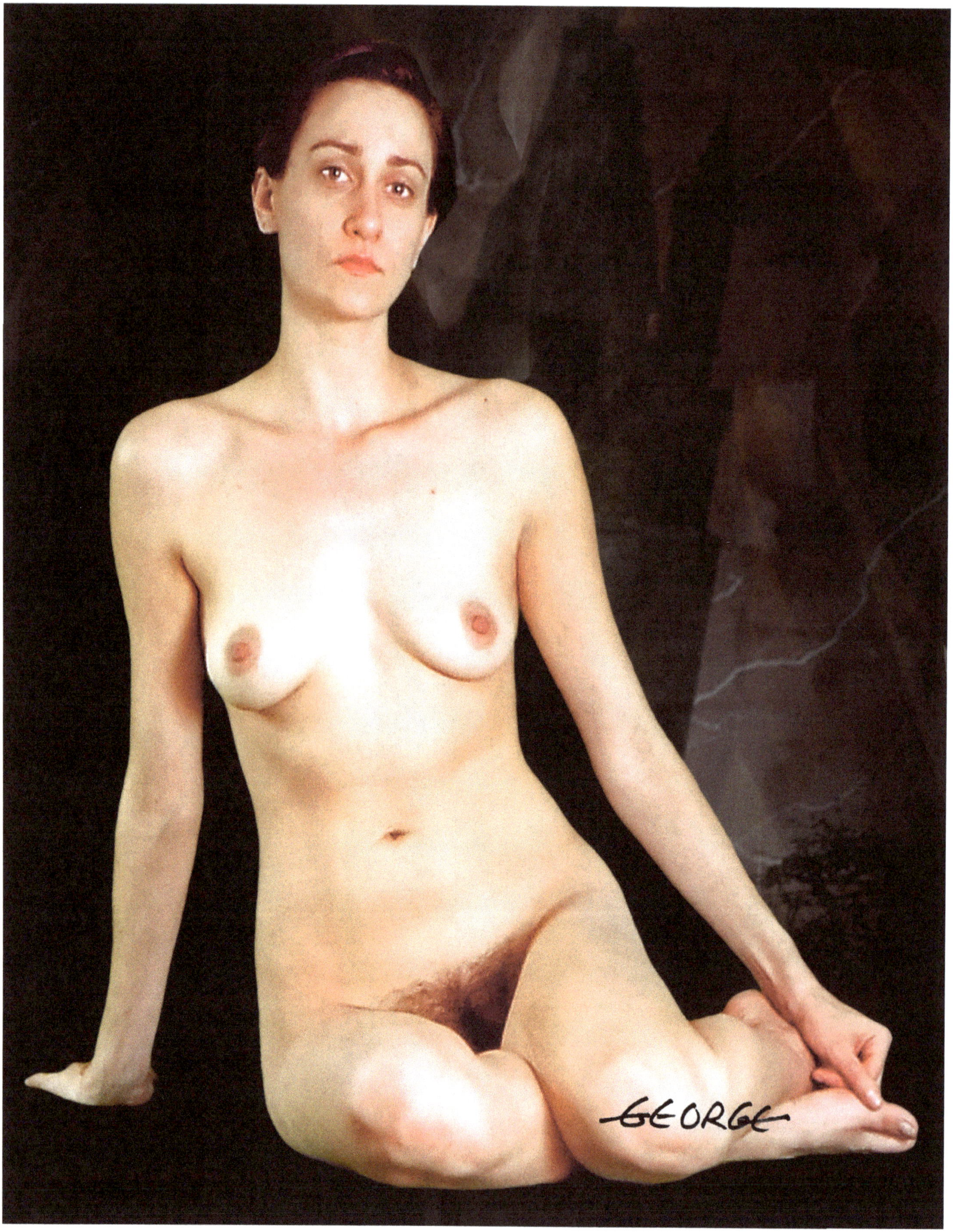
GEORGE

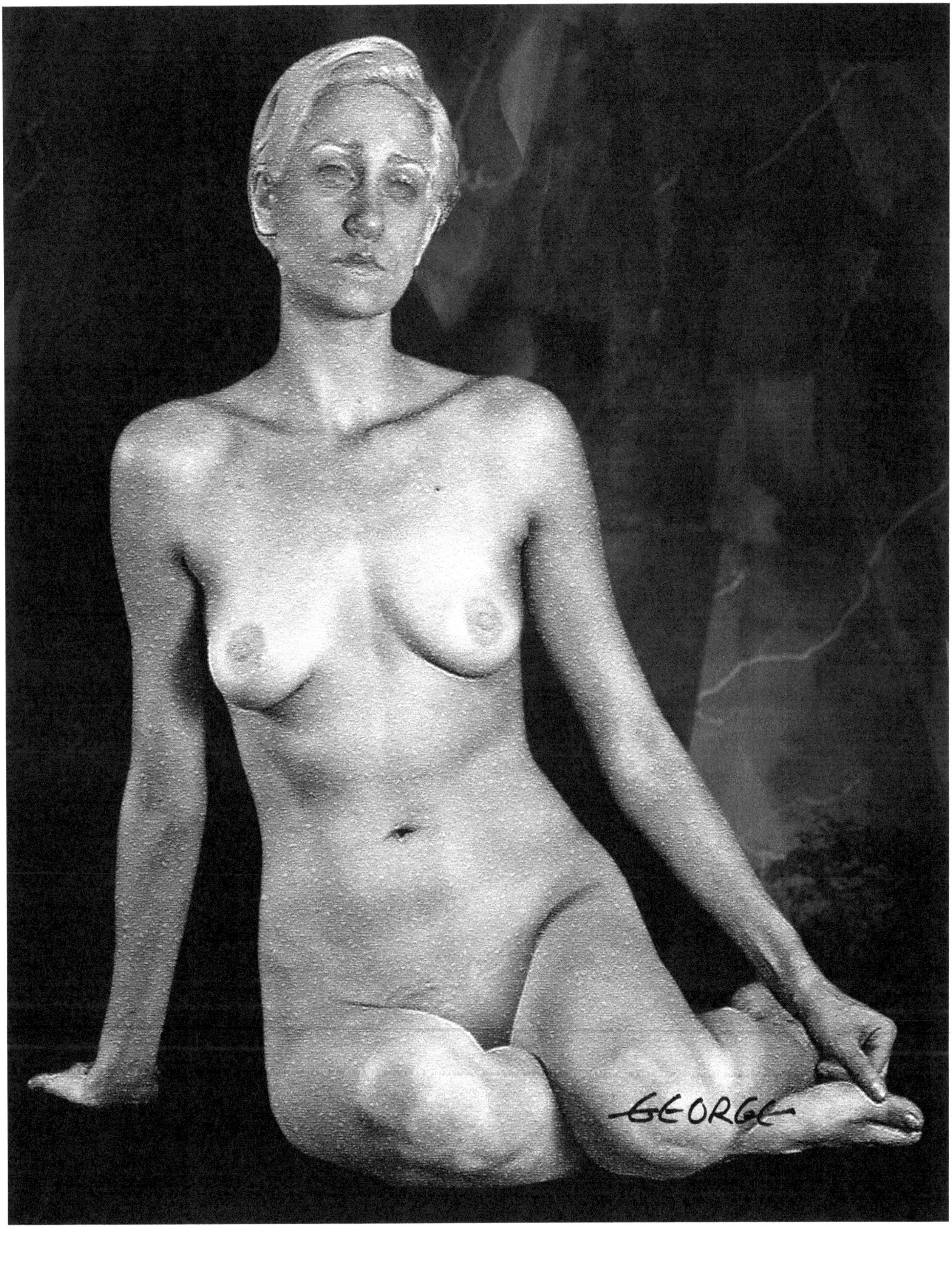
GEORGE

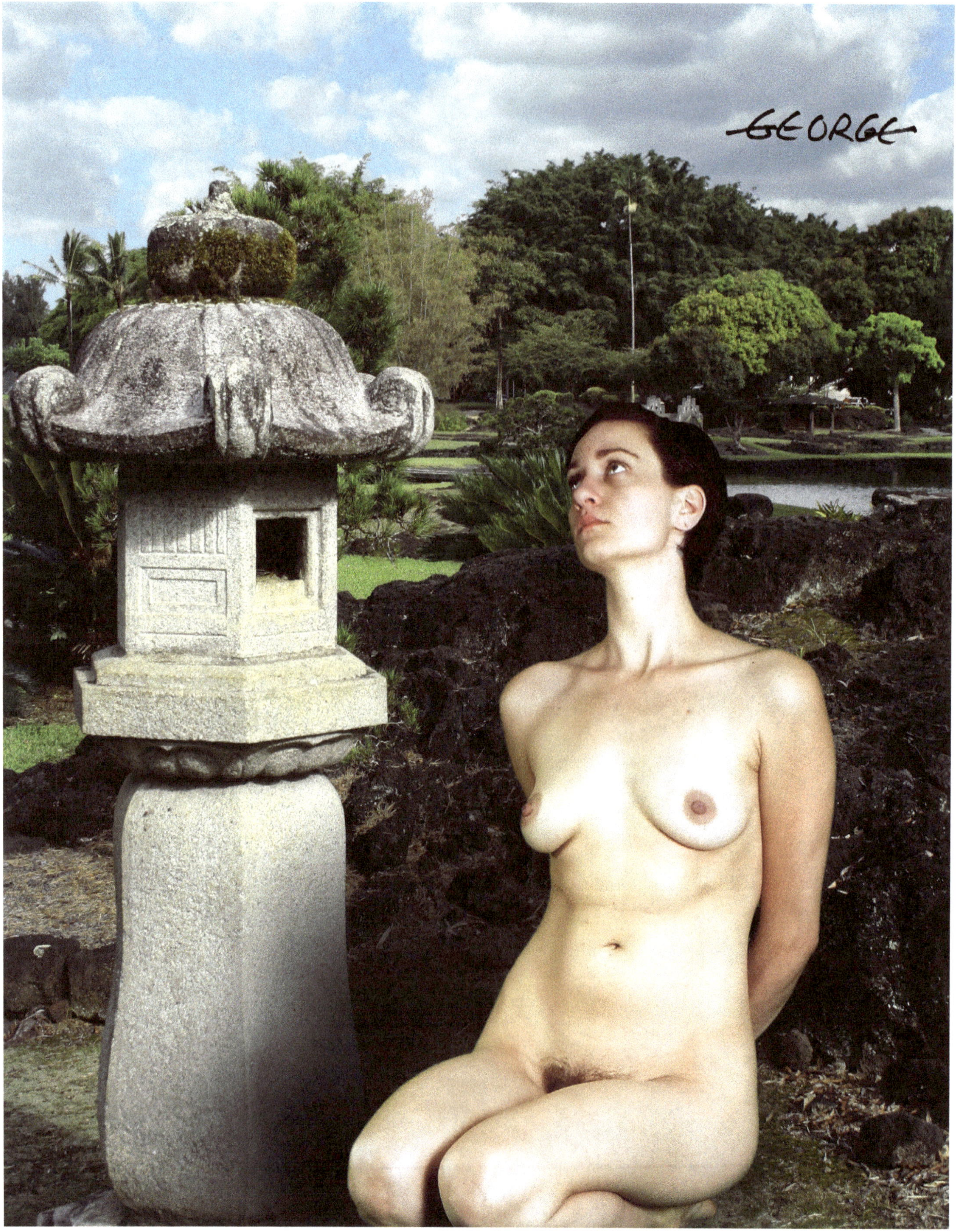
GEORGE

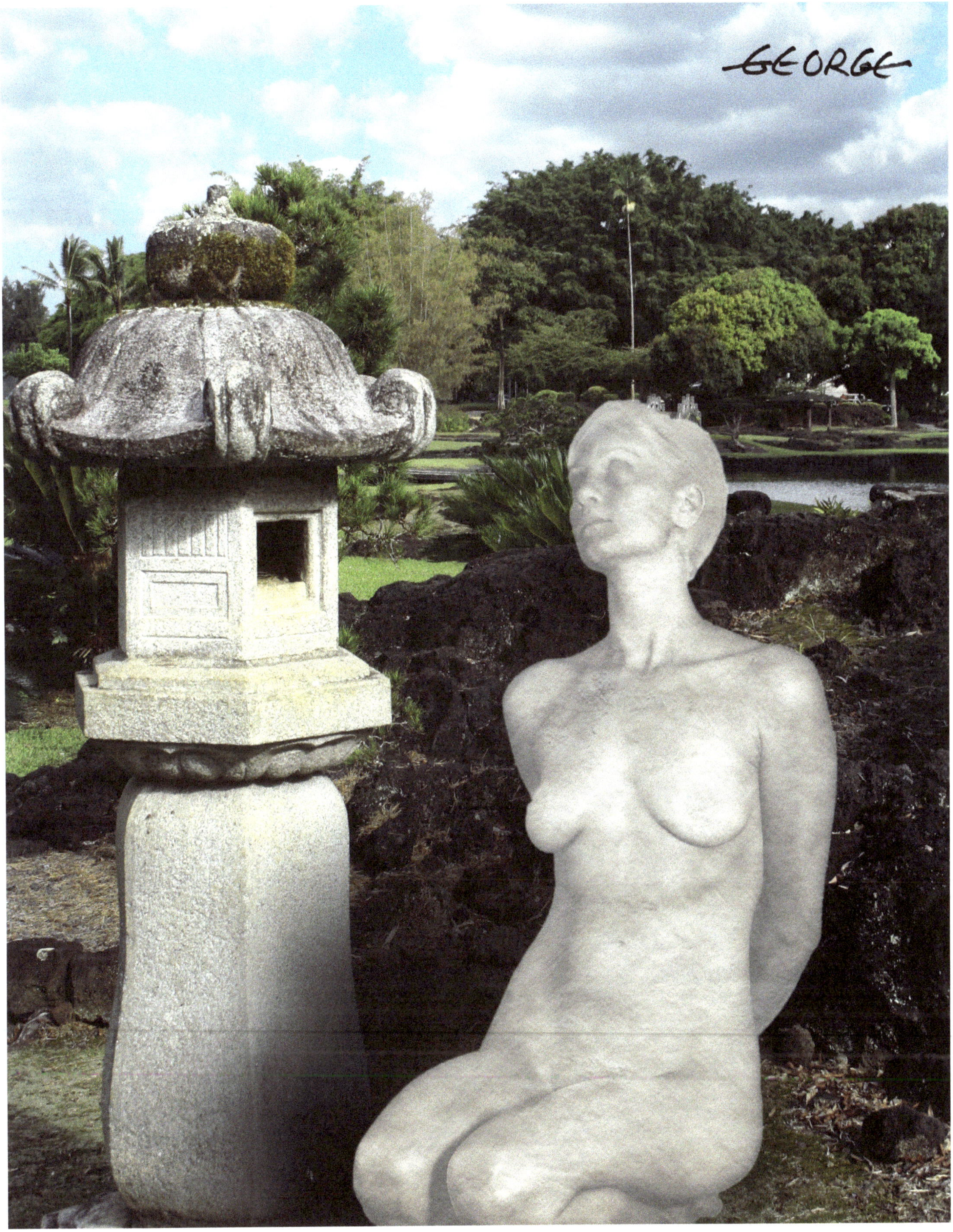
GEORGE

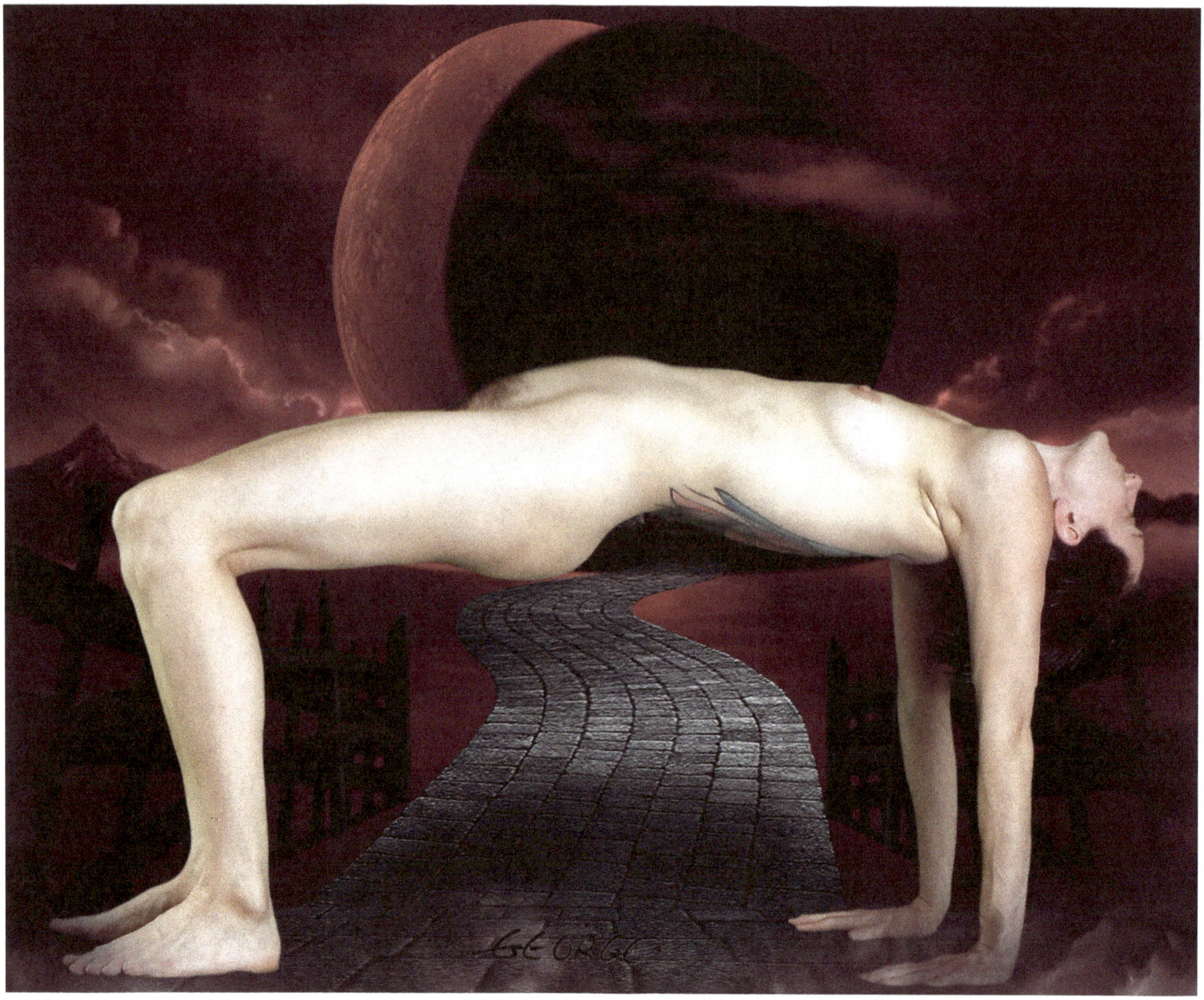

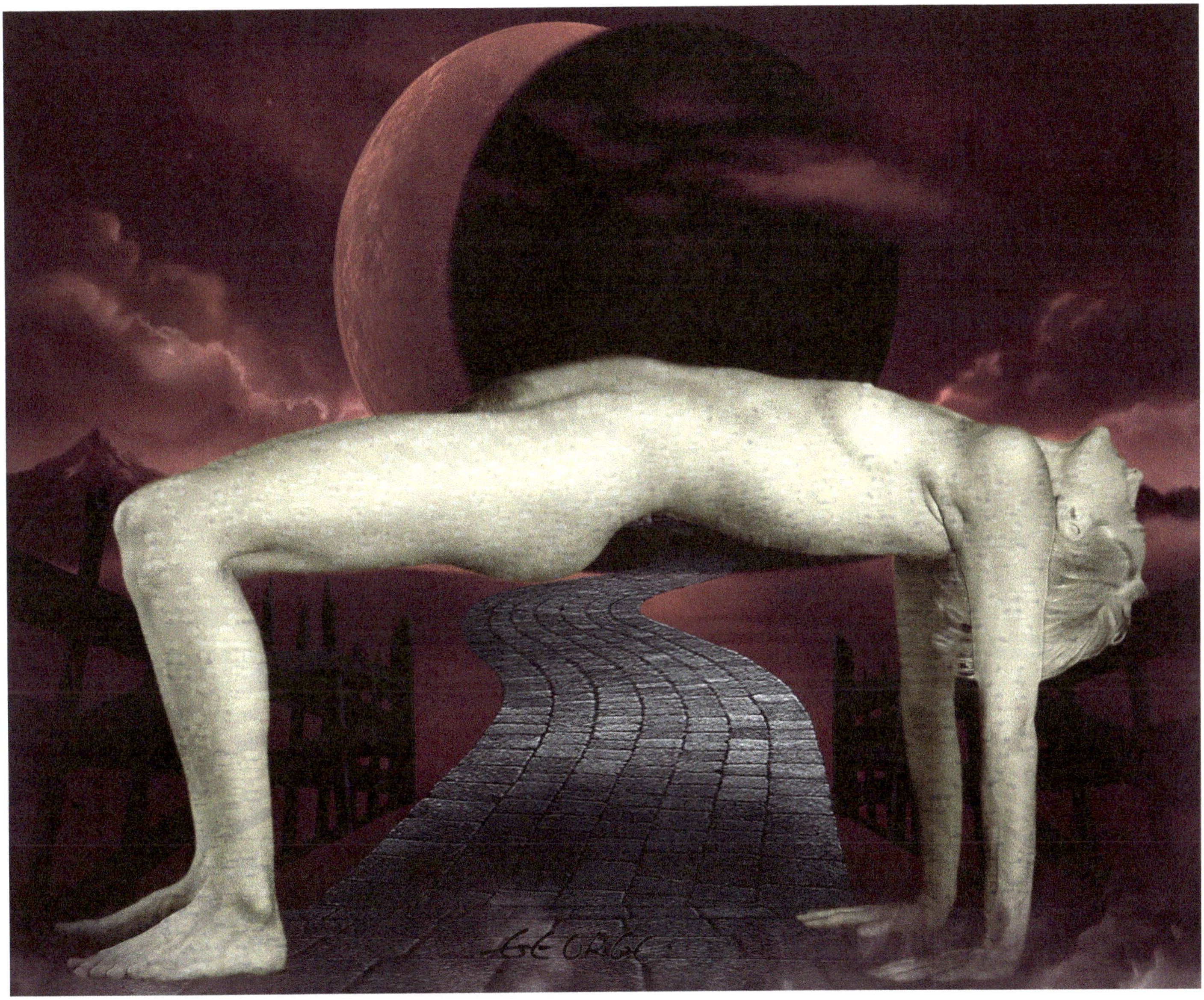

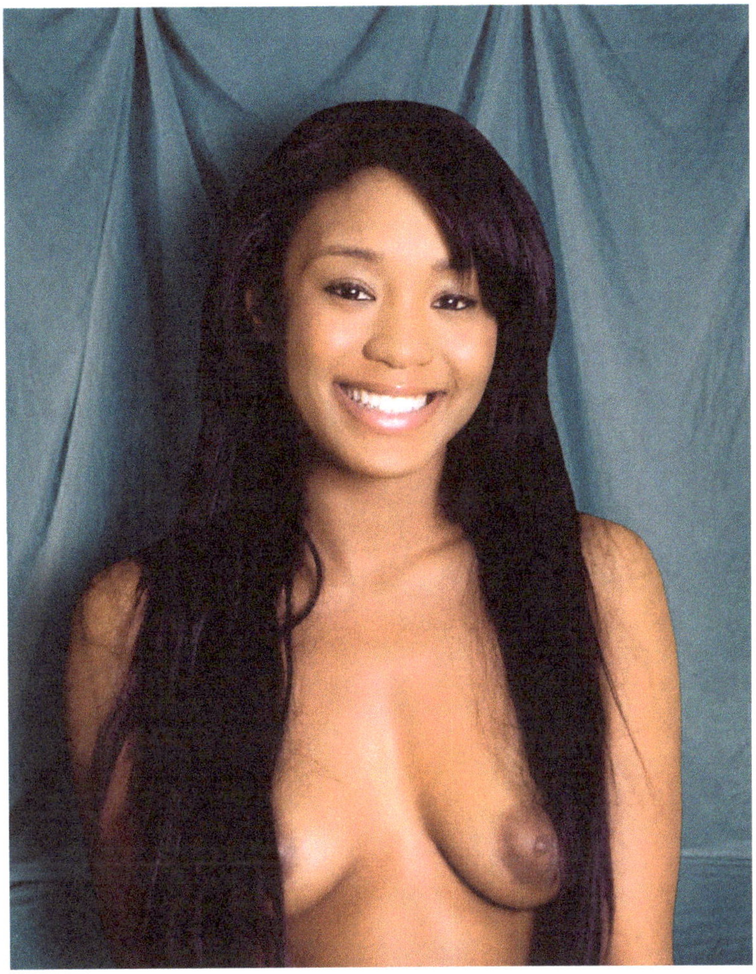

ARIKA BALA

Height 5'4" Weight 115 lbs Bust 34" Waist 30" Hips 39" Cup C

I discovered my interest in modeling two years ago and I have been lucky to have opportunities for modeling in many genres. This experience makes me very ambitious to climb the modeling ladder of success. I am always amazed to see the photos from each shoot, and ask, is that me?

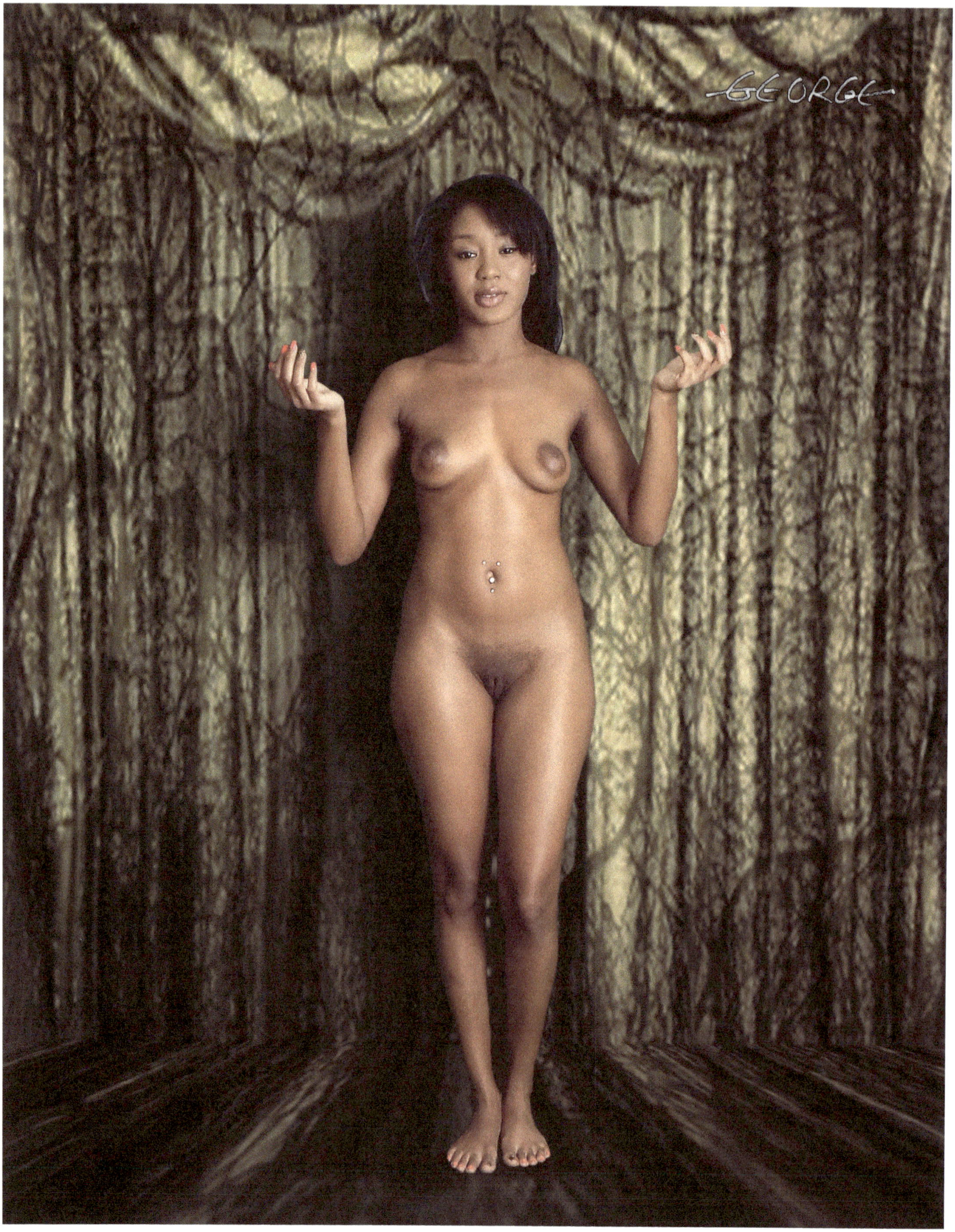
GEORGE

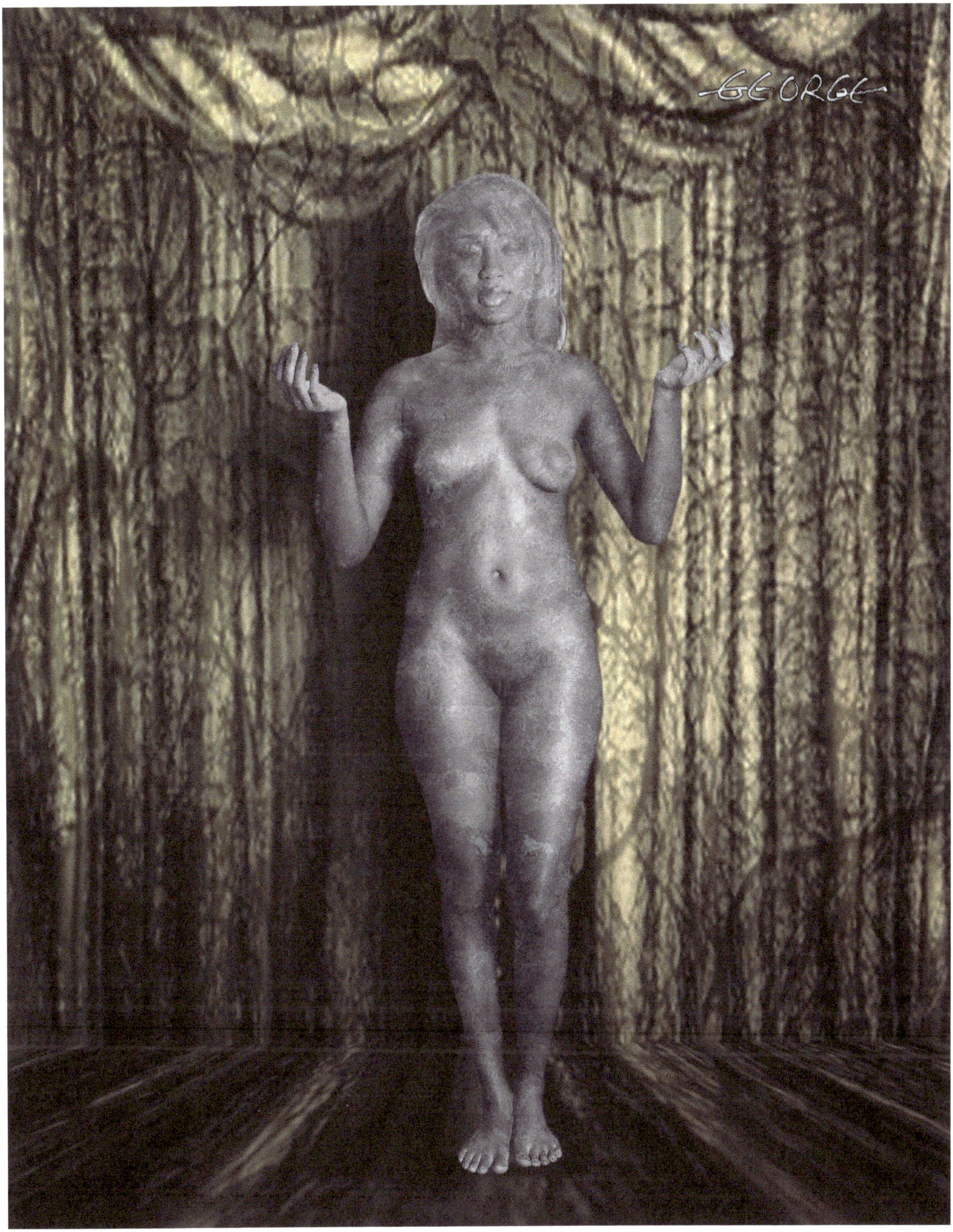
GEORGE

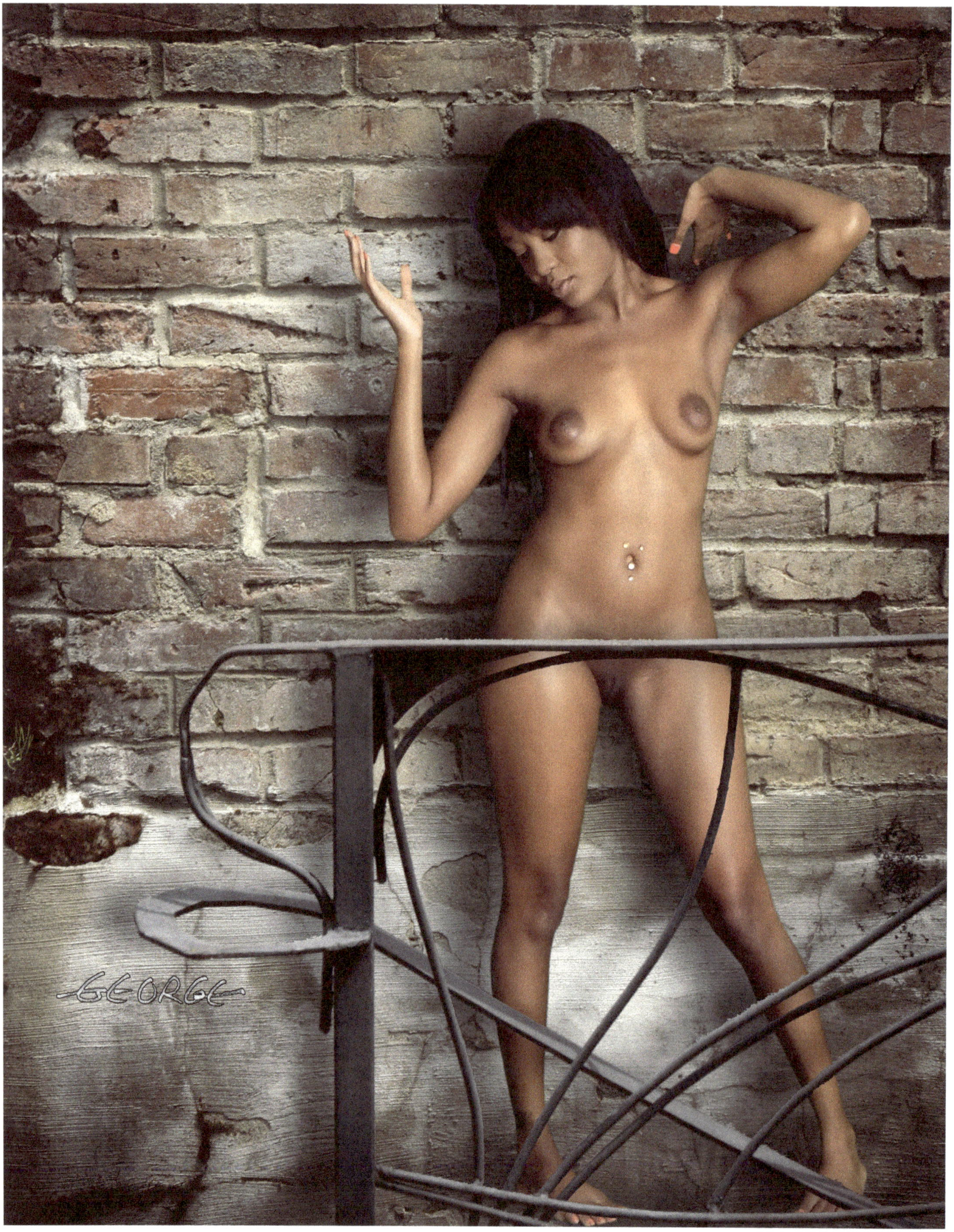
GEORGE

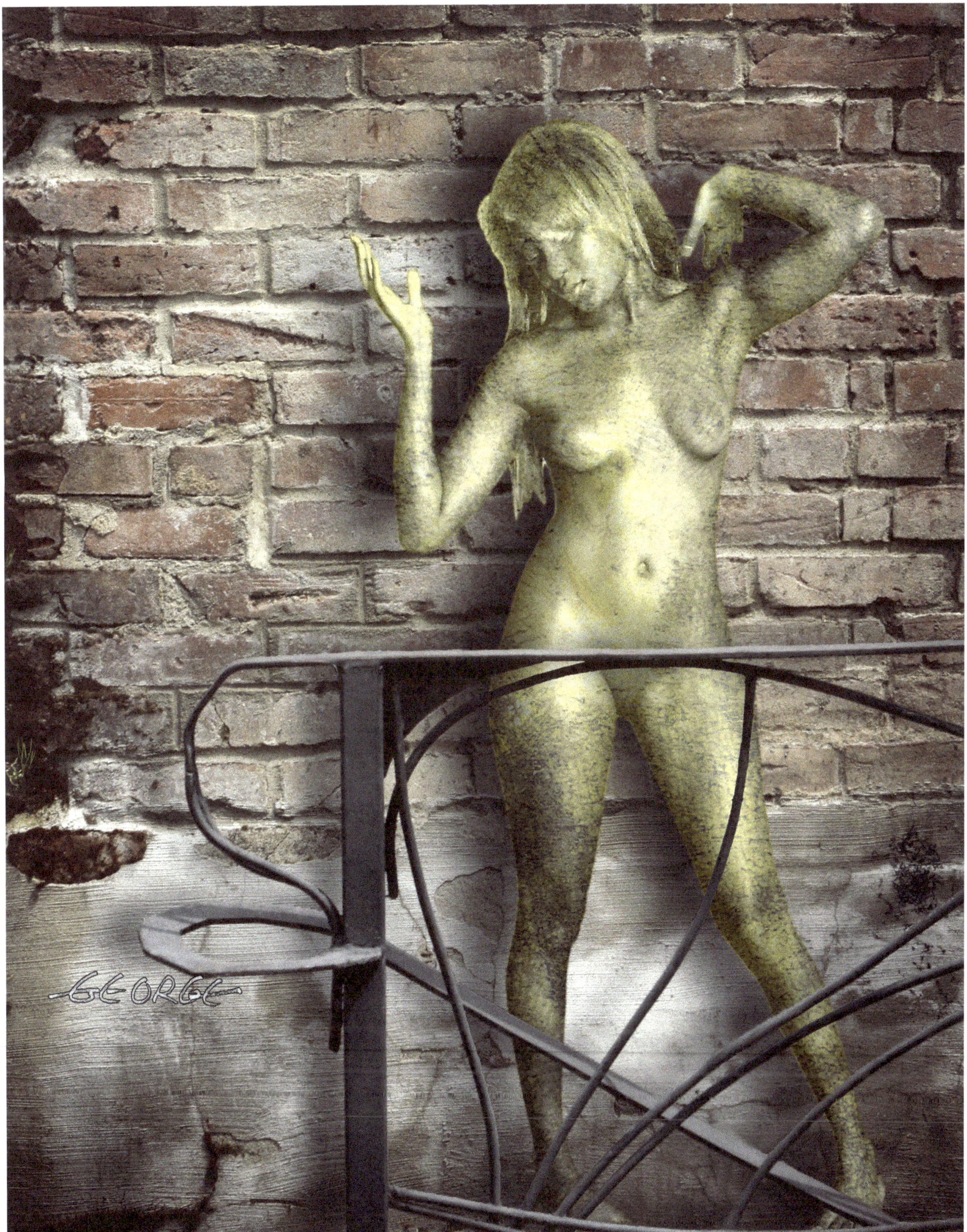
GEORGE

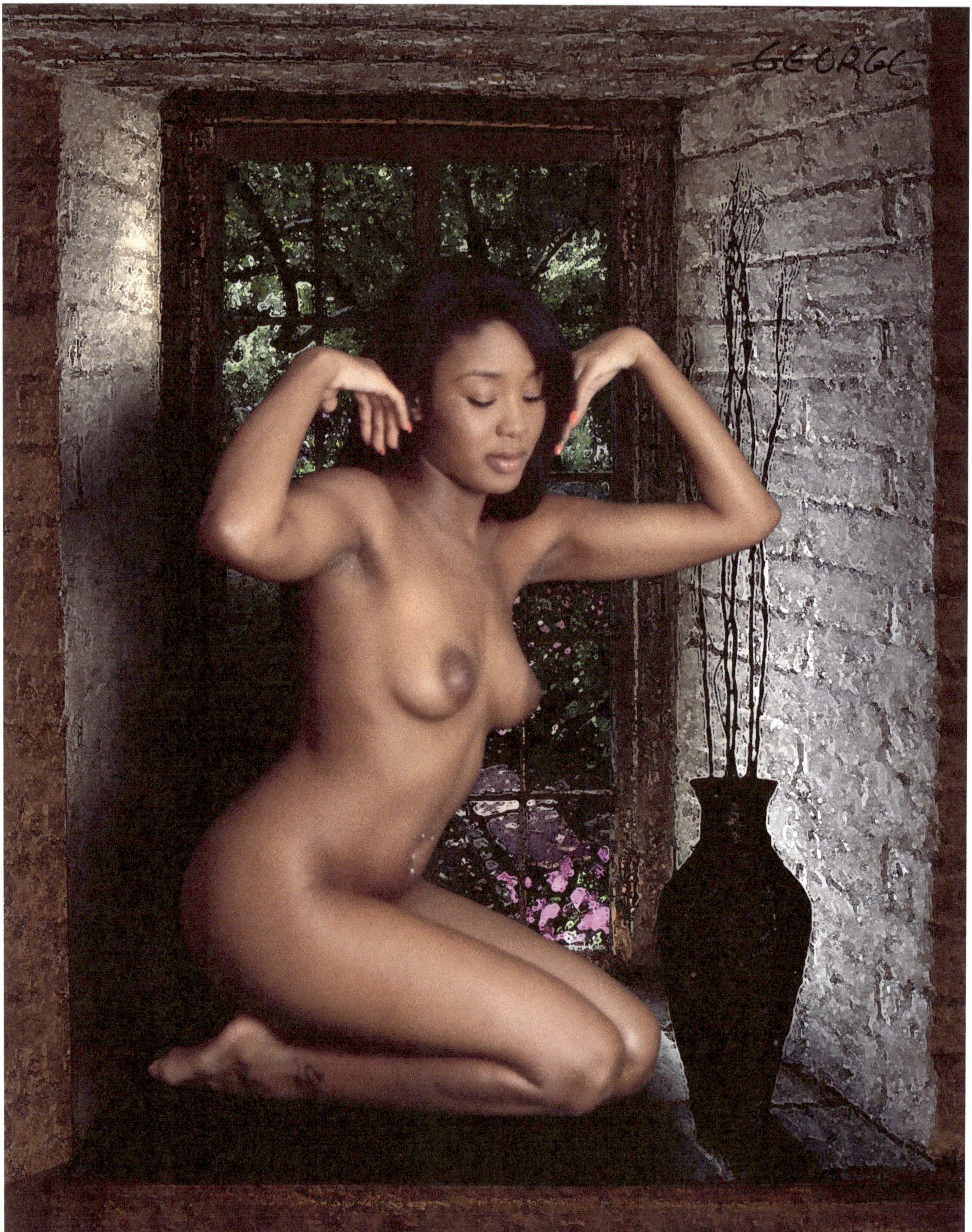

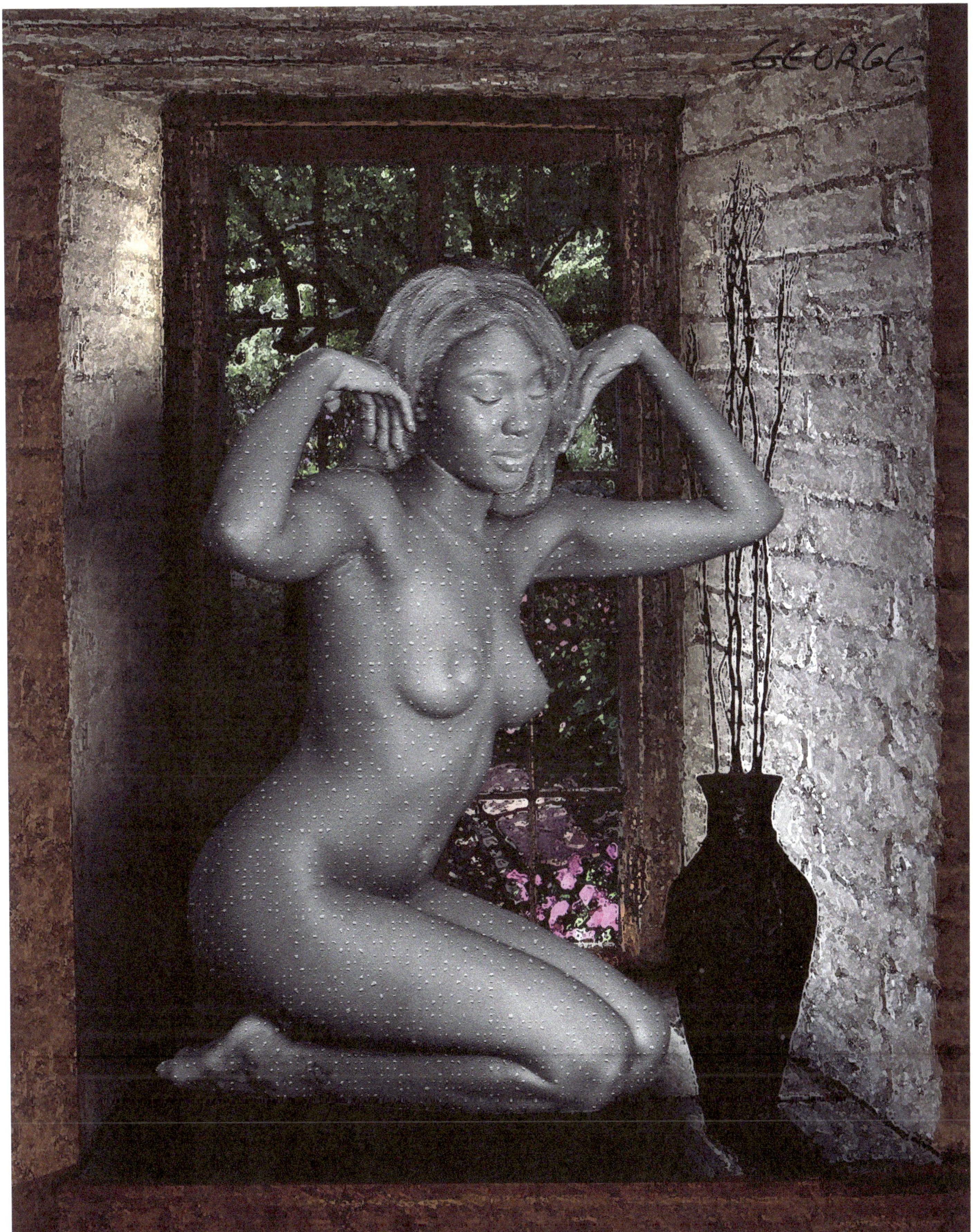
GEORGE

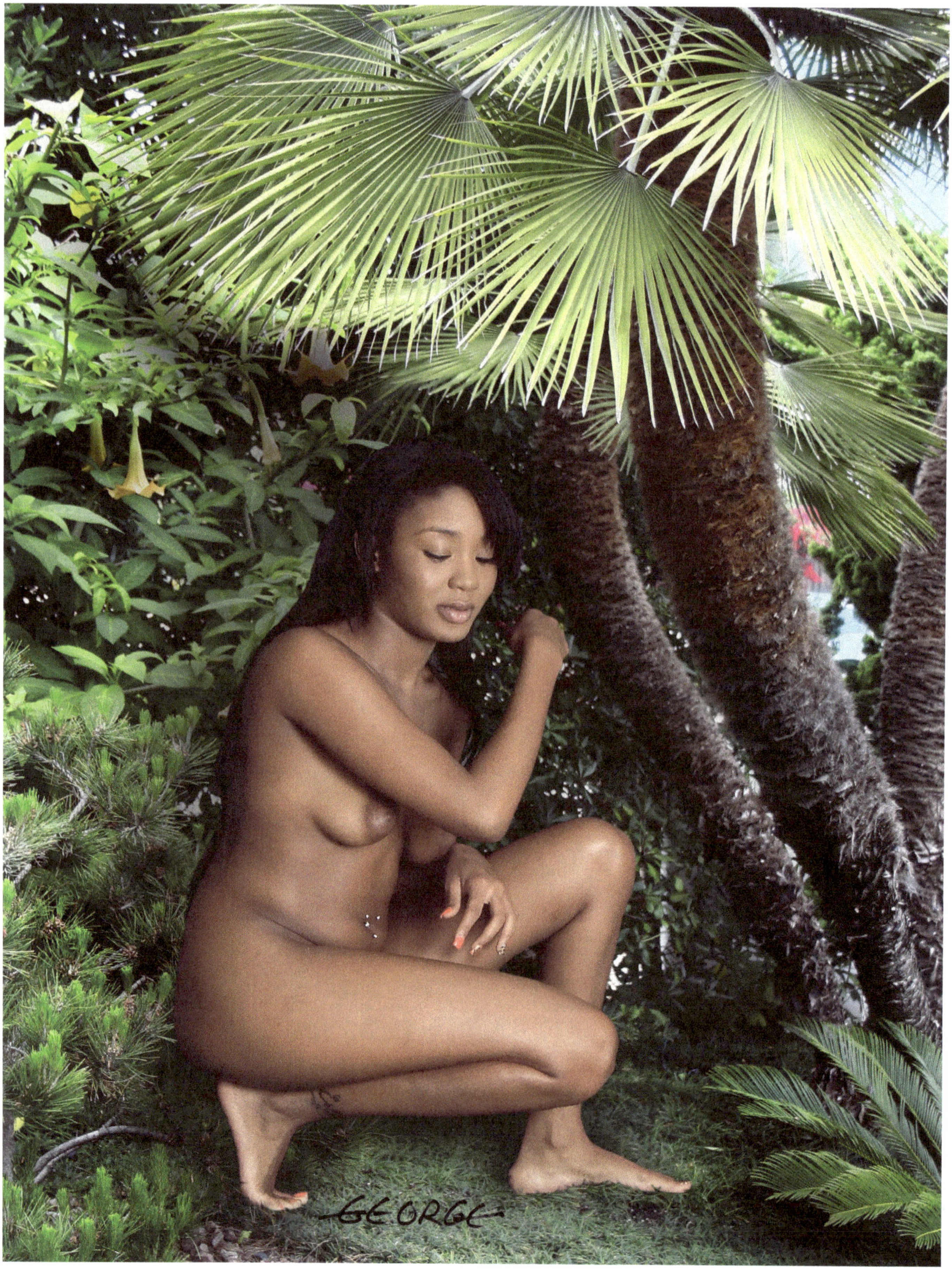
GEORGE

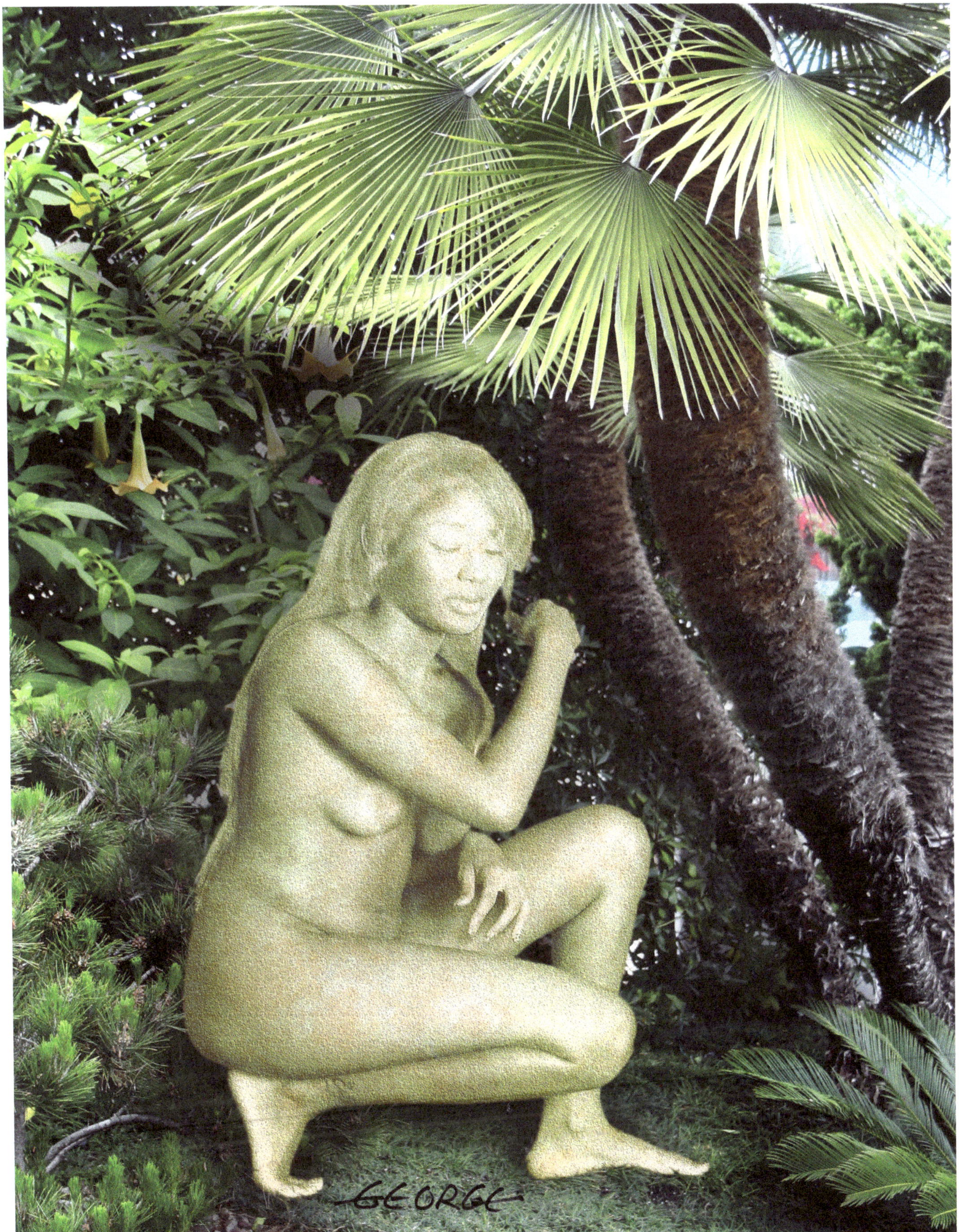
GEORGE

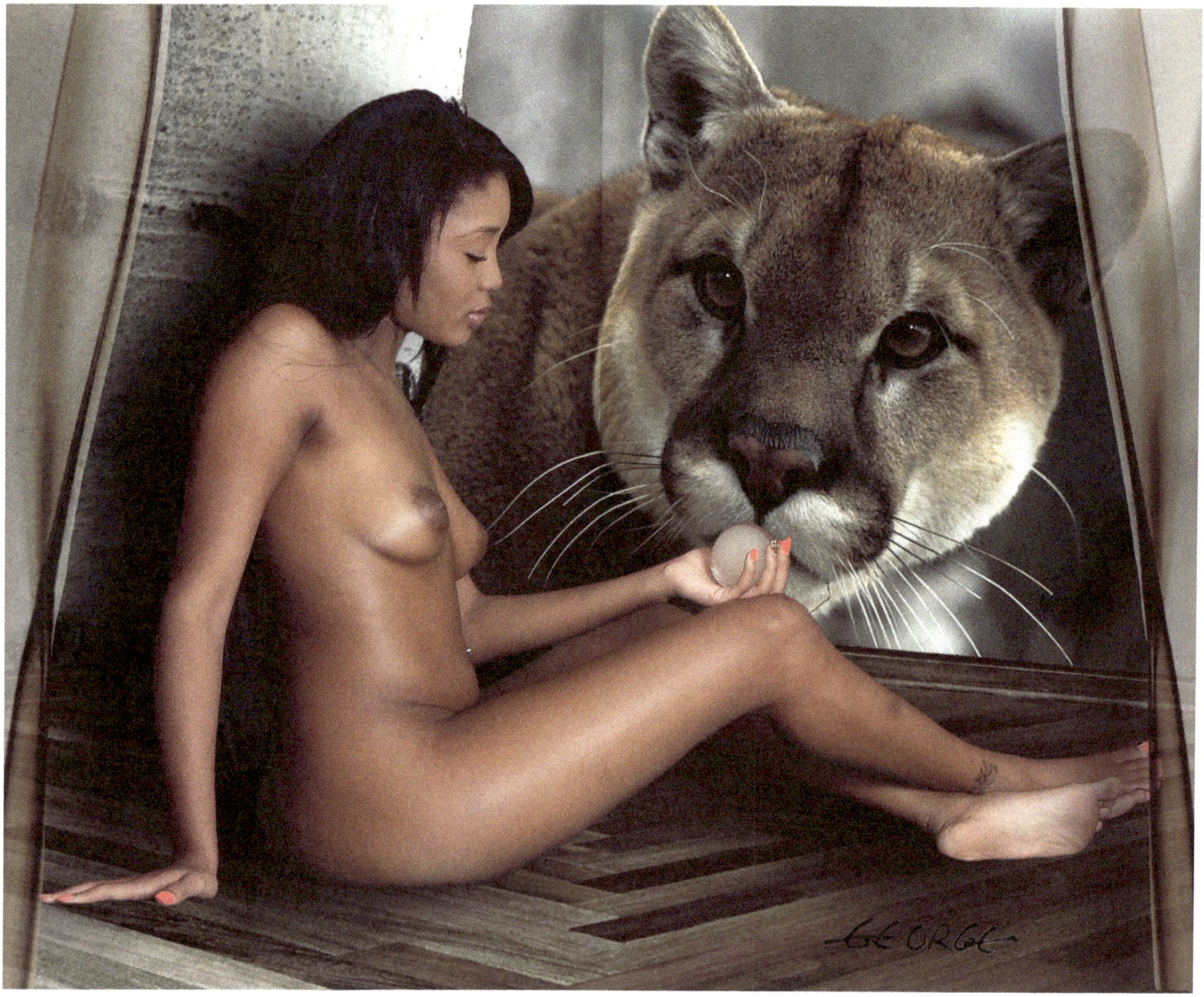
GEORGE

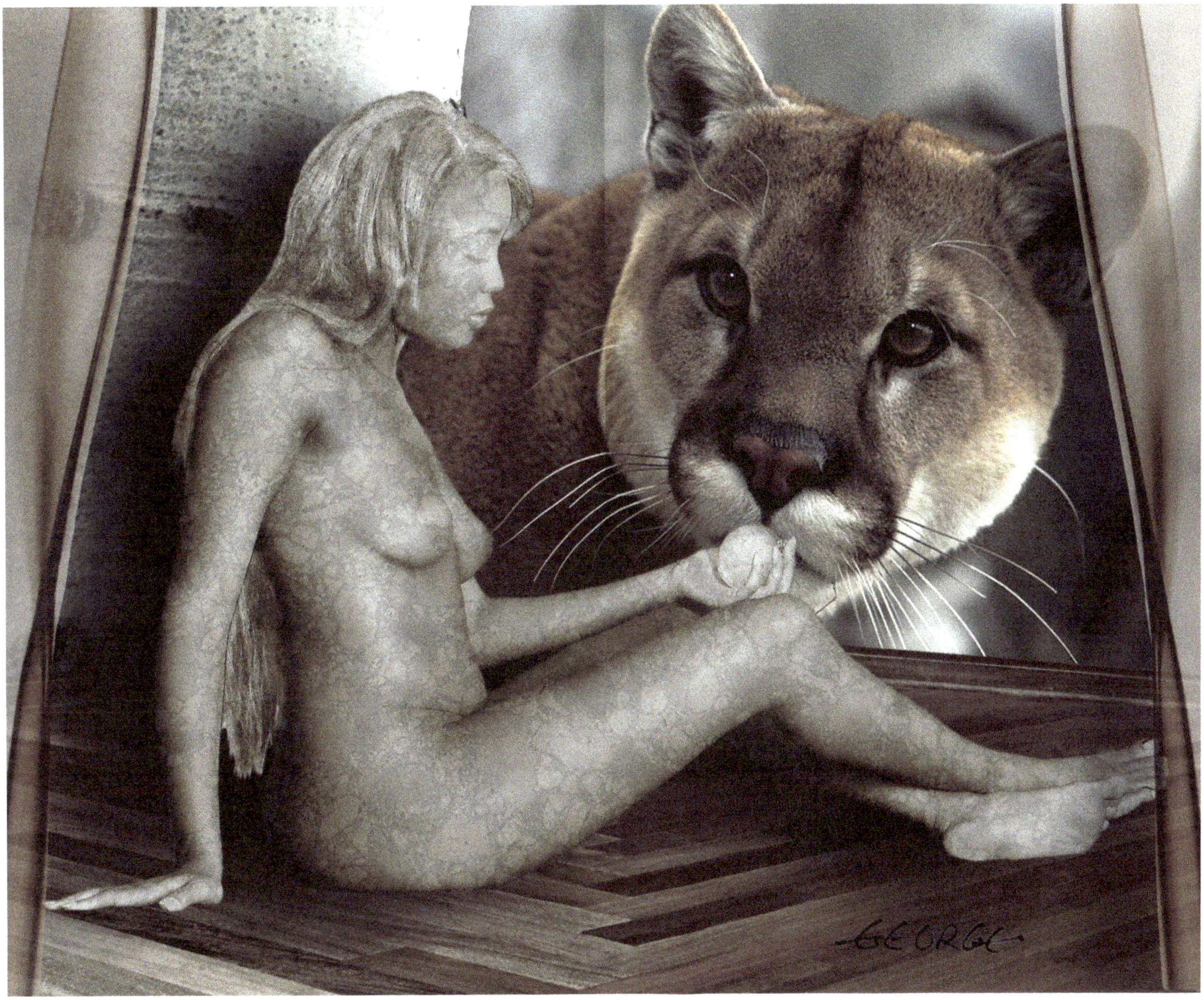
GEORGE

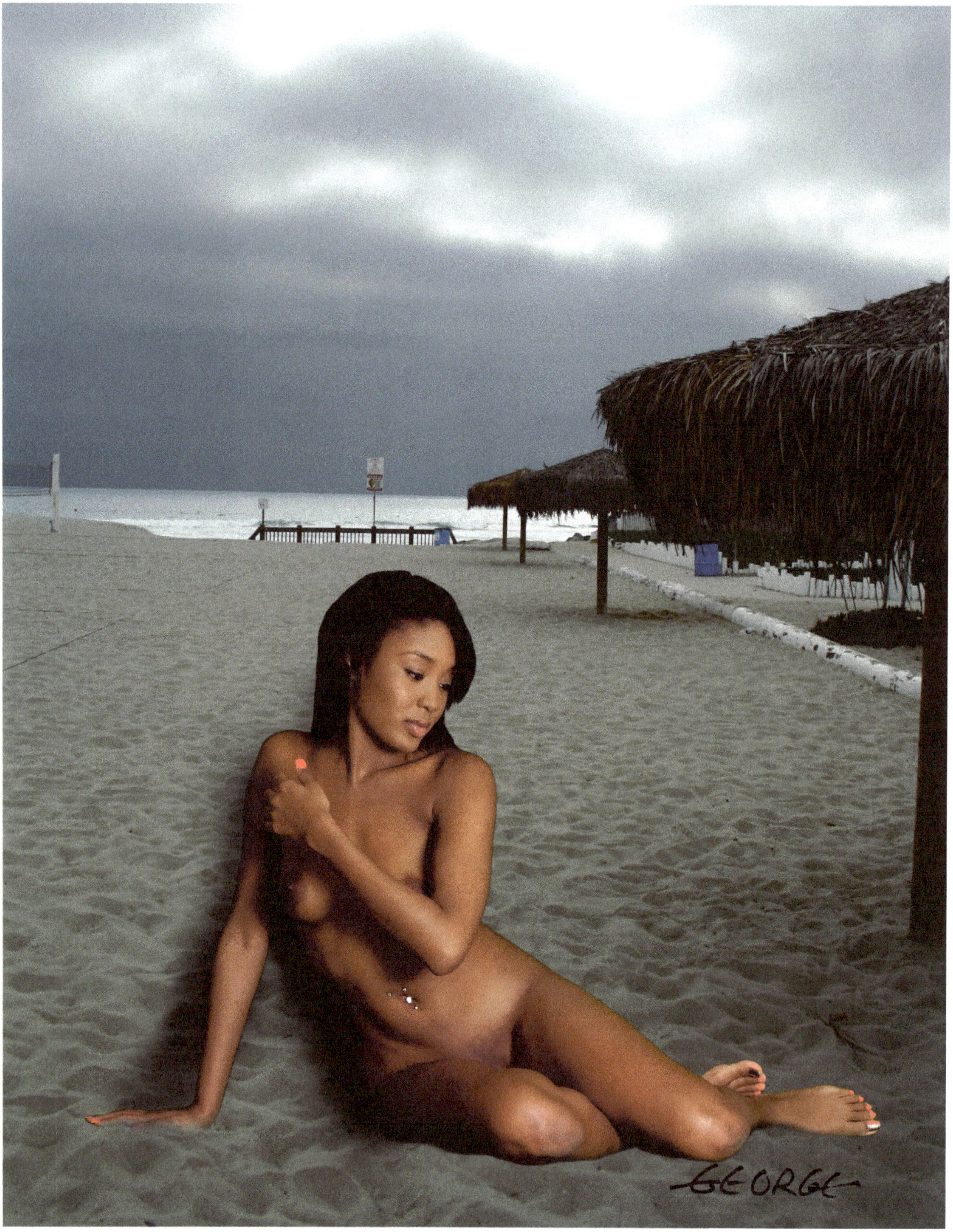
GEORGE

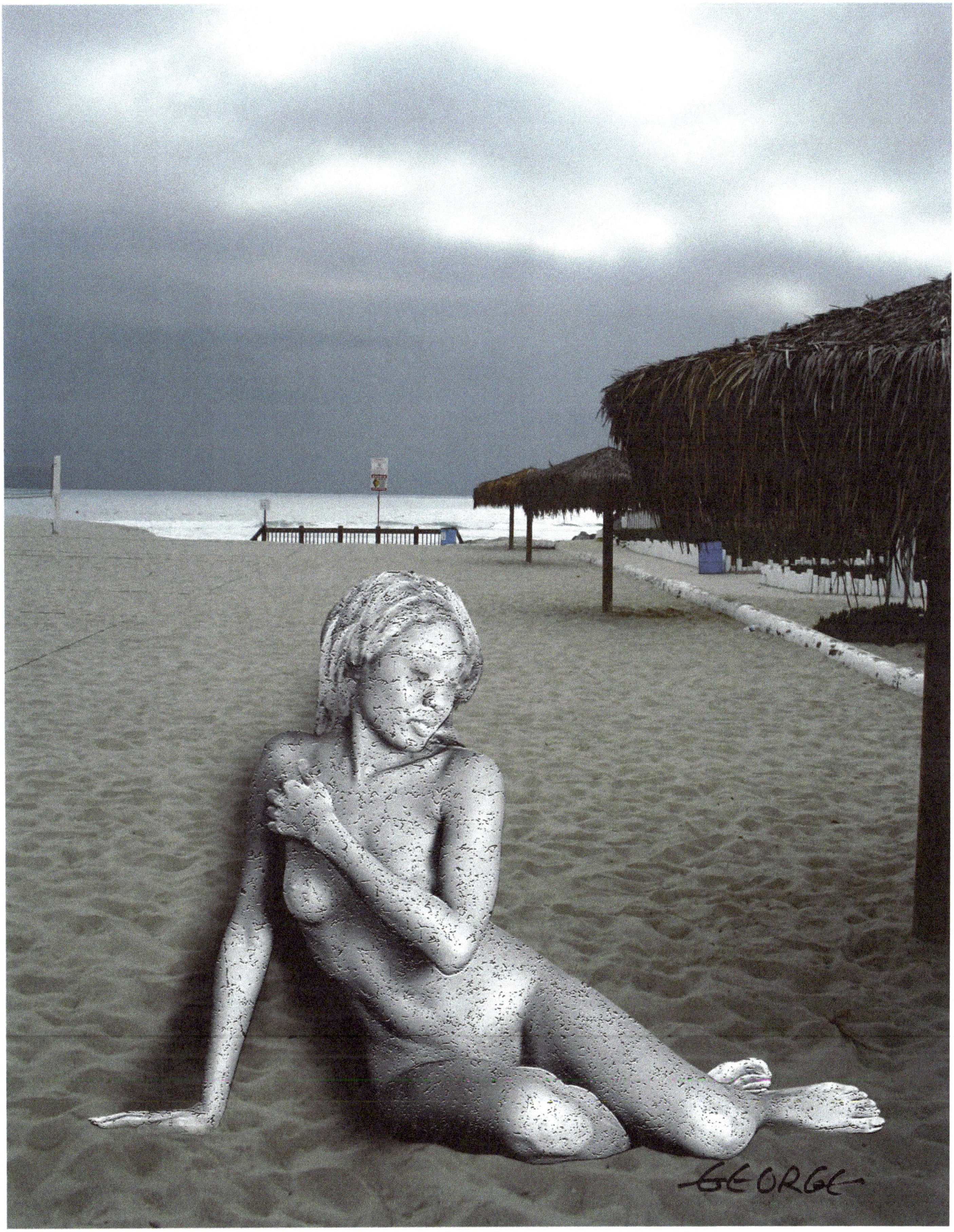
GEORGE

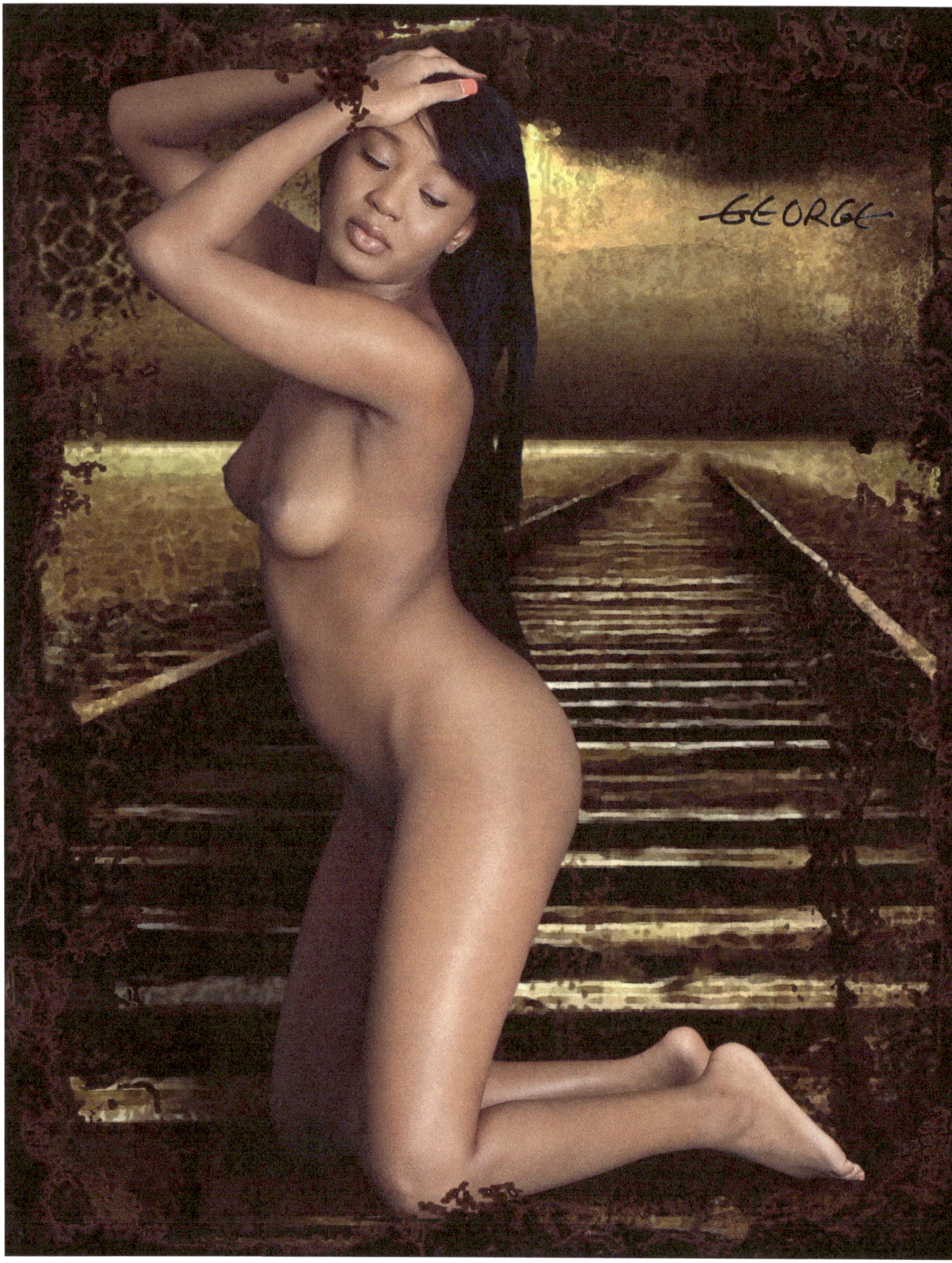
GEORGE

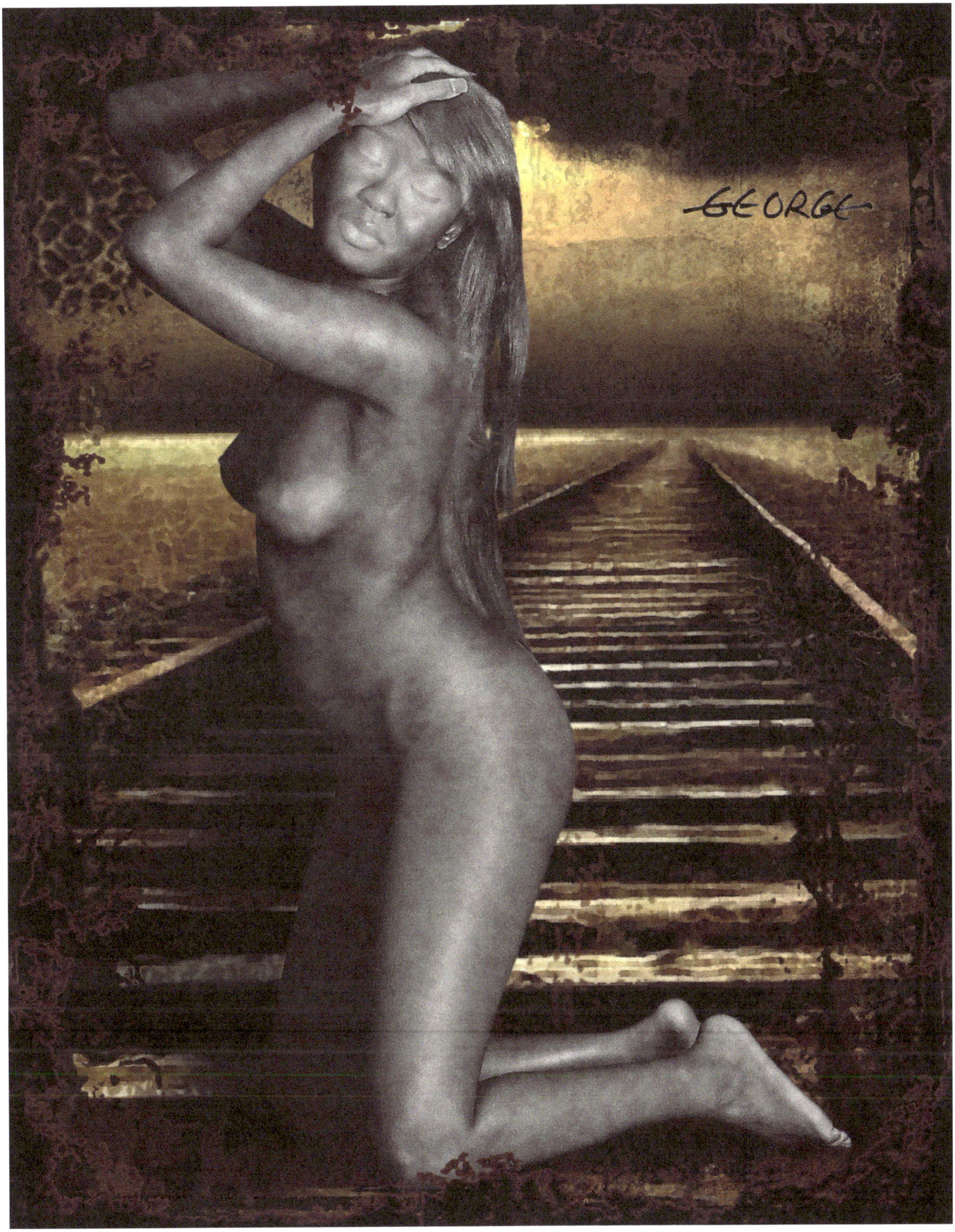
GEORGE

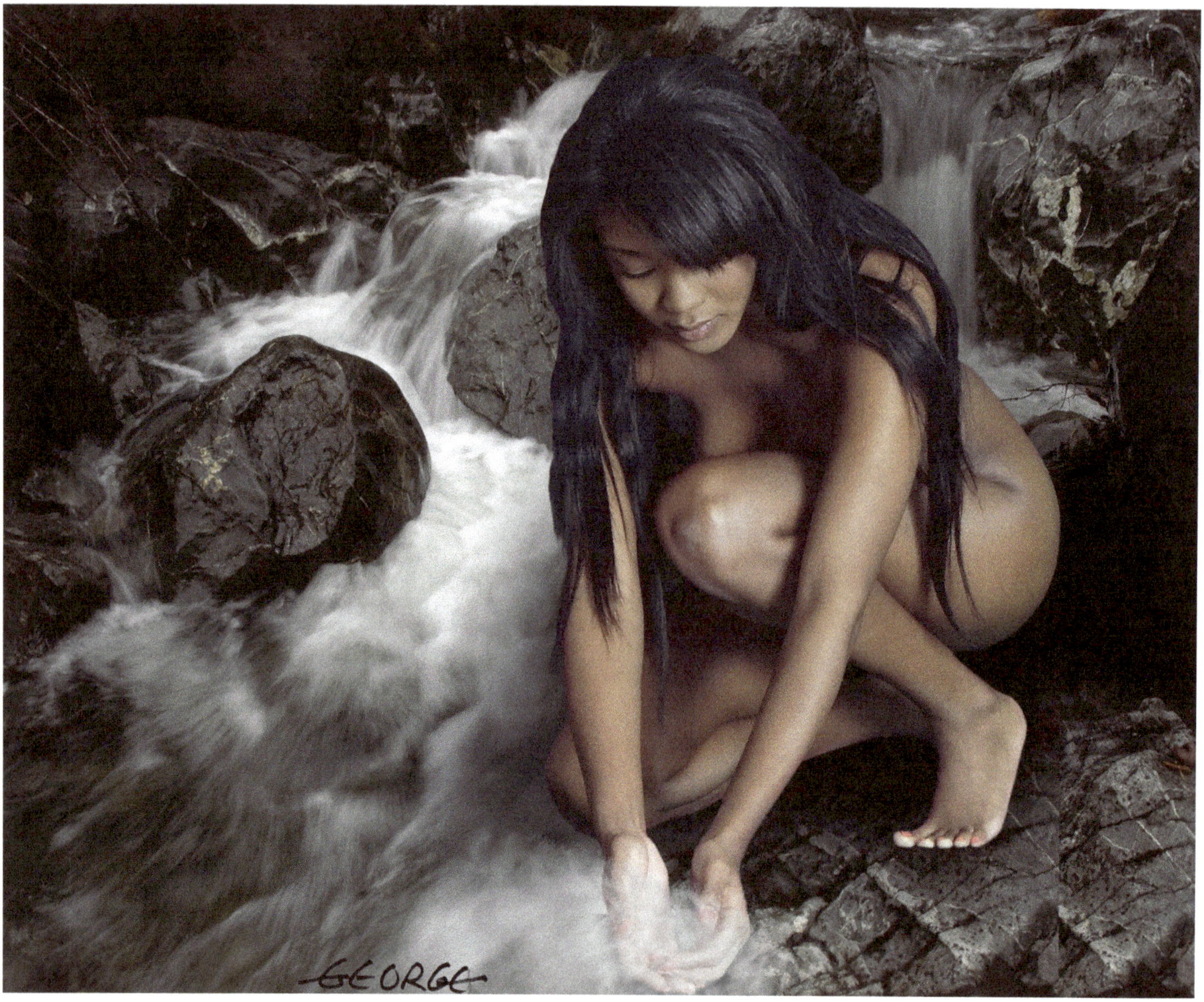
GEORGE

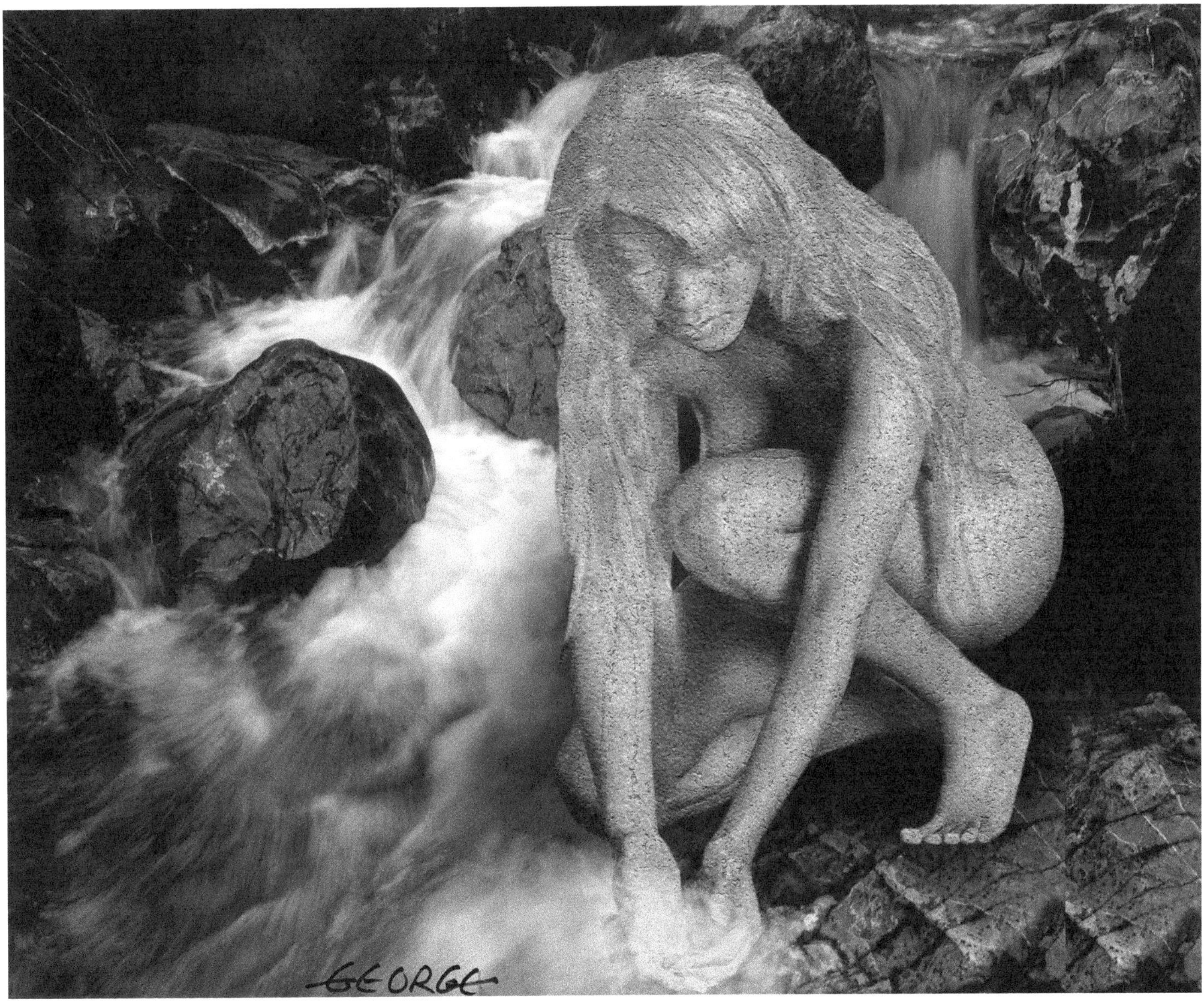
GEORGE

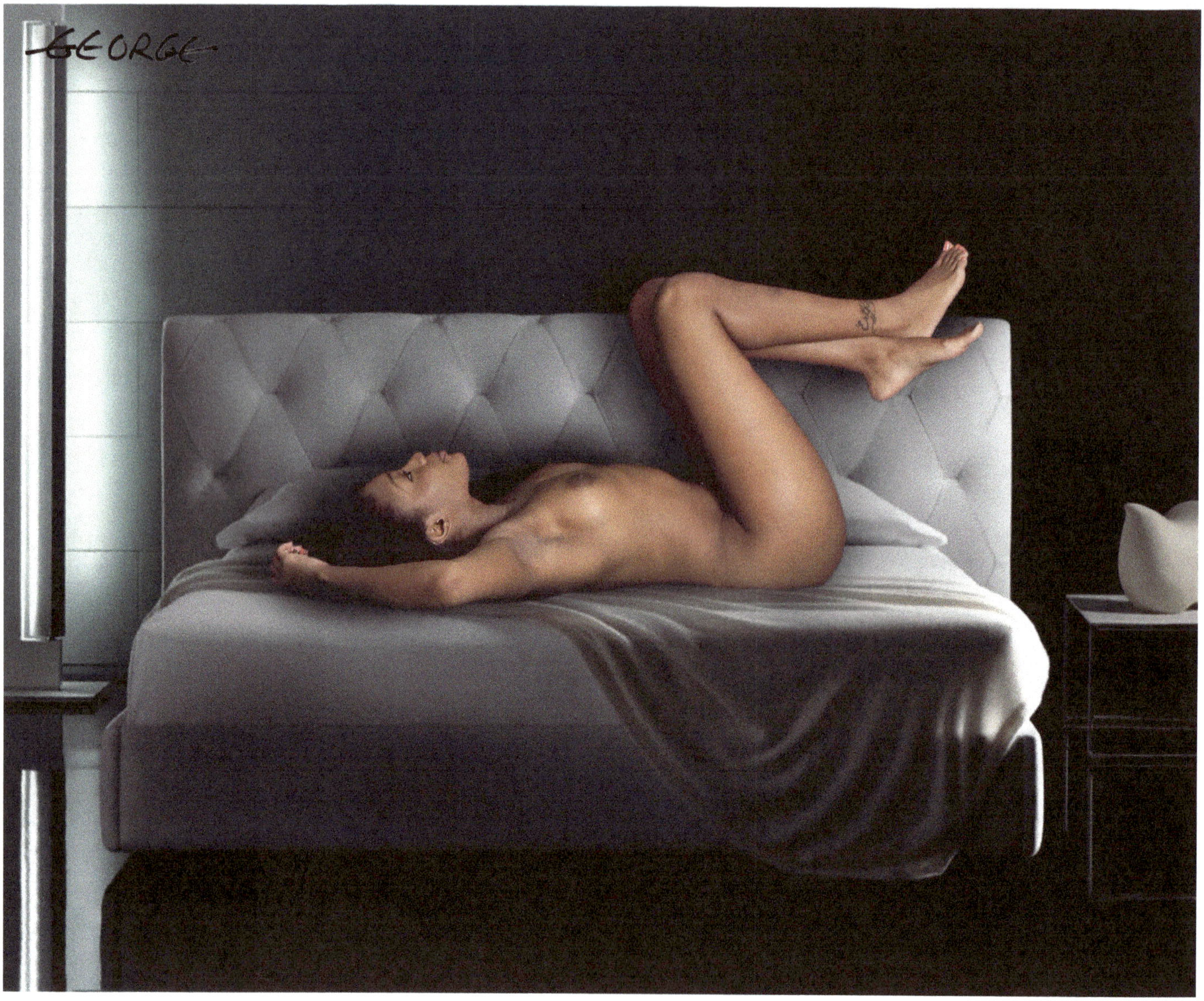
GEORGE

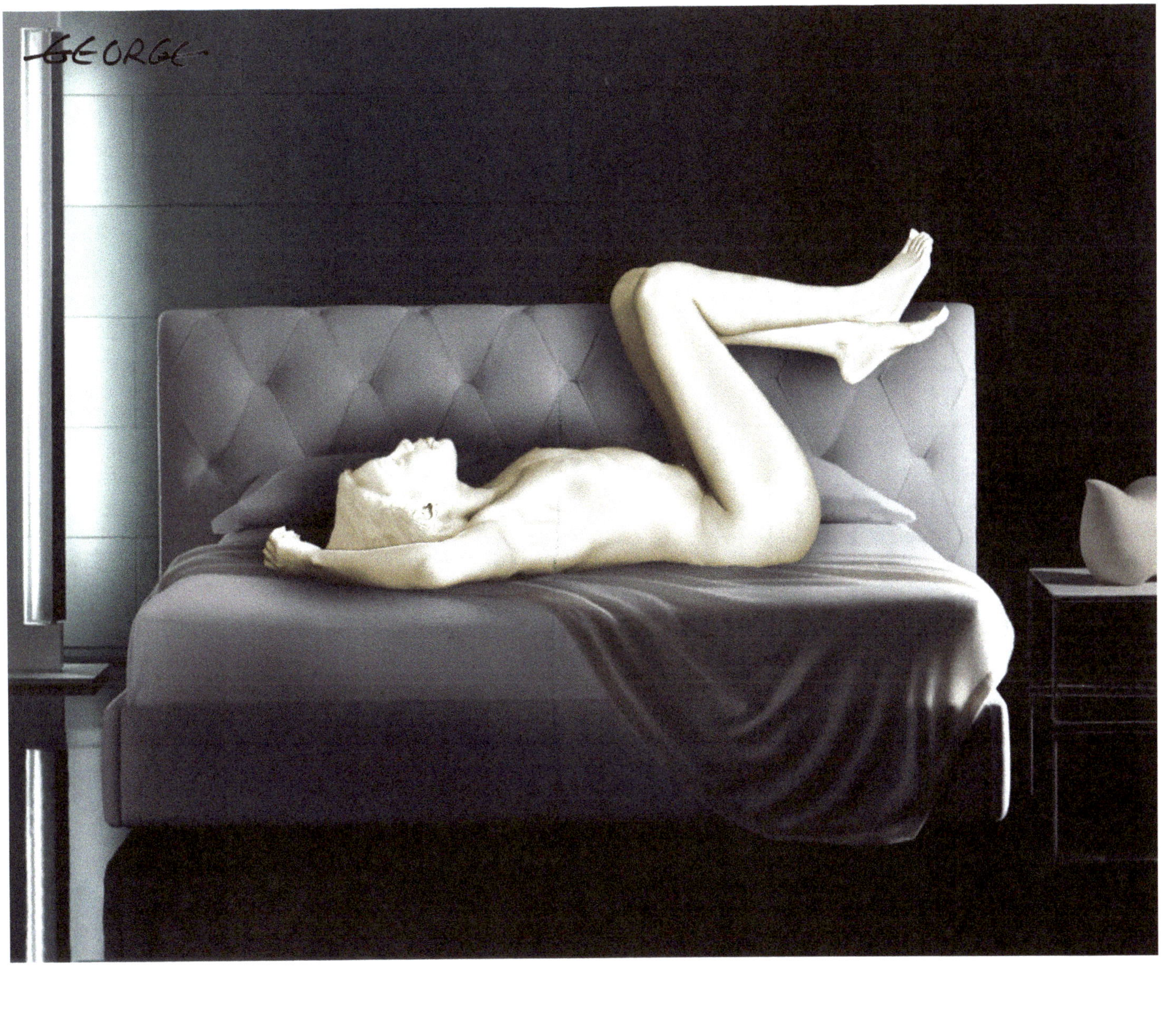
GEORGE

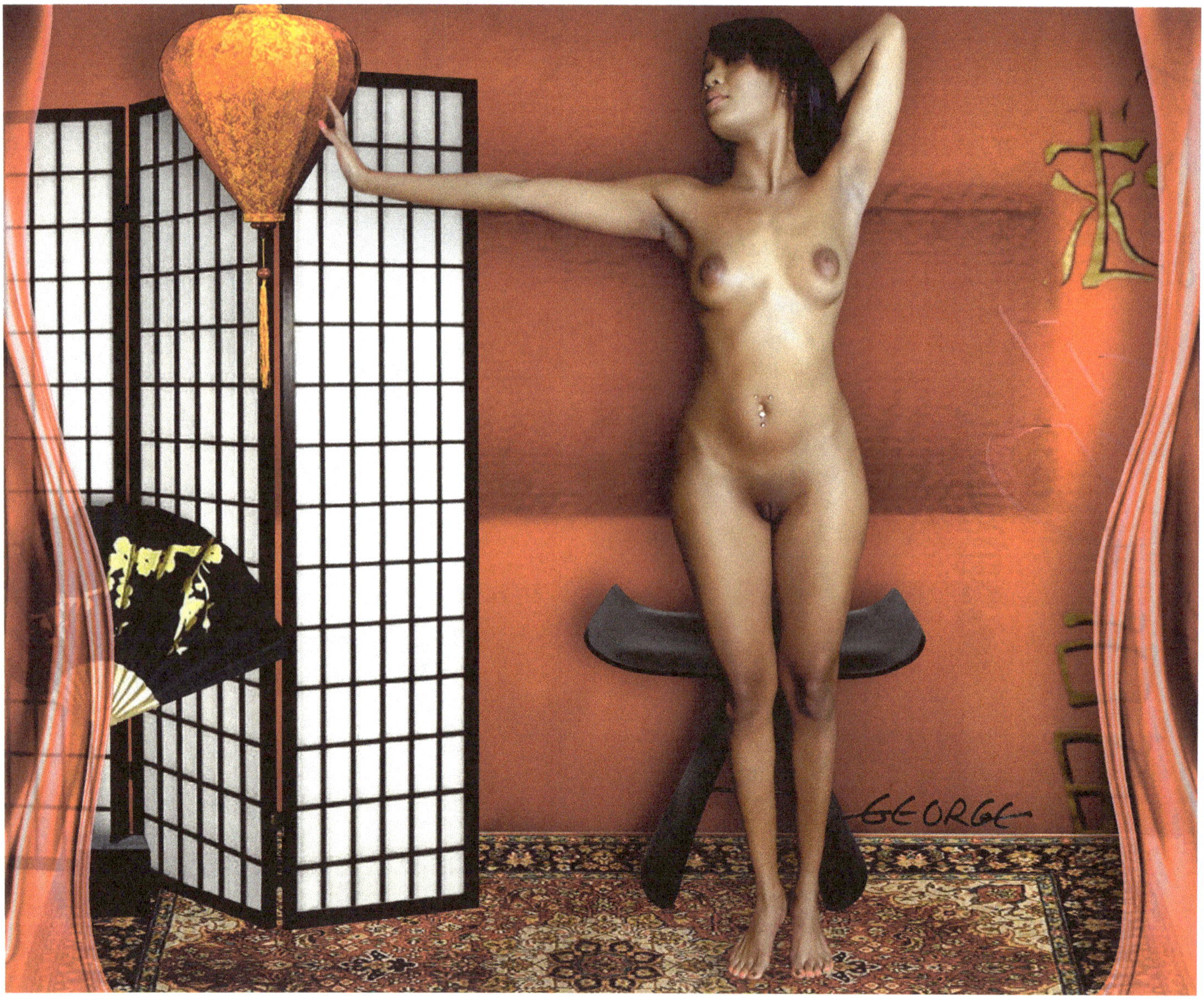
GEORGE

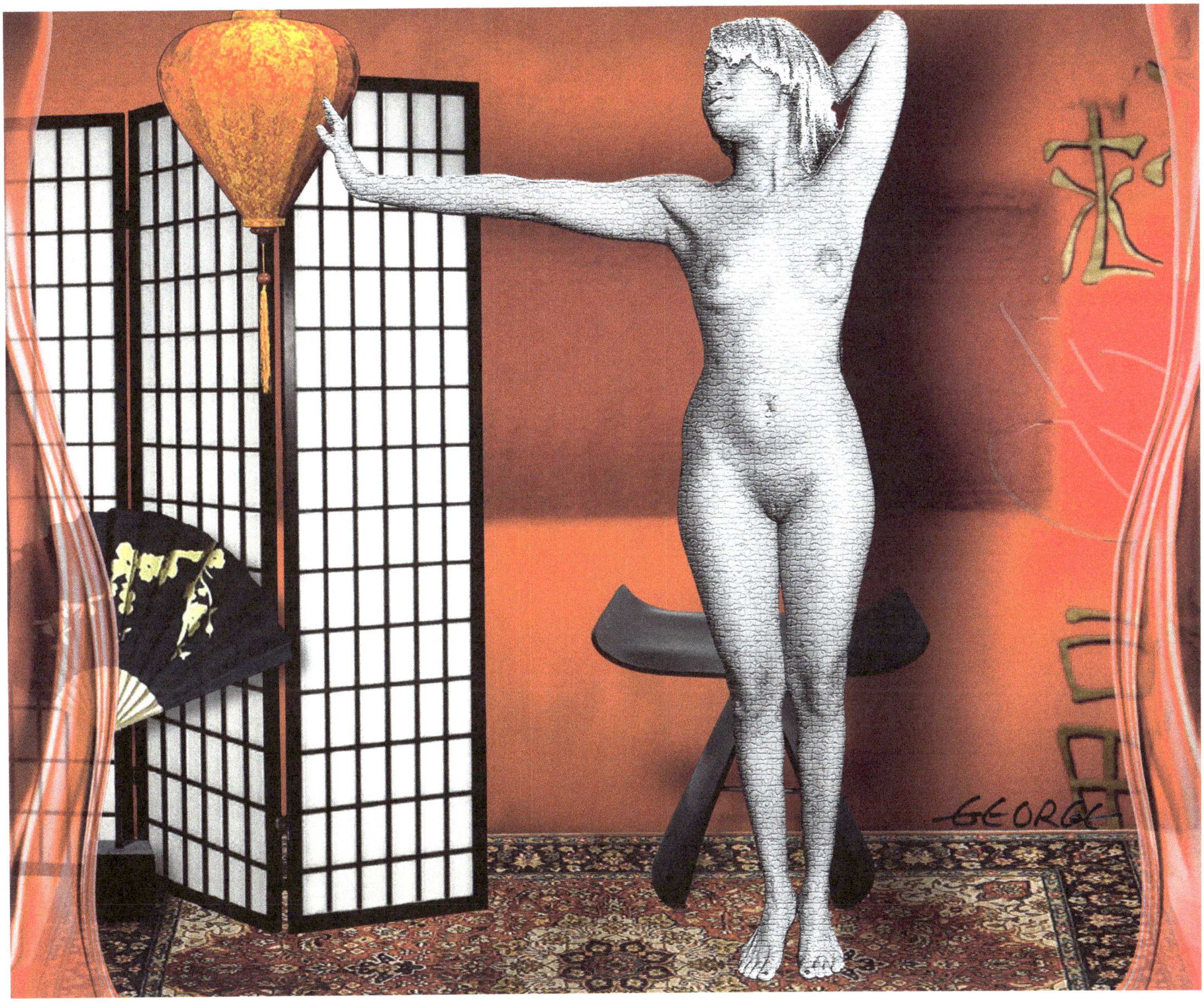

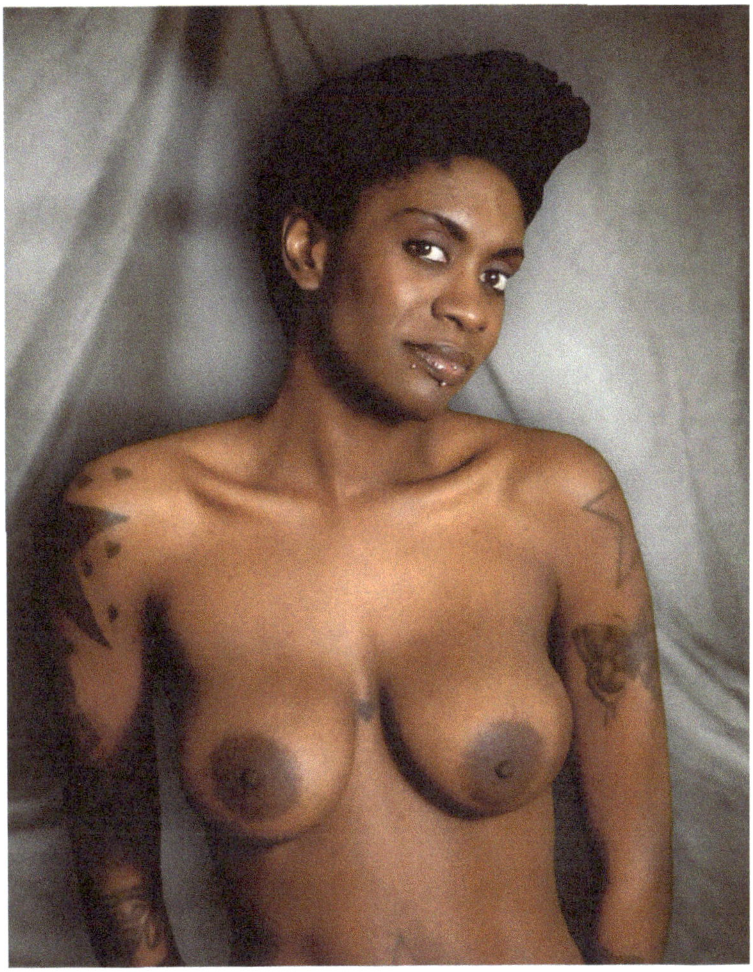

AVA DARKNESS

Height 5'9" Weight 125 lbs Bust 36" Waist 26" Hips 36" Cup D

I am a professional fine art model with over four years of experience in live/figure modeling. I love all things glamorous, stylized, classic, controversial, offensive, silly, edgy, funky, messy, crazy, kinky, sexy, dirty, arty, creepy, funny and freaky... especially if nude.

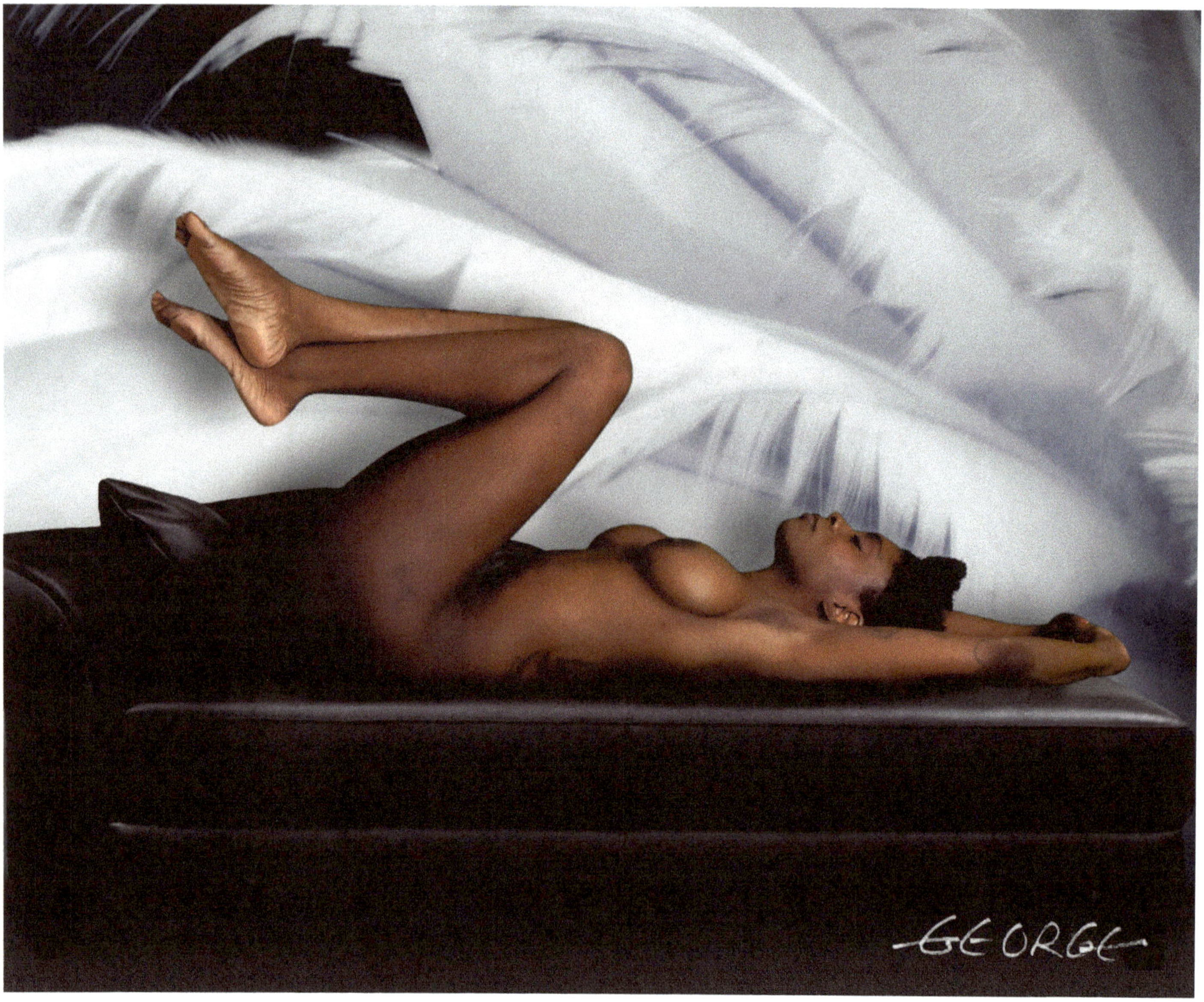
GEORGE

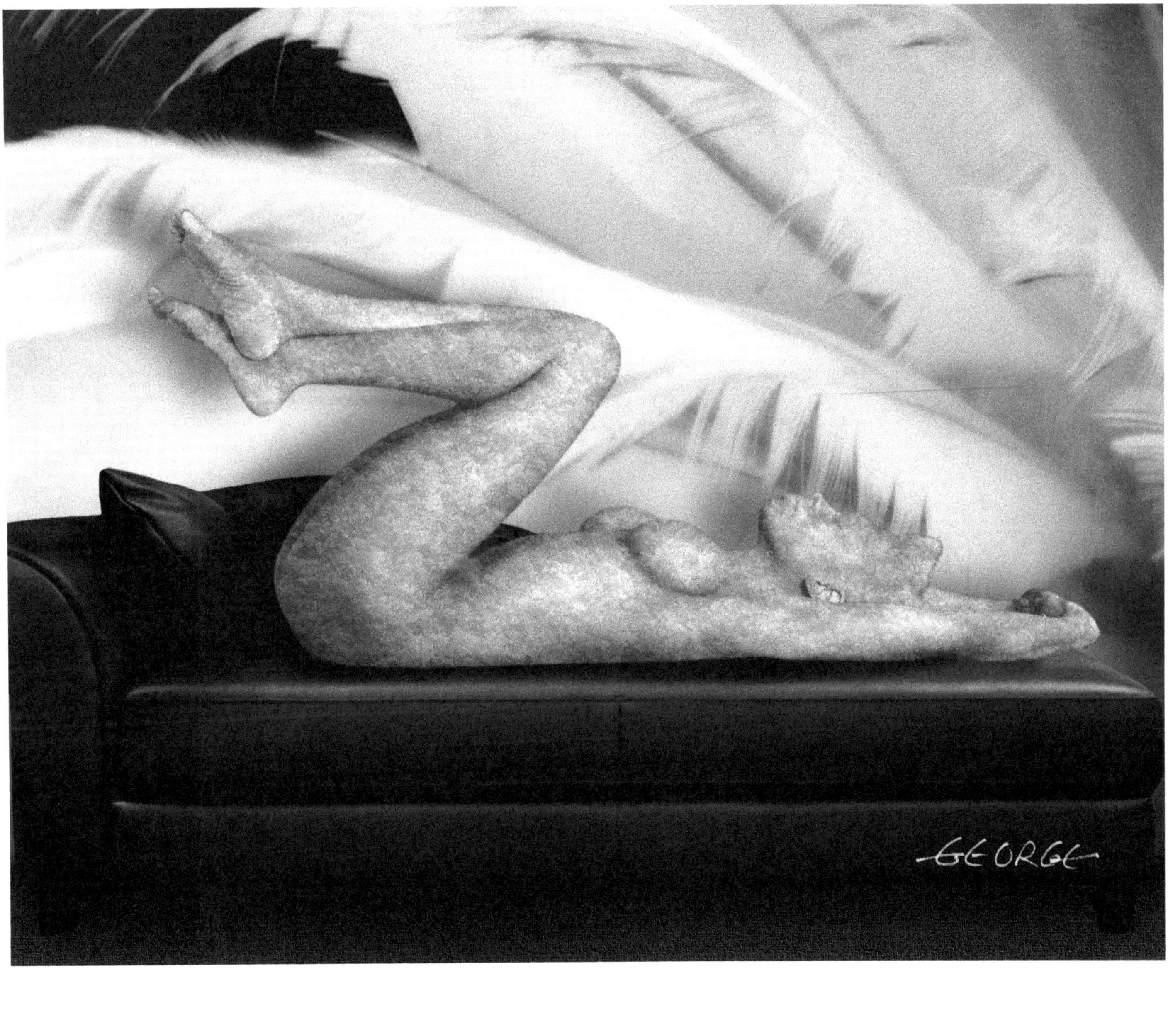
GEORGE

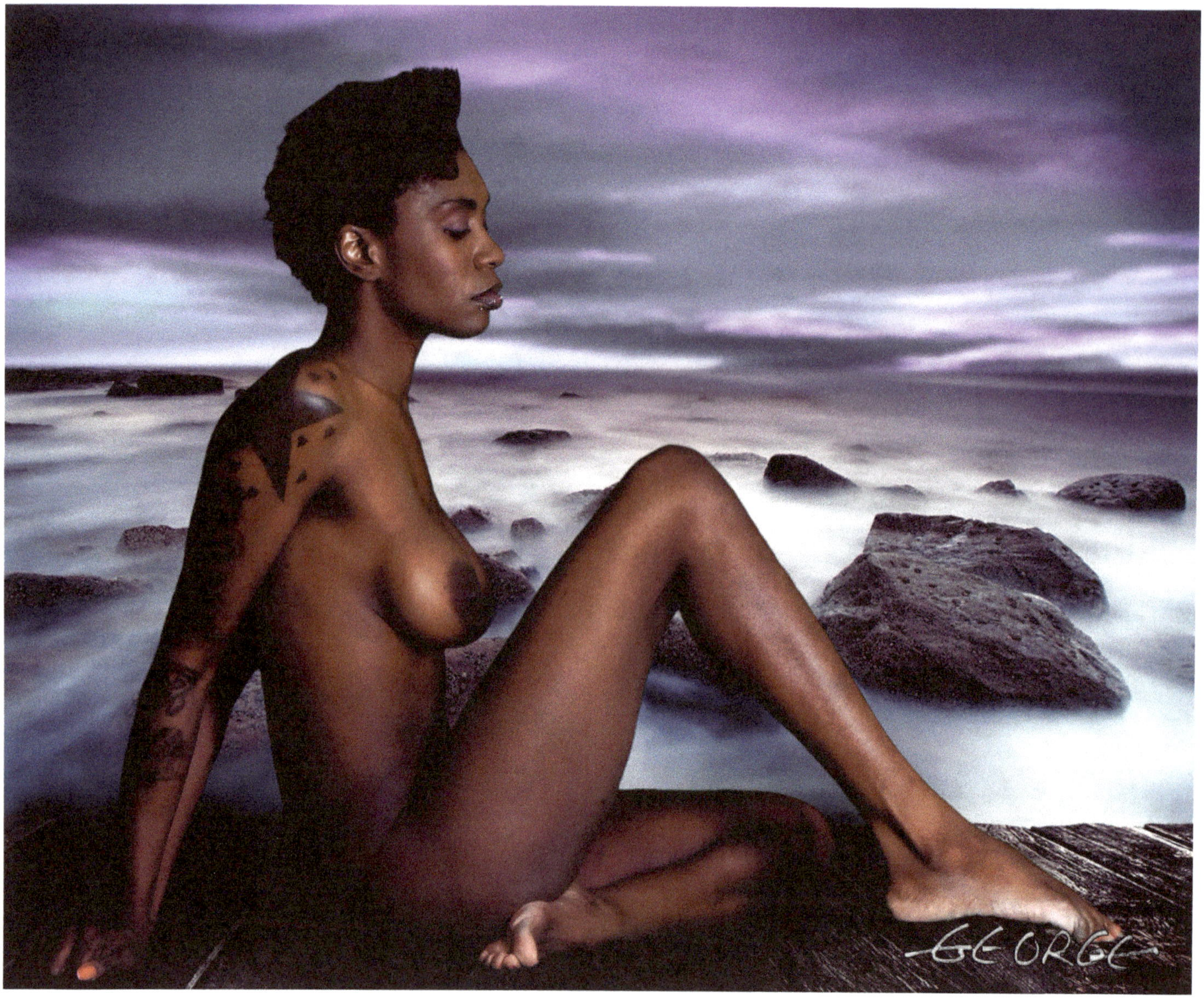
GEORGE

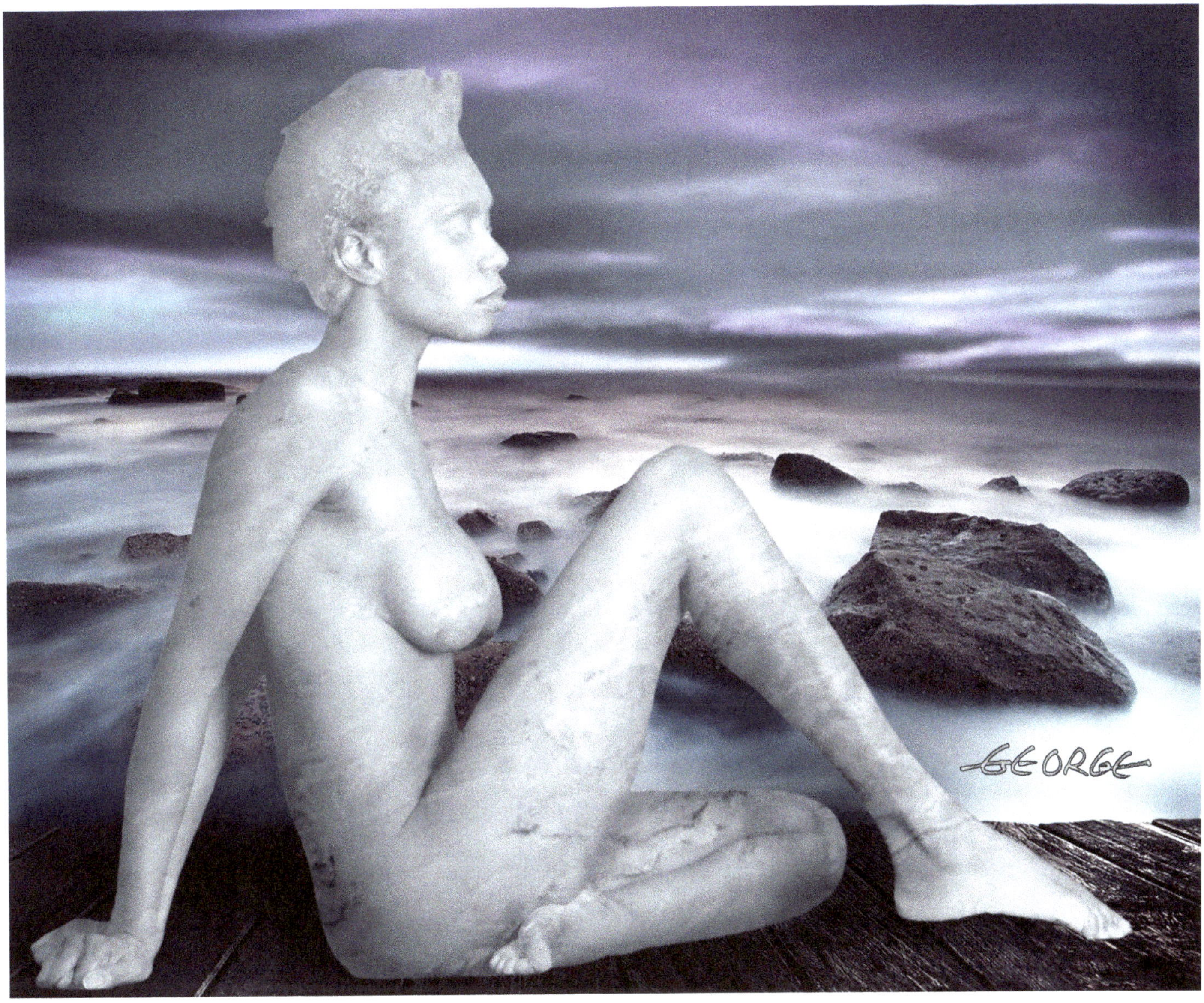
GEORGE

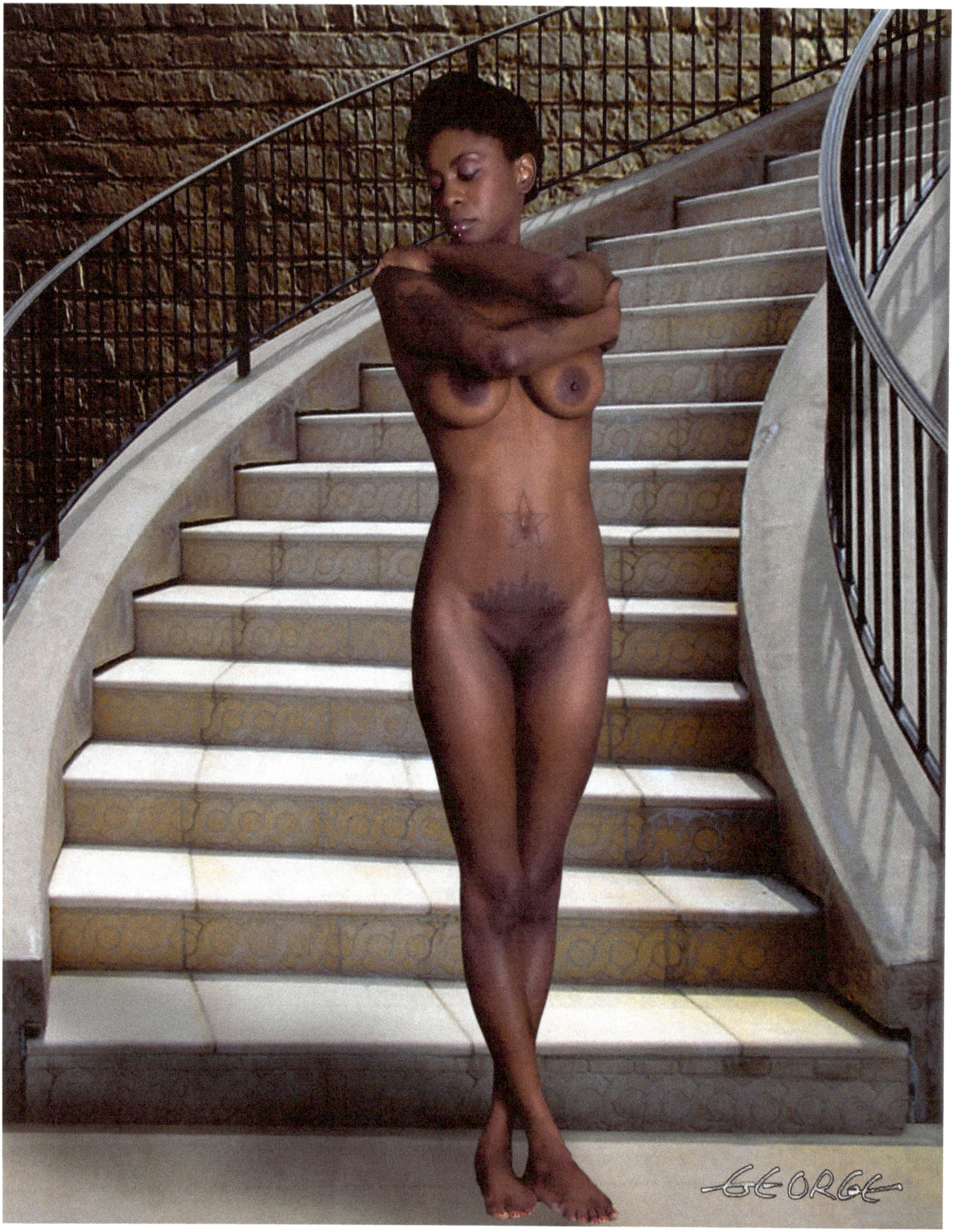
GEORGE

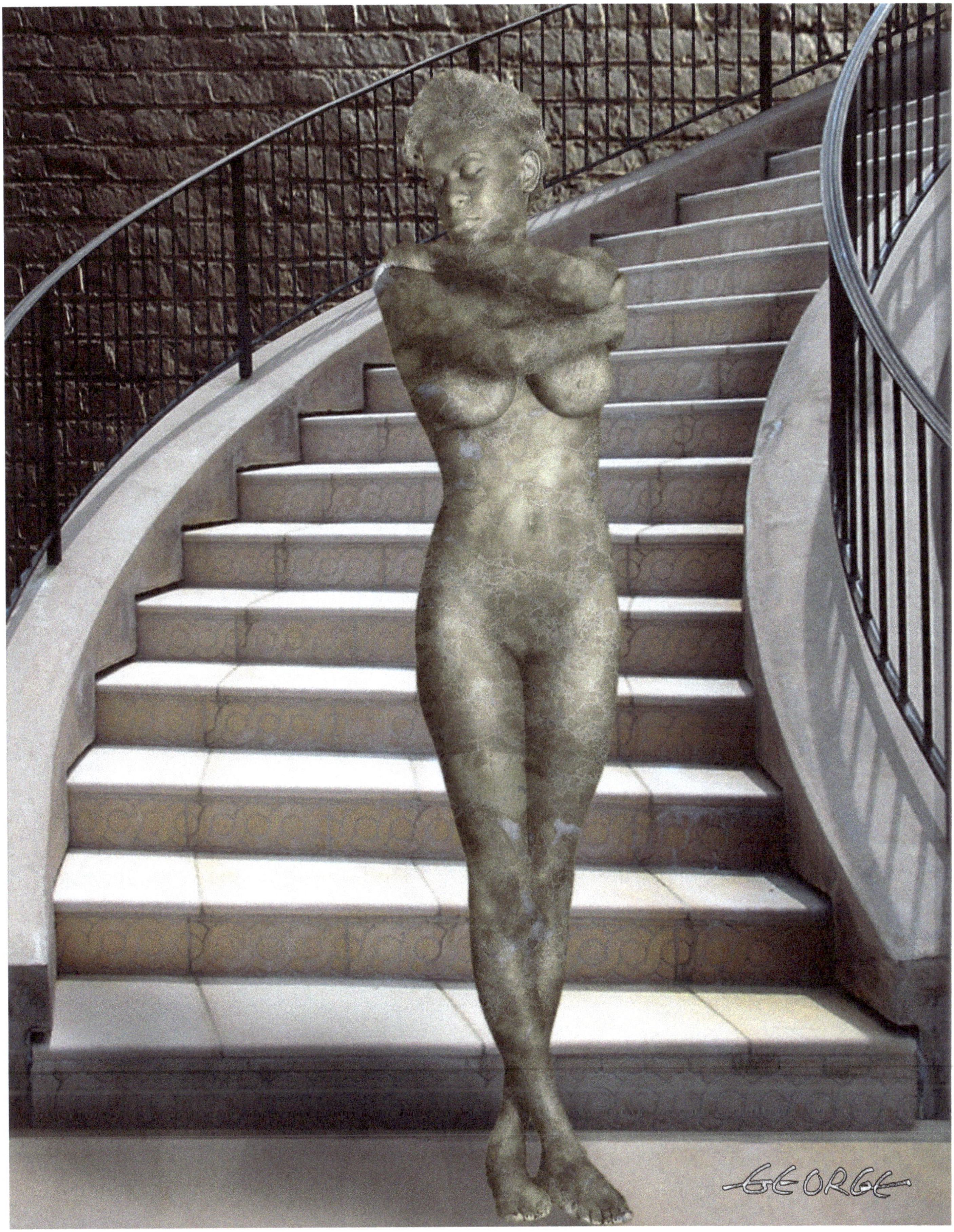
GEORGE

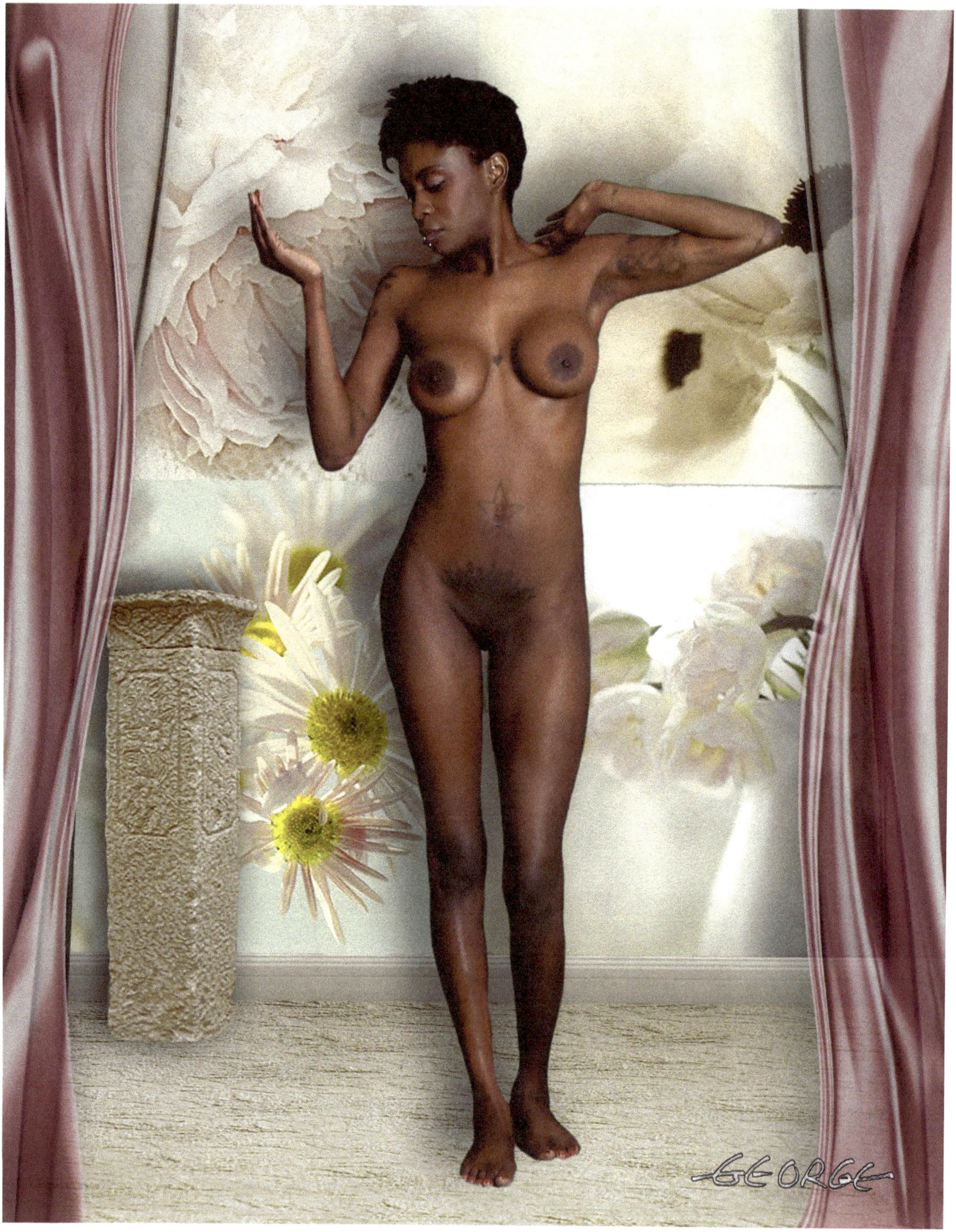
GEORGE

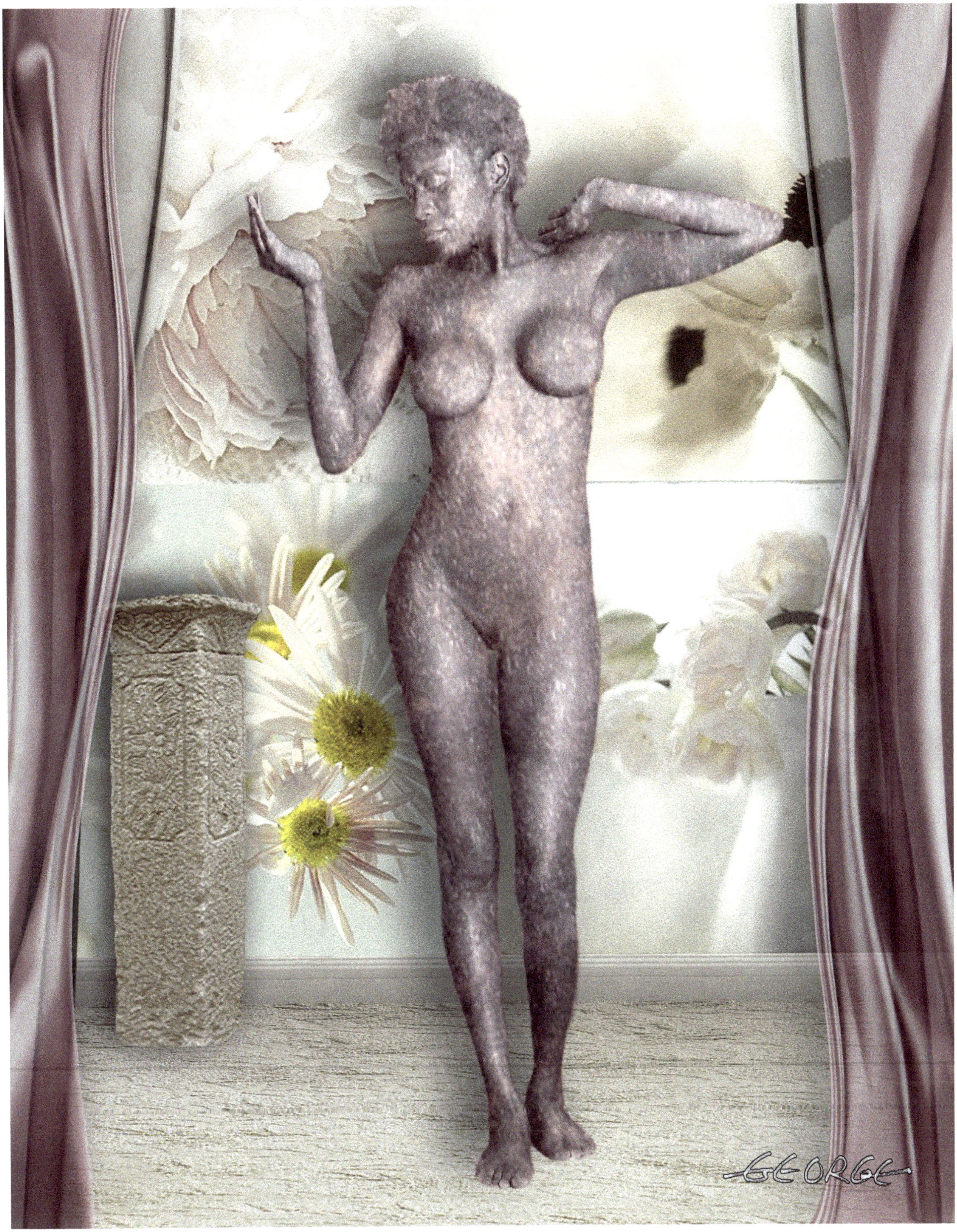
GEORGE

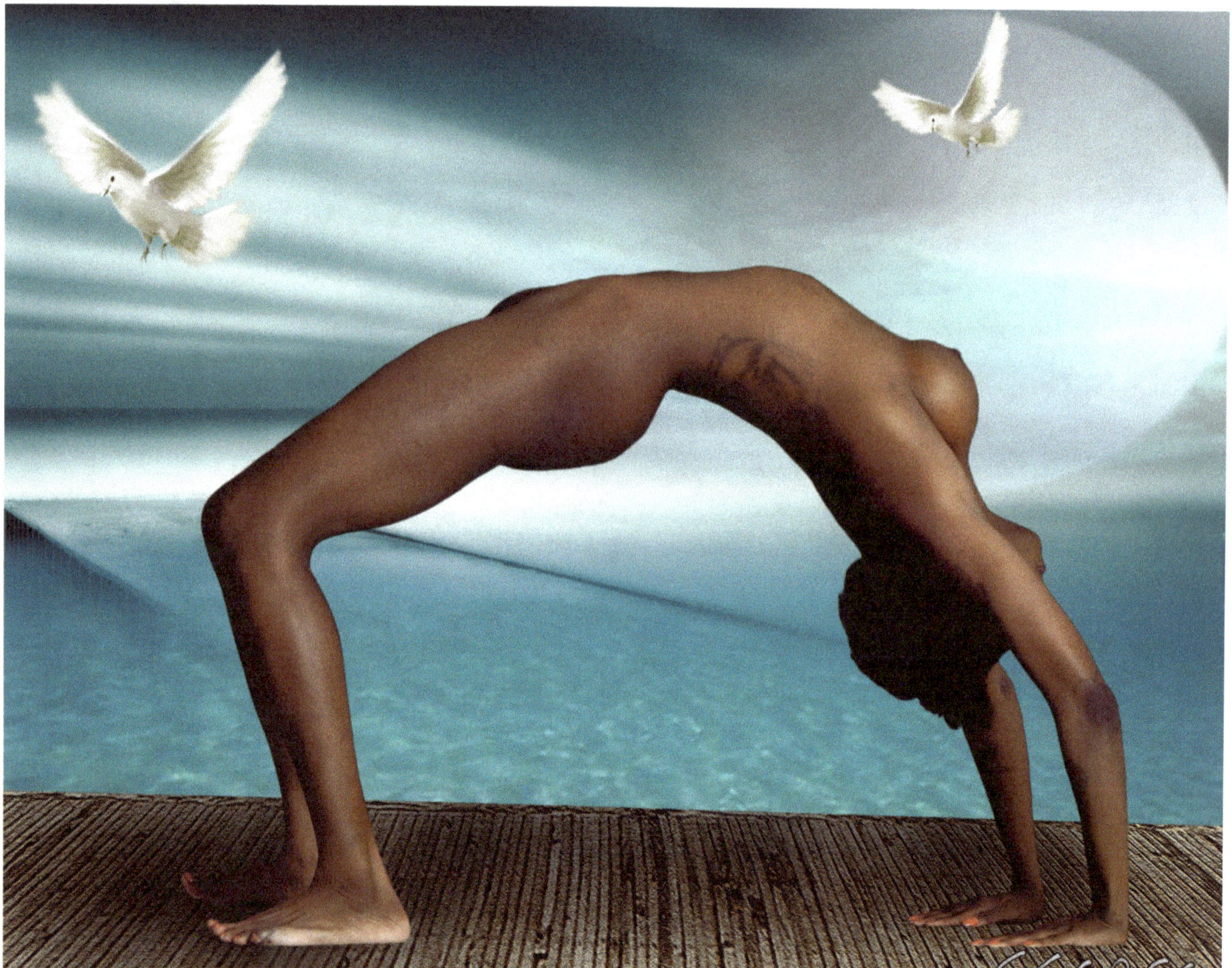
GEORGE

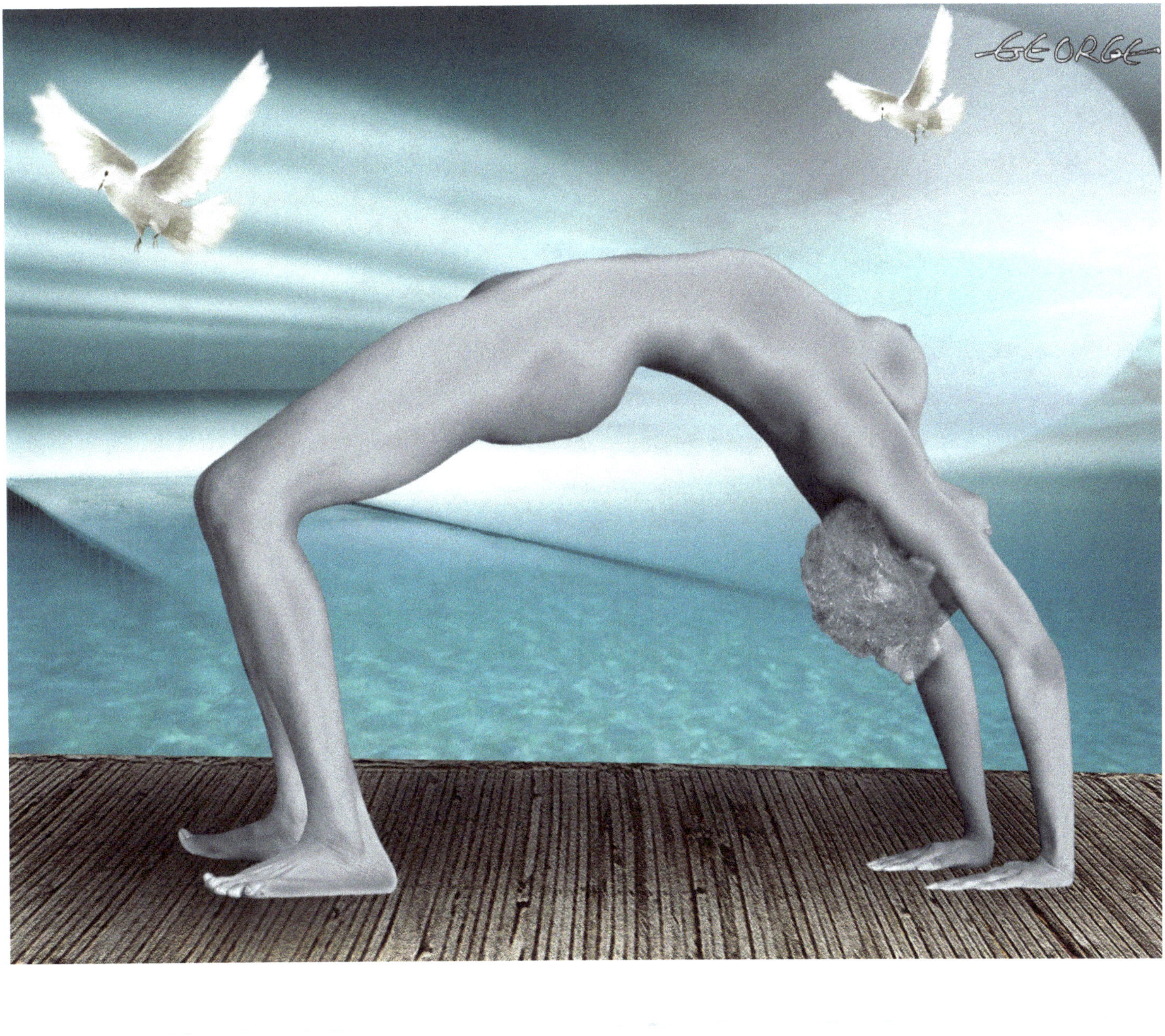
GEORGE

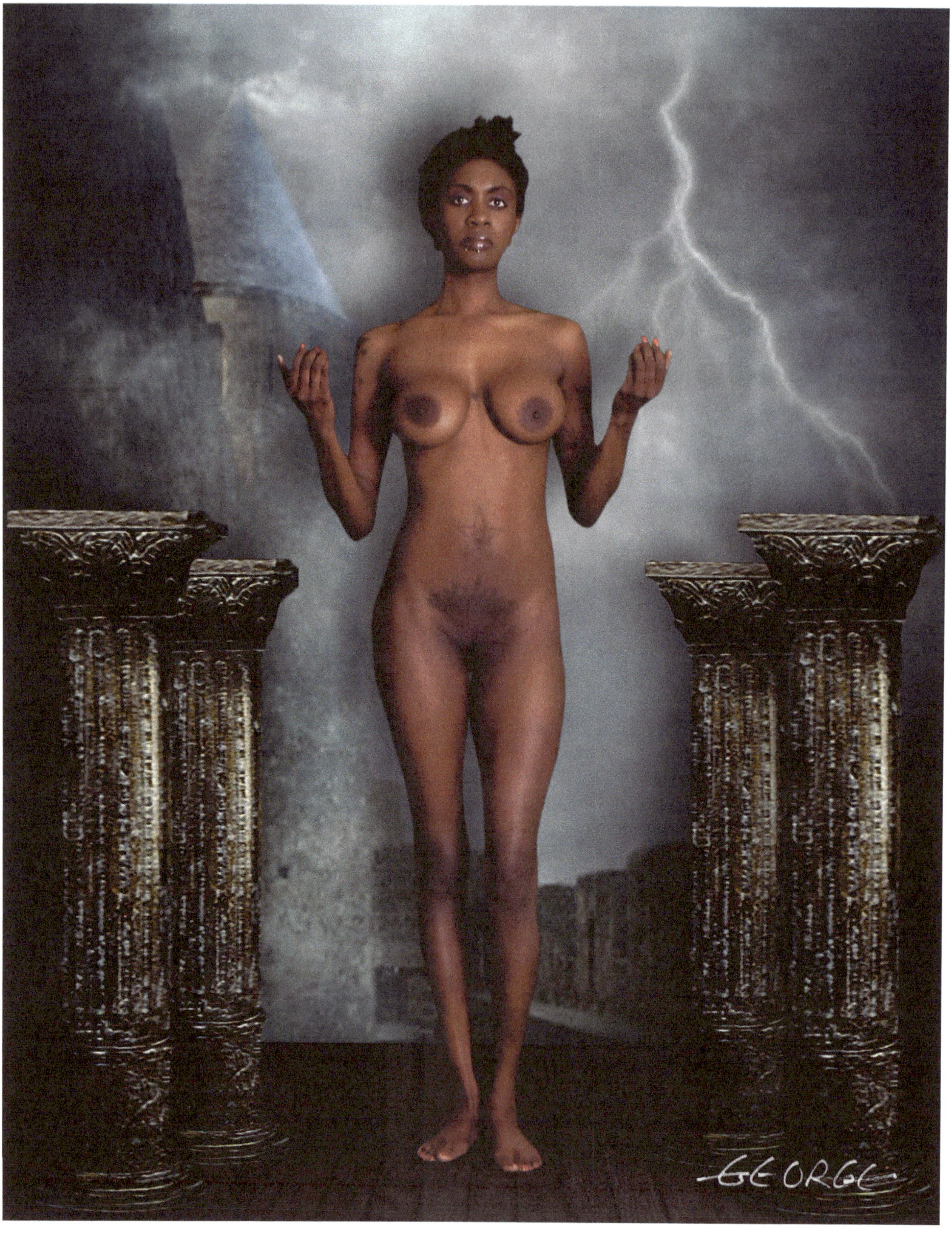
GEORGE

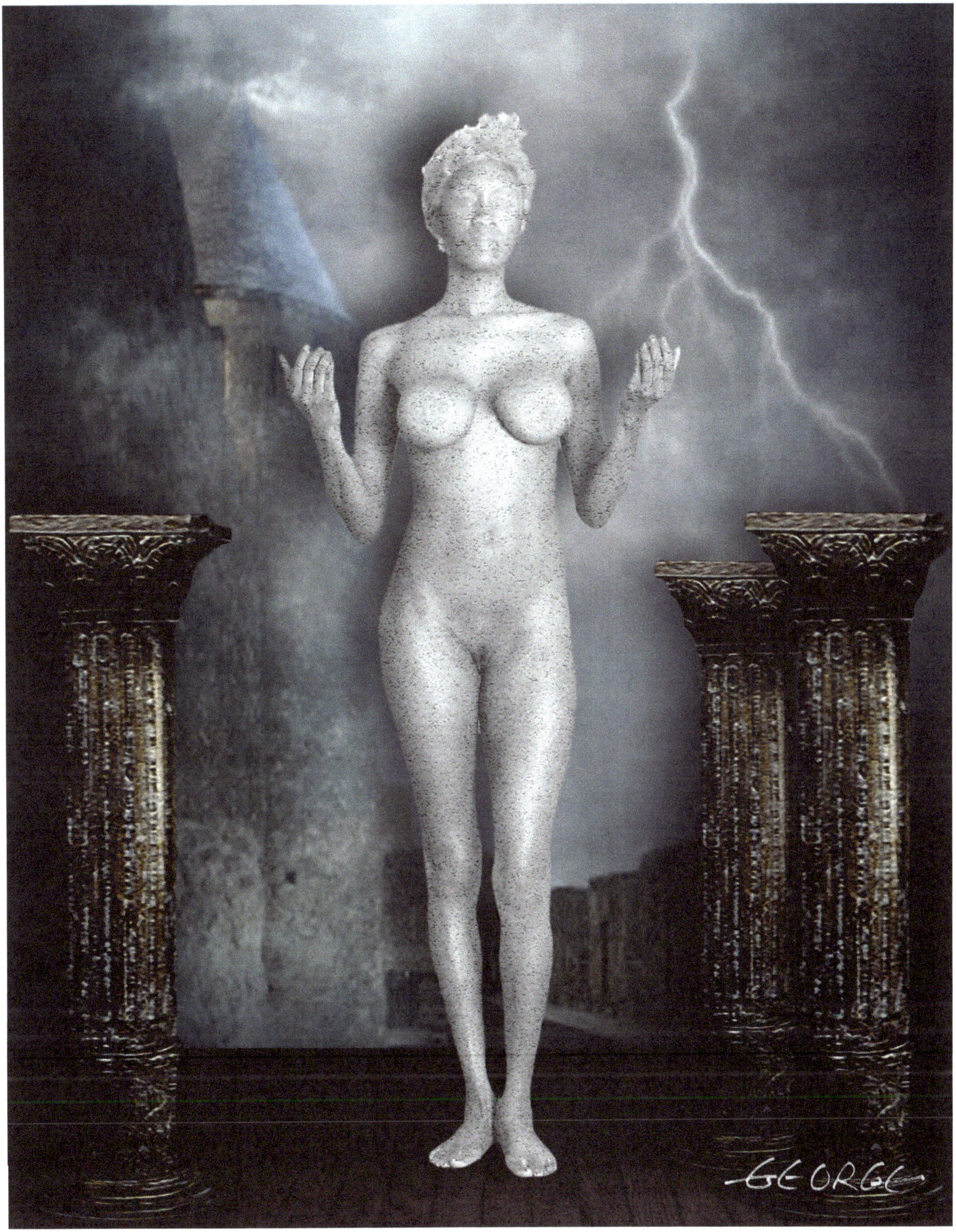
GEORGE

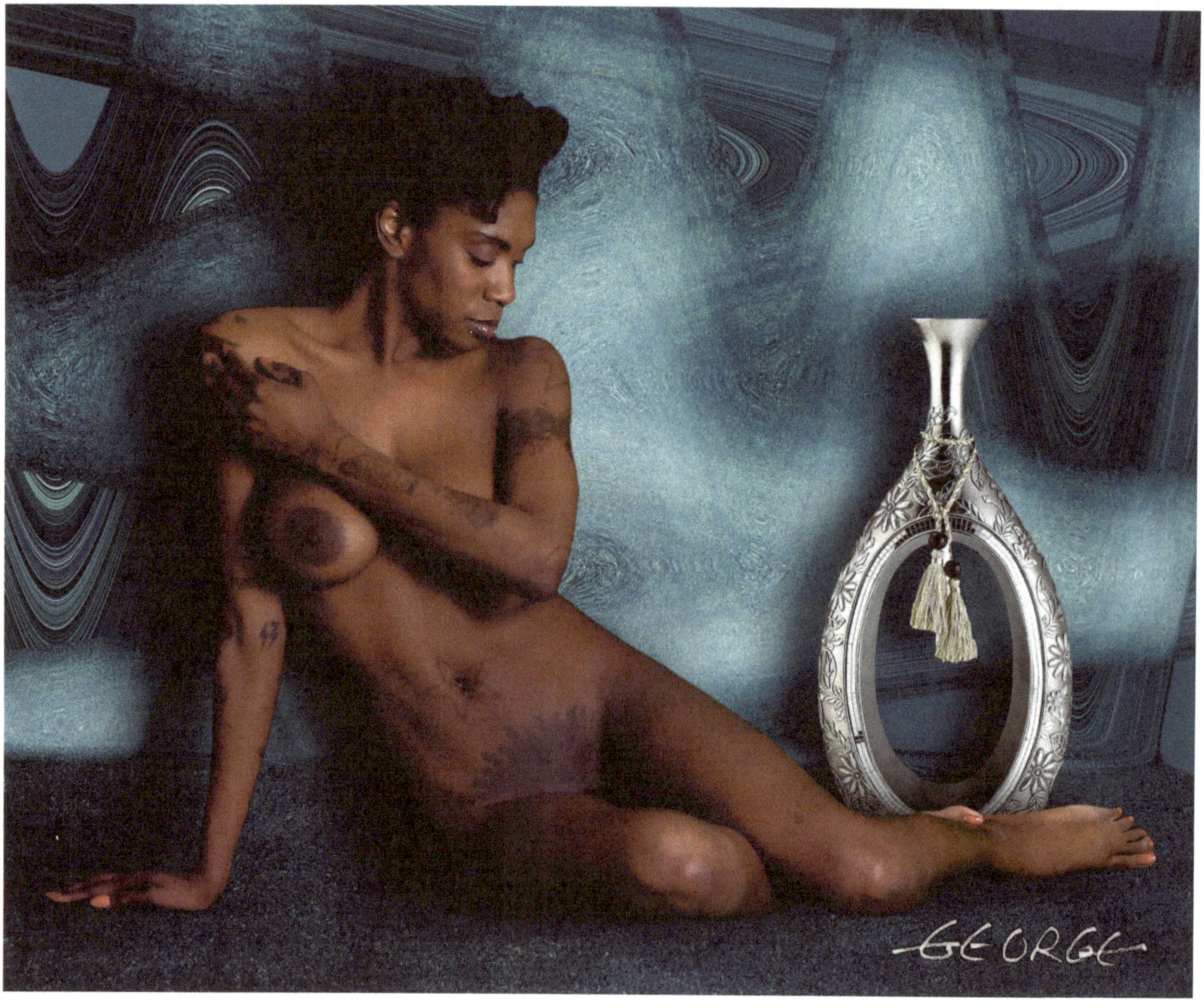
GEORGE

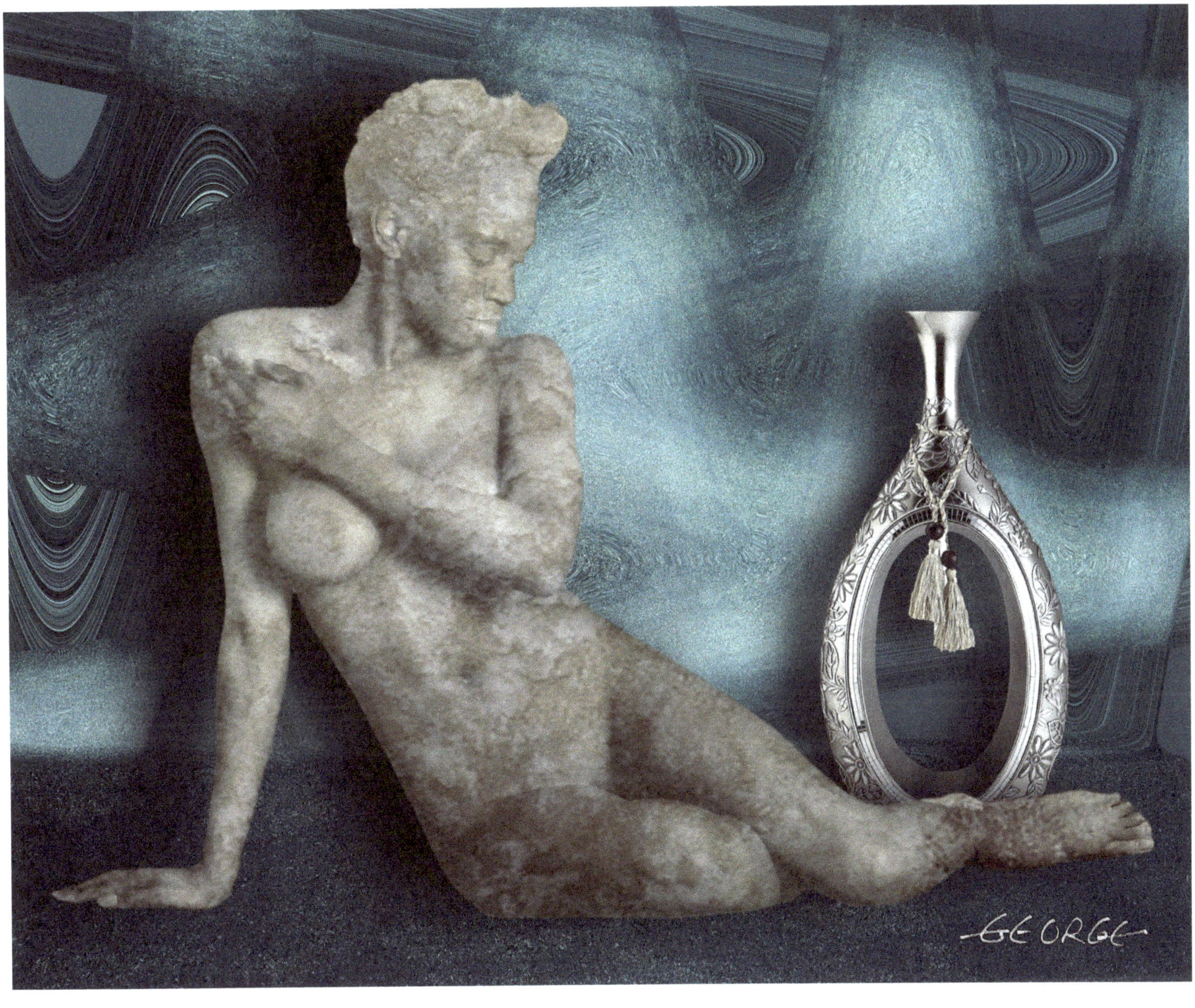
GEORGE

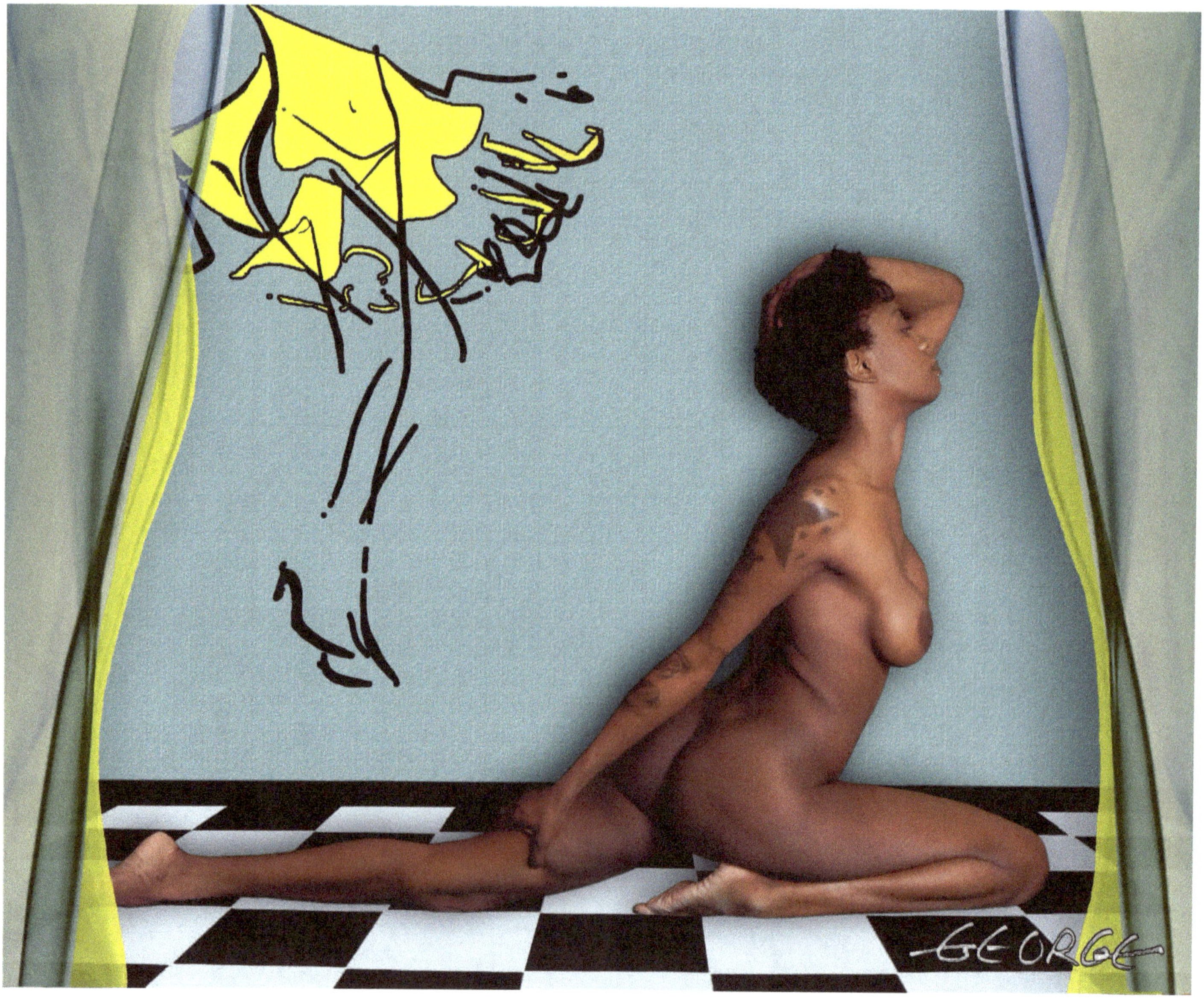
GEORGE

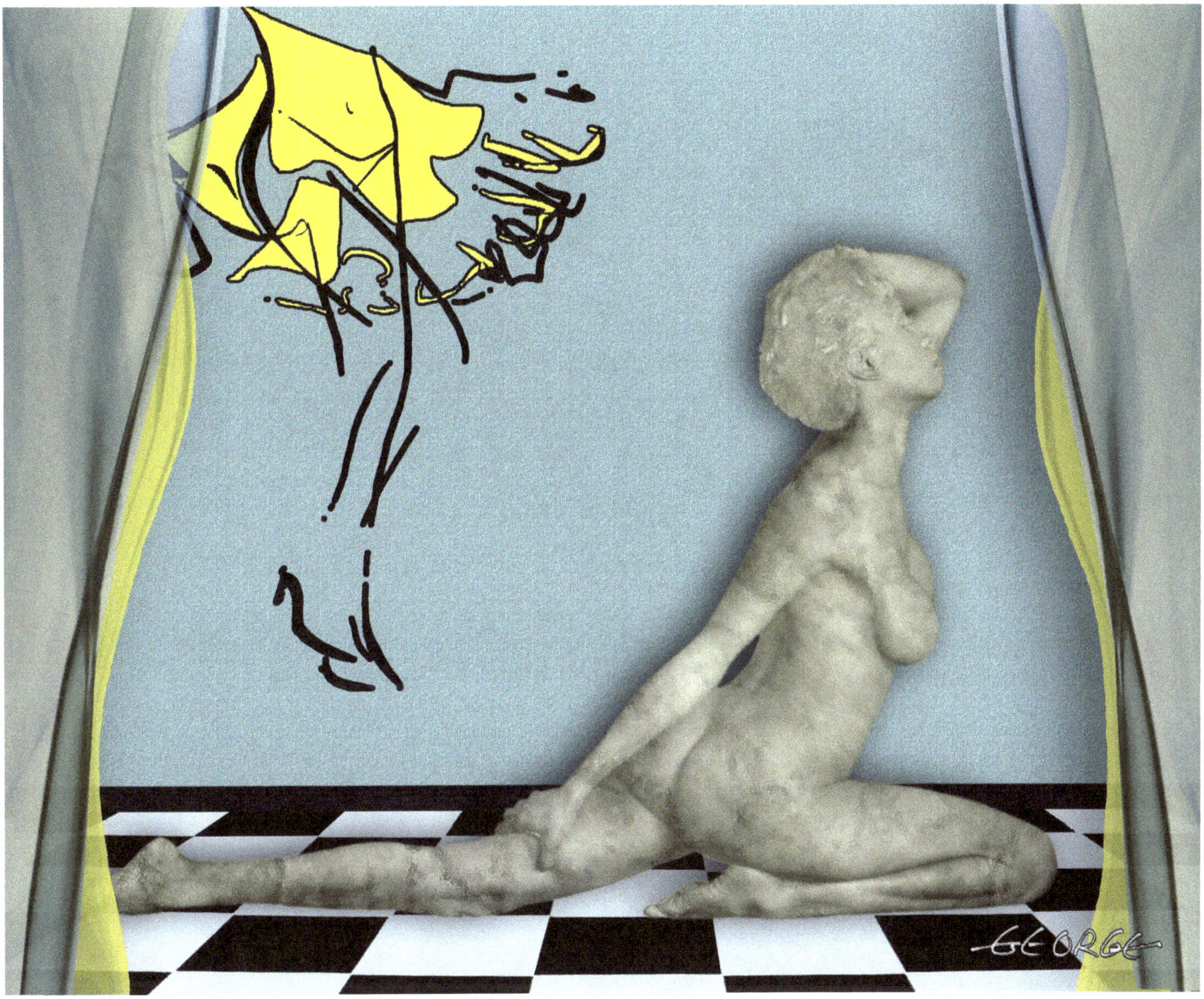
GEORGE

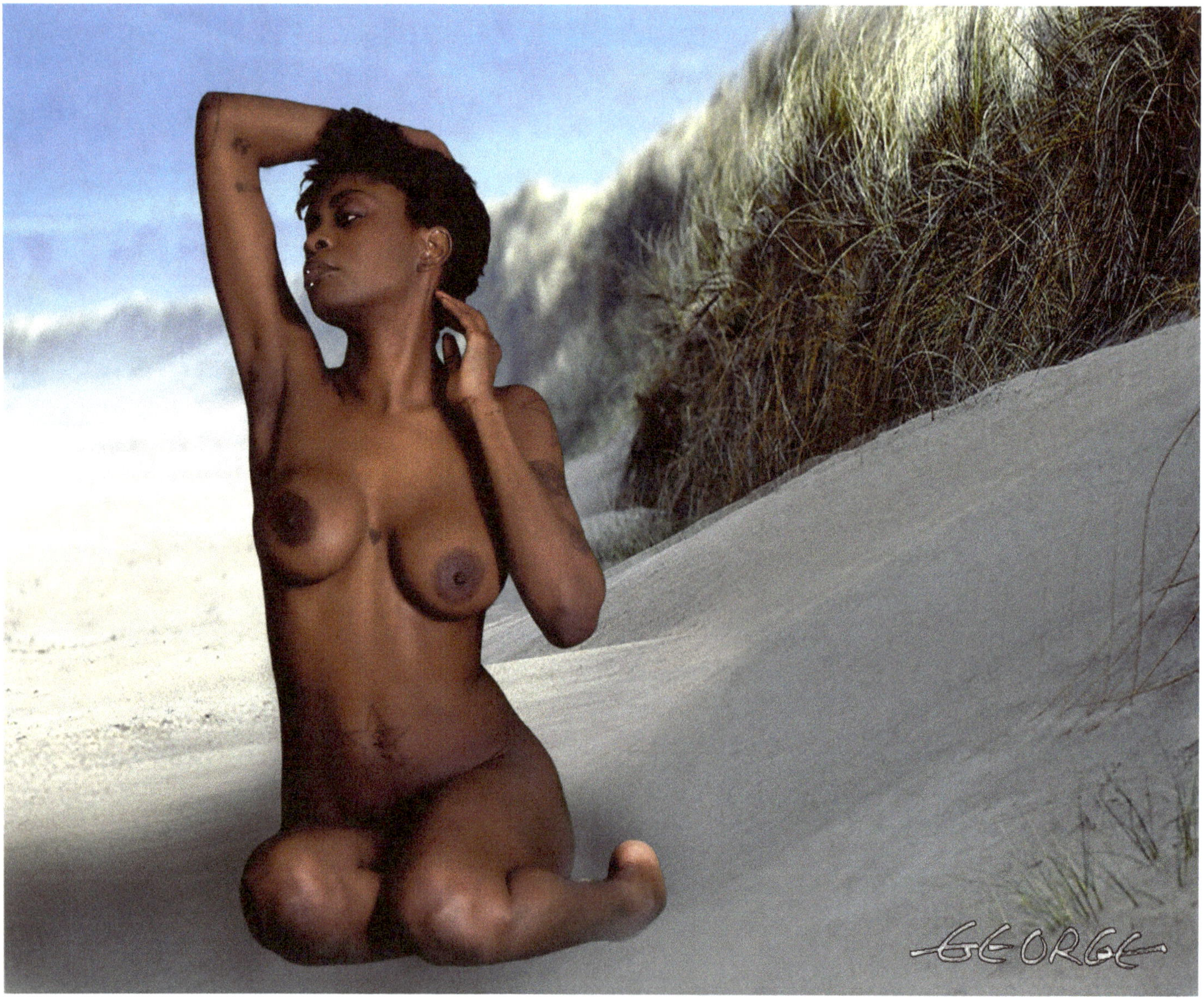
GEORGE

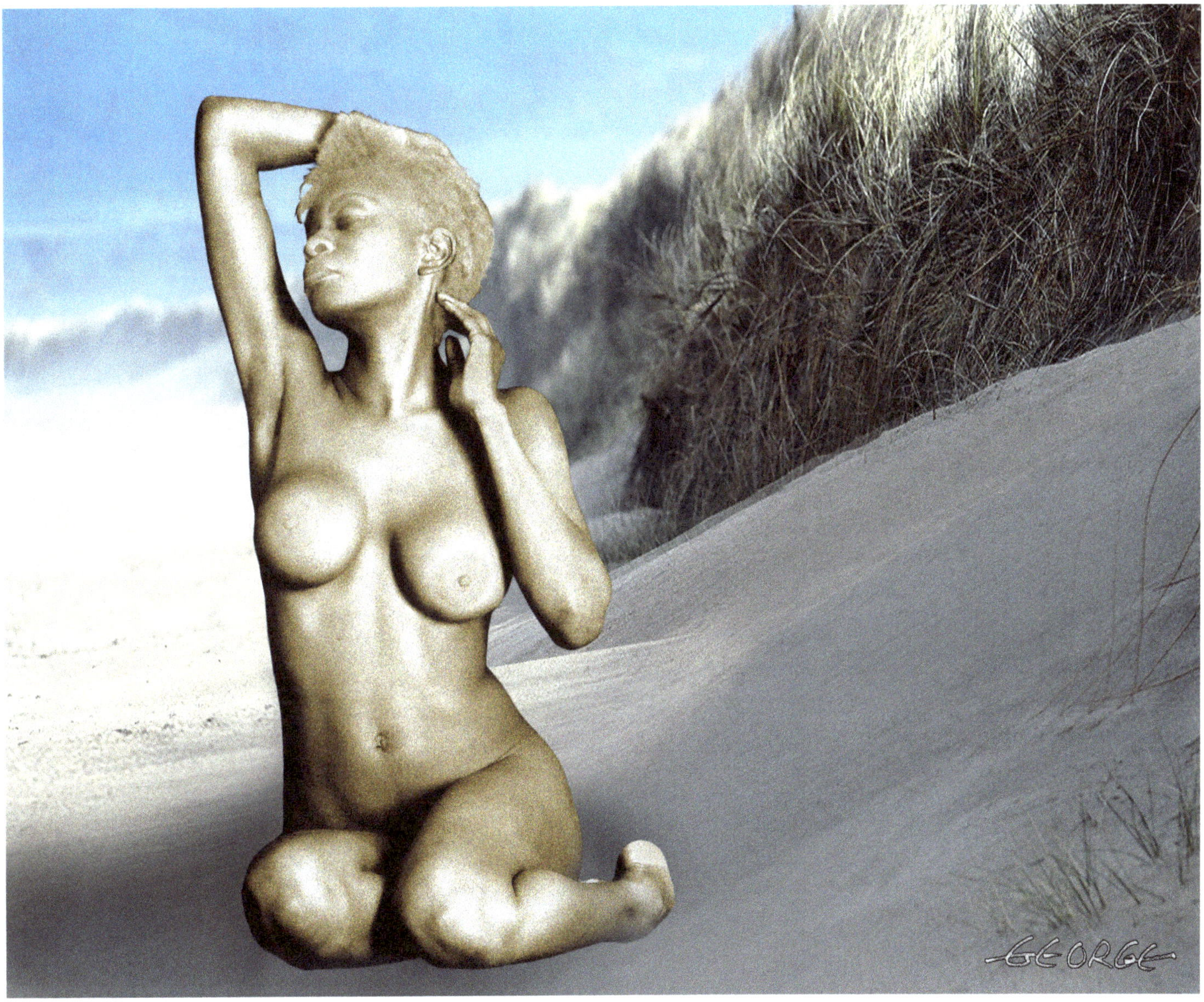
GEORGE

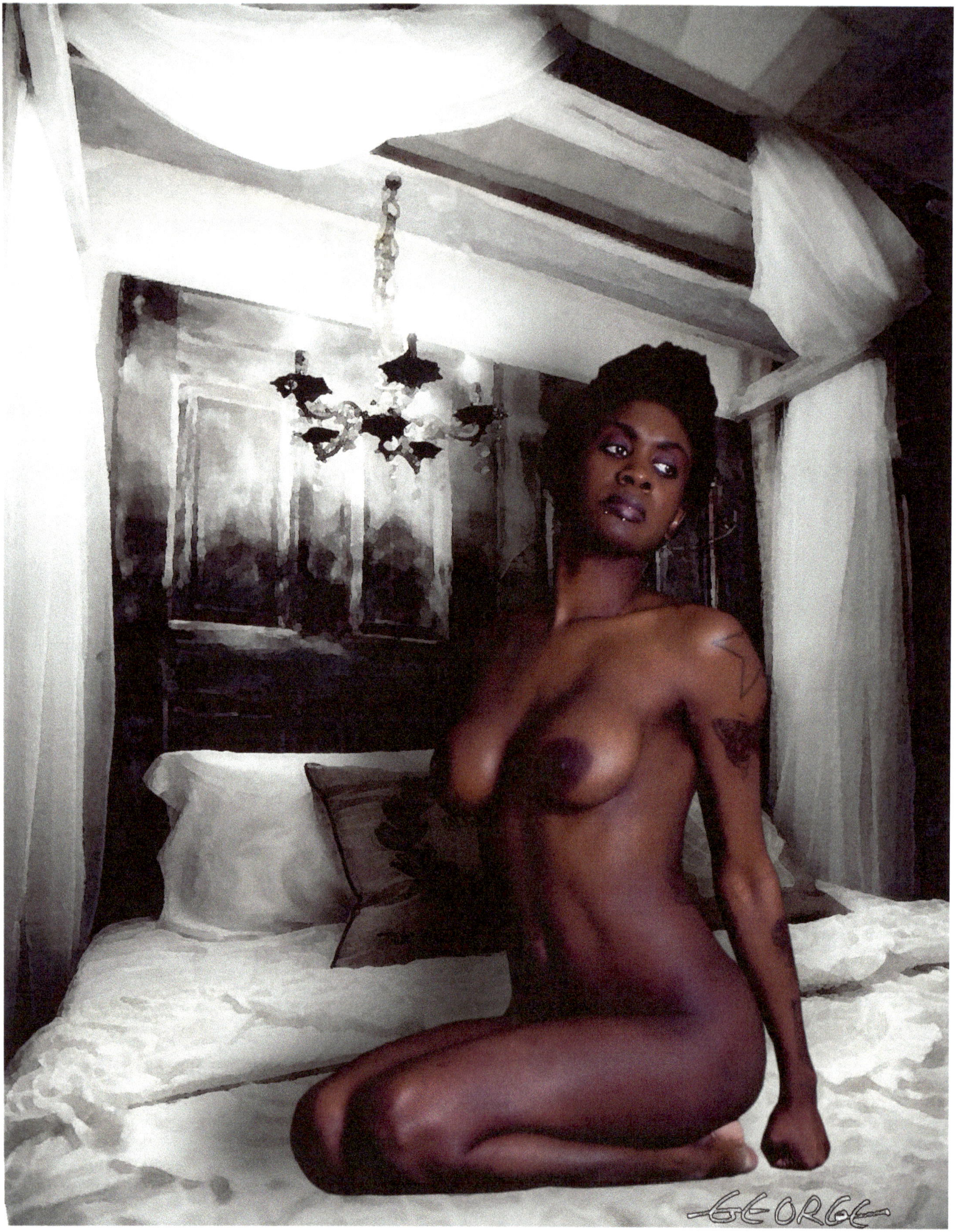
GEORGE

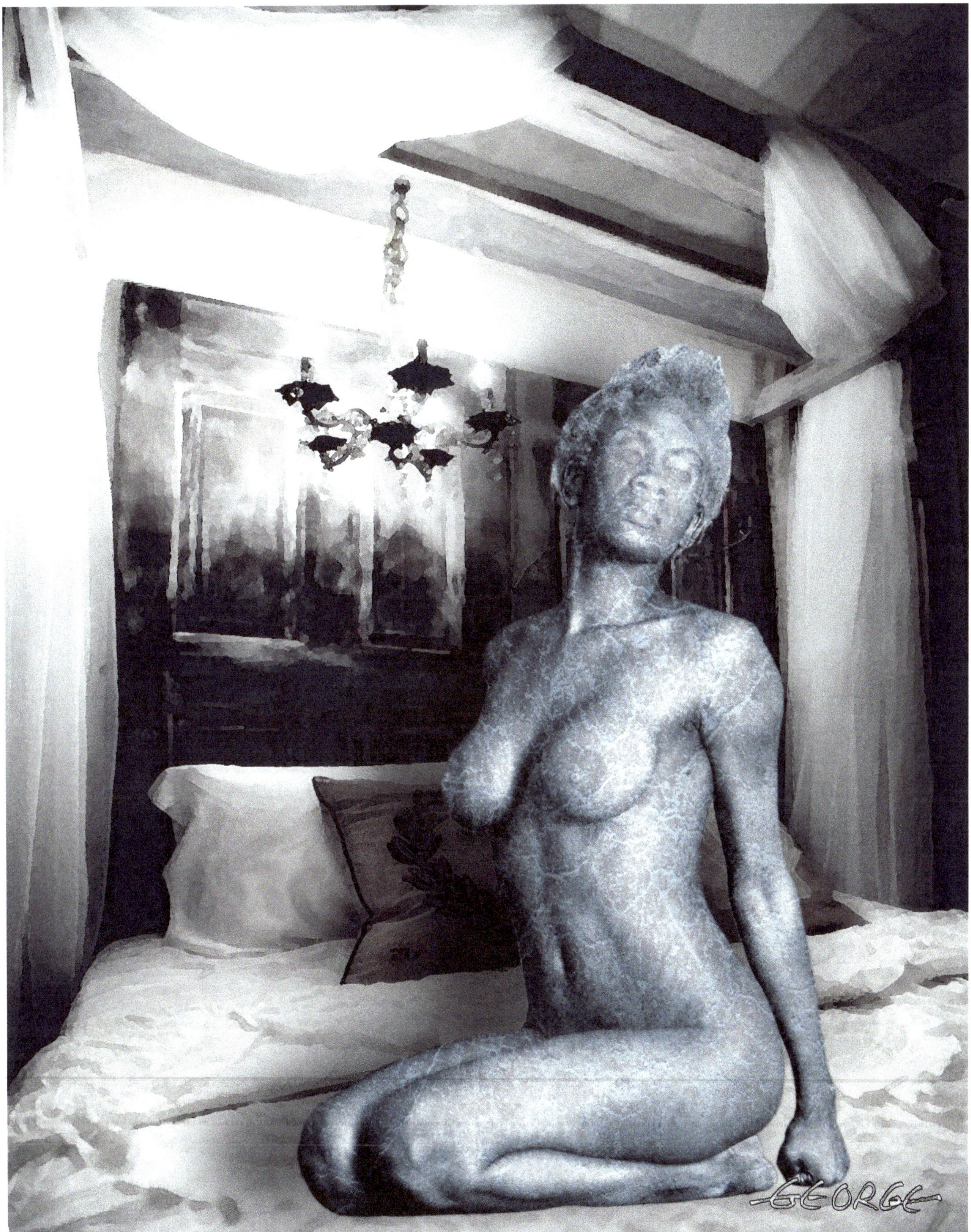
GEORGE

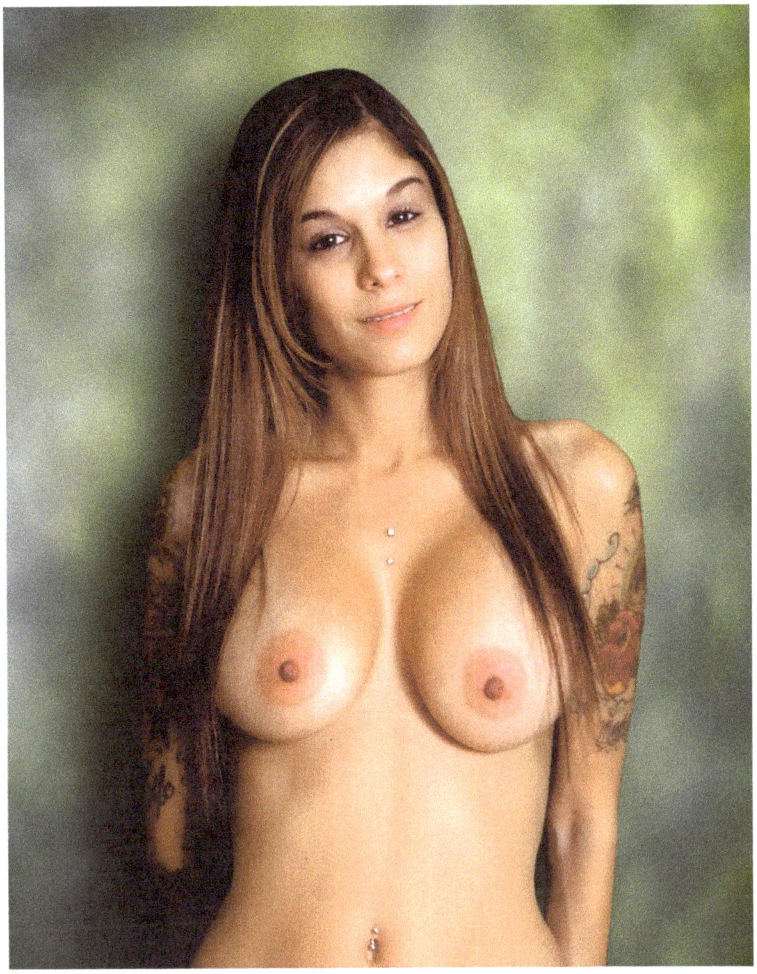

EMILY MARIE

Height 5'1" Weight 95 lbs Bust 34" Waist 24" Hips 36" Cup

After taking a break from modeling for a few years to take care of my daughter, I was ready to get back into it again the summer of 2013. I am so glad that I have this opportunity to show the world that the human body is a beautiful work of art that should be documented.

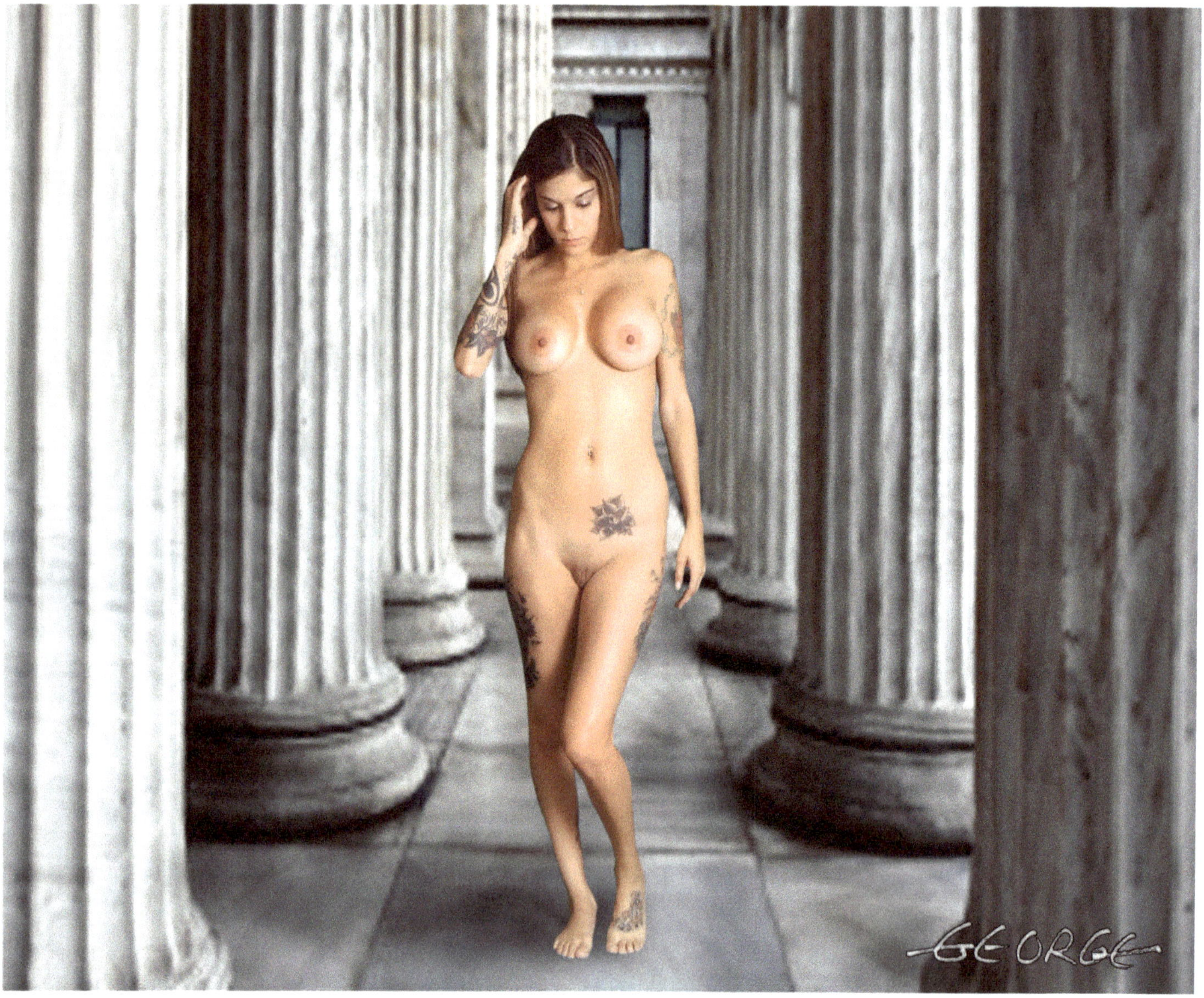
GEORGE

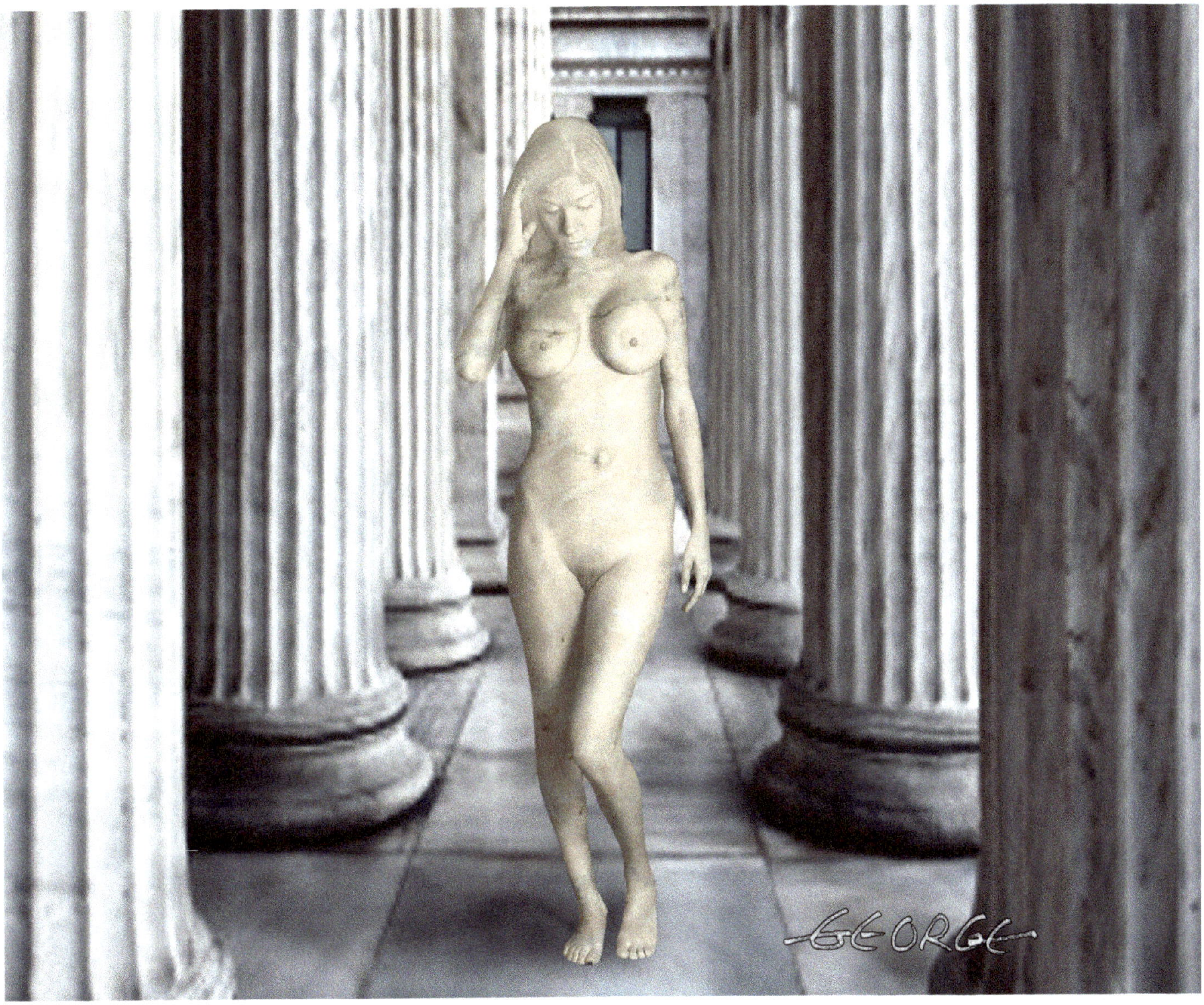
GEORGE

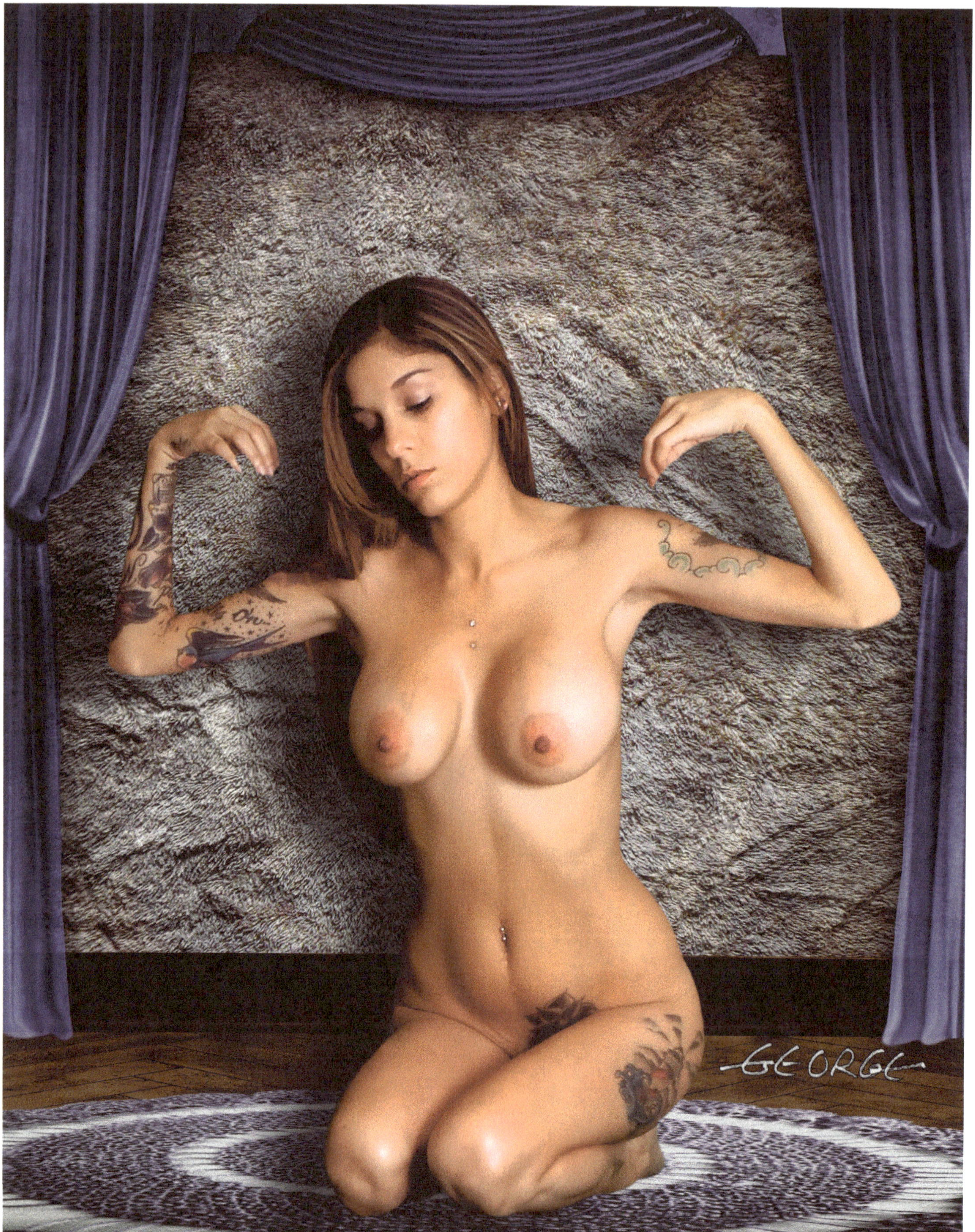
GEORGE

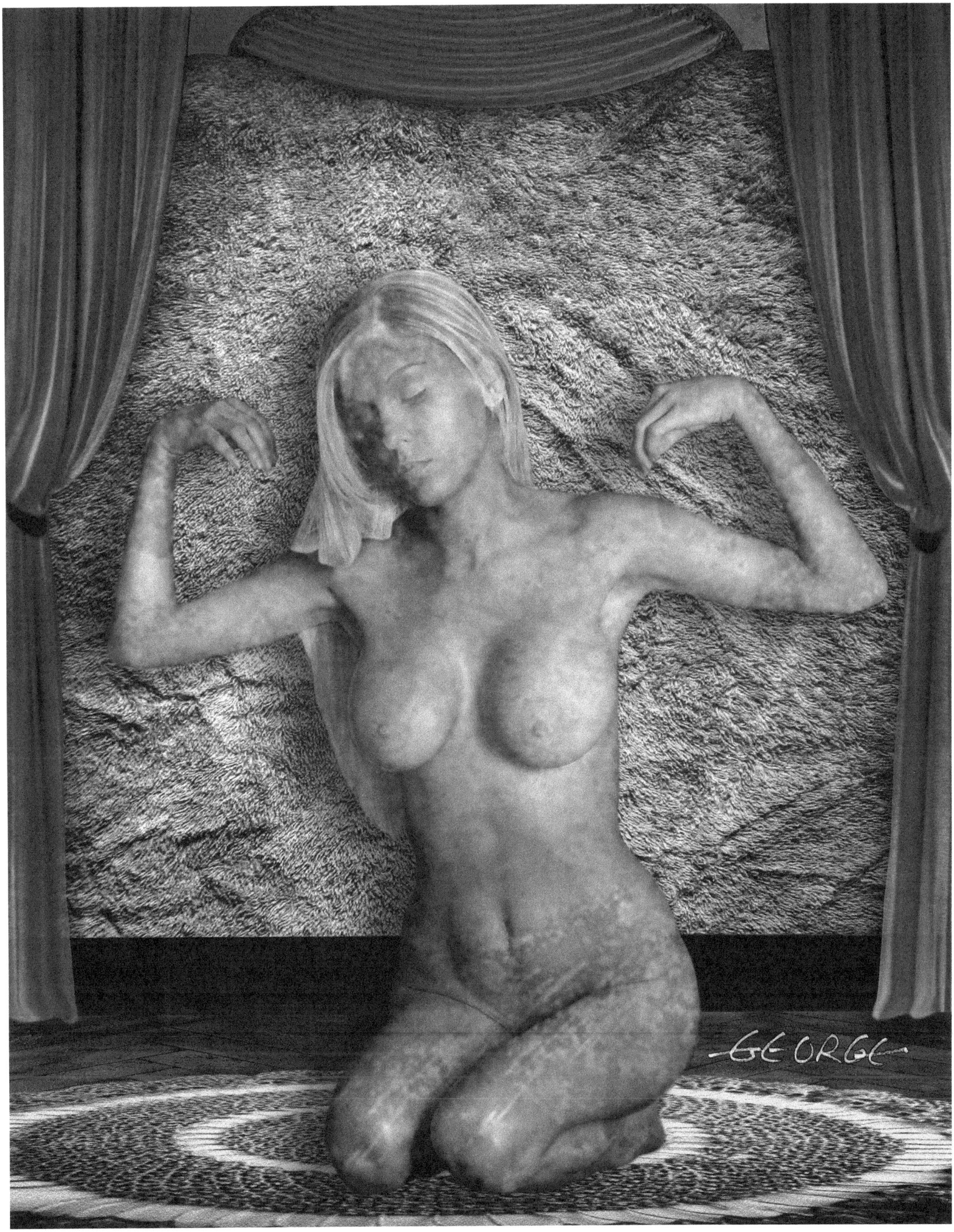
GEORGE

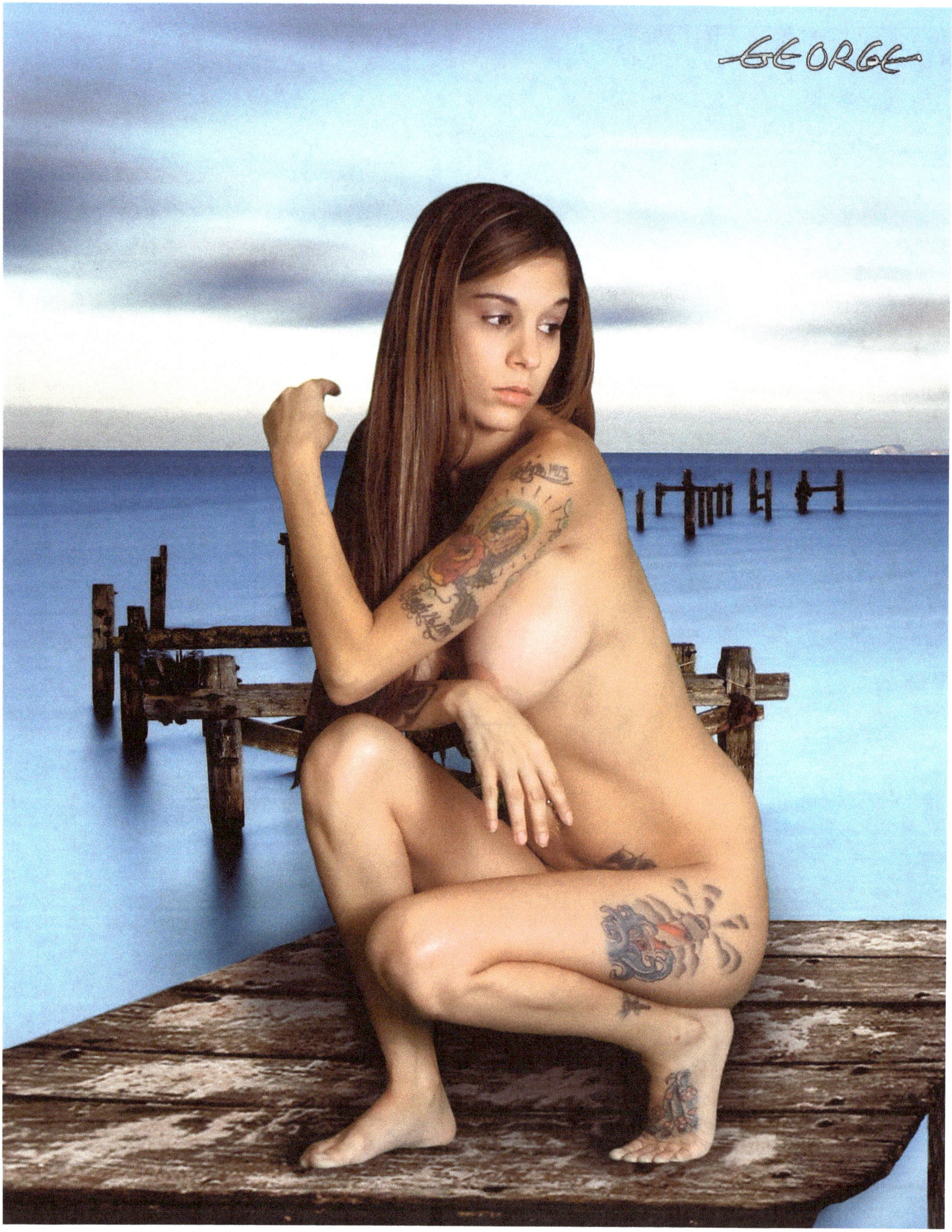
GEORGE

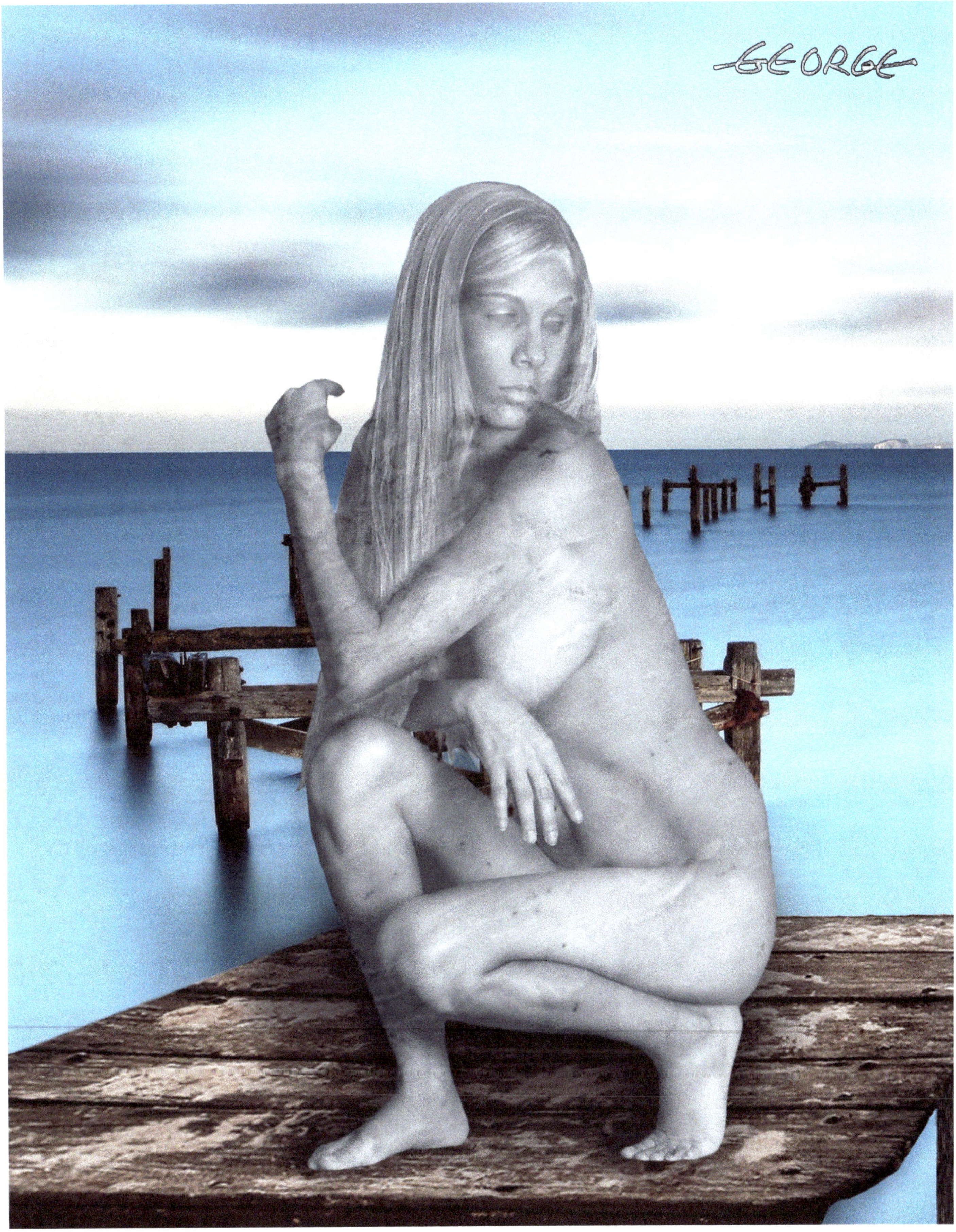
GEORGE

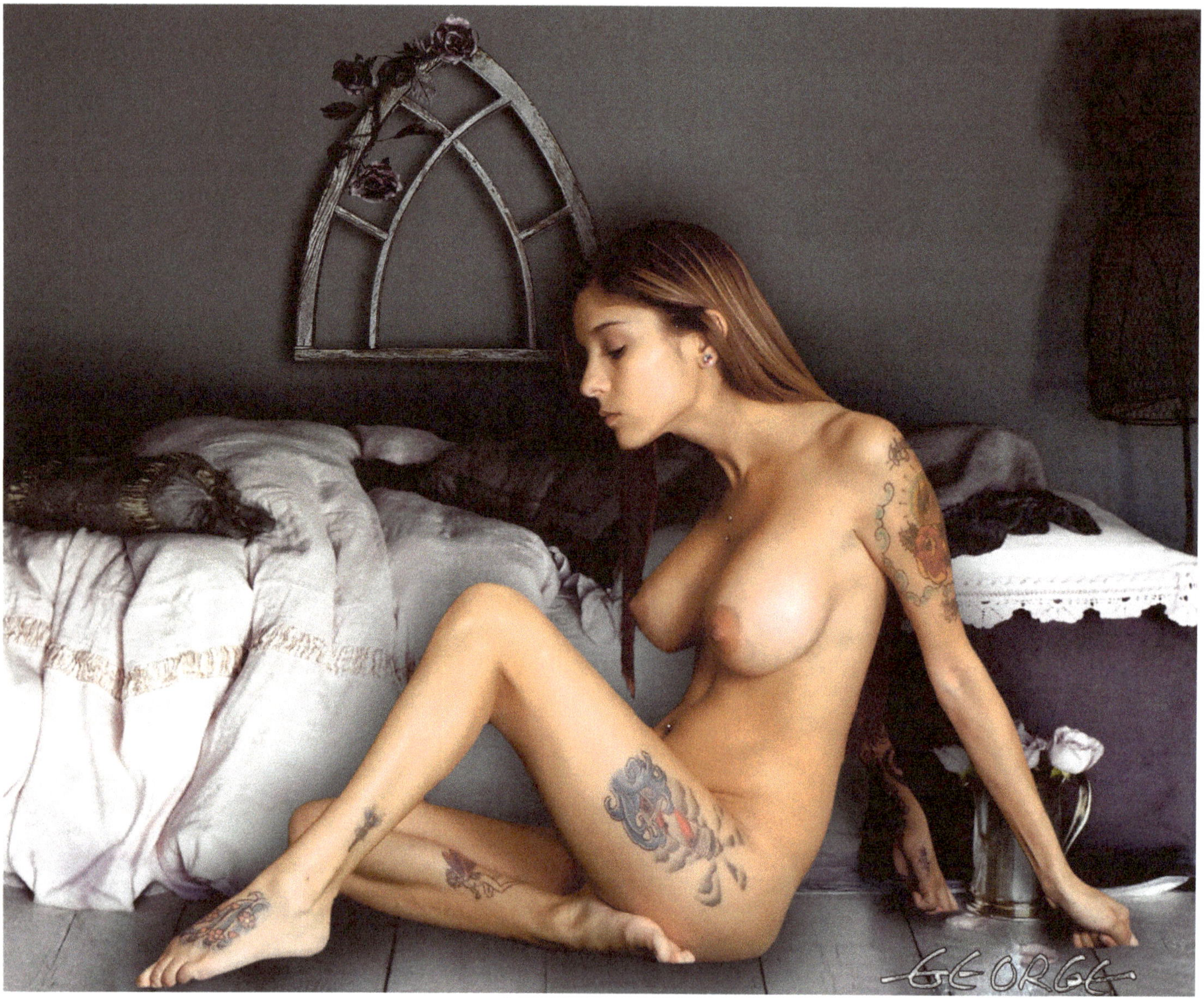
GEORGE

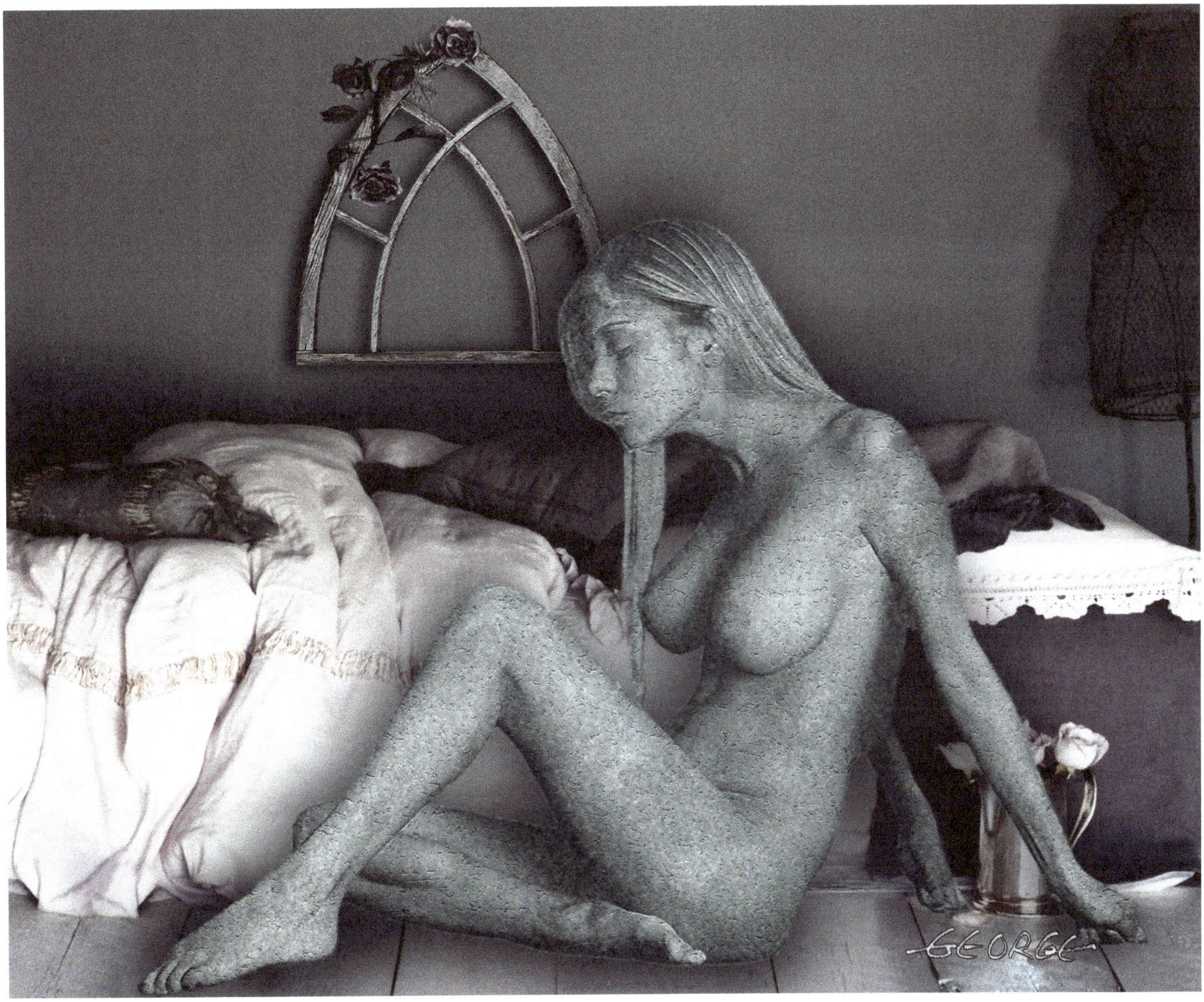
GEORGE

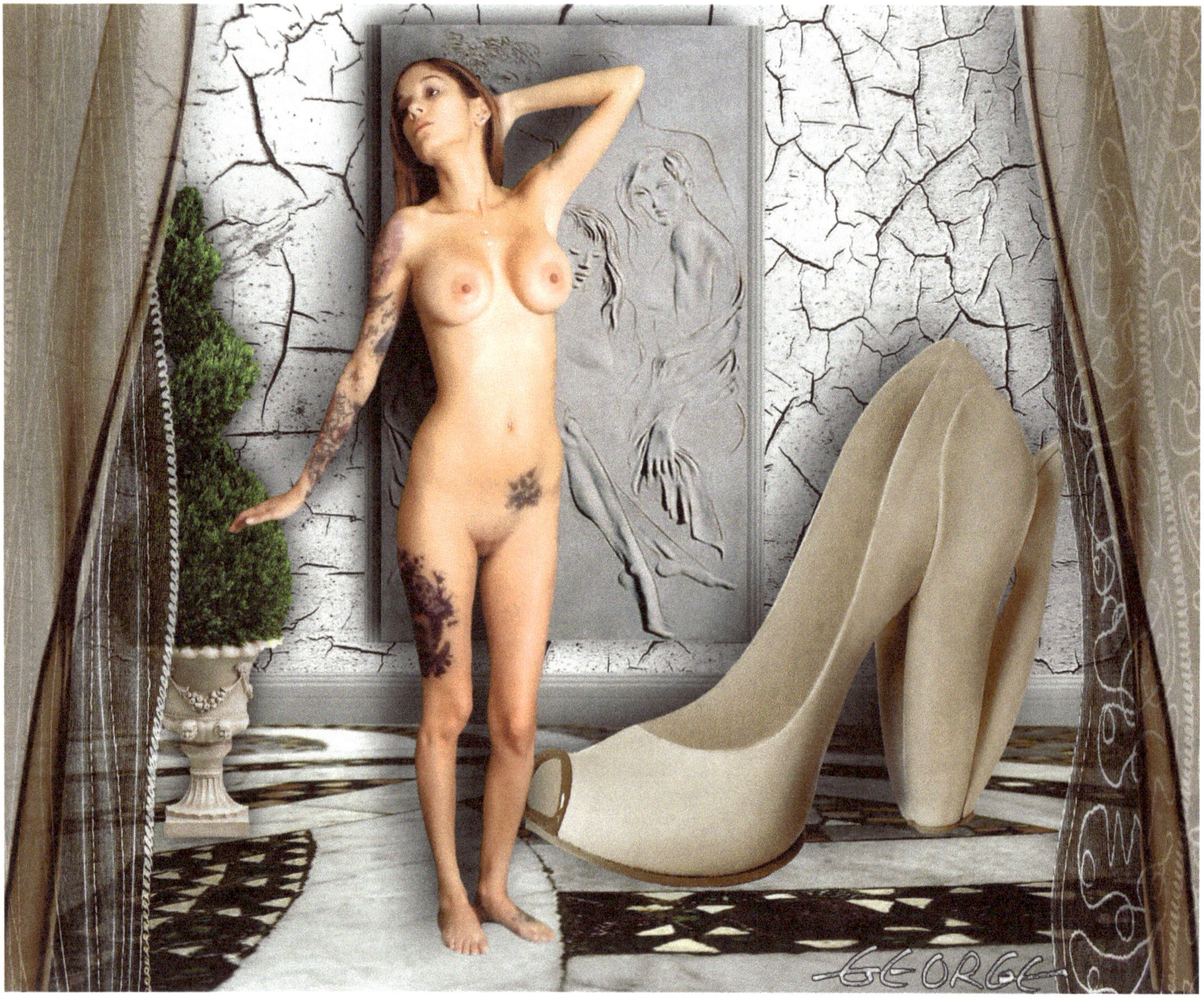
GEORGE

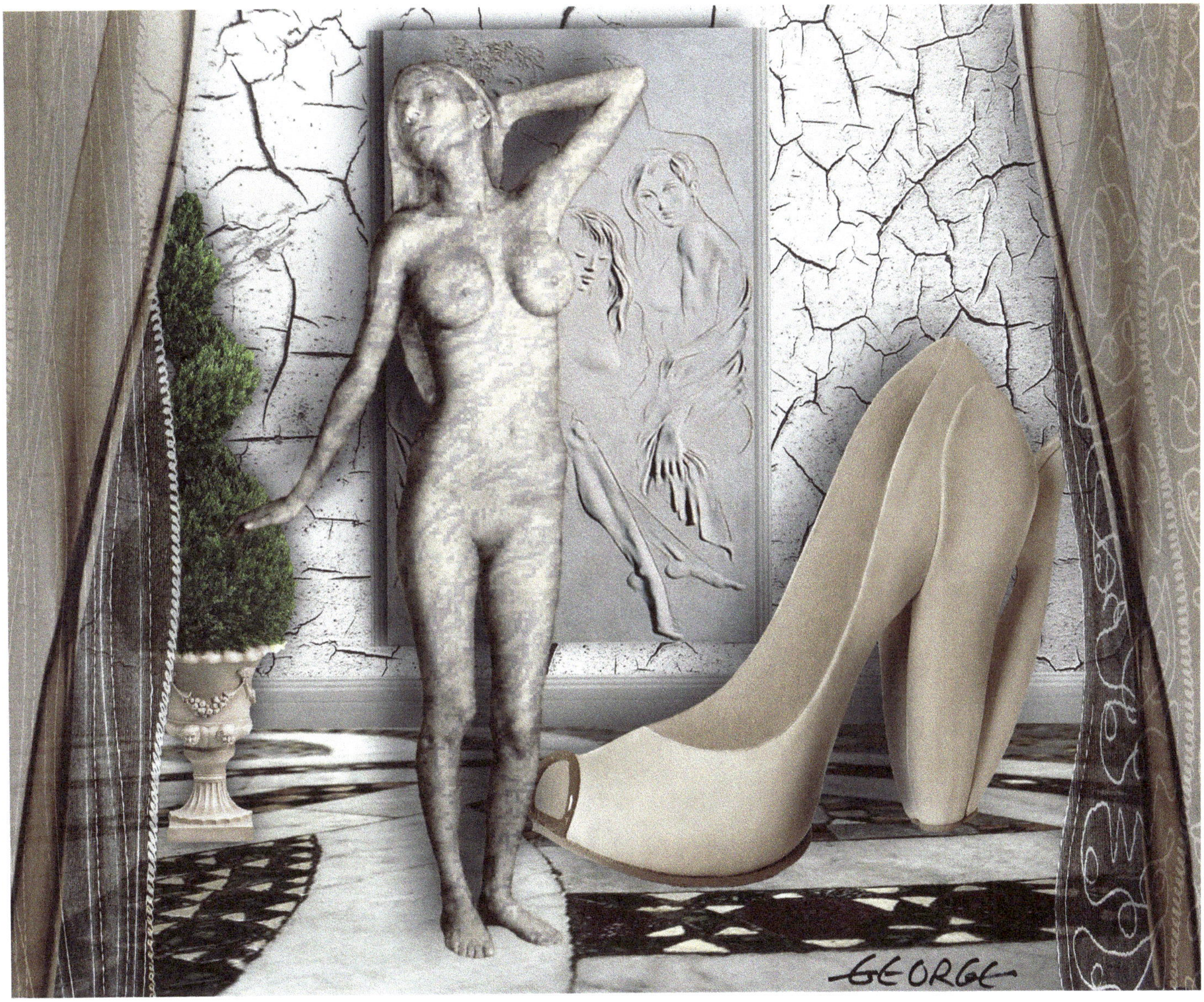
GEORGE

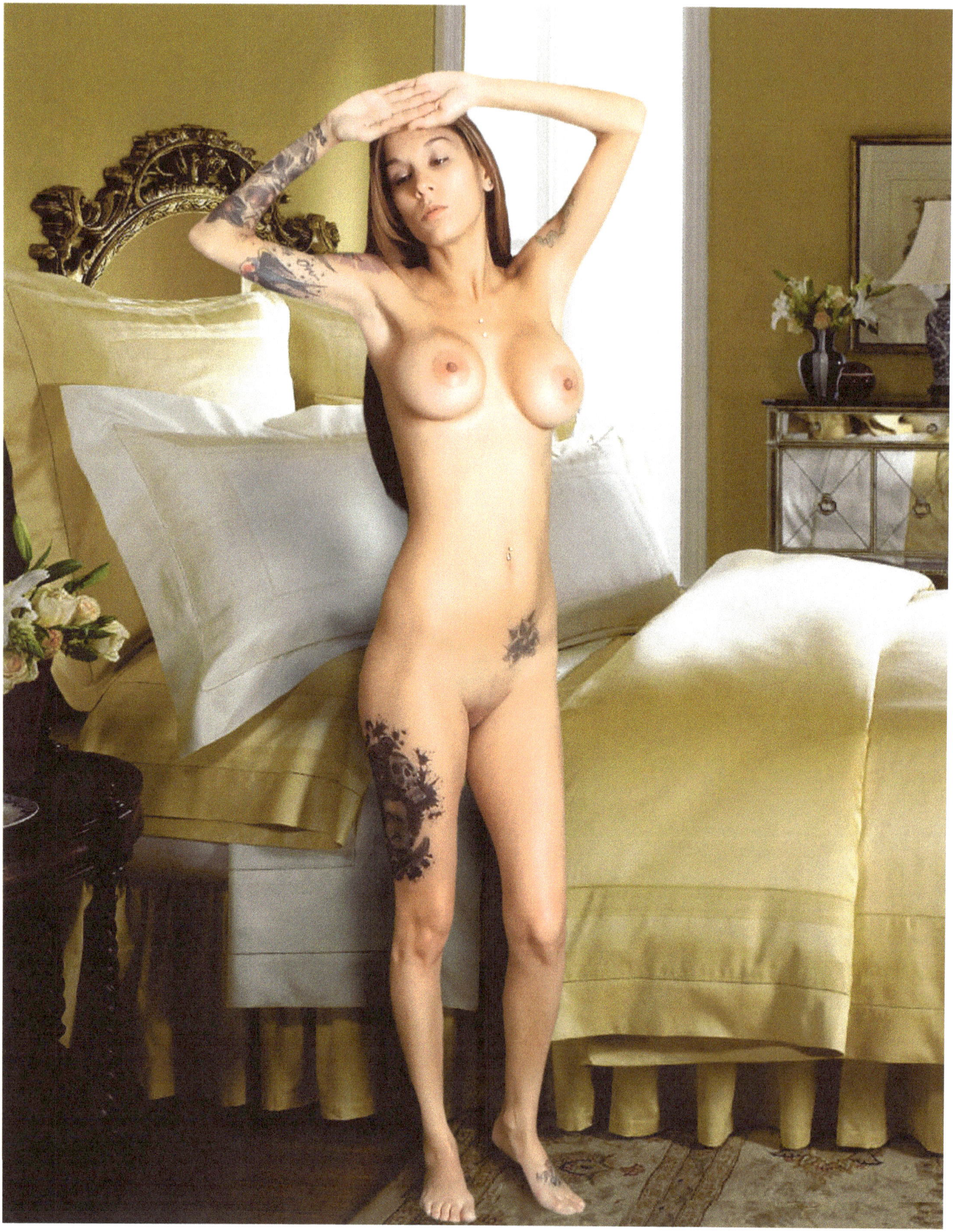

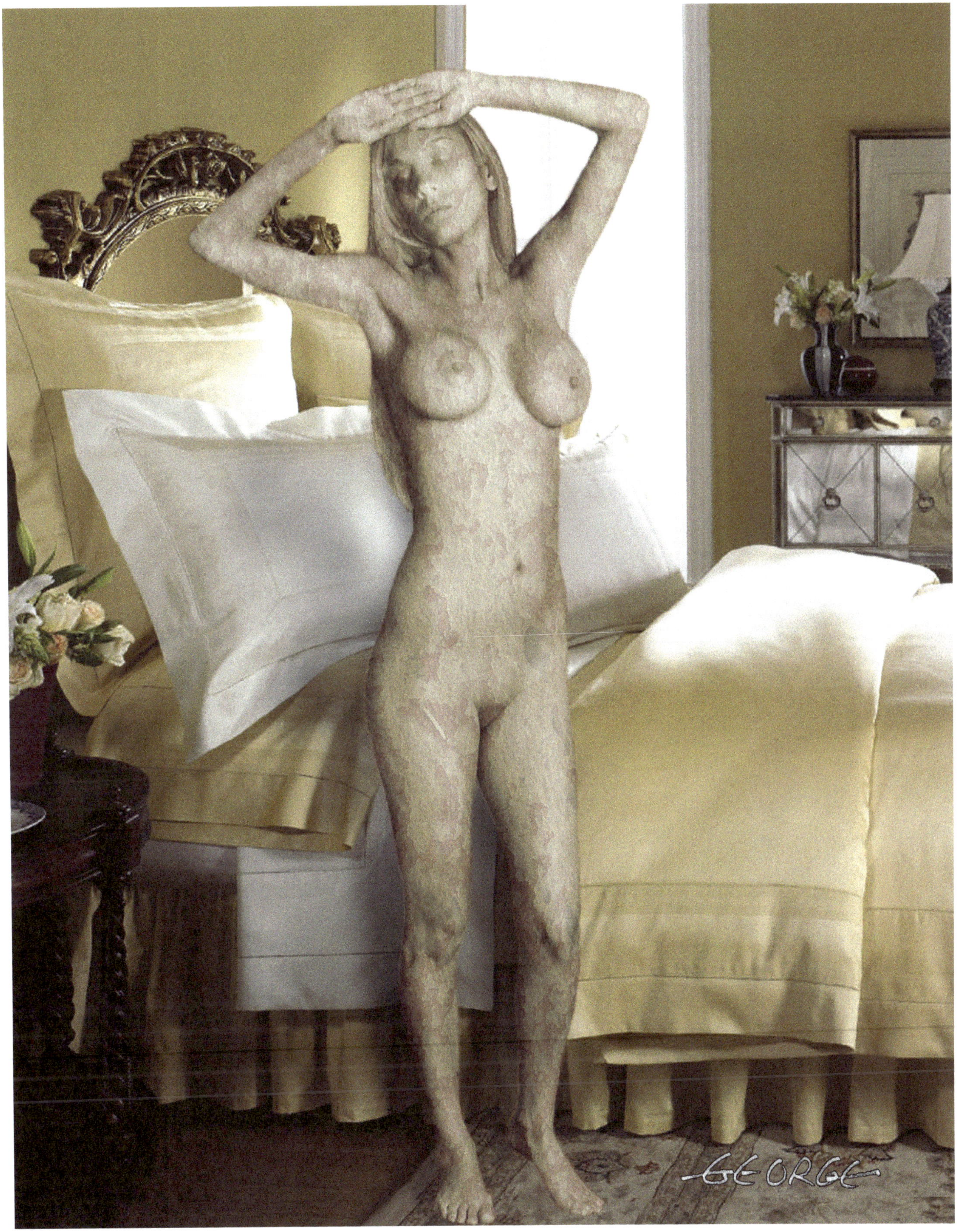
GEORGE

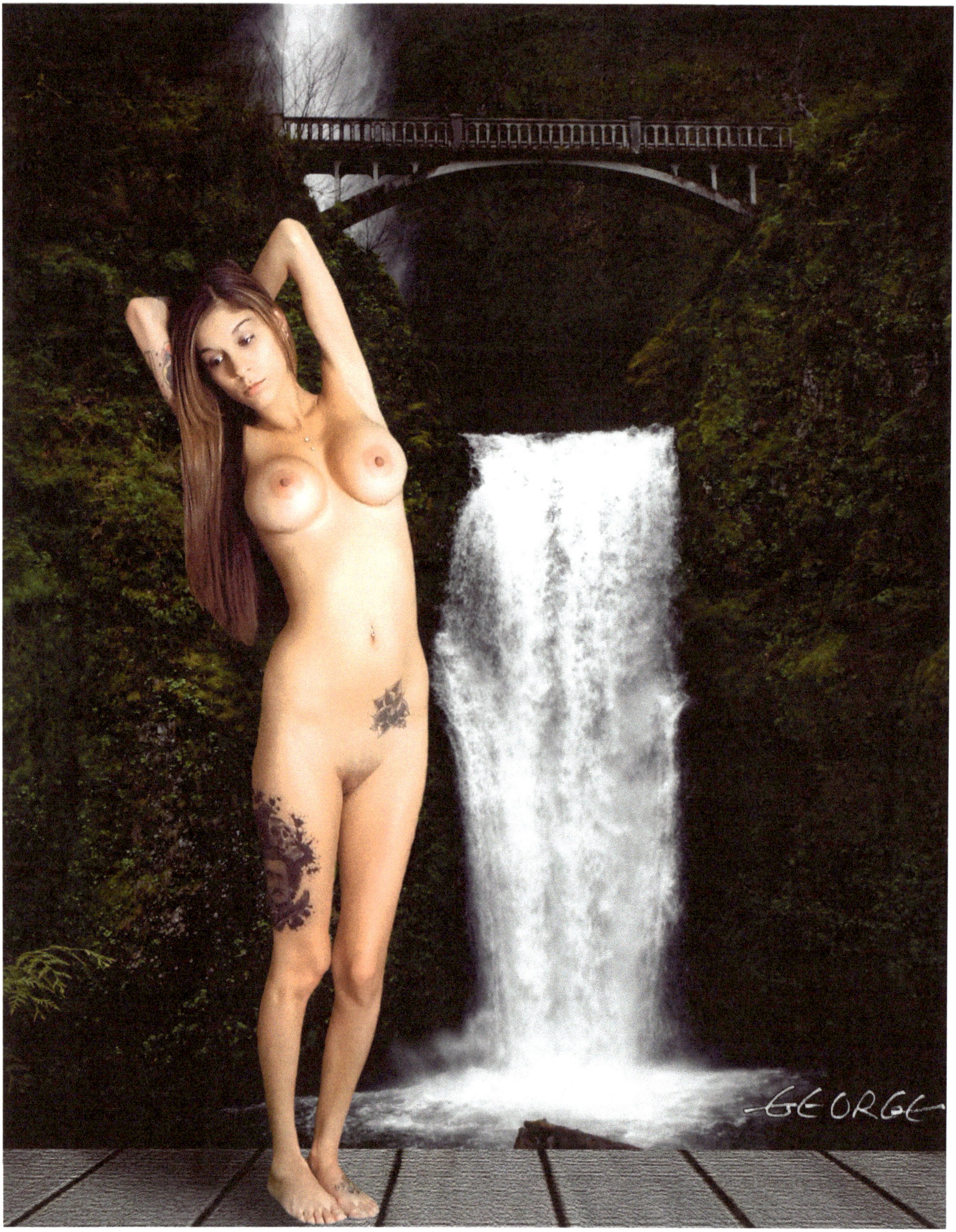
GEORGE

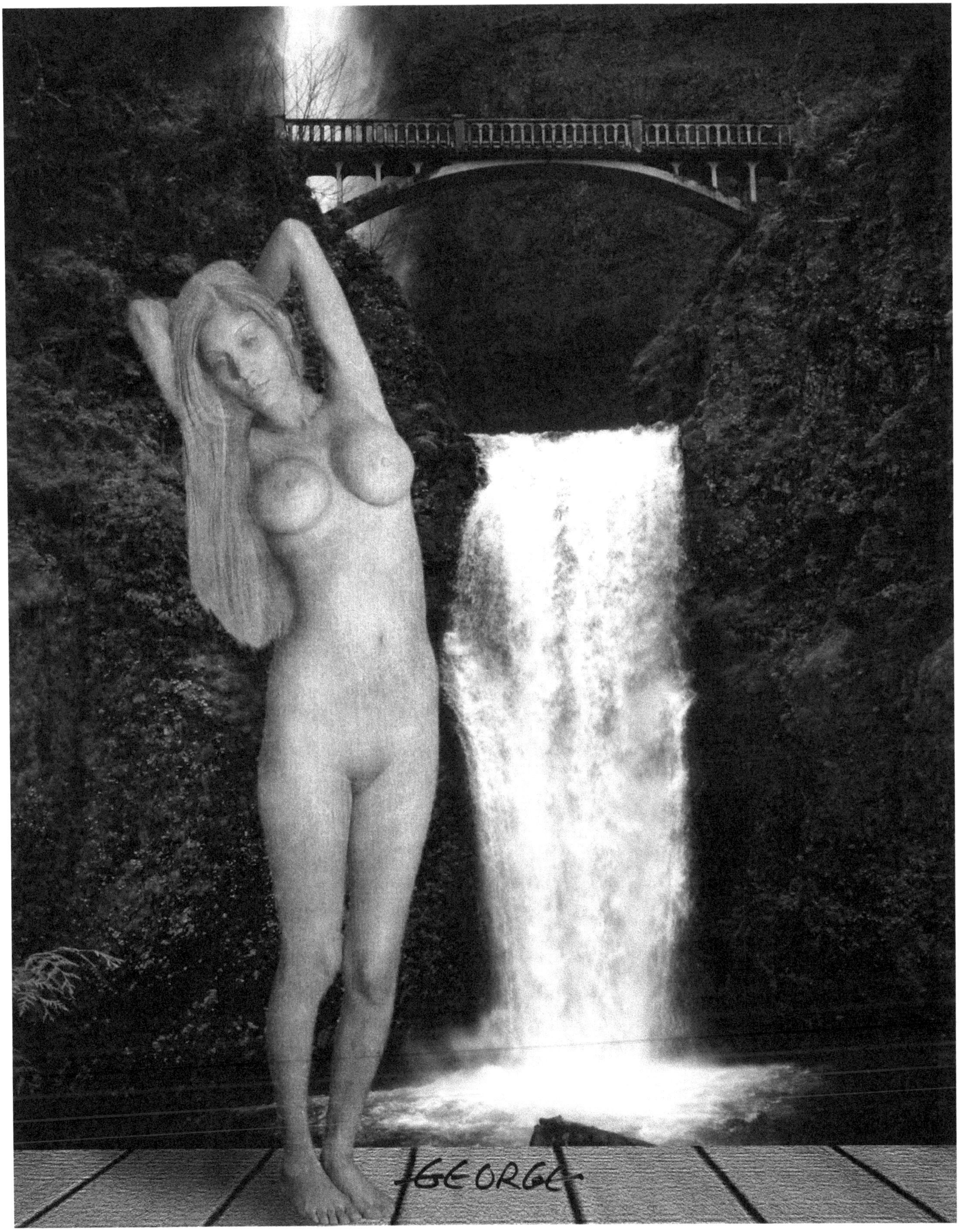
GEORGE

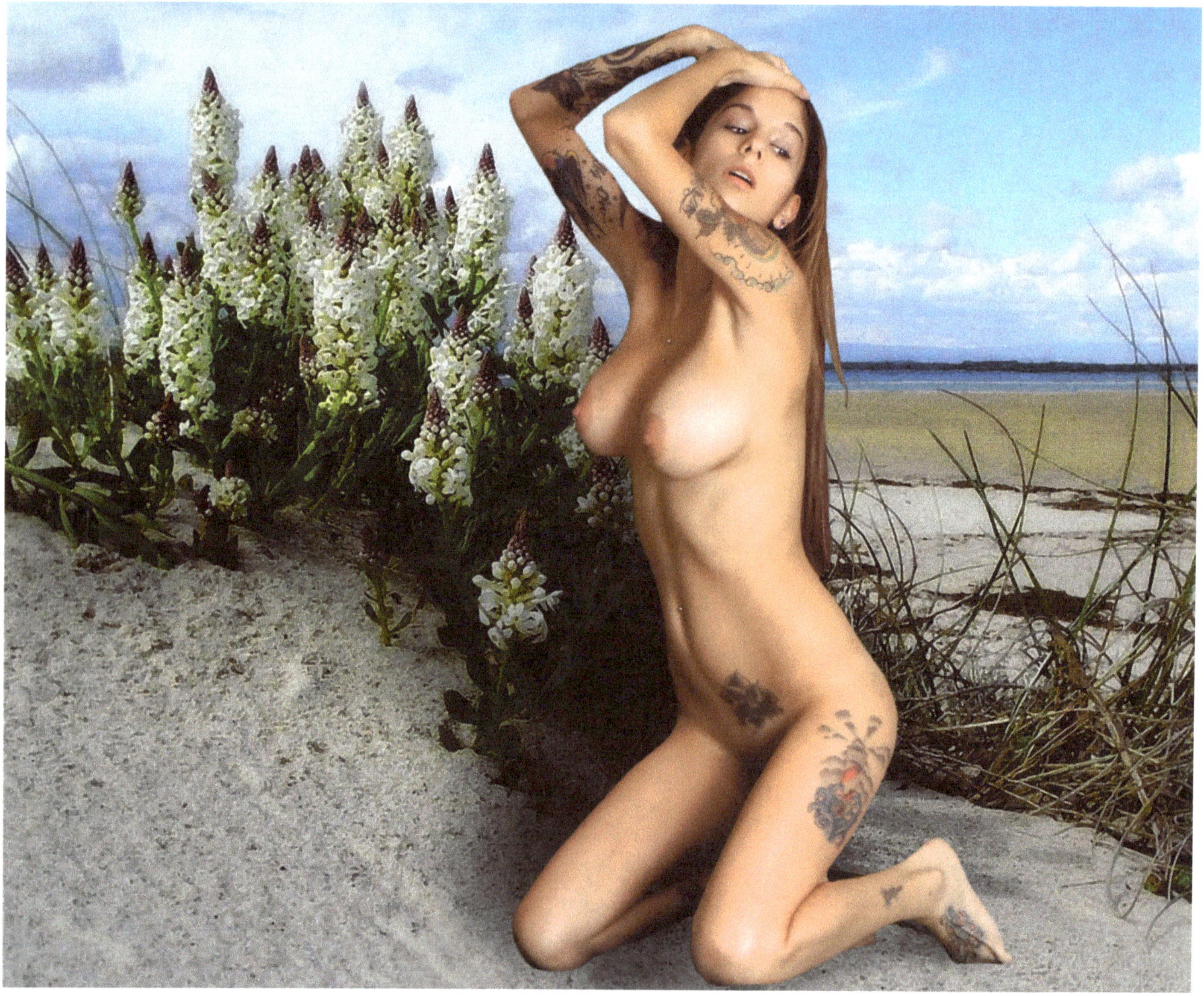

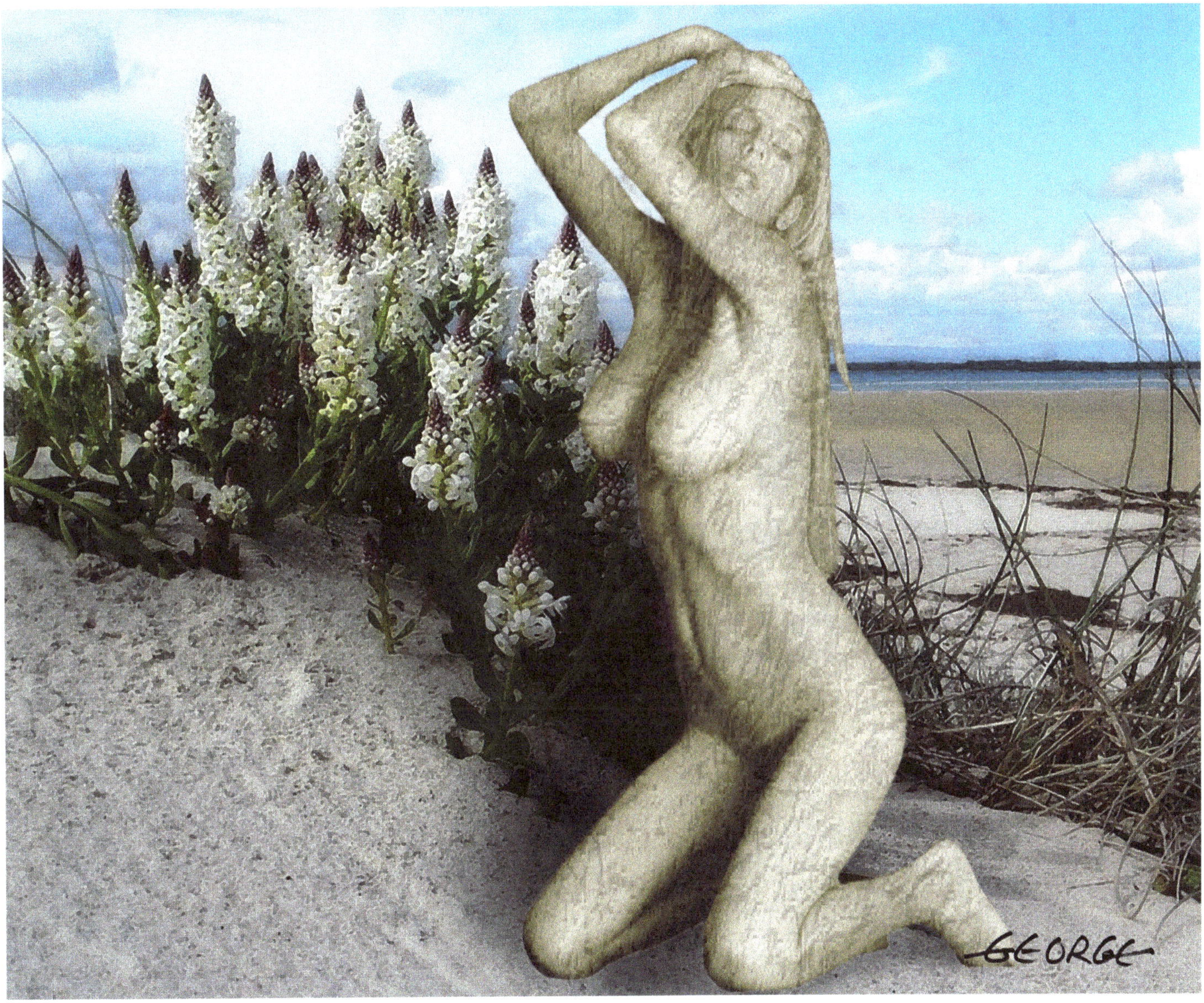
GEORGE

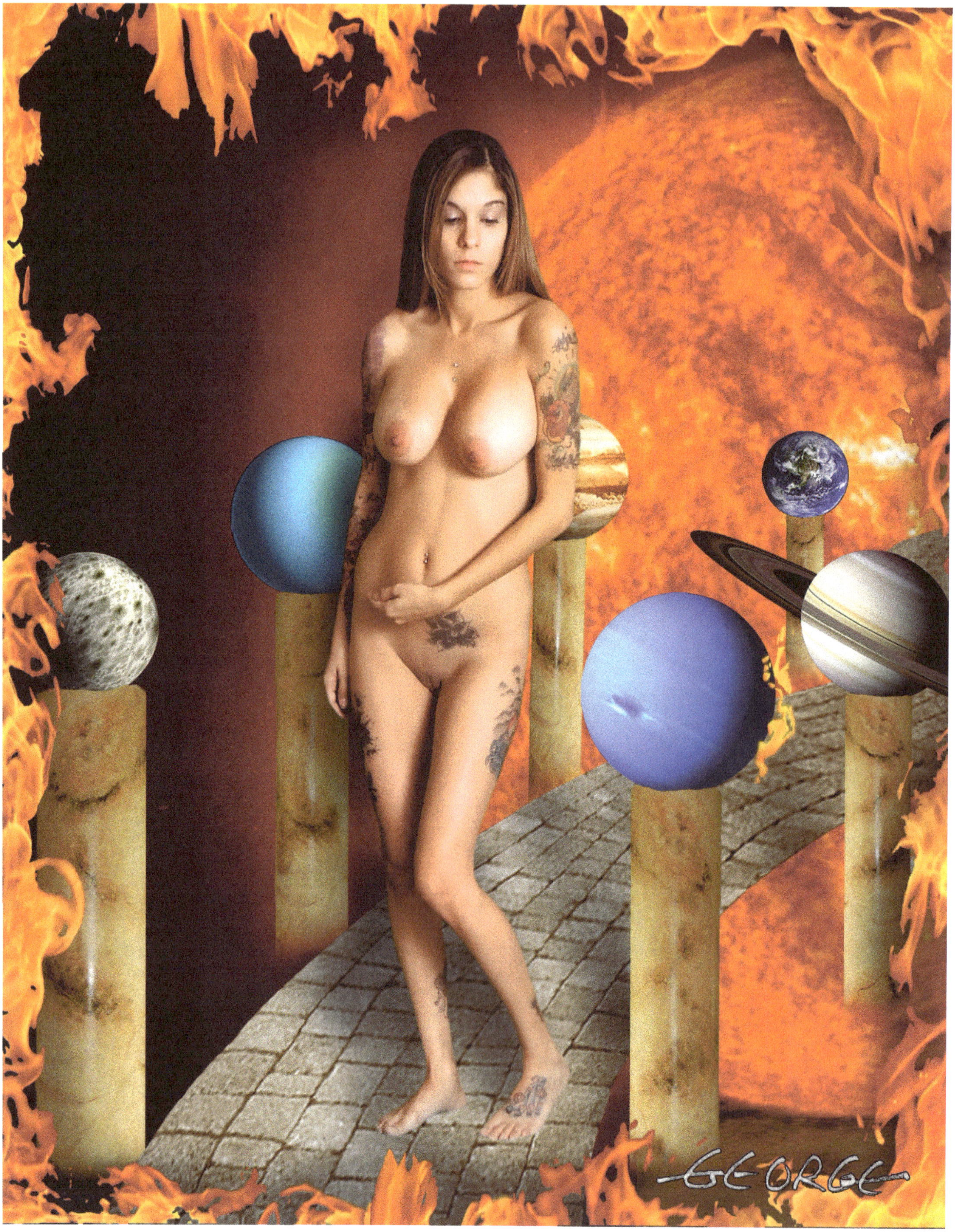
GEORGE

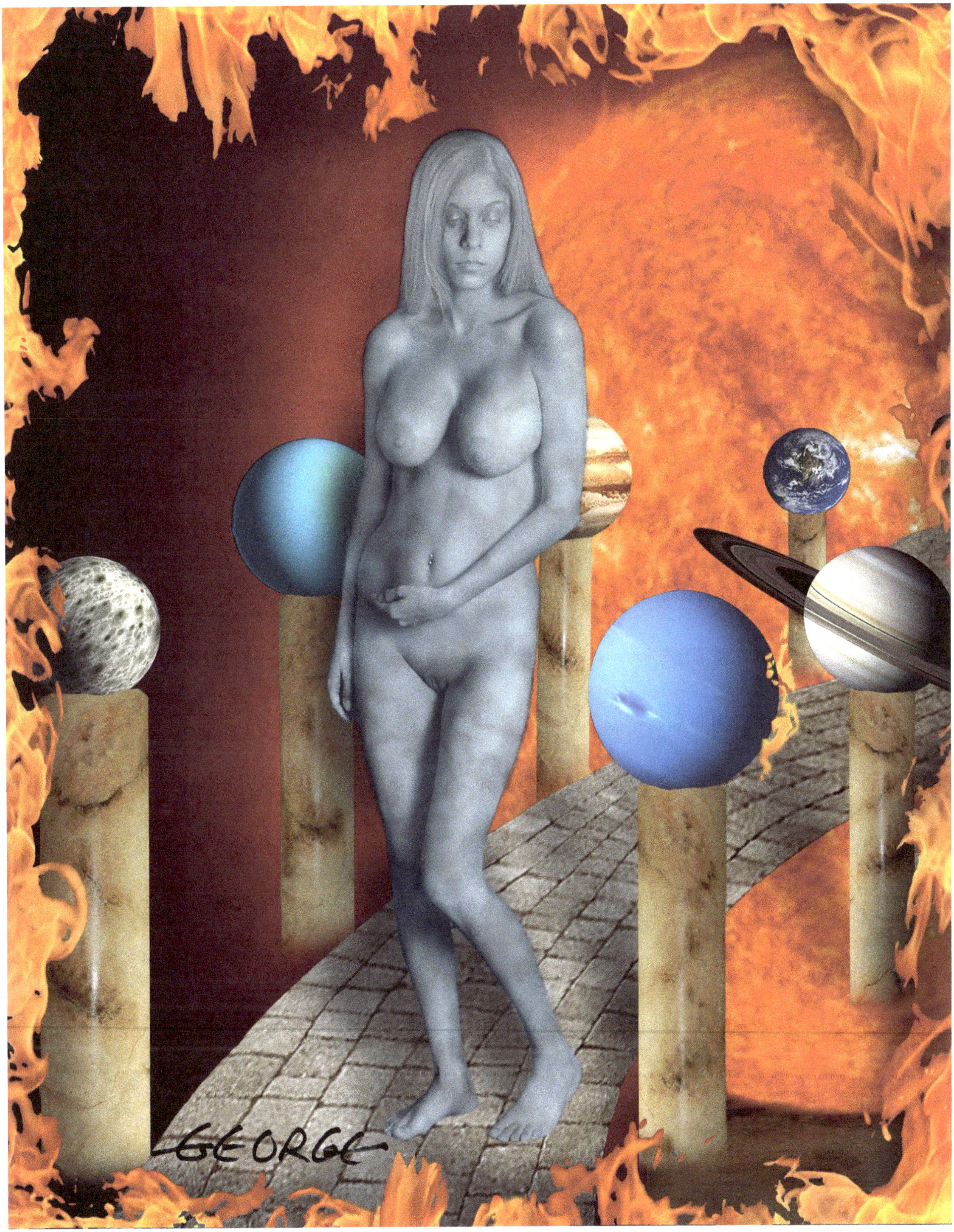
GEORGE

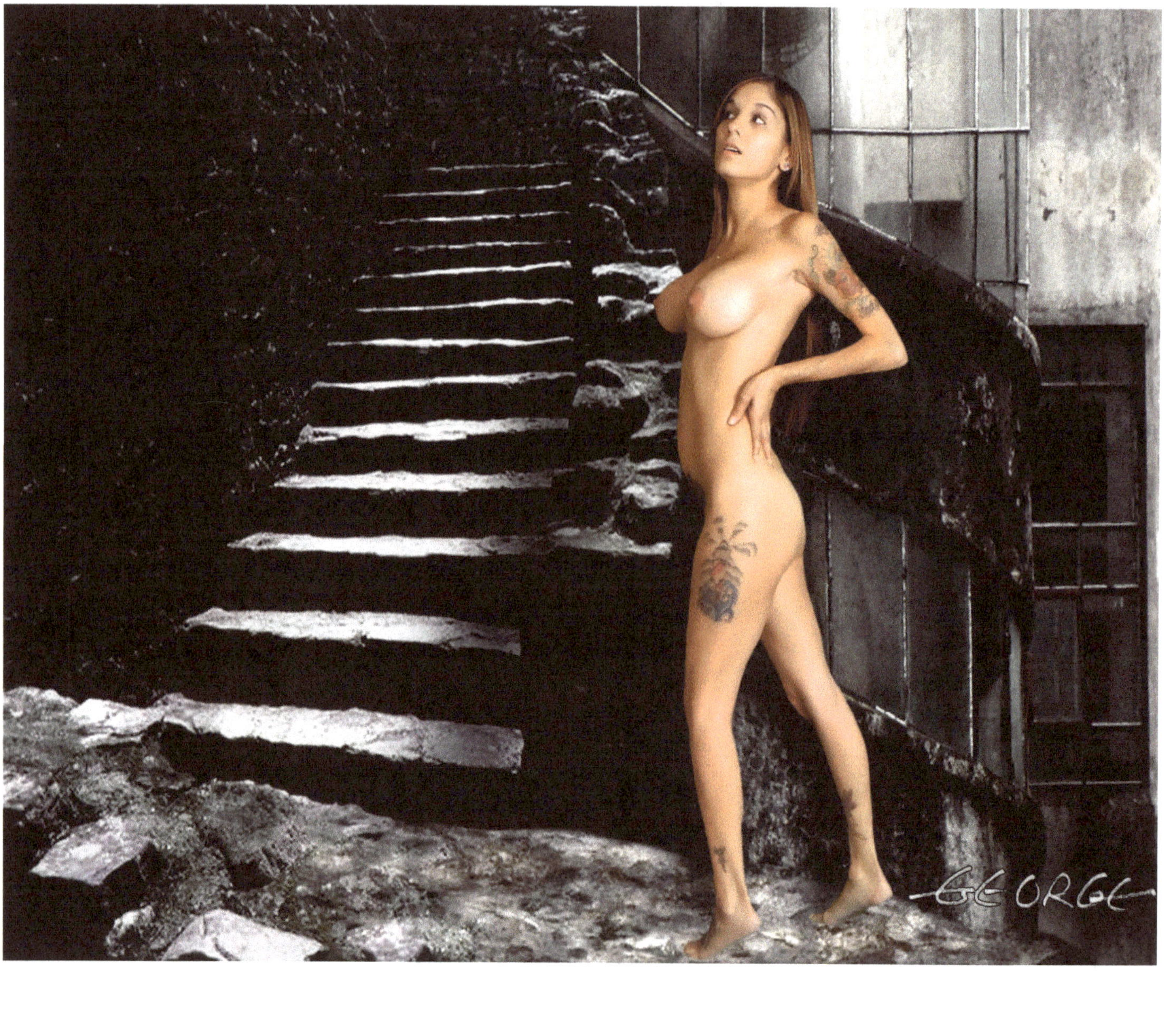
GEORGE

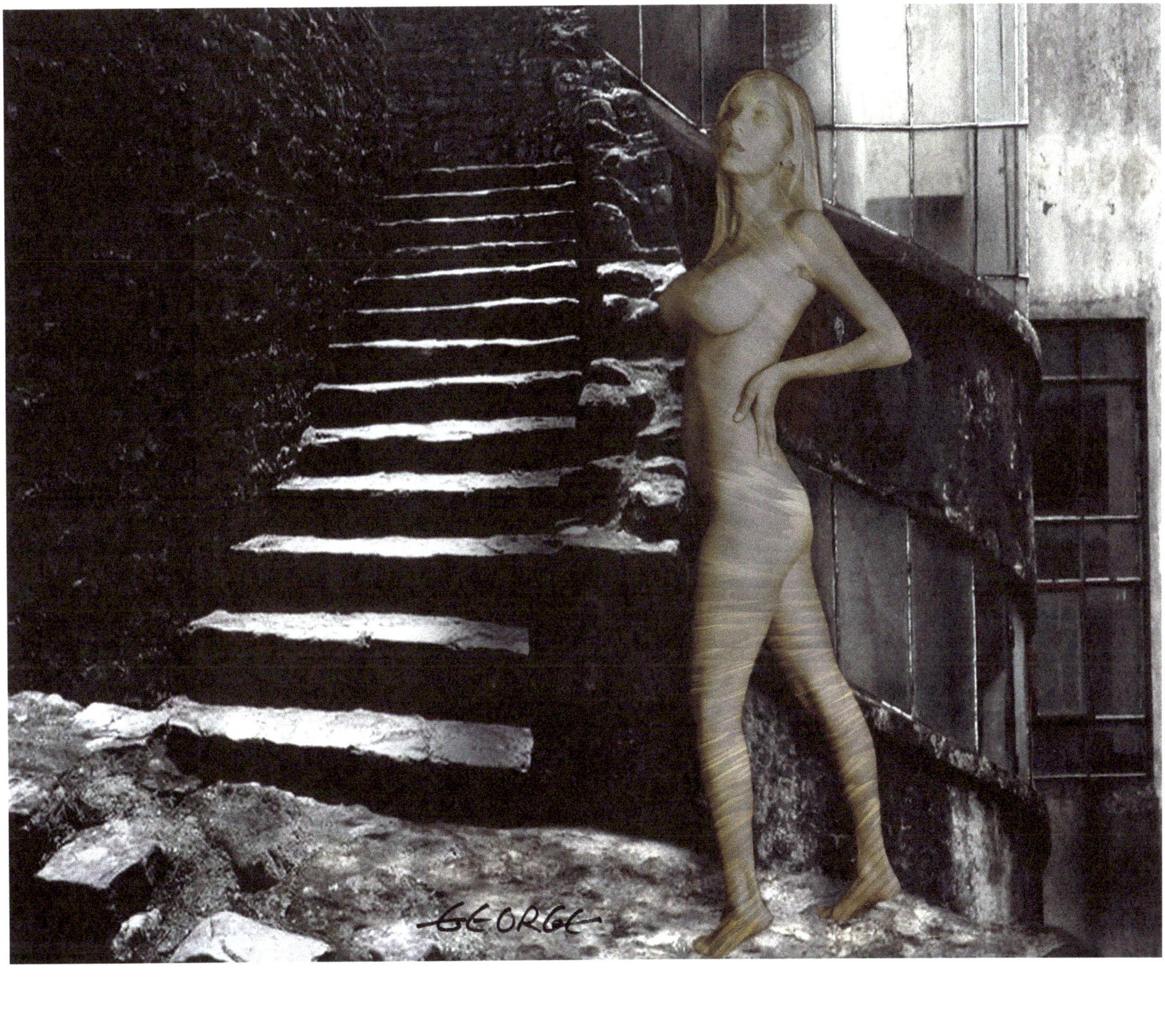
GEORGE

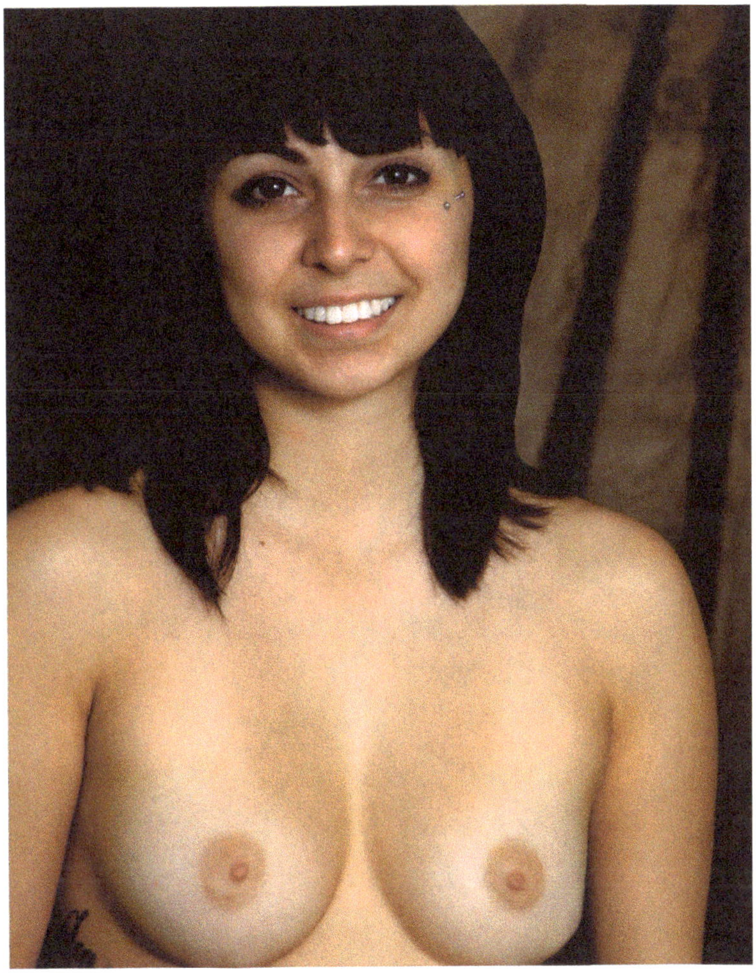

FRANCHESCA JO

Height 5'3" Weight 95 lbs Bust 32" Waist 0?" Hips 0?" Cup B

I have more of a punk style but I'm completely open to any style, idea or opportunity to help my portfolio grow. I'm tattooed and hope to be featured in a tattoo magazine. I'm a fun, vivacious person to work with, easy going, spunky and I take direction well.

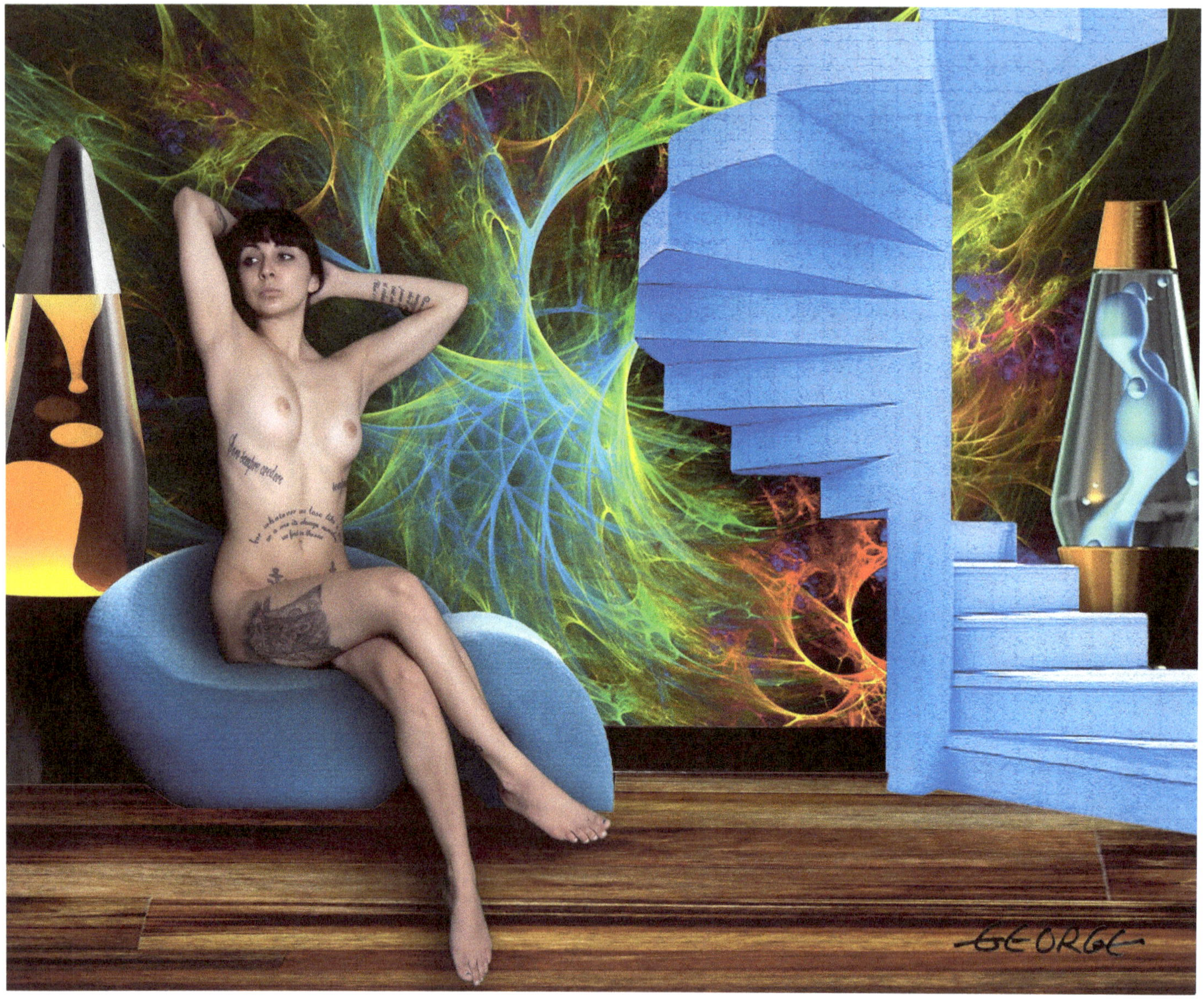
GEORGE

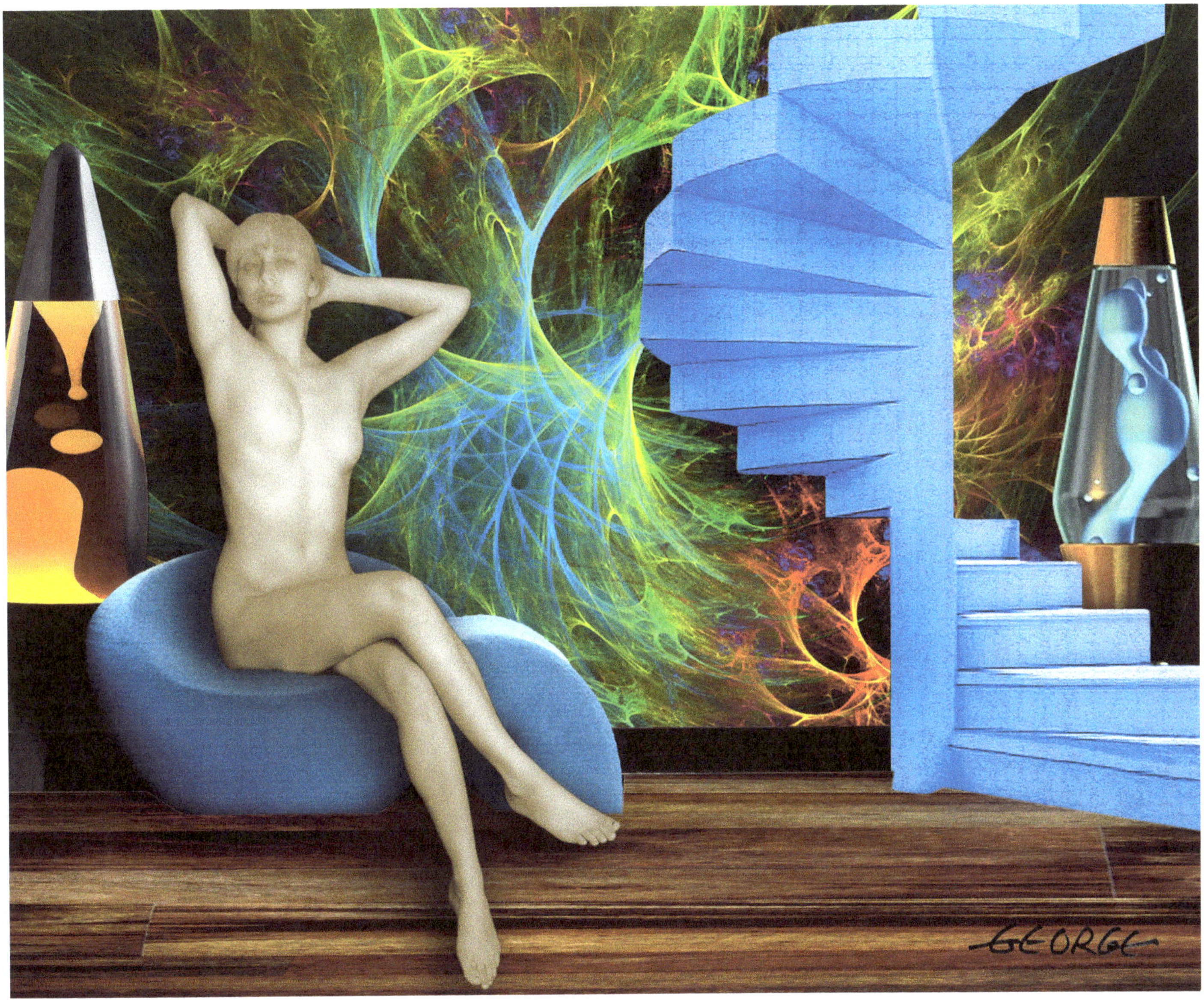
GEORGE

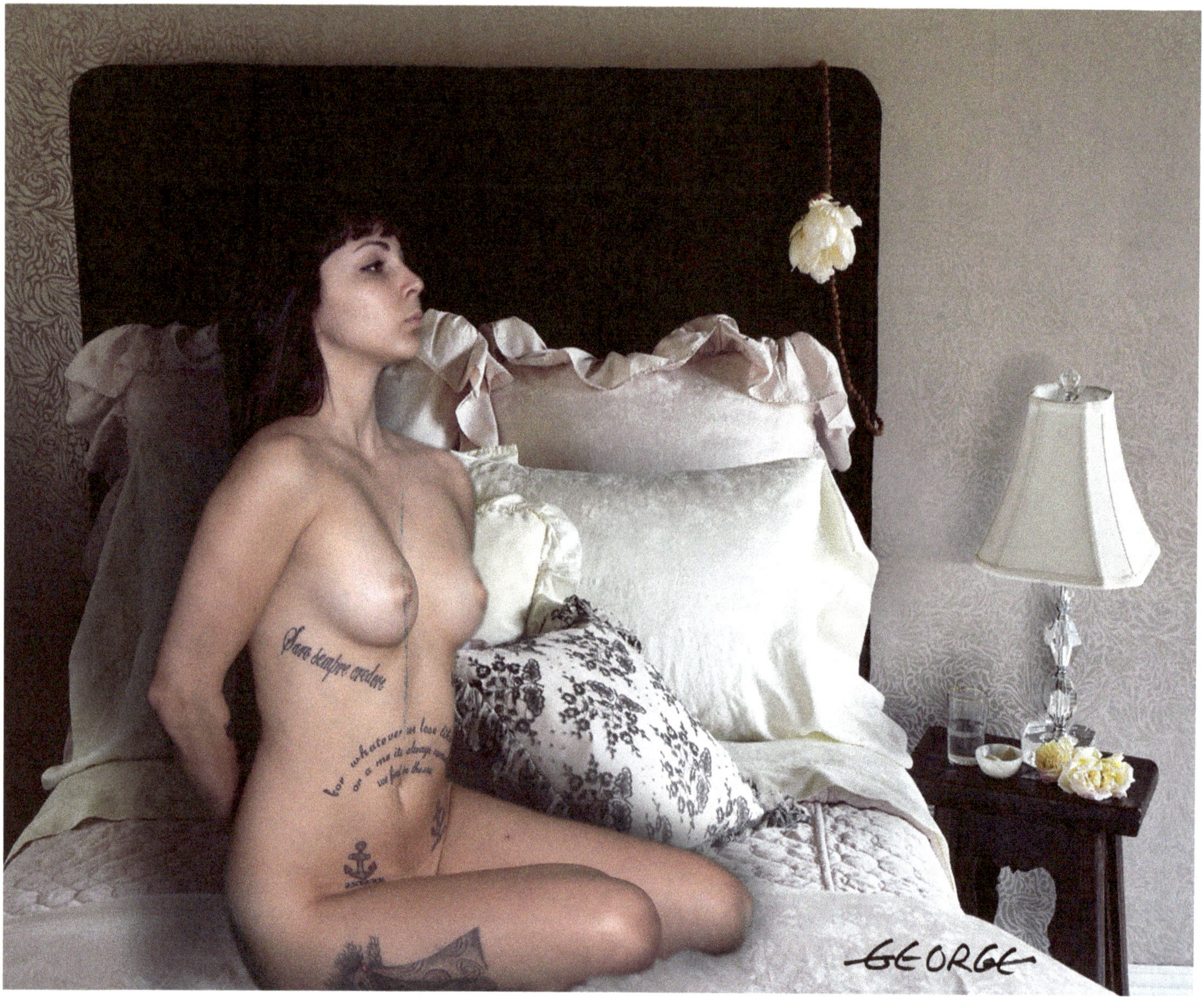
GEORGE

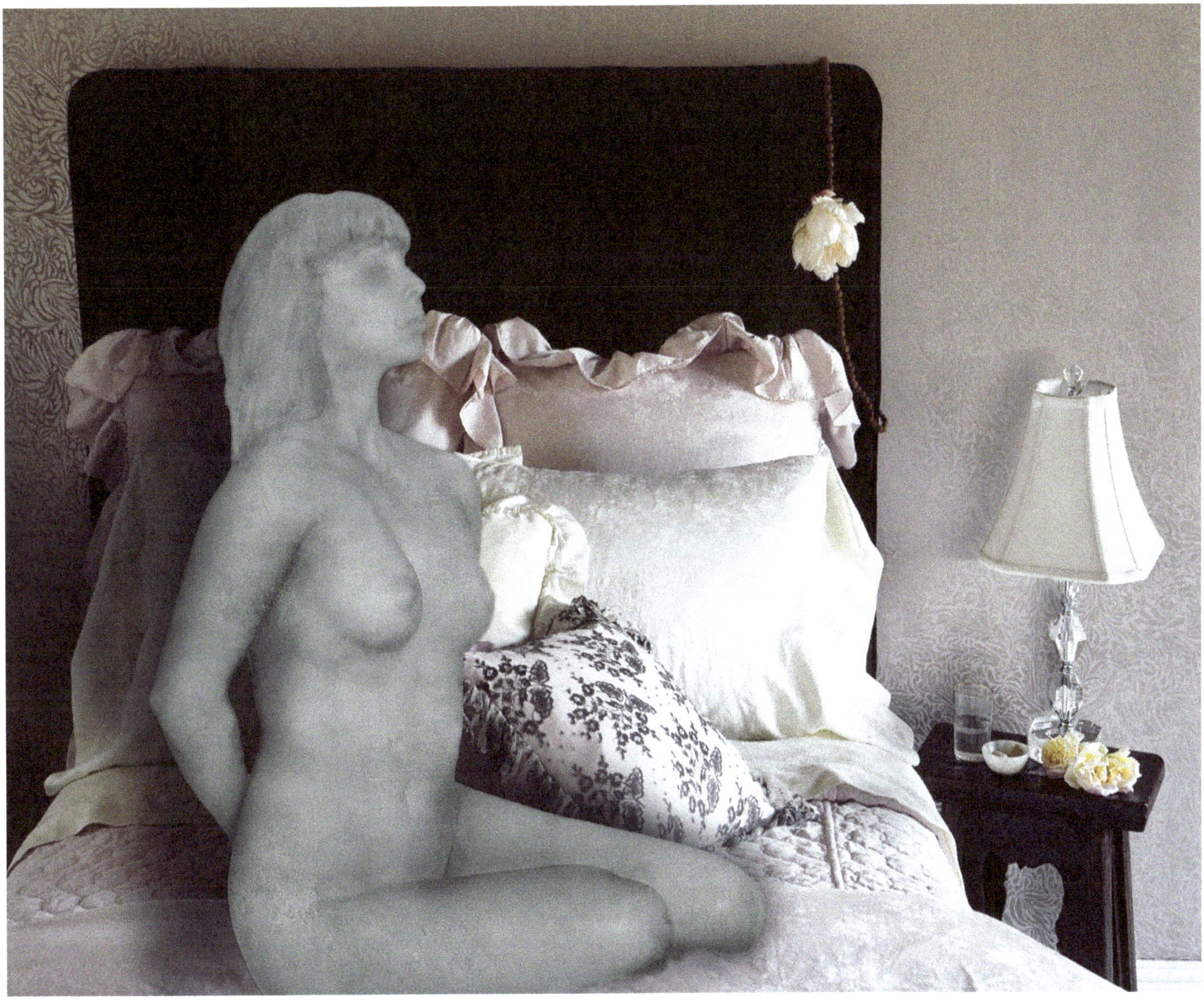

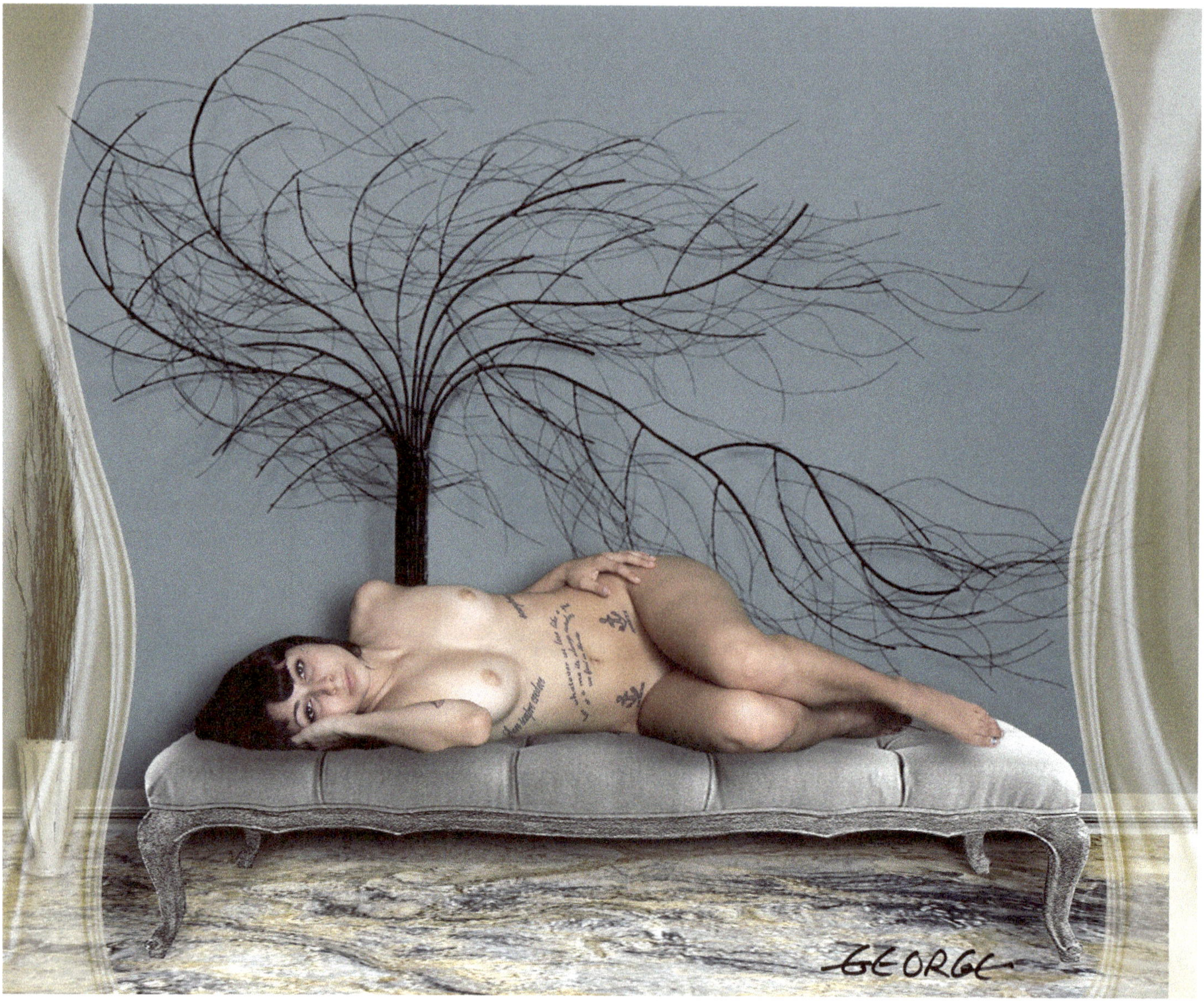
GEORGE

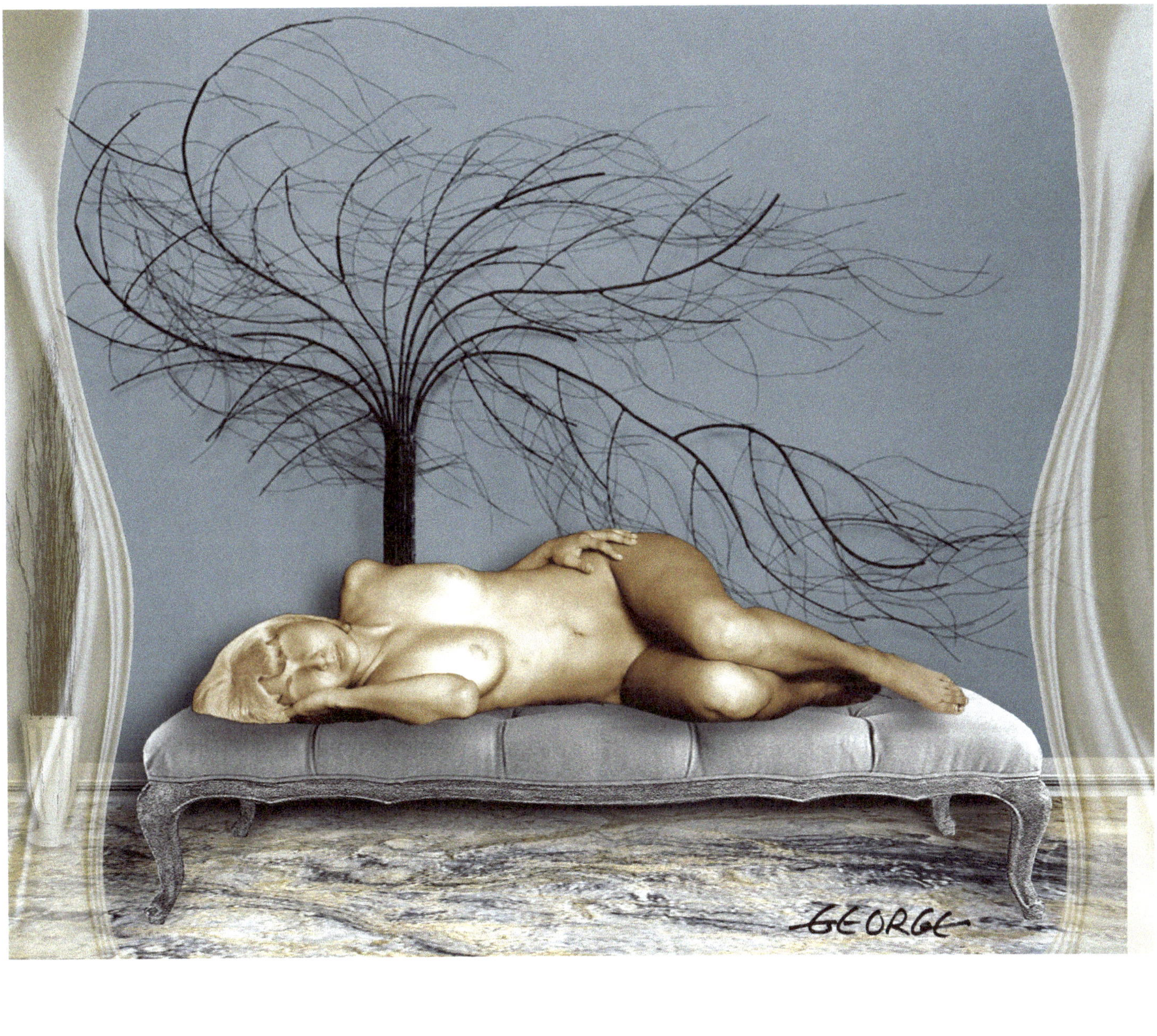
GEORGE

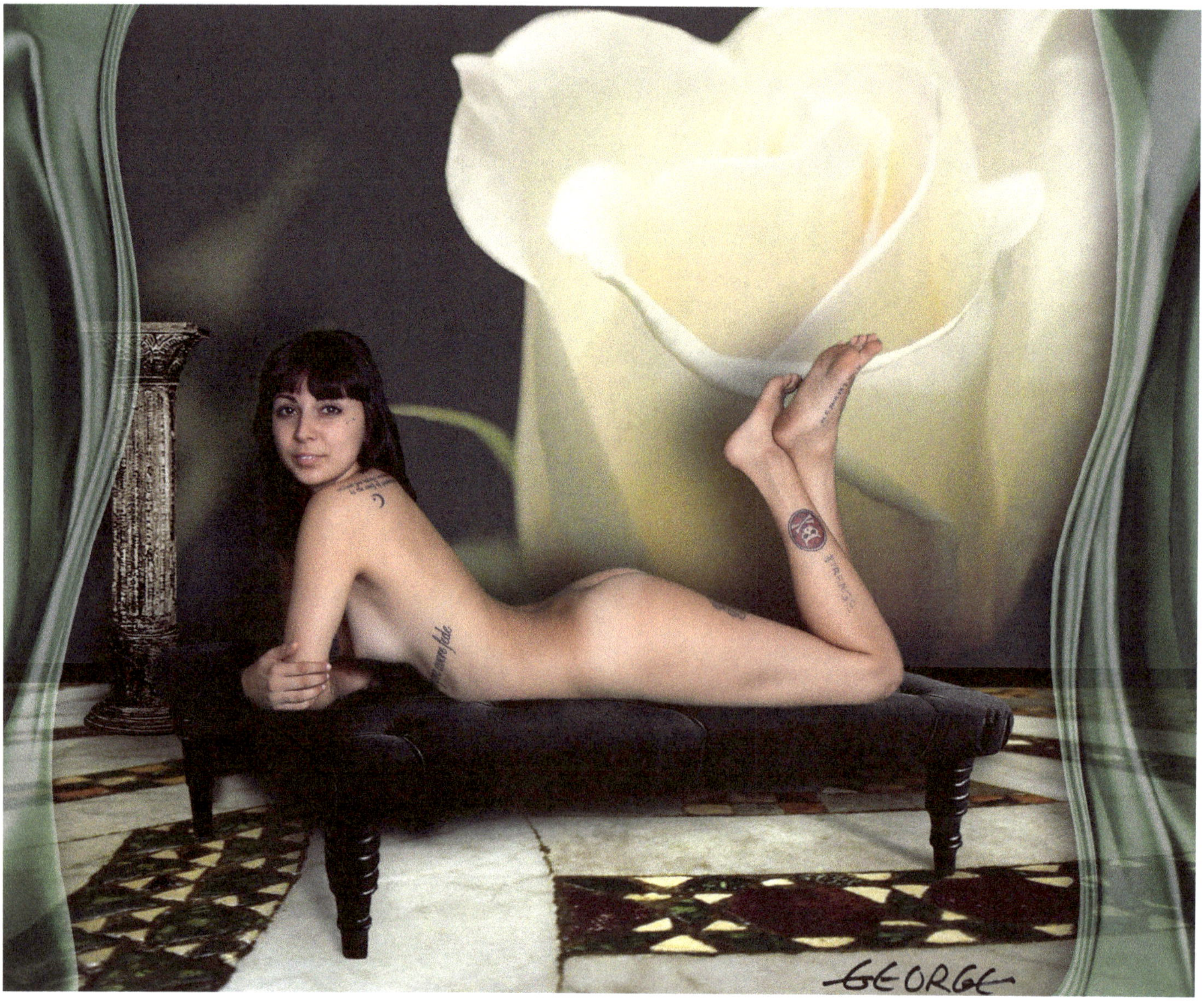
GEORGE

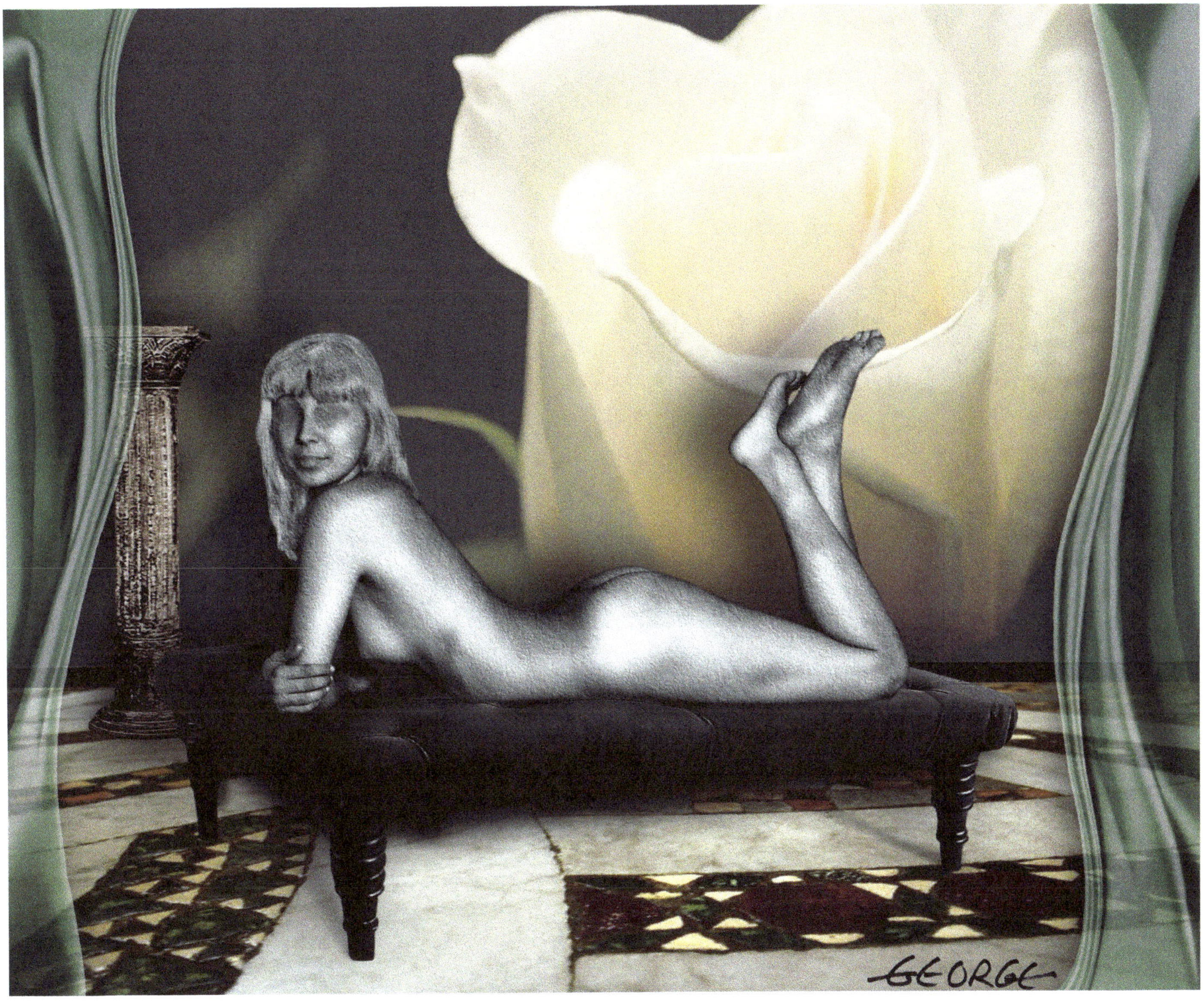
GEORGE

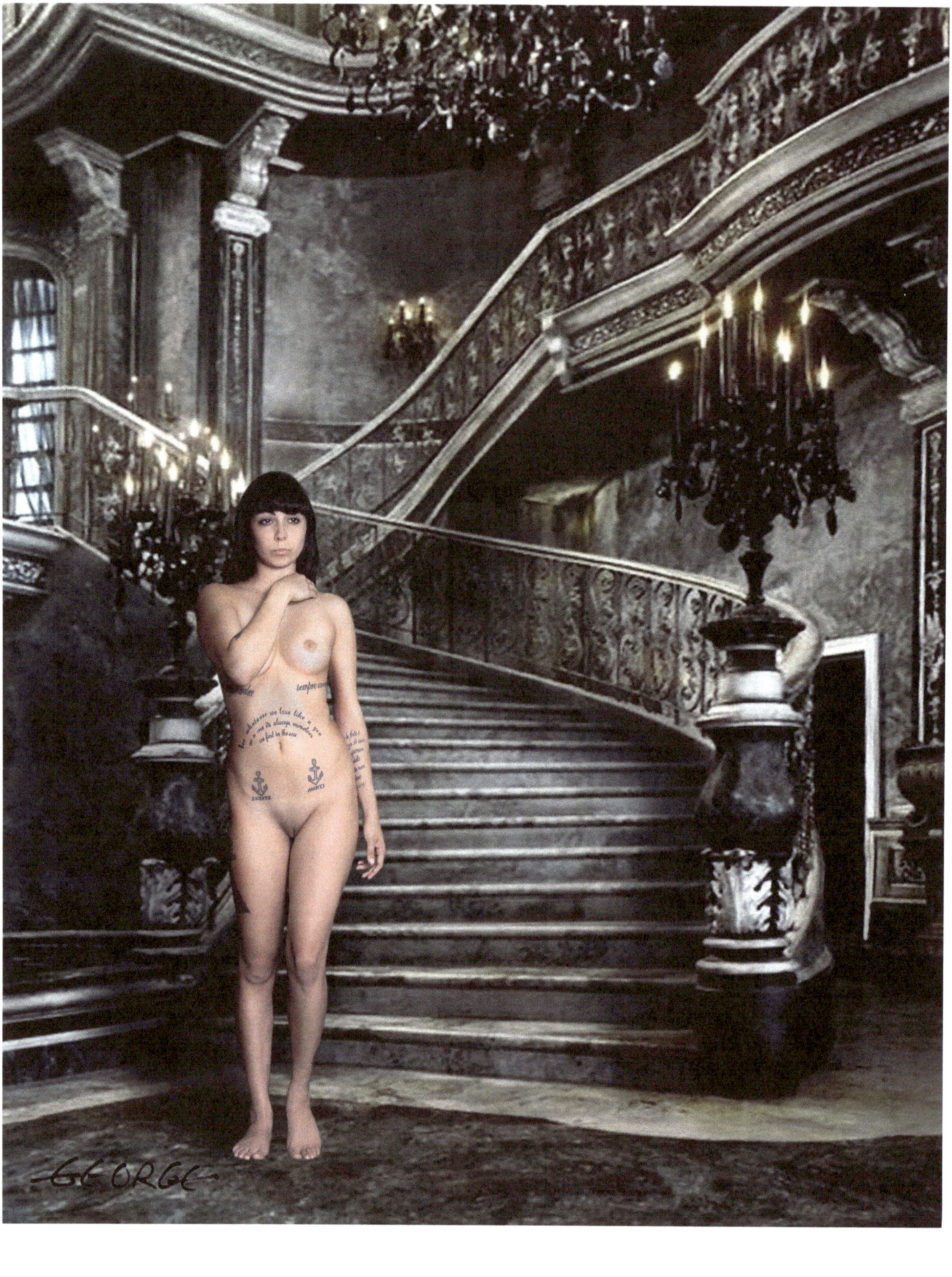
GEORGE

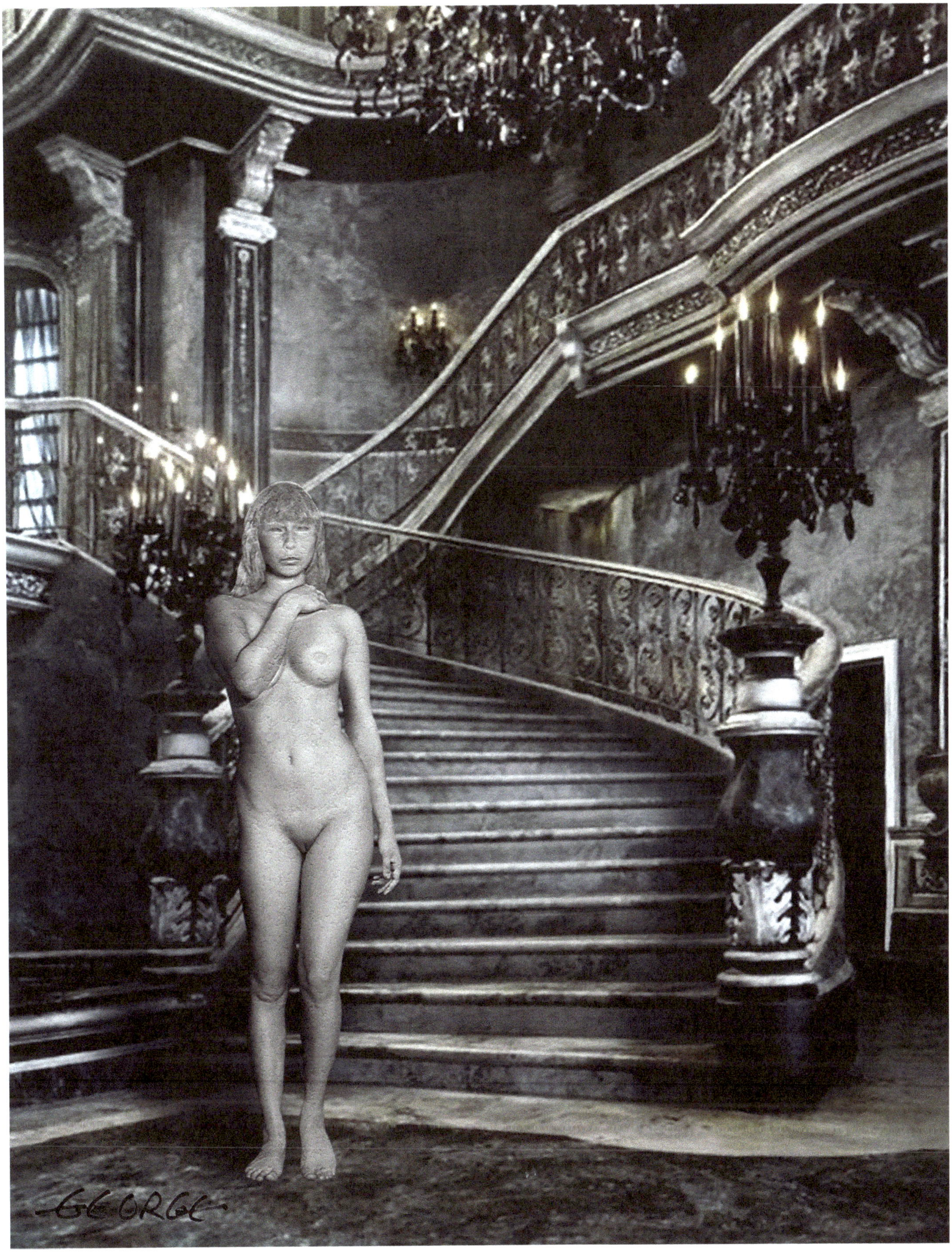
GEORGE

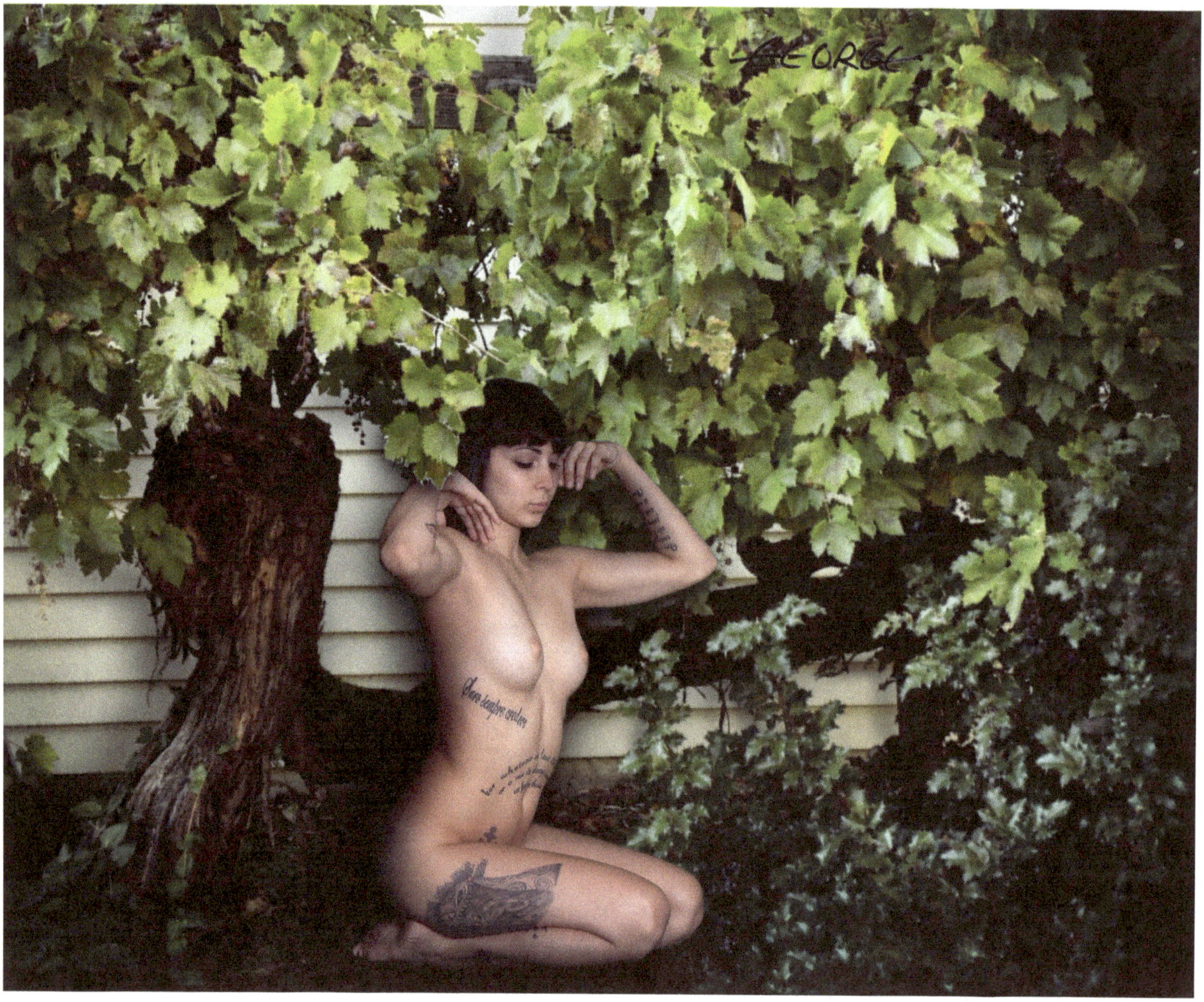

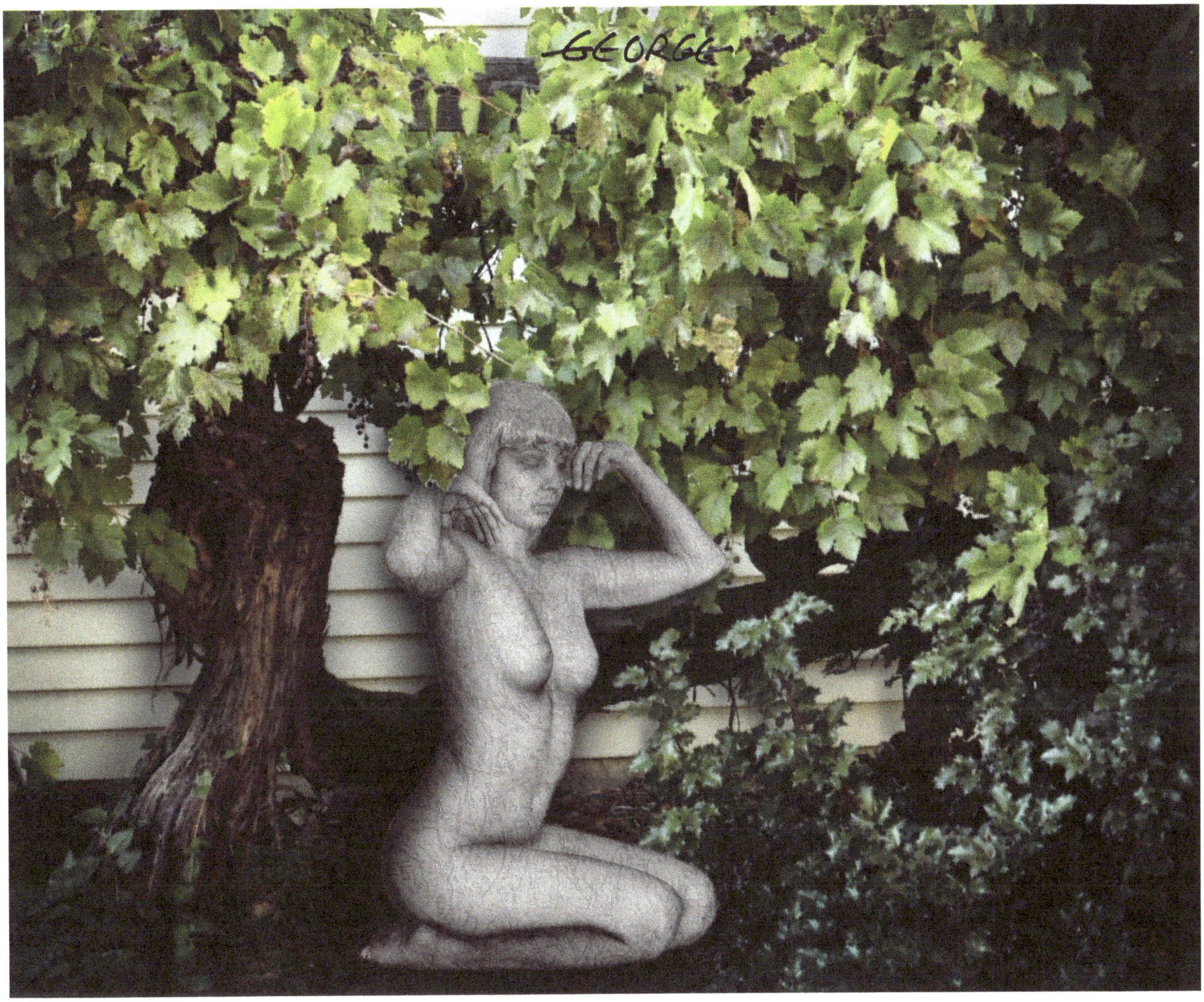
GEORGE

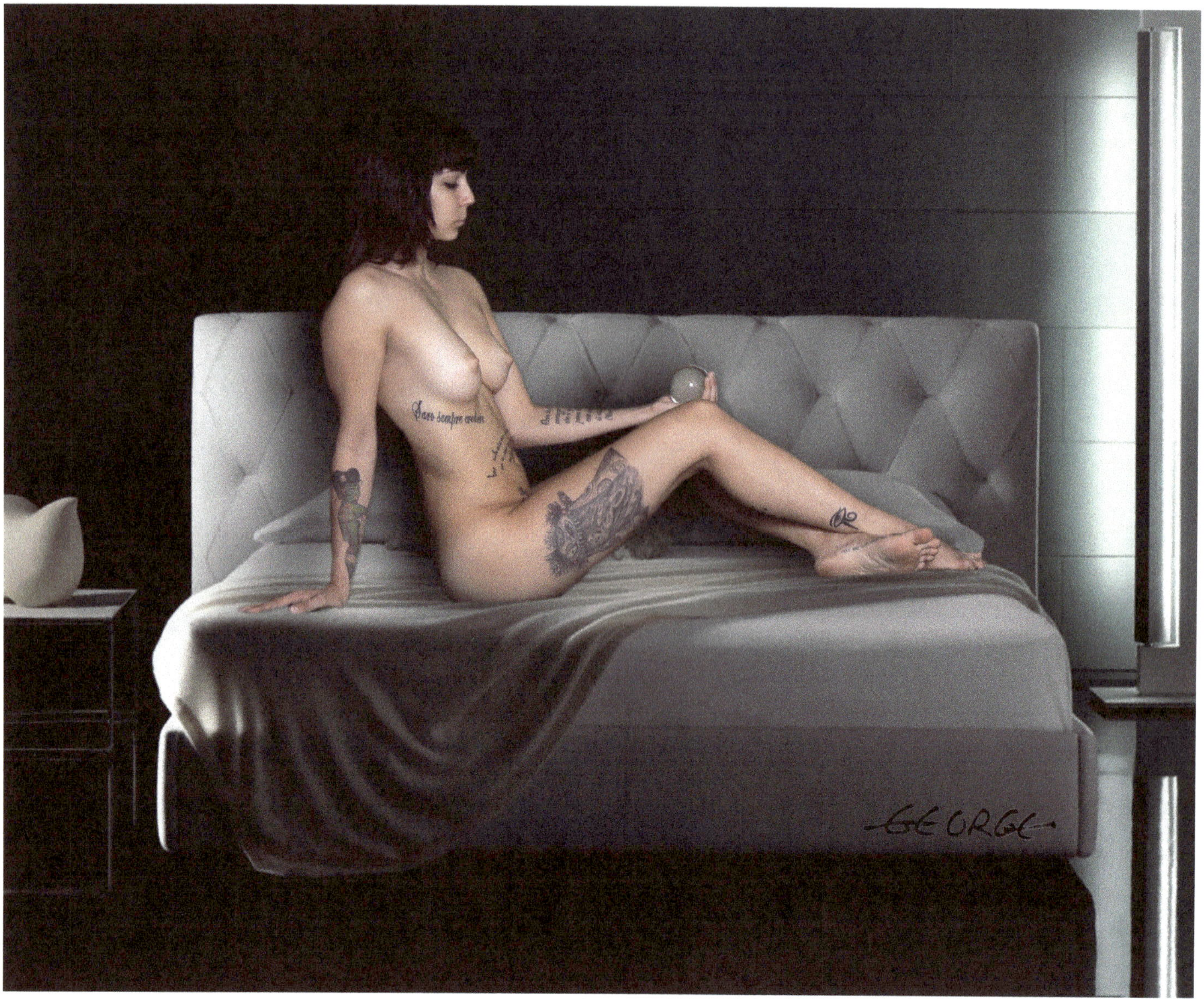
GEORGE

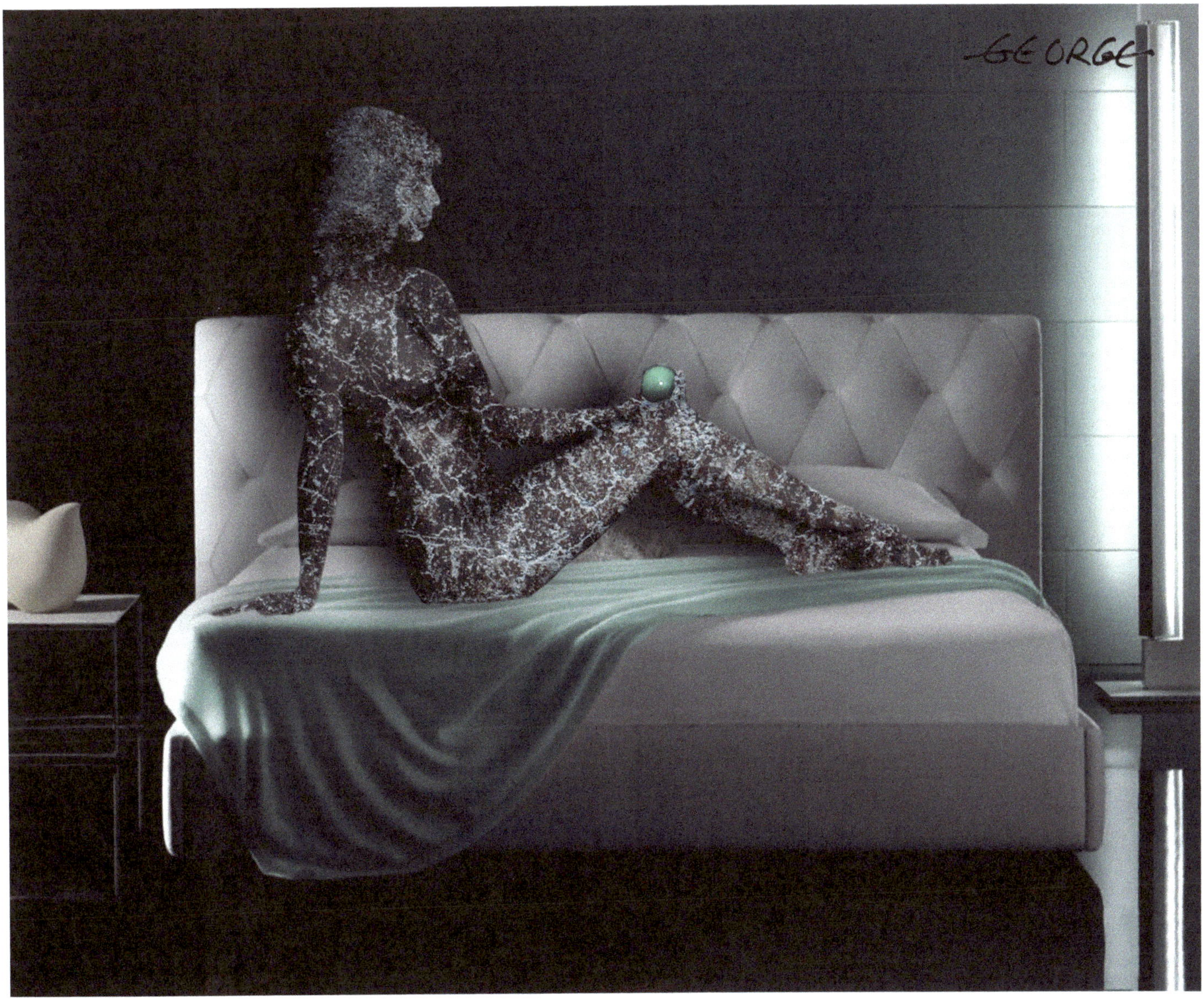
GEORGE

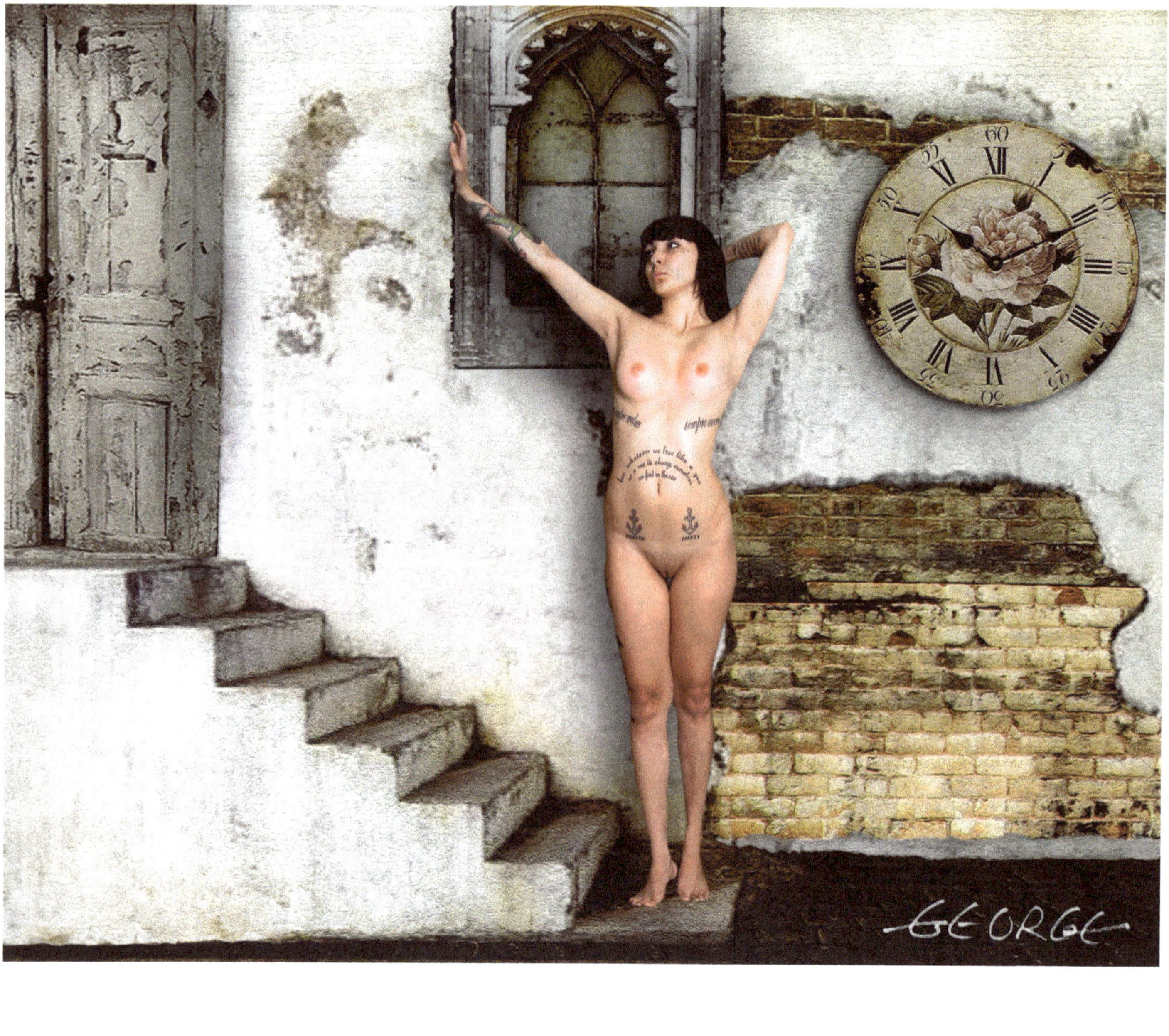
GEORGE

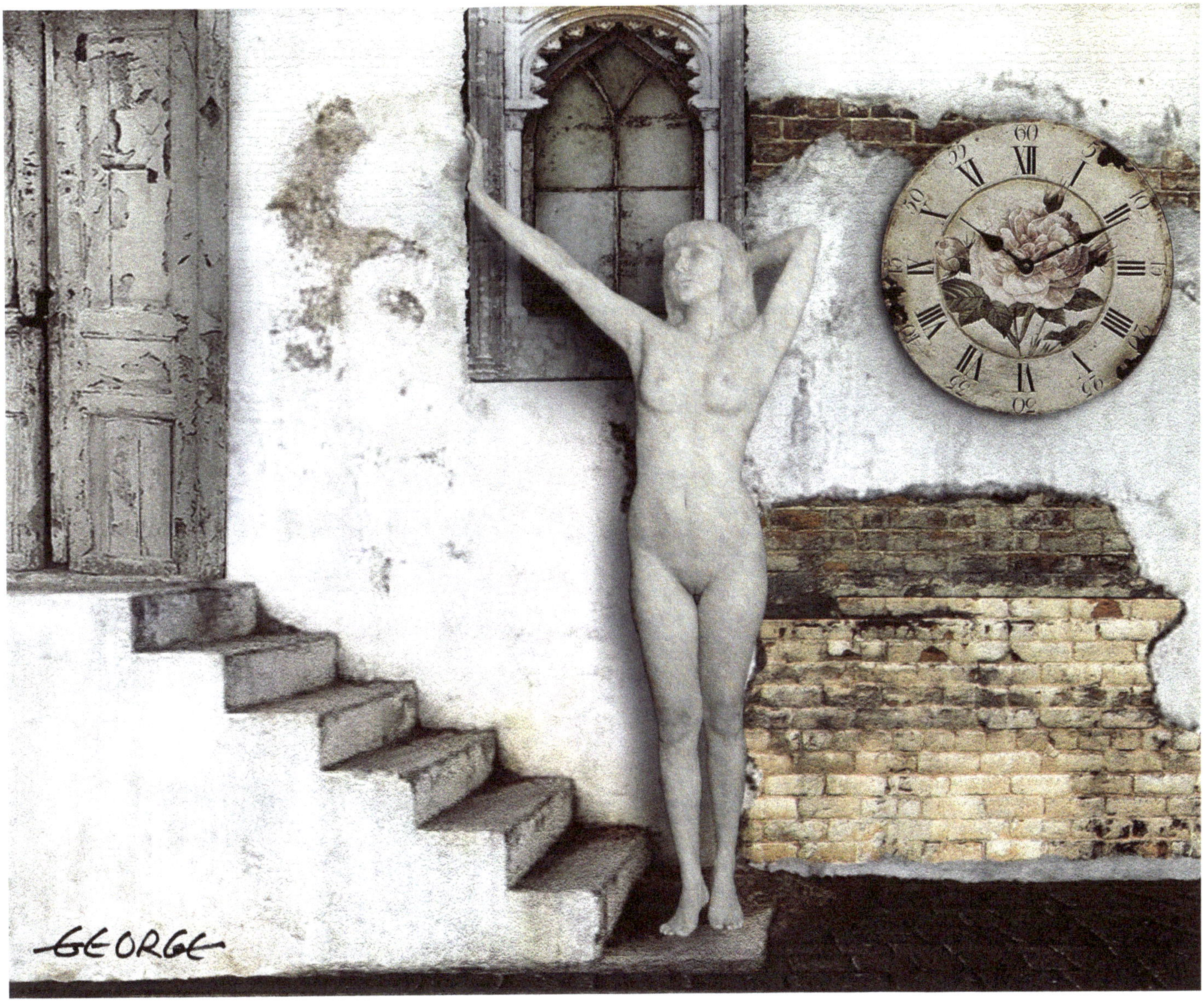
GEORGE

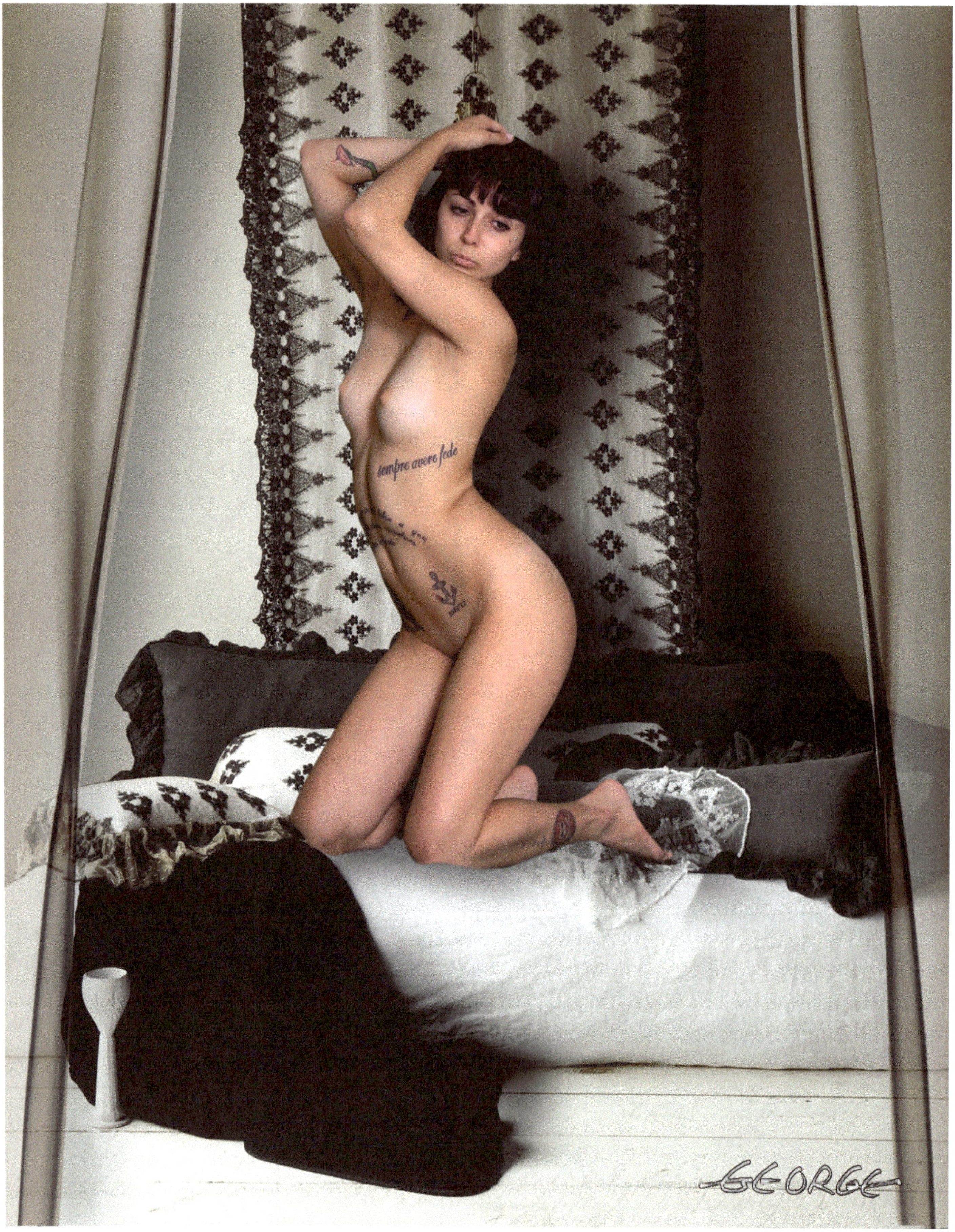
sempre avere fede
GEORGE

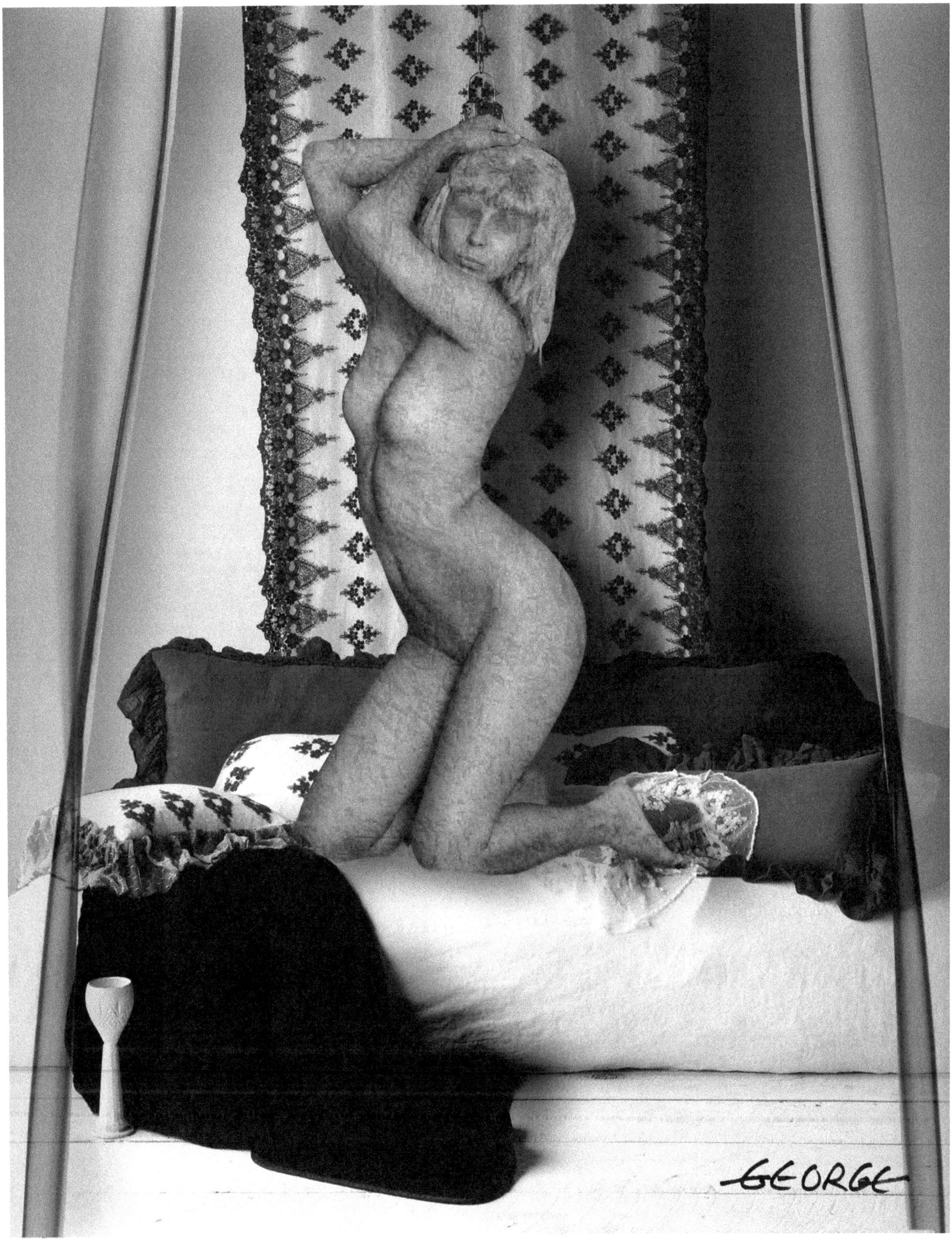
GEORGE

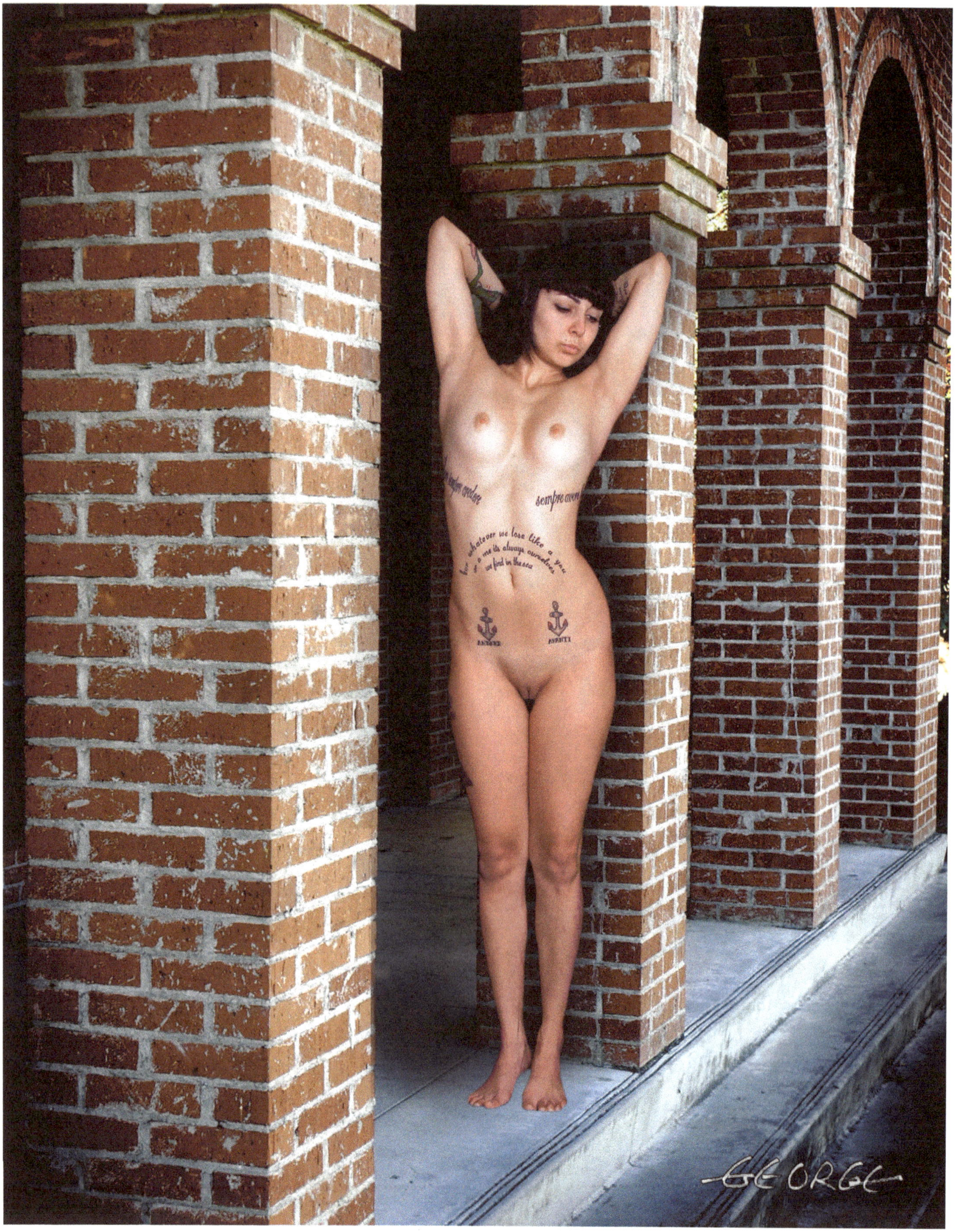
GEORGE

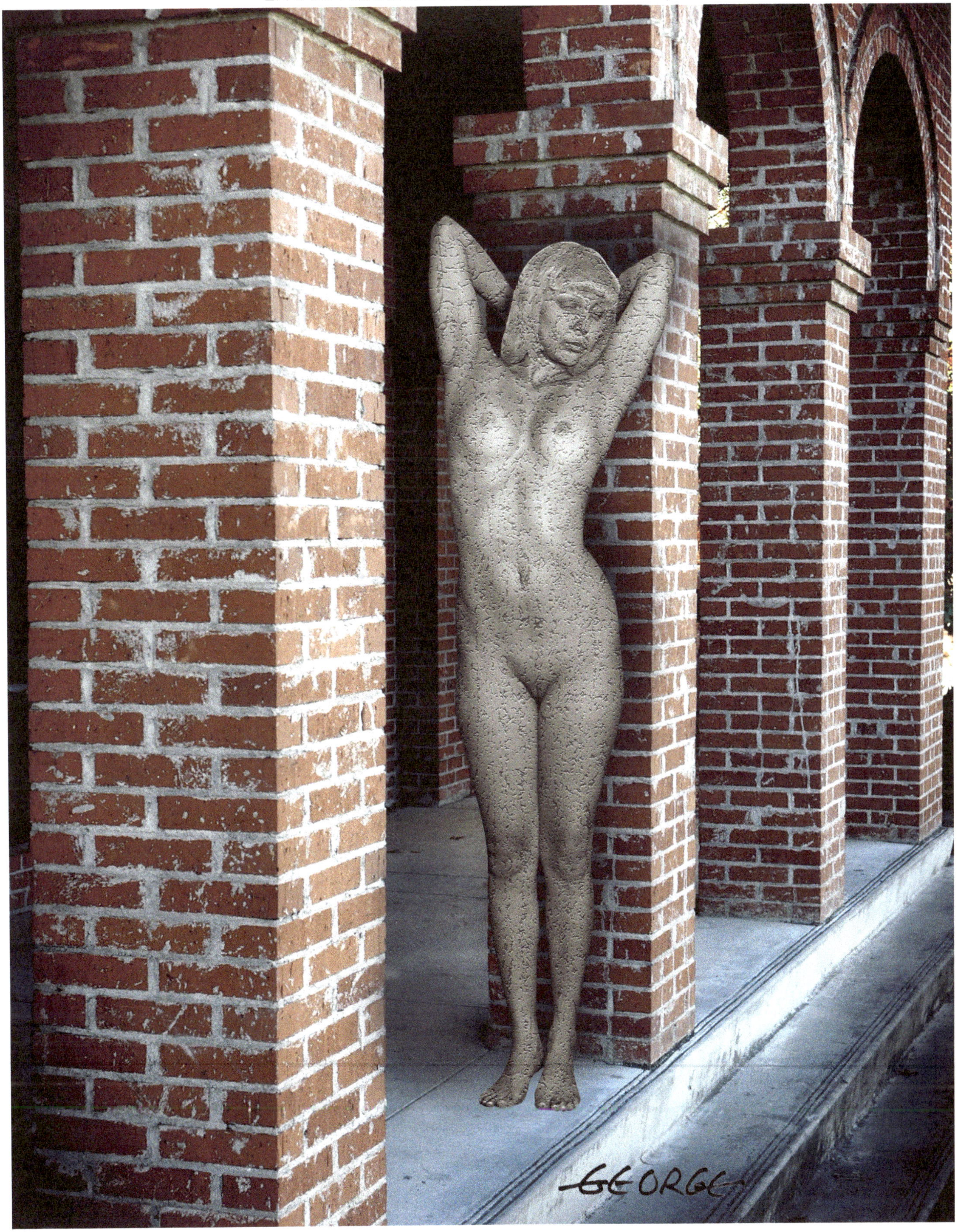
GEORGE

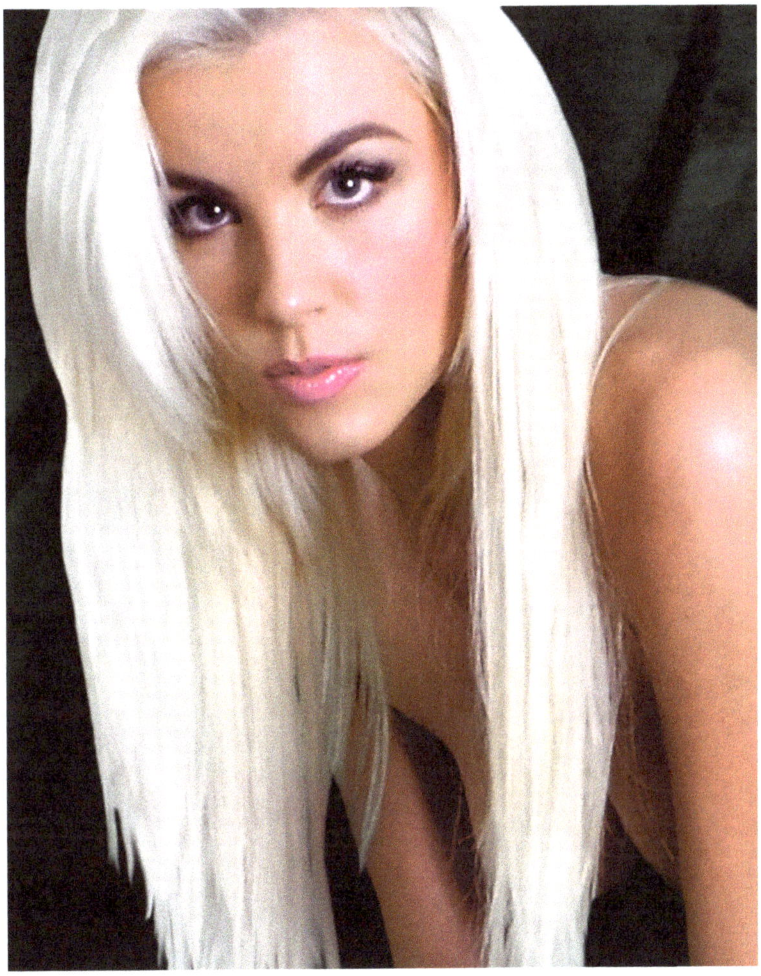

JESSICA

Height 5'7" Weight 112 lbs Bust 32" Waist 24" Hips 34" Cup B

My name is Jessica and I love all forms of art and beauty but my favorite art form is the human body. I love to express my artistic side by celebrating the beauty of my body by taking photos that express the artistic side of my personality.

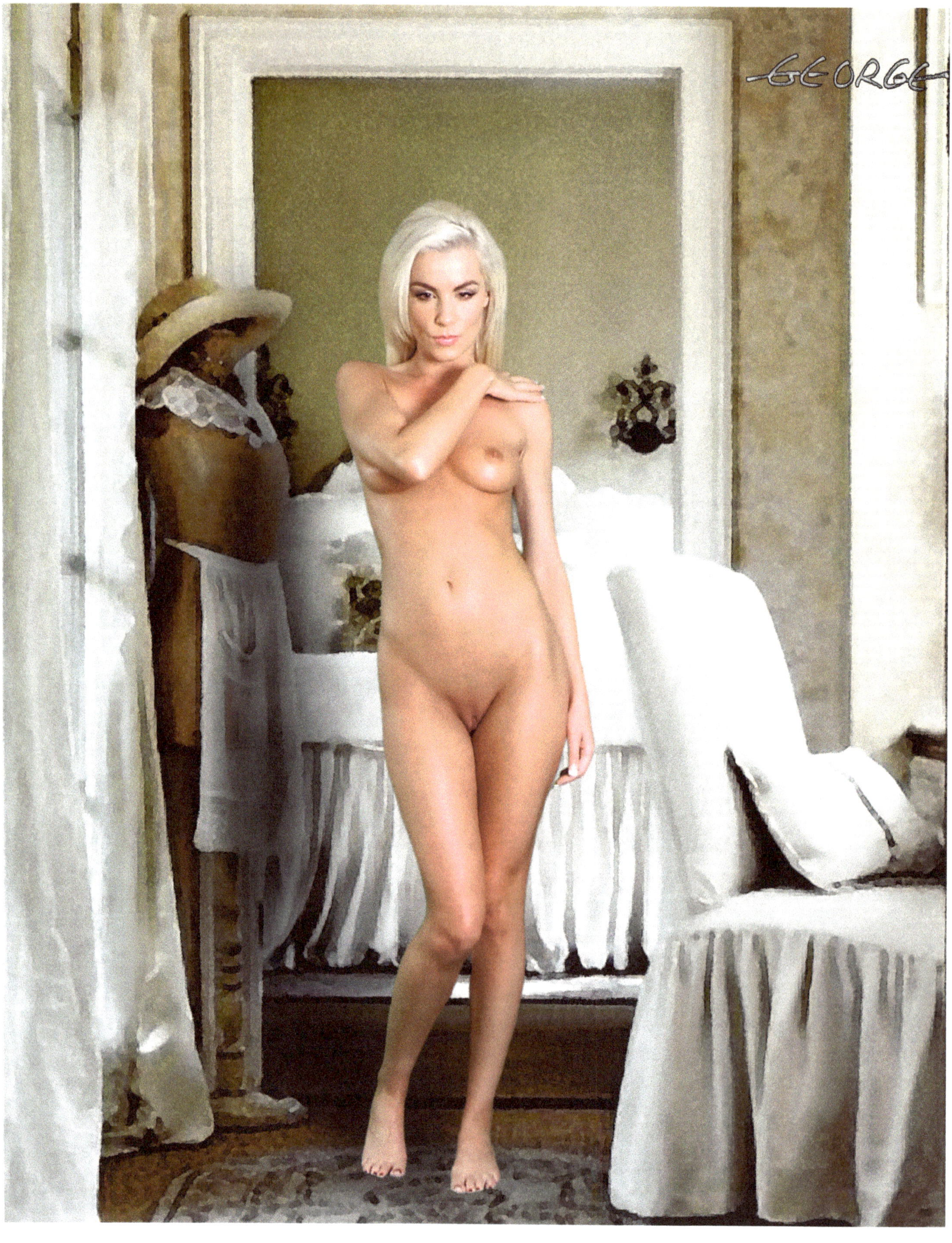
GEORGE

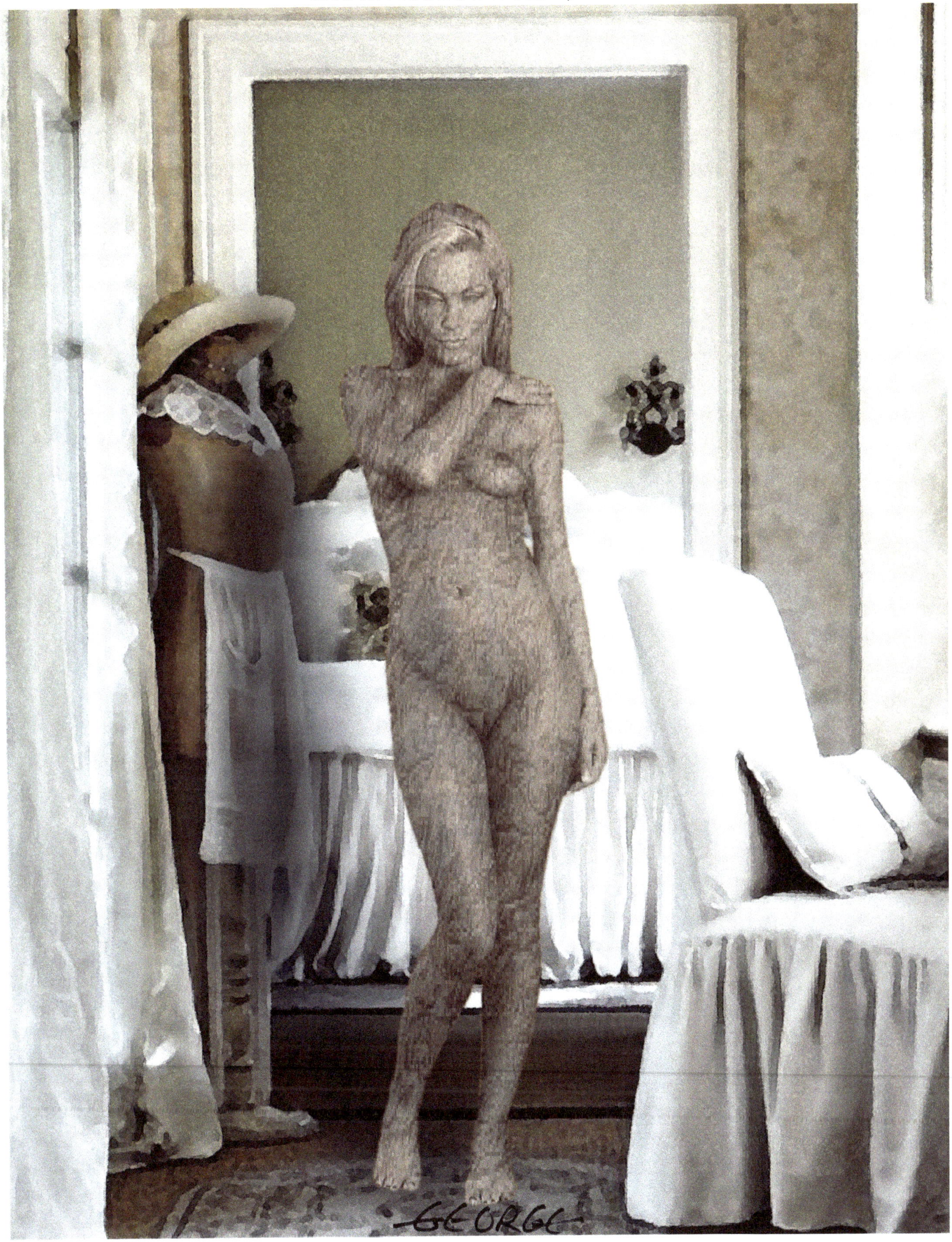
GEORGE

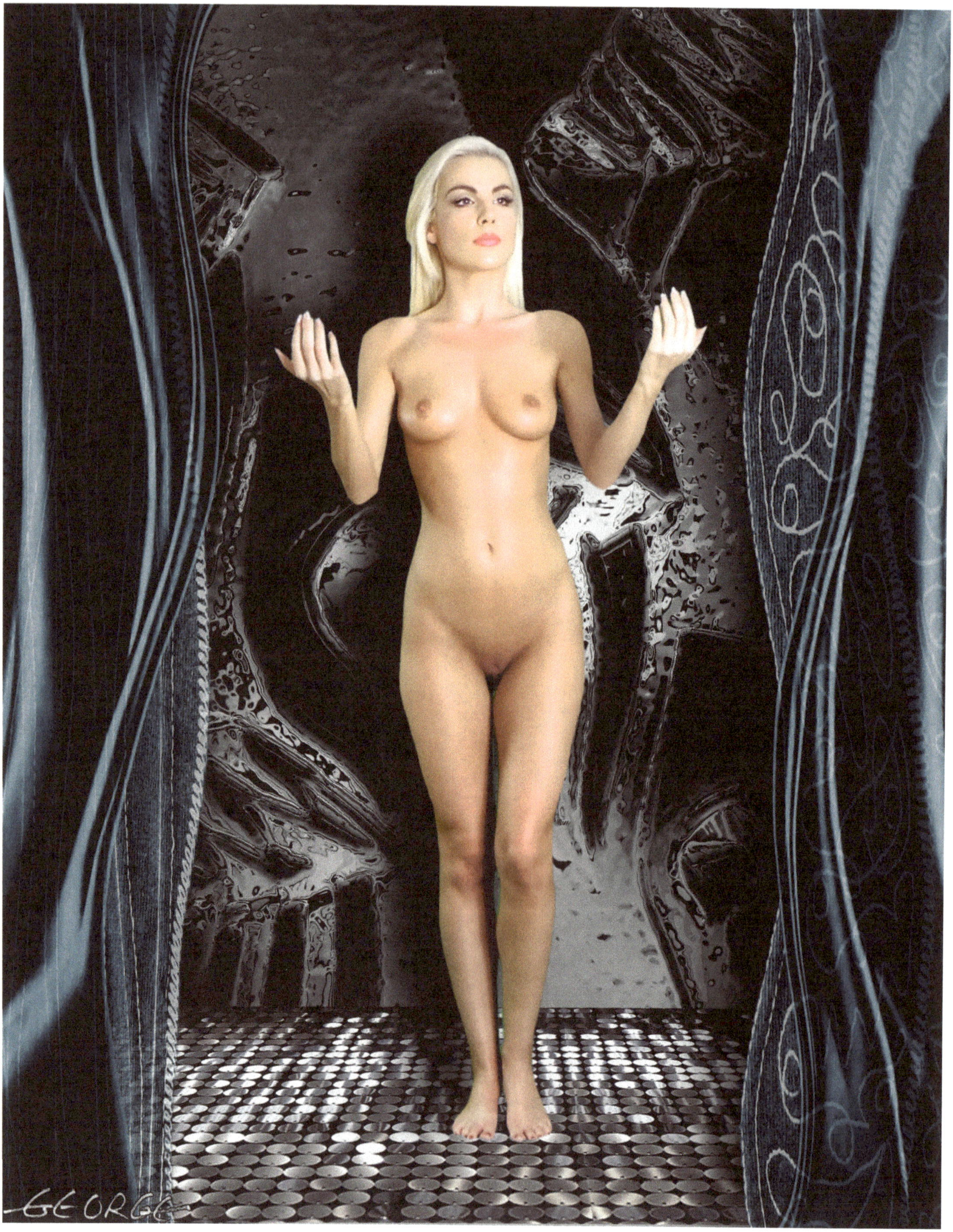

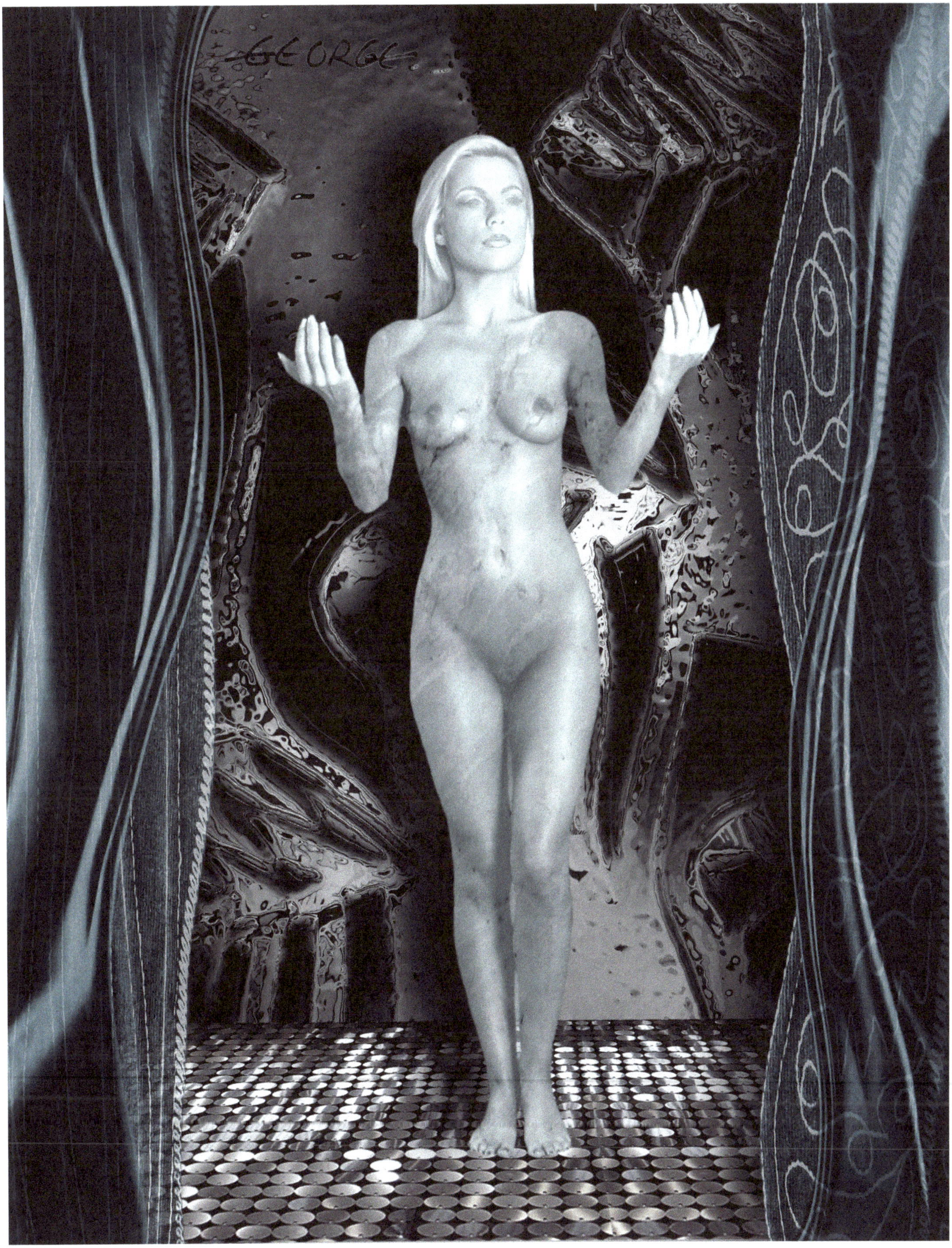
GEORGE

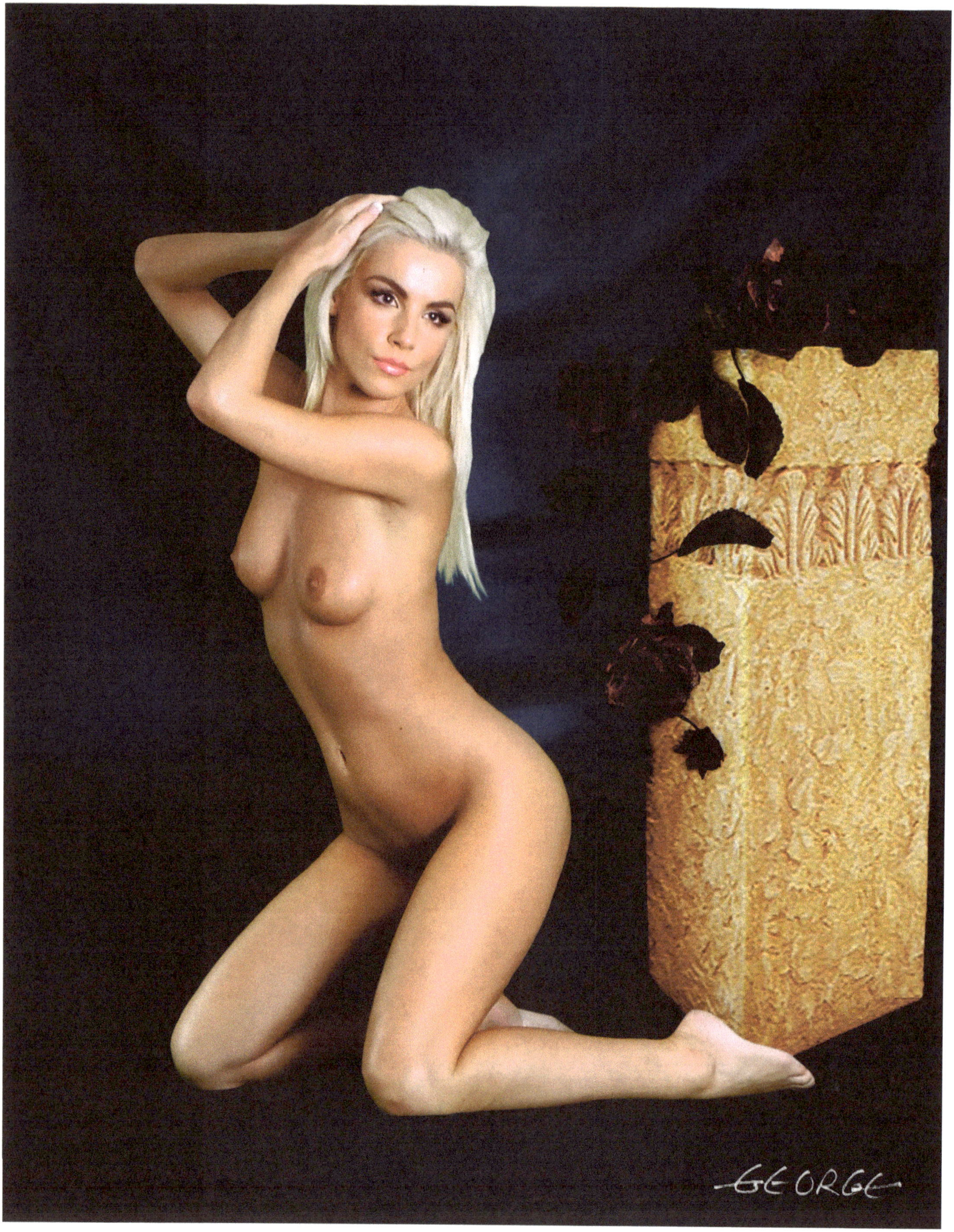
GEORGE

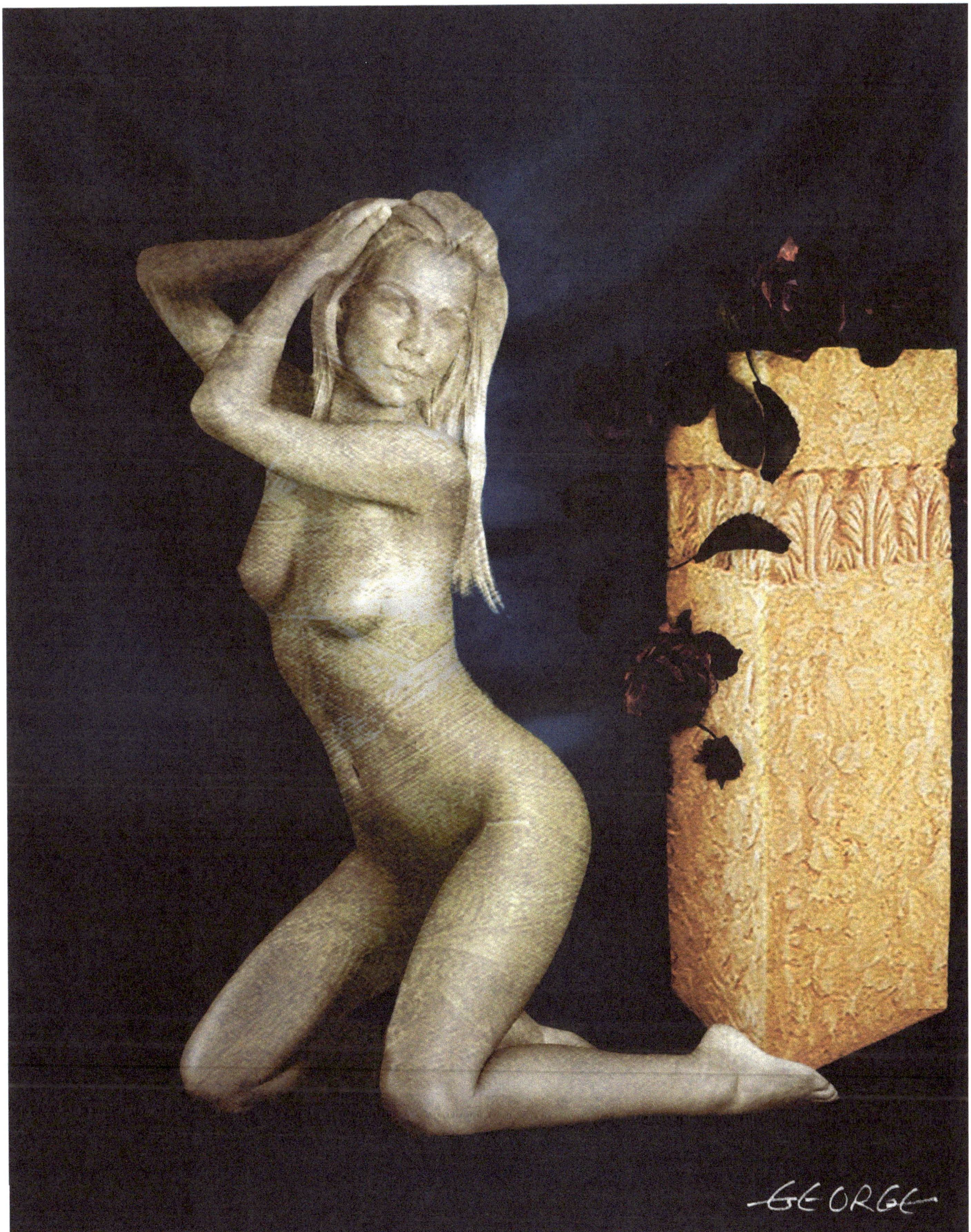
GEORGE

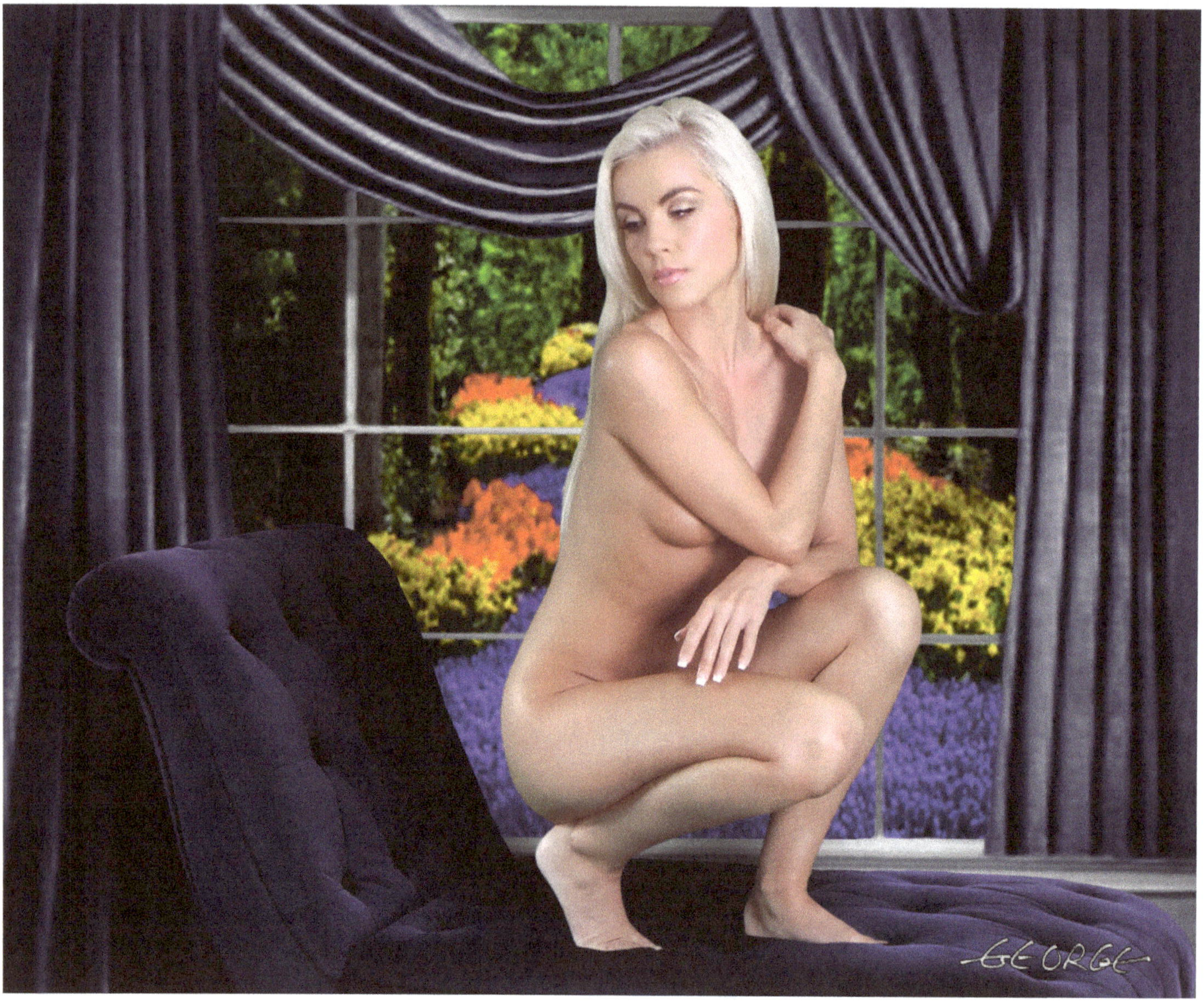
GEORGE

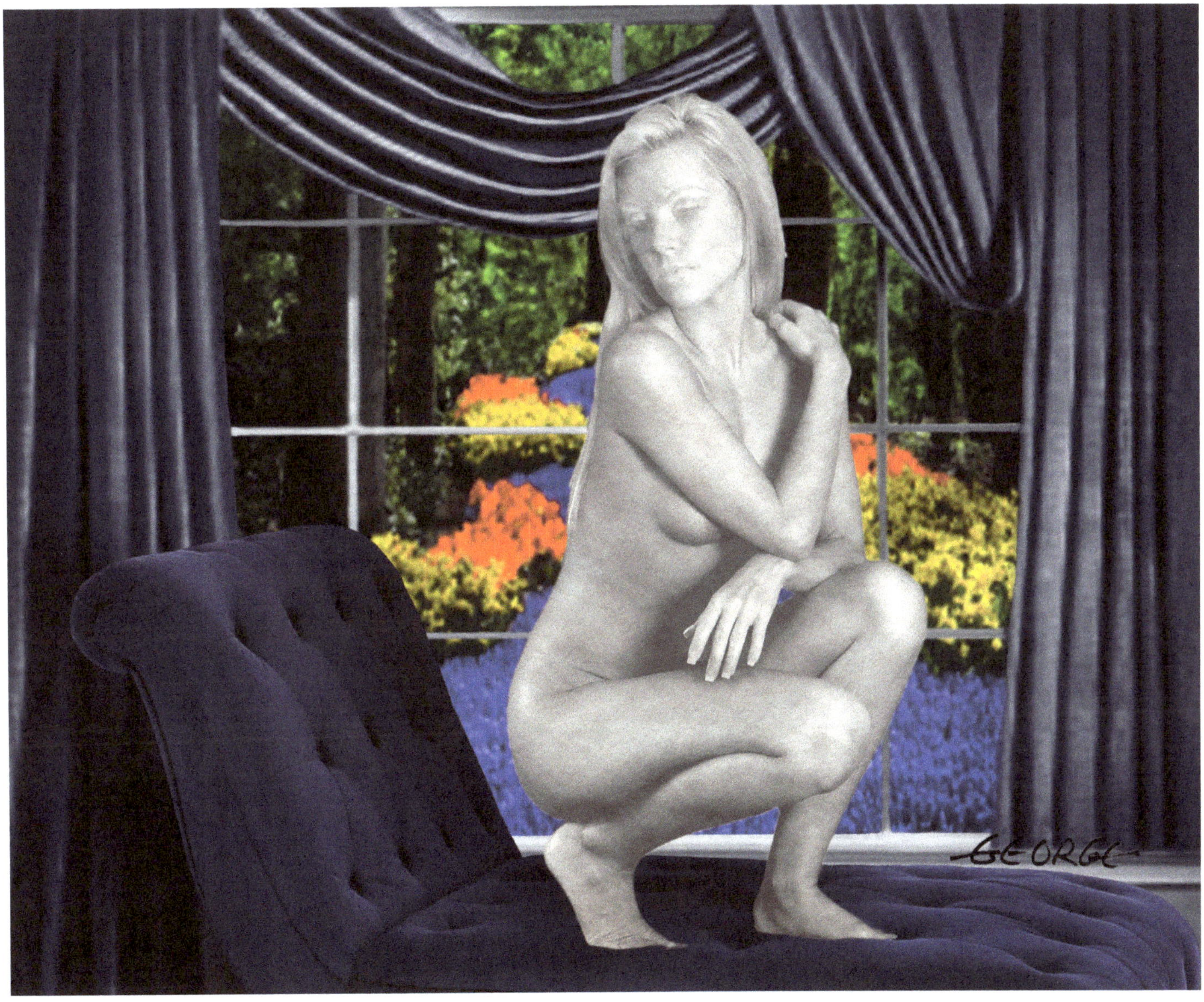
GEORGE

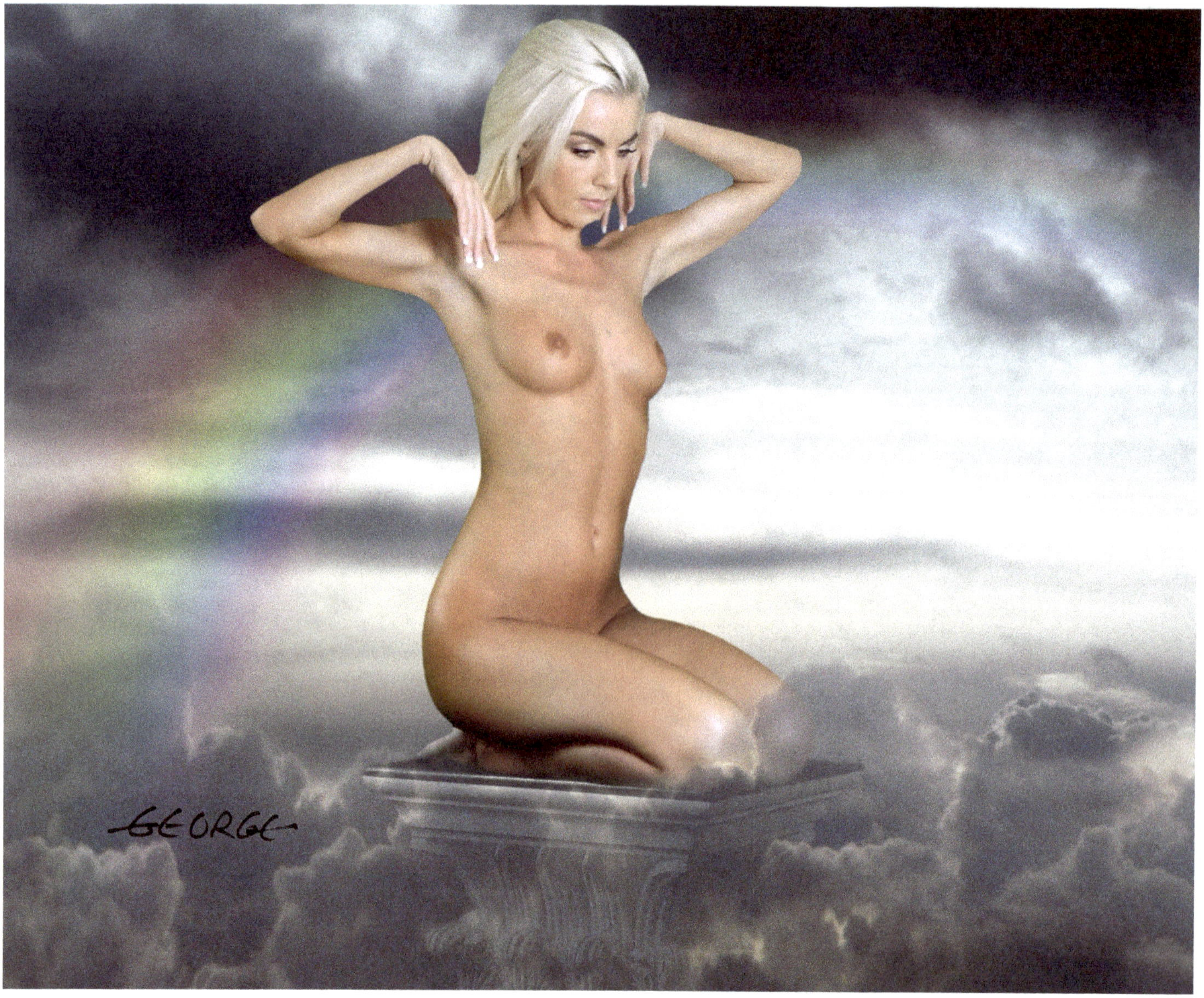
GEORGE

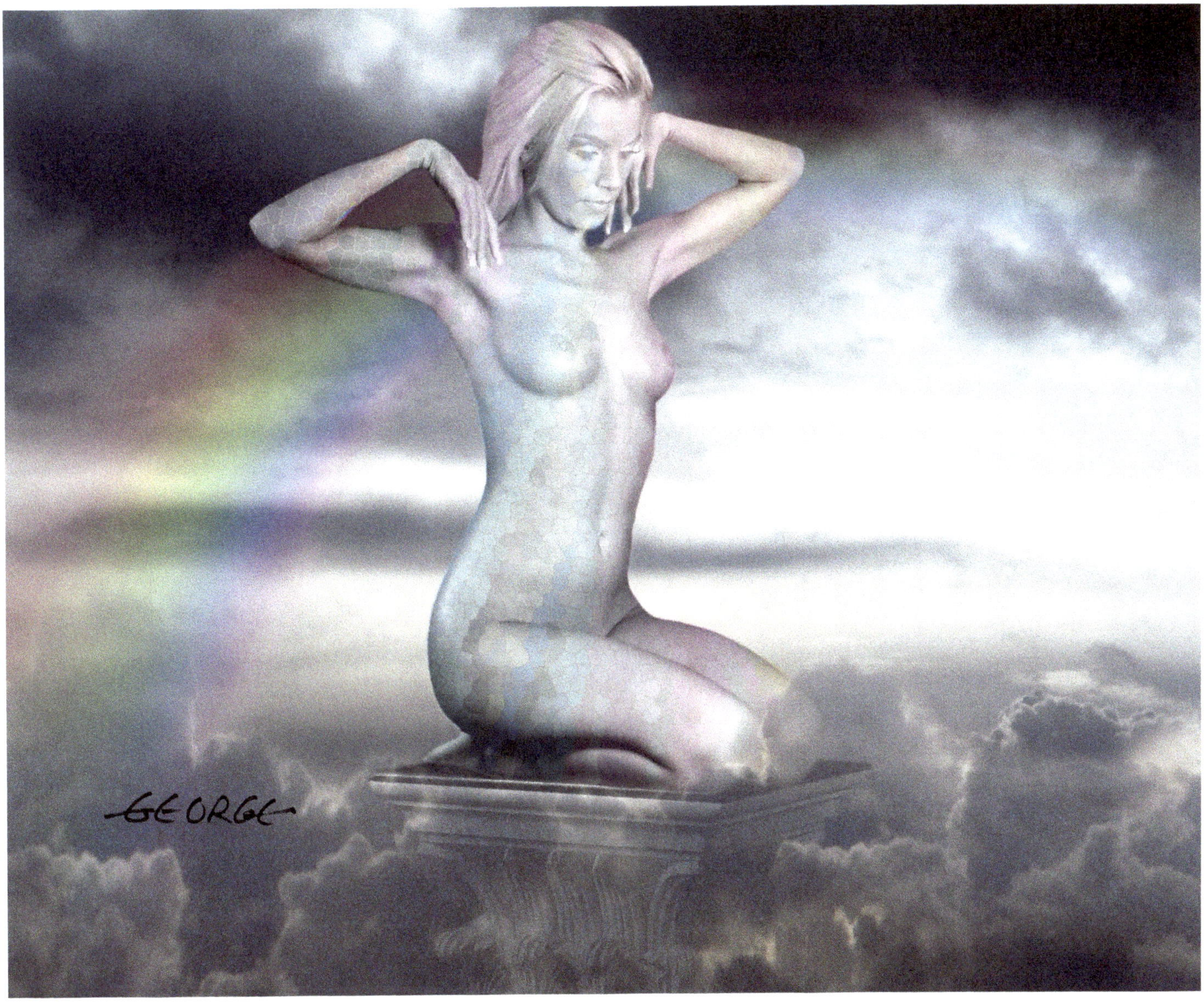
GEORGE

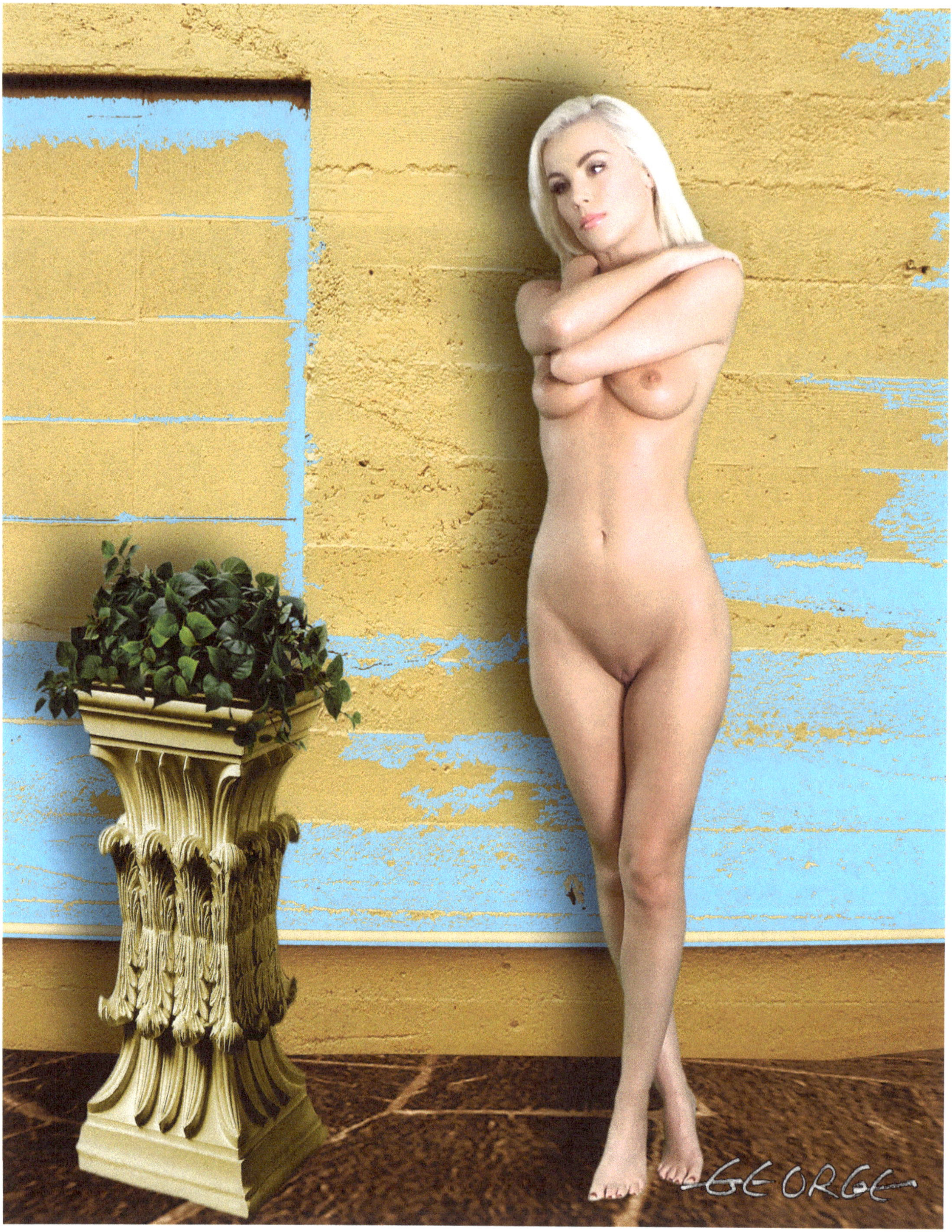
GEORGE

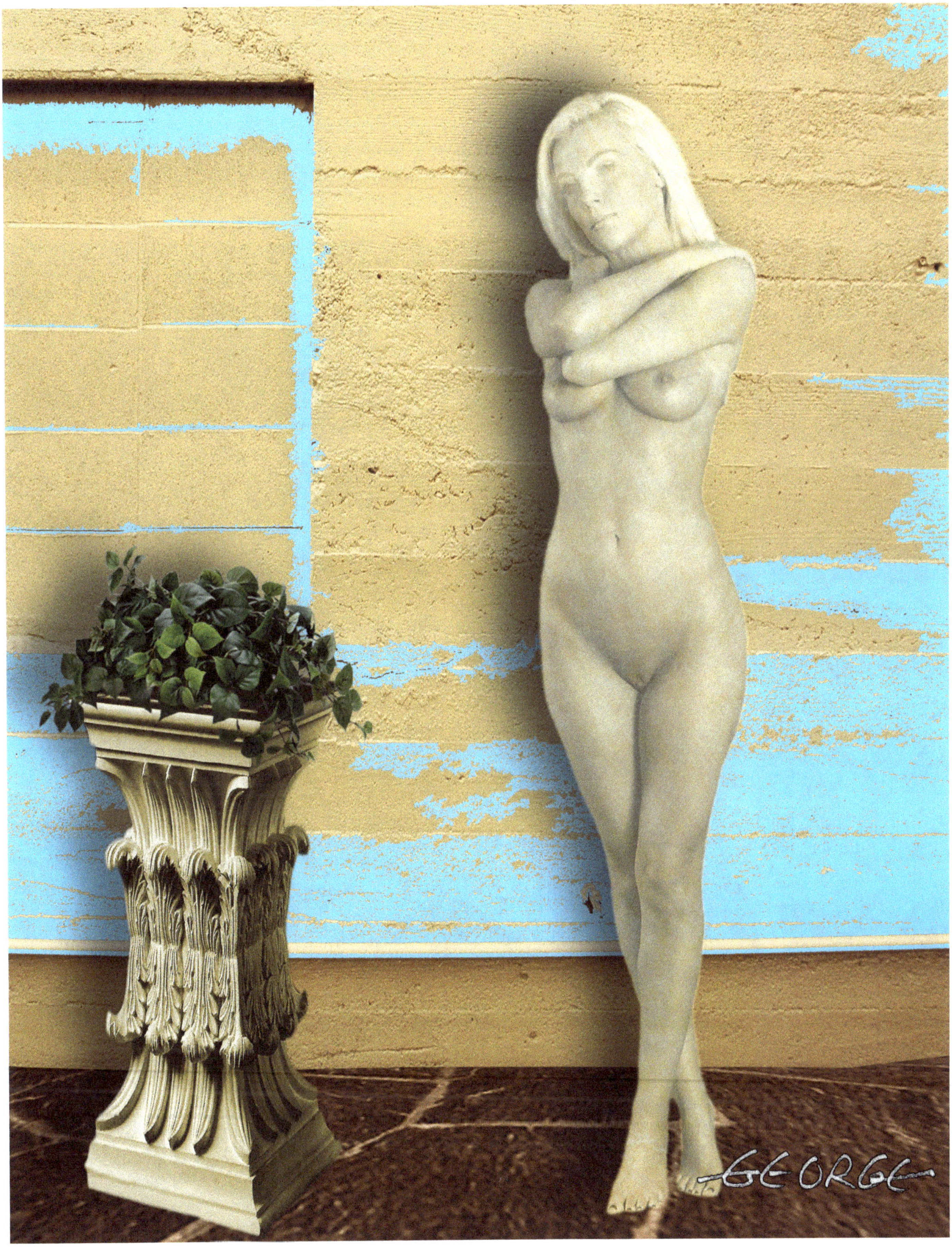
GEORGE

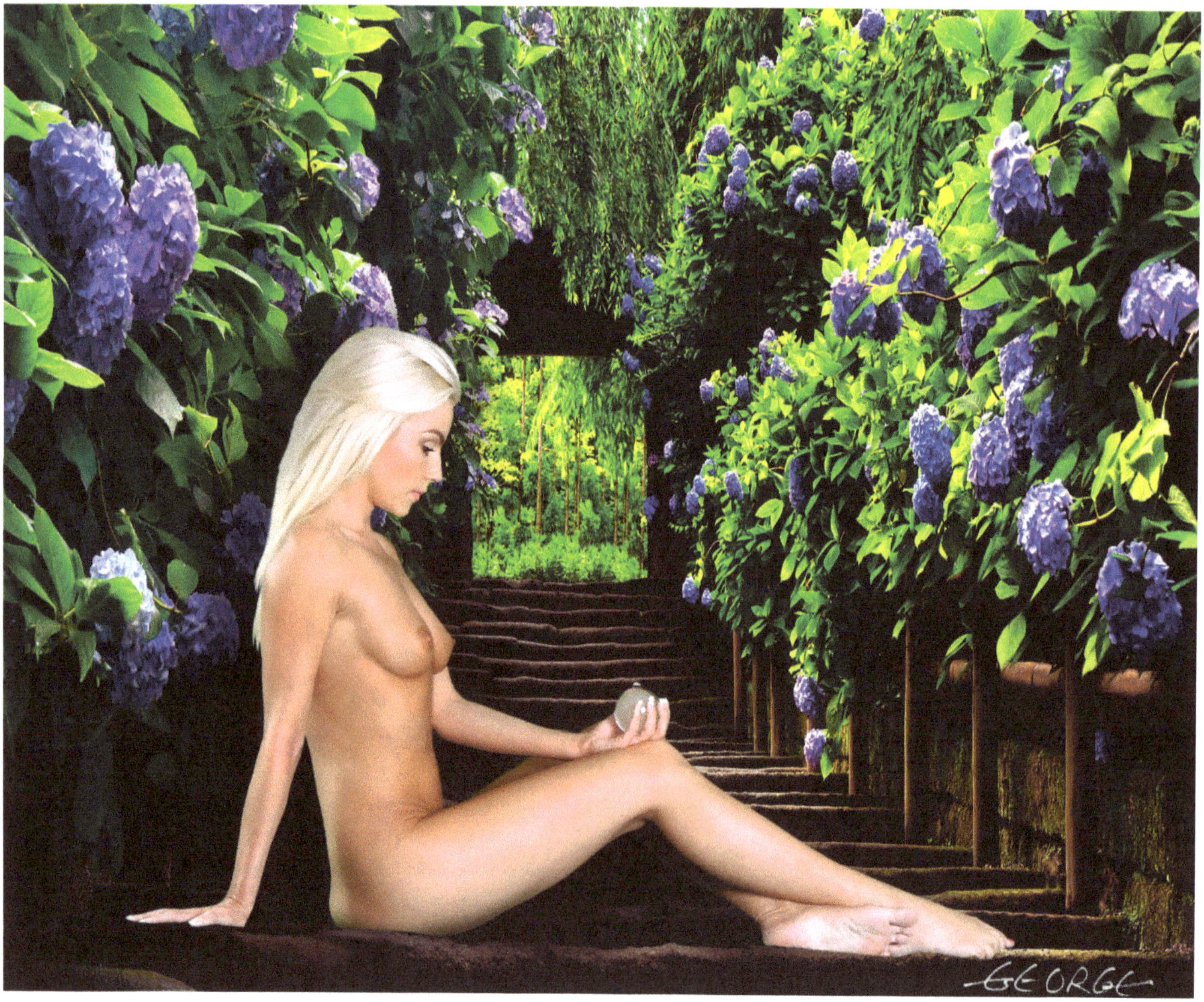
GEORGE

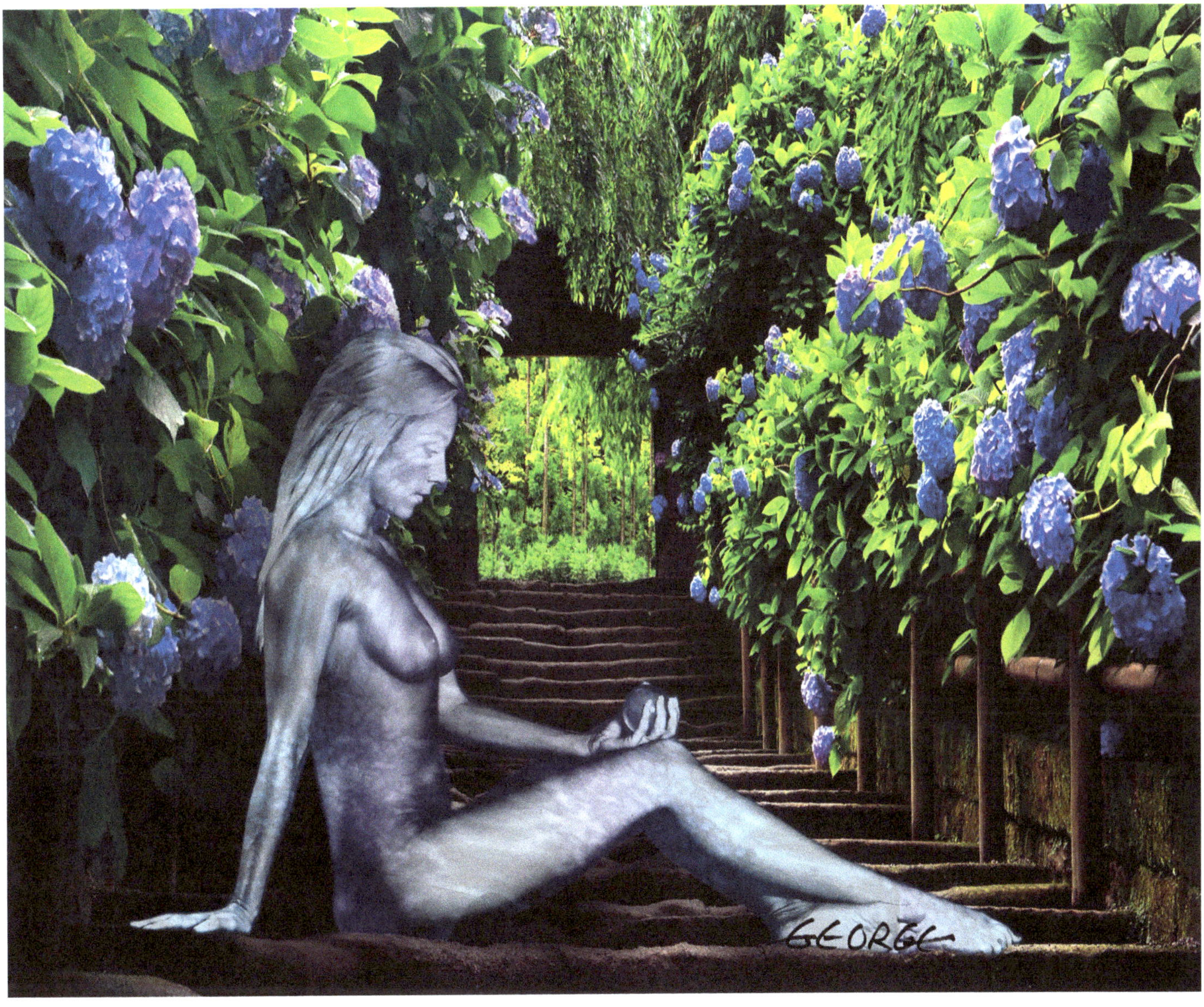
GEORGE

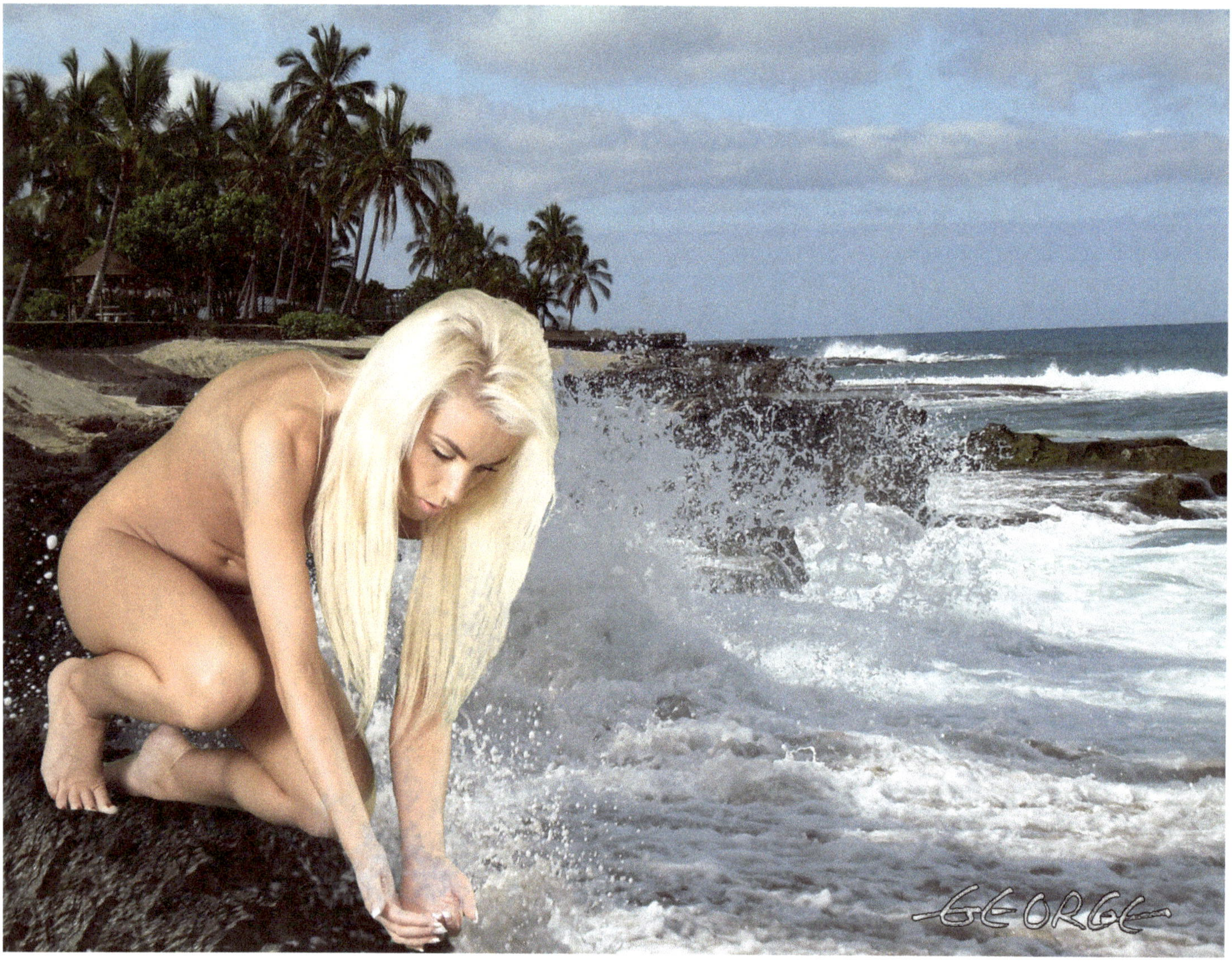
GEORGE

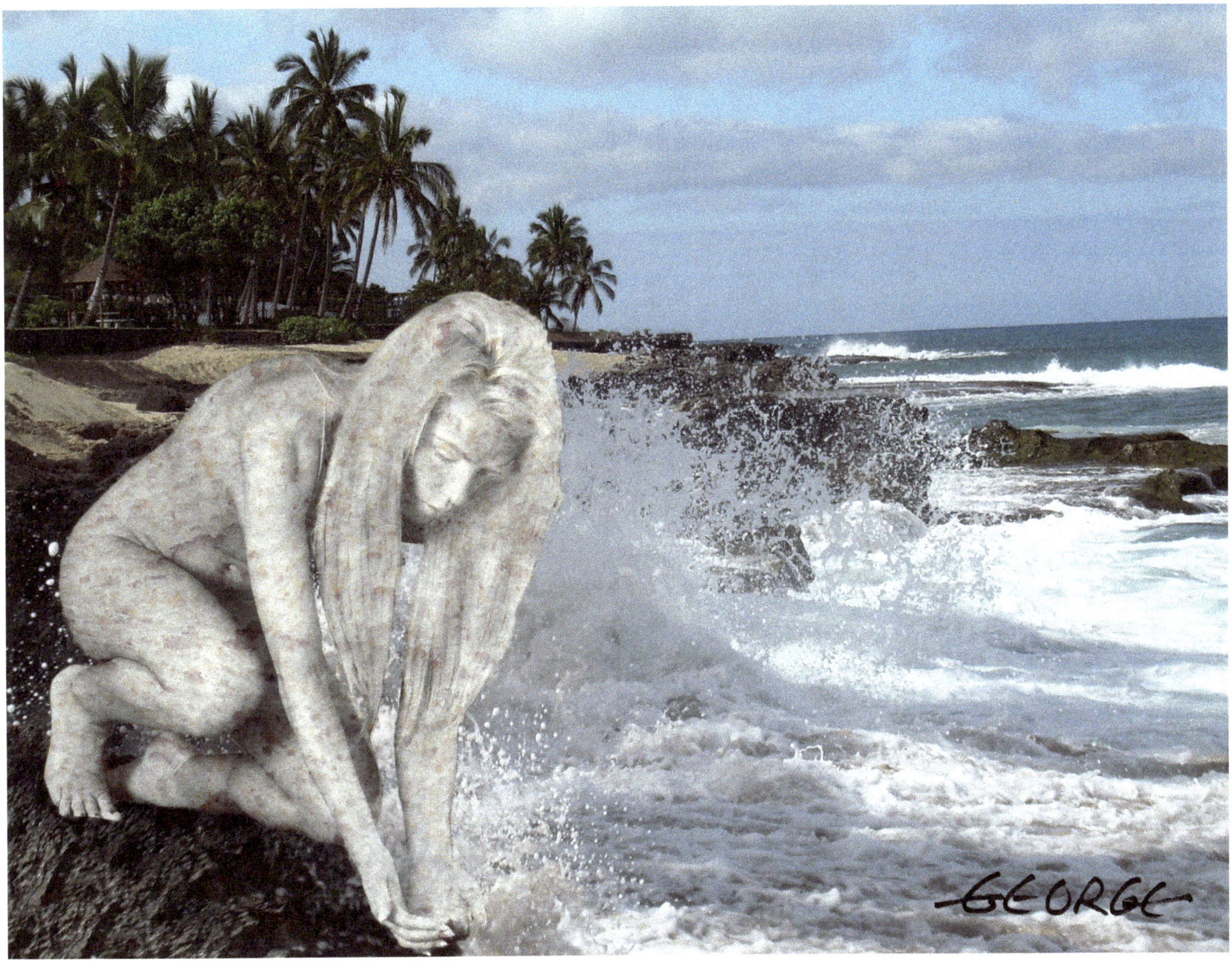
GEORGE

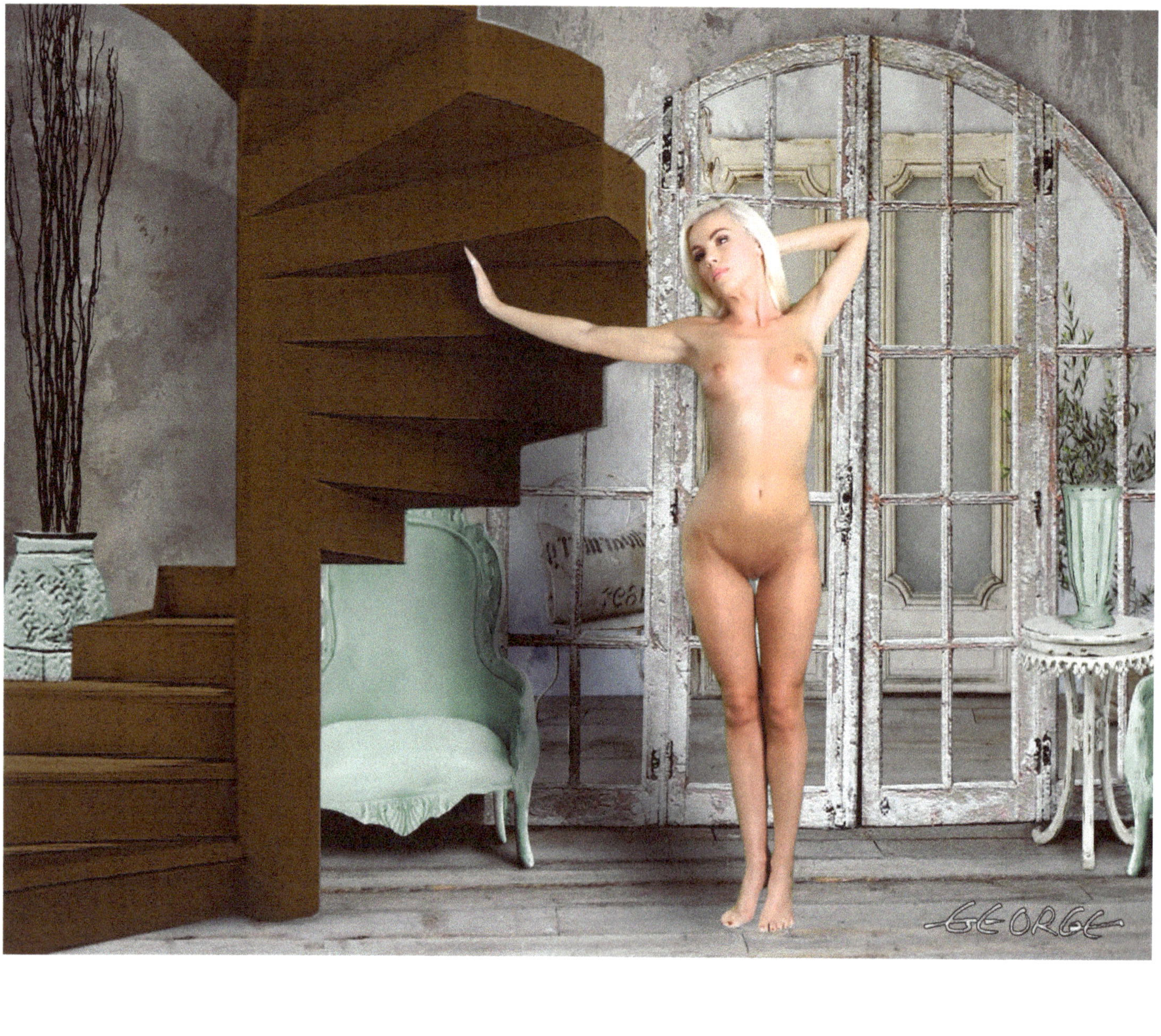
GEORGE

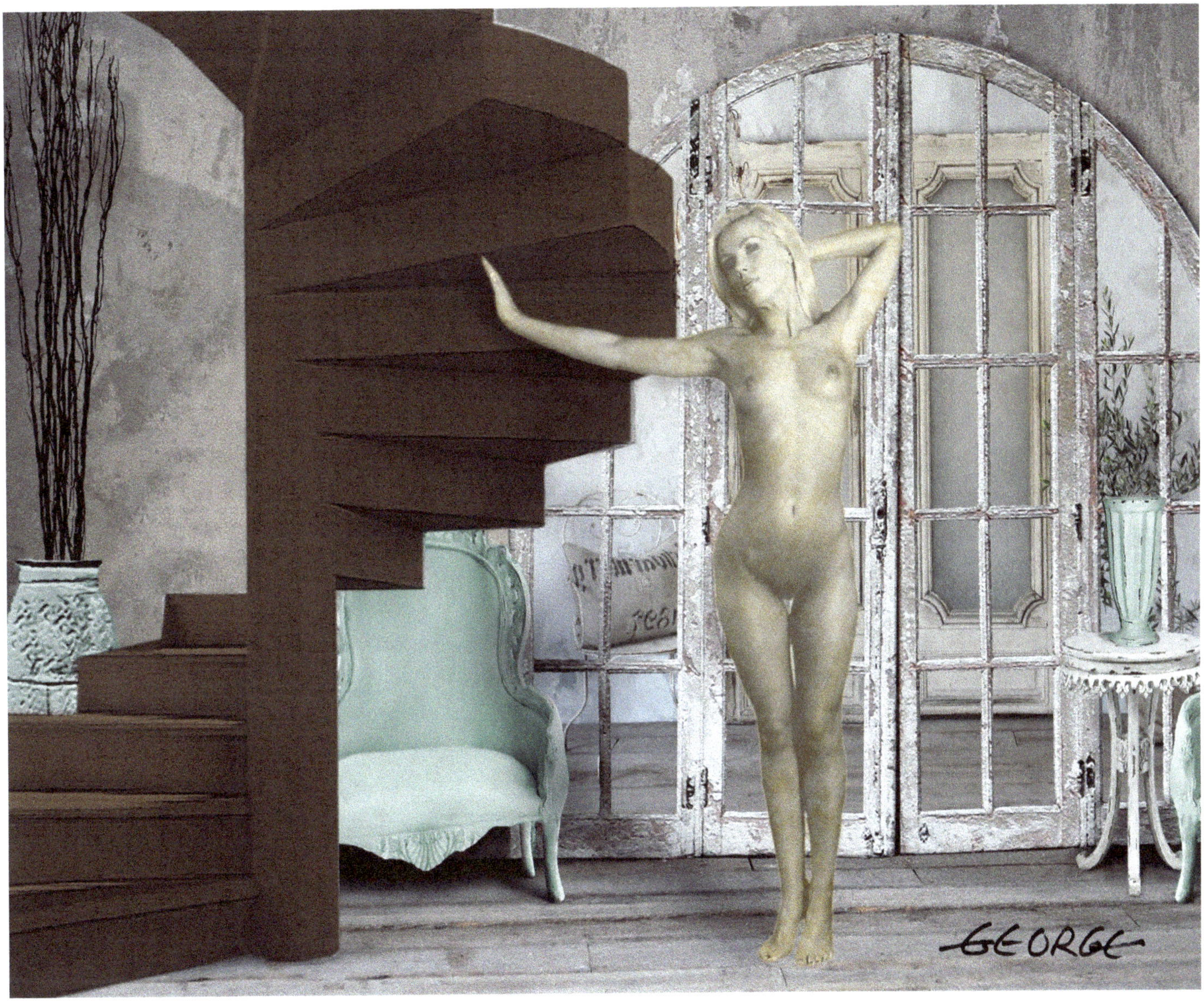
GEORGE

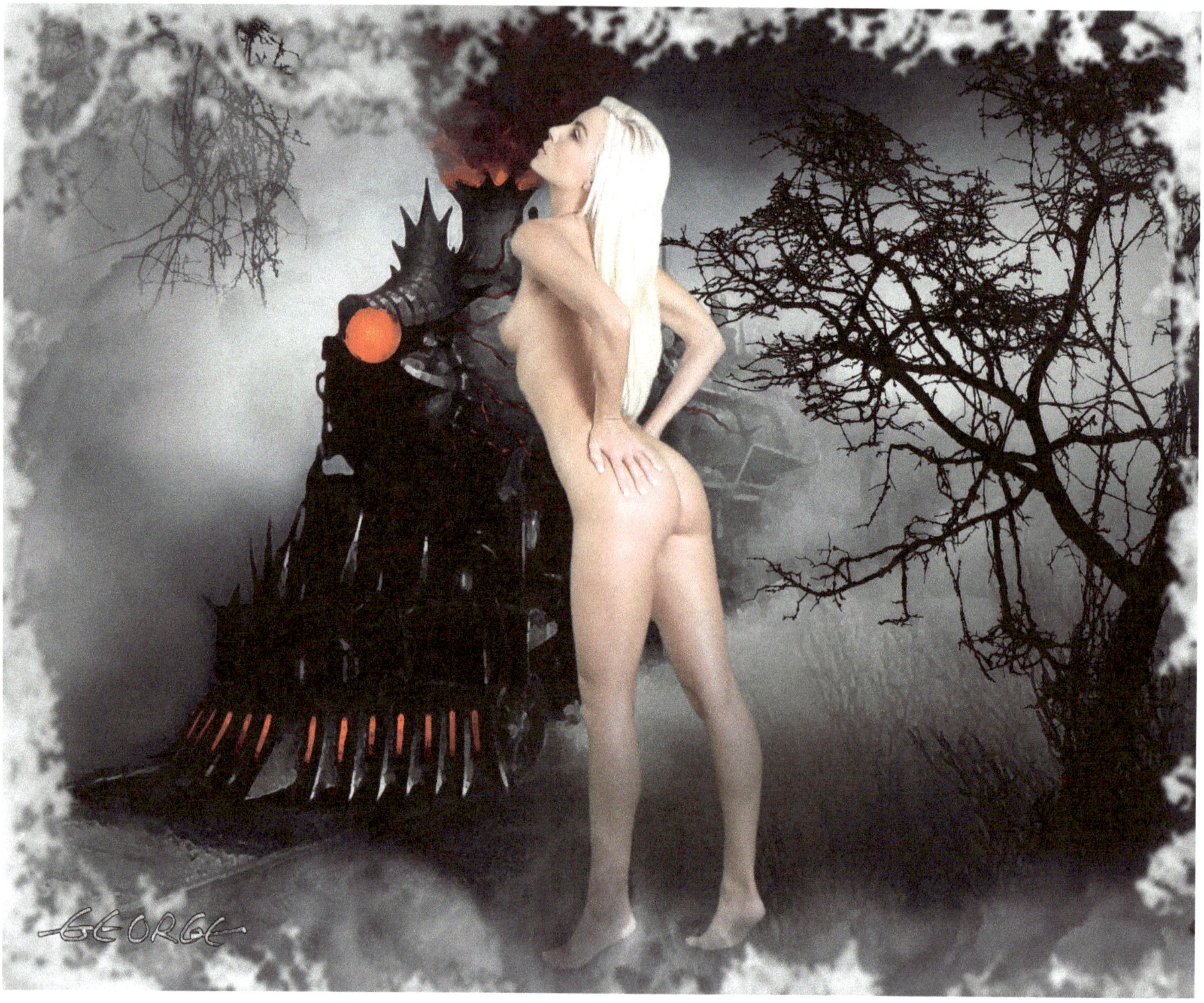
GEORGE

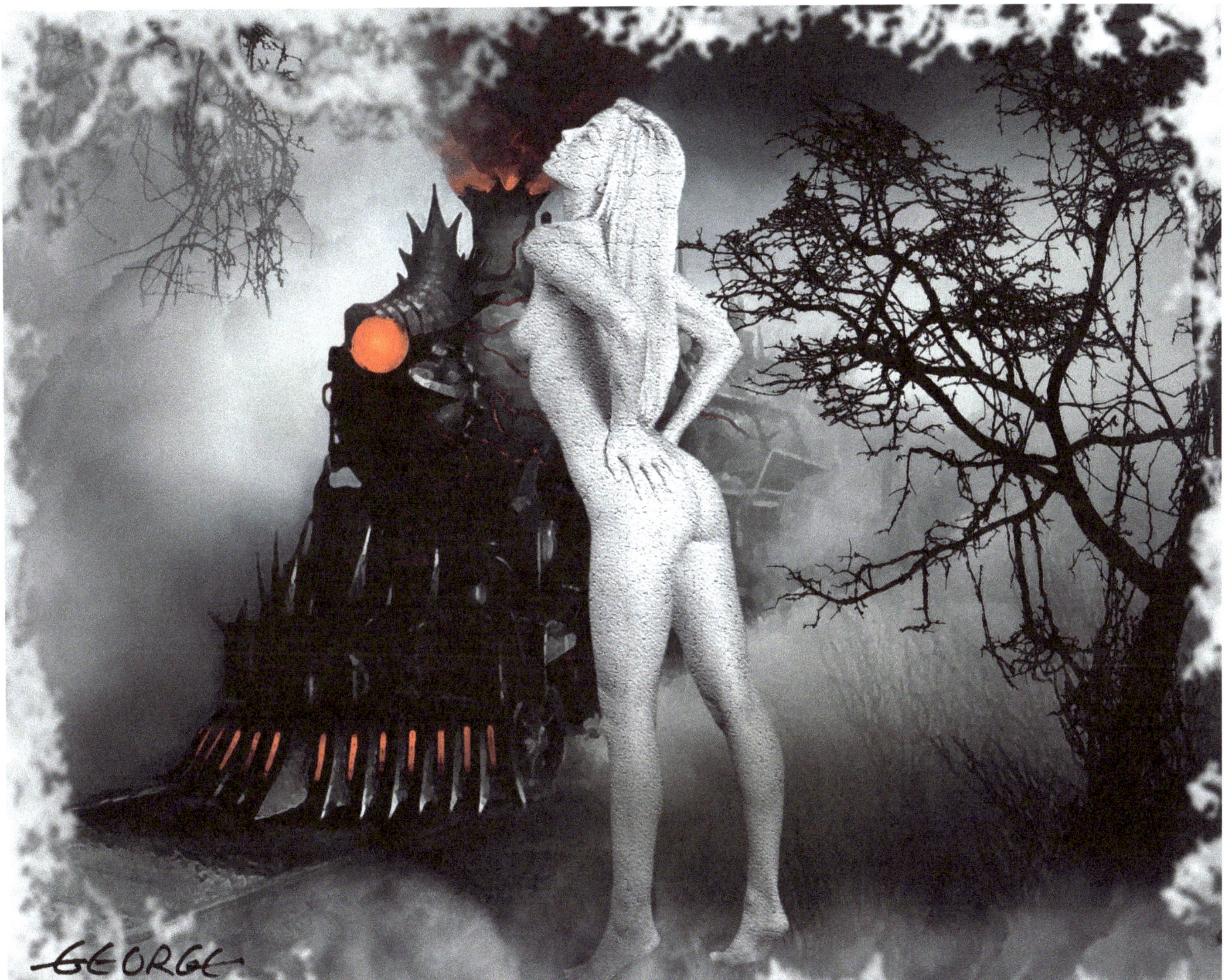
GEORGE

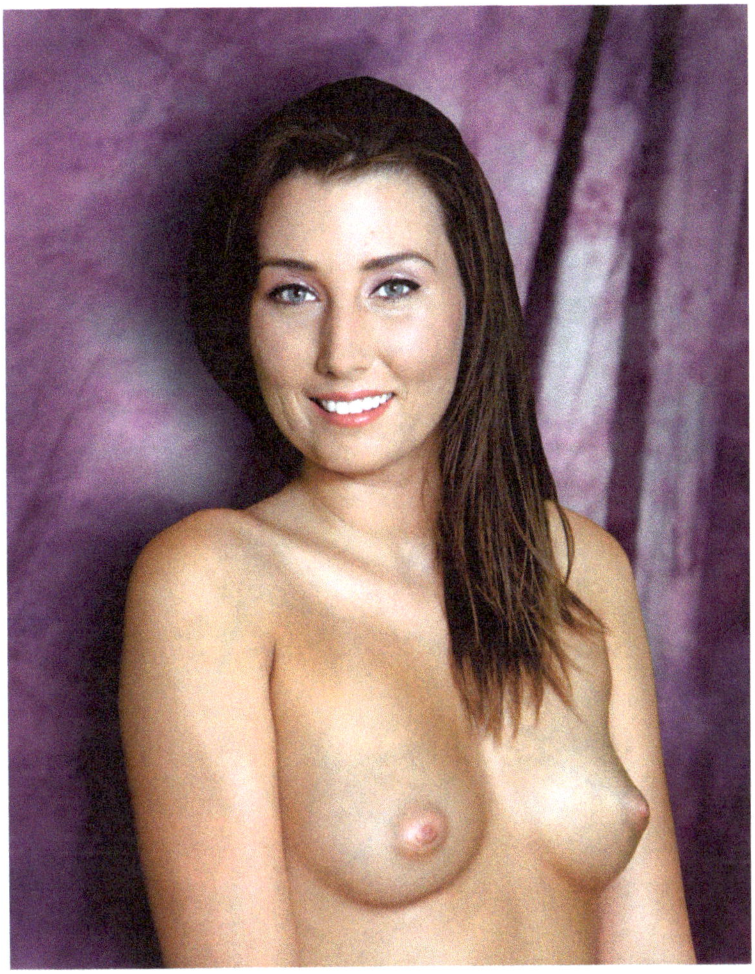

KATY JO

Height 5'8" Weight 135 lbs Bus 36" Waist 26" Hips 40" Cup A

I am very creative and down to Earth. I love meeting new people and exploring new places. I am an open-minded, creative, free spirit. I enjoy cooking (I adhere to a strict Paleo diet), reading, networking, swimming, working out, tanning, doing yoga, and bettering myself.

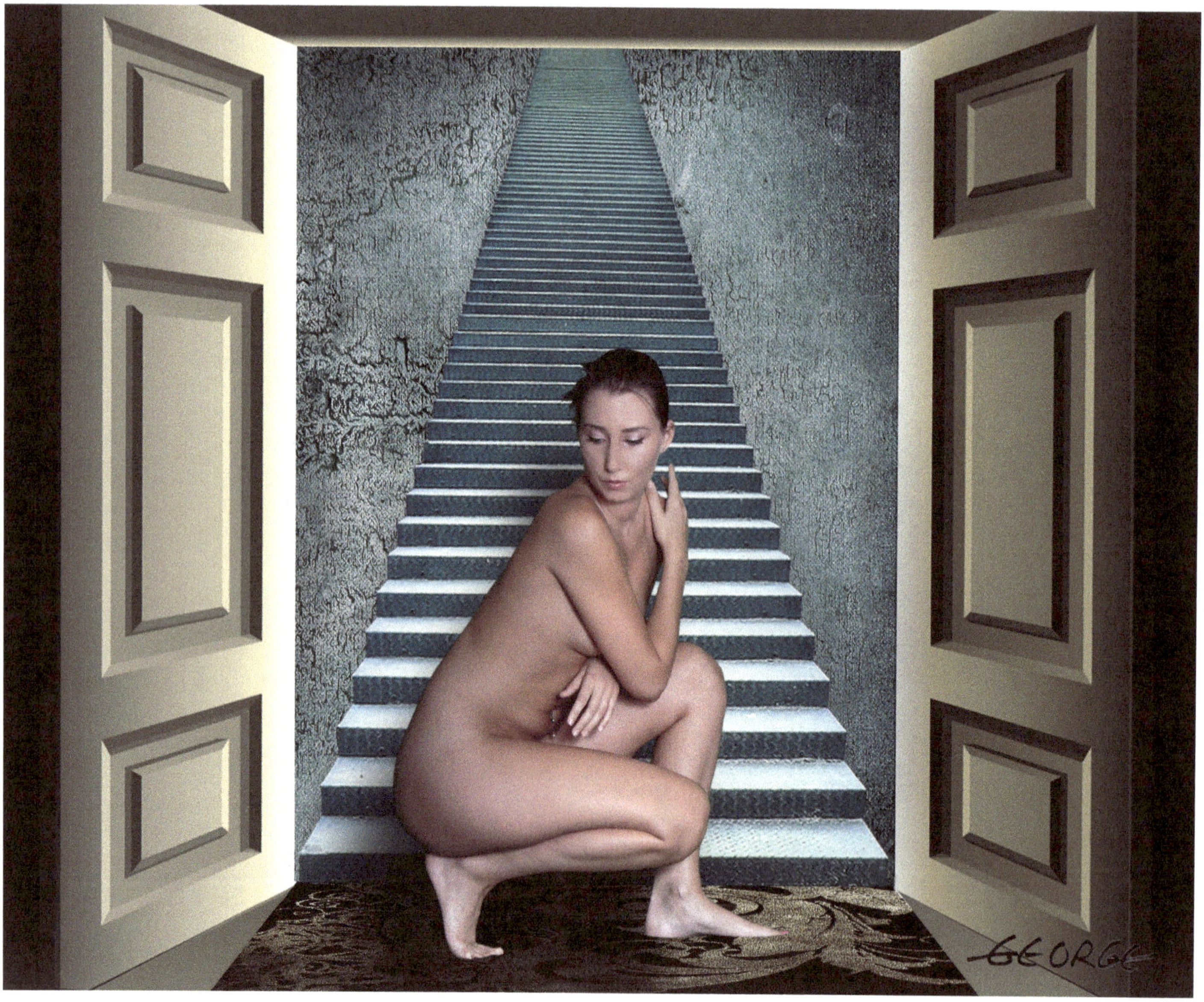
GEORGE

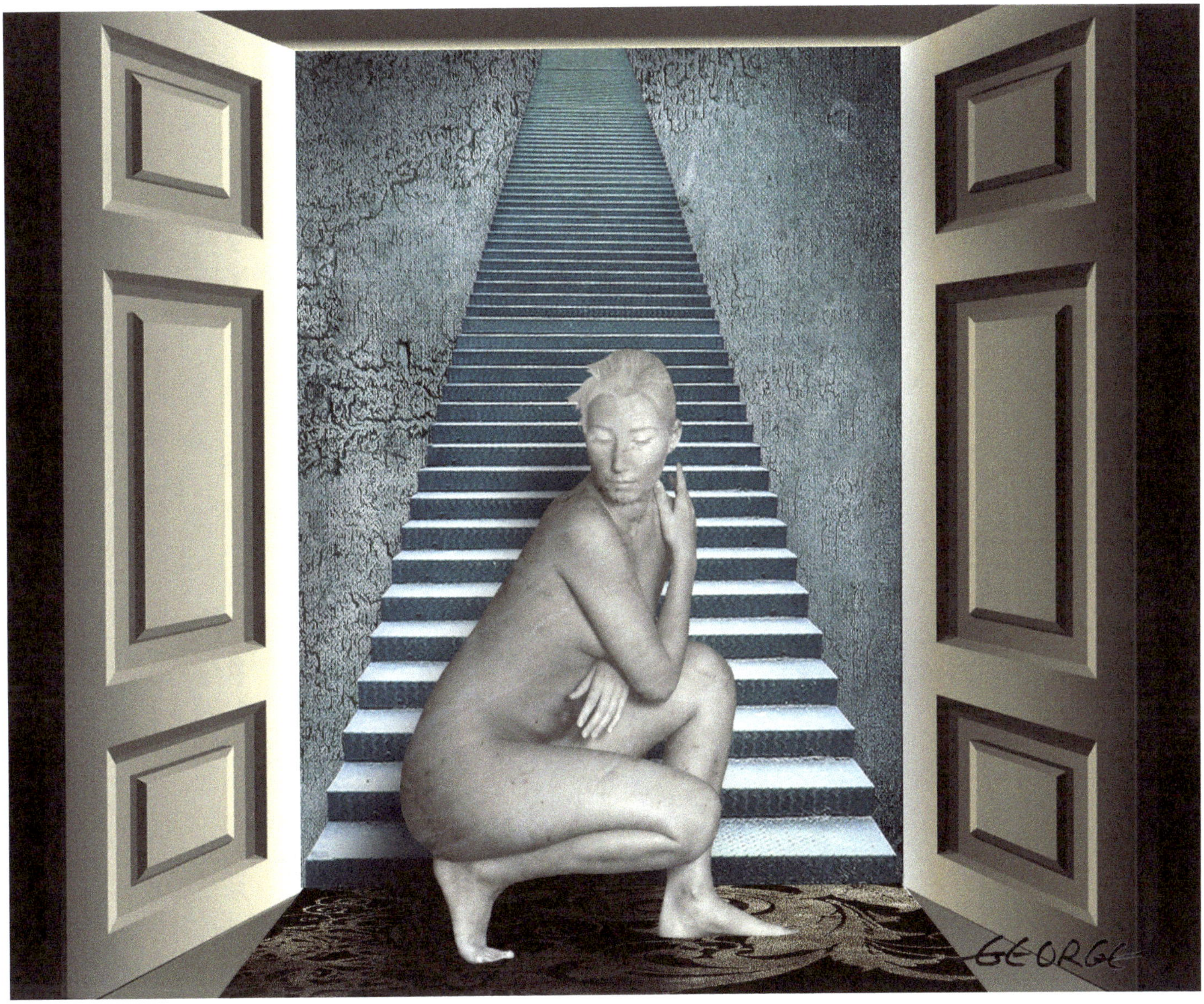
GEORGE

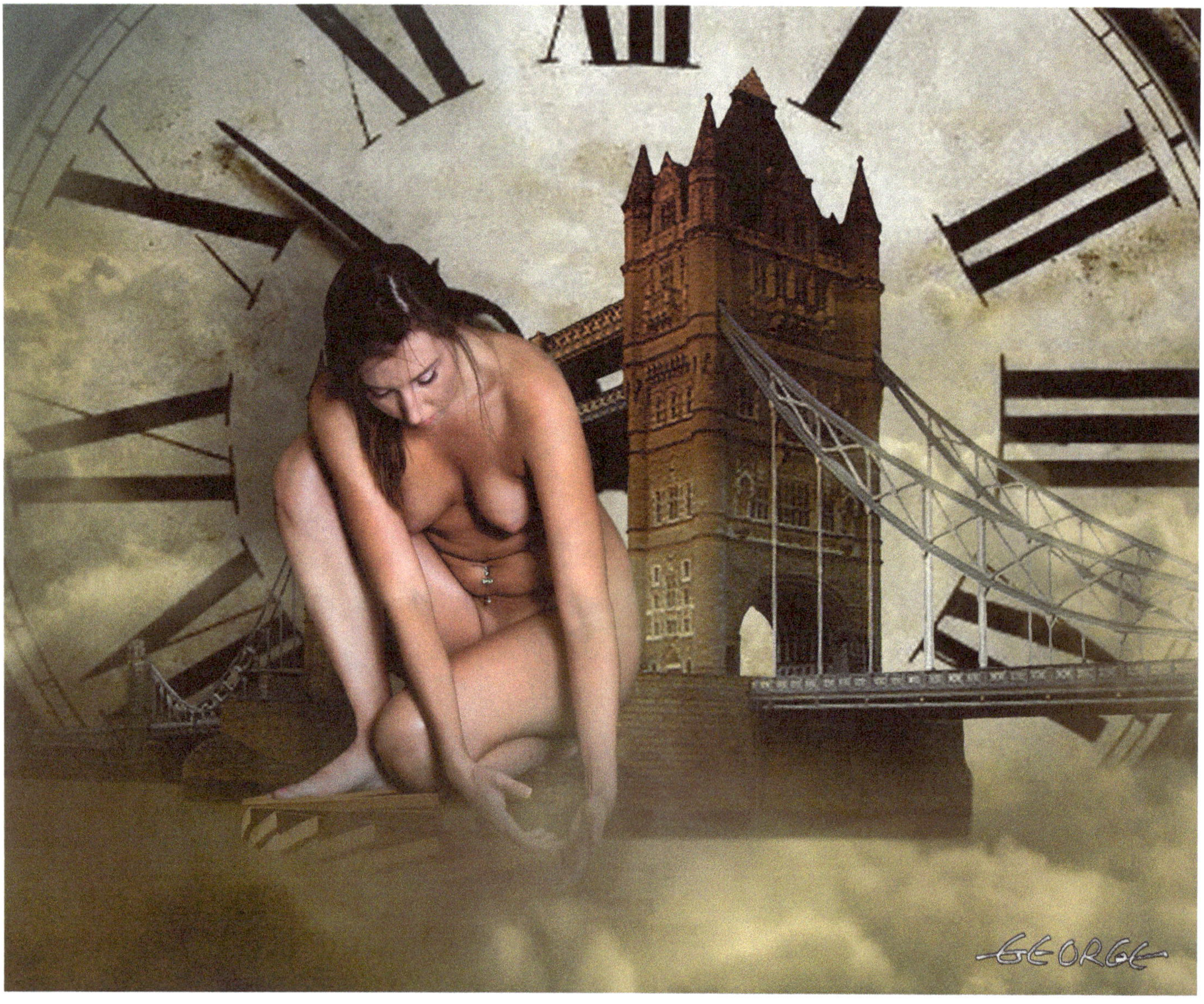
GEORGE

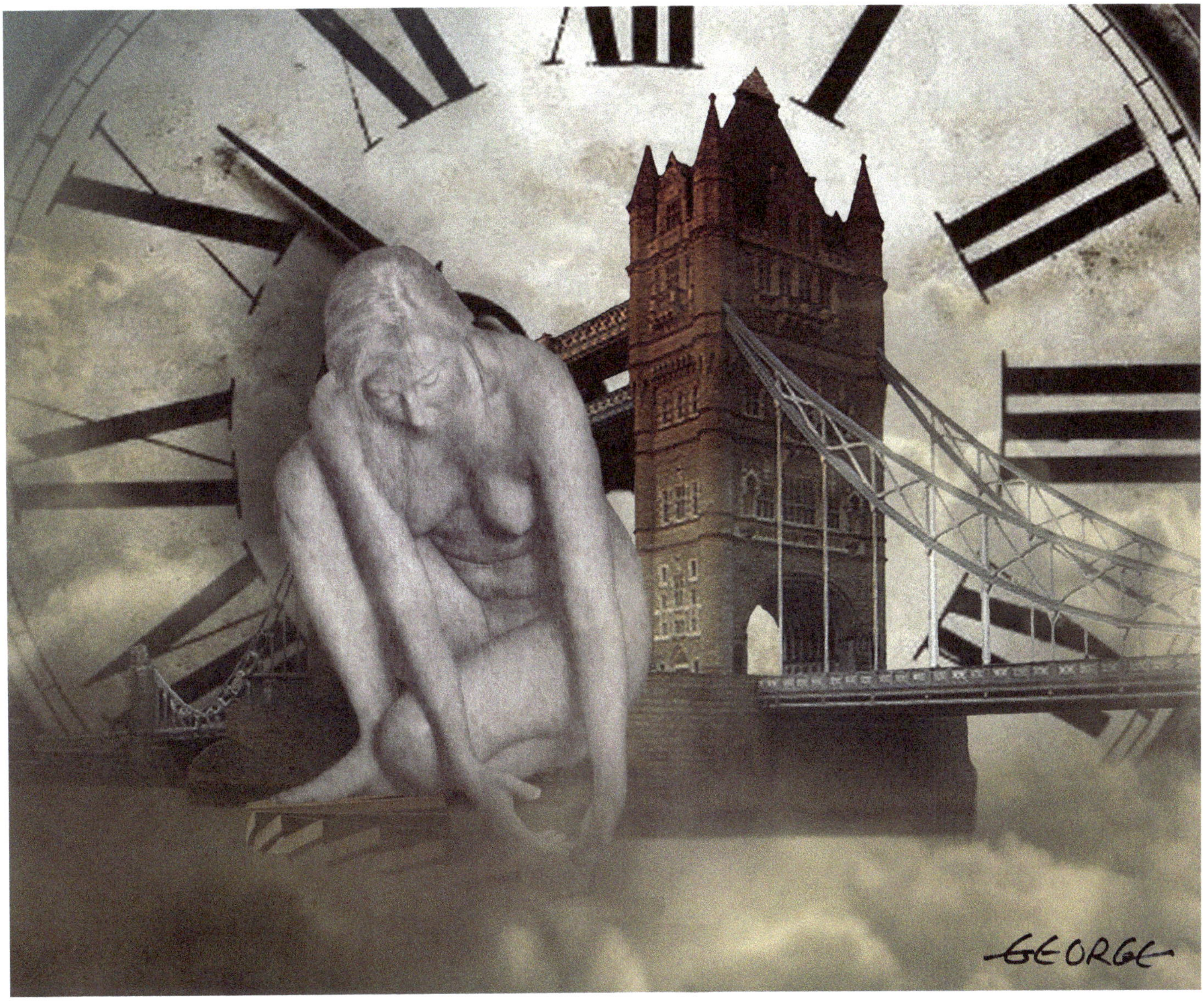
GEORGE

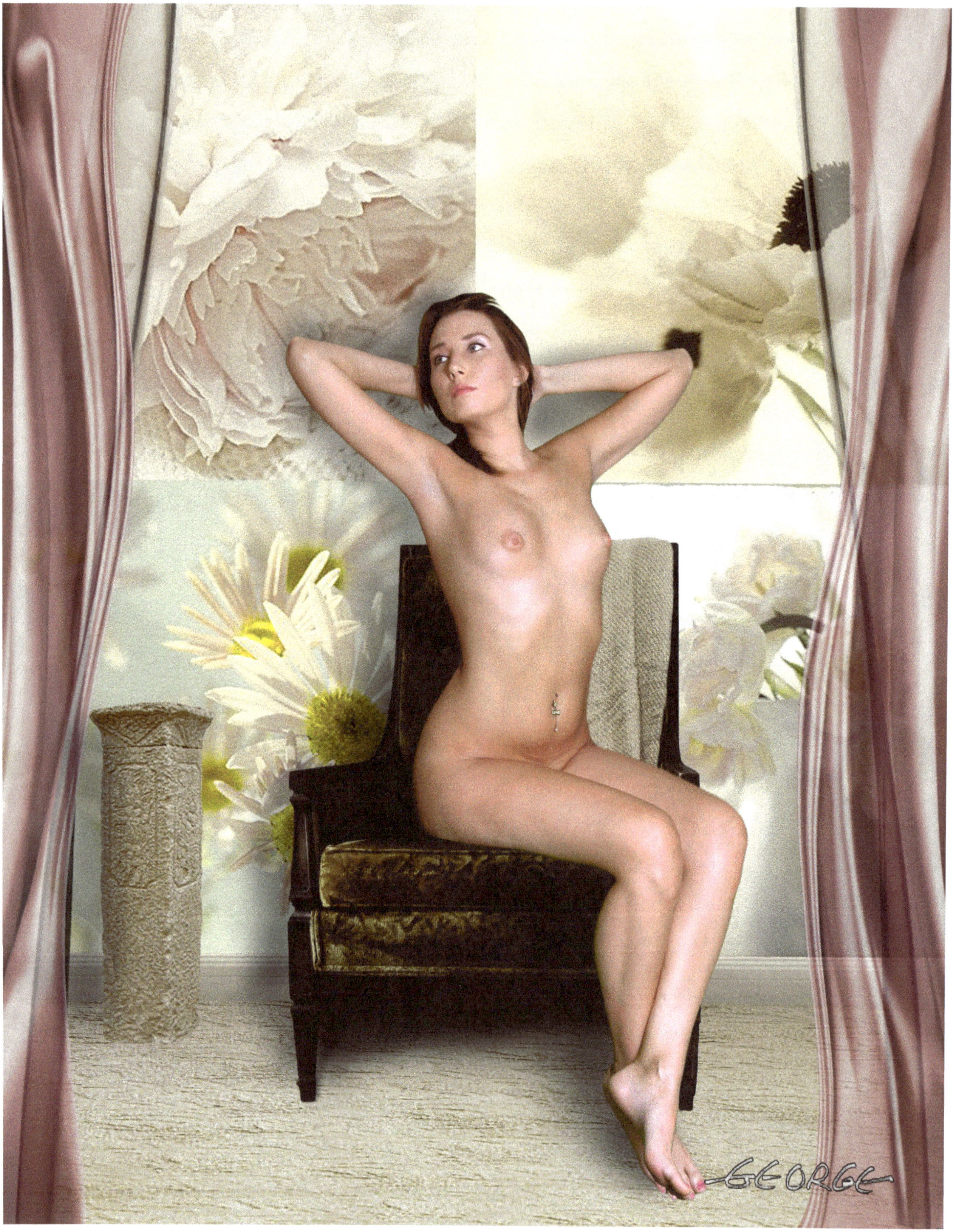
GEORGE

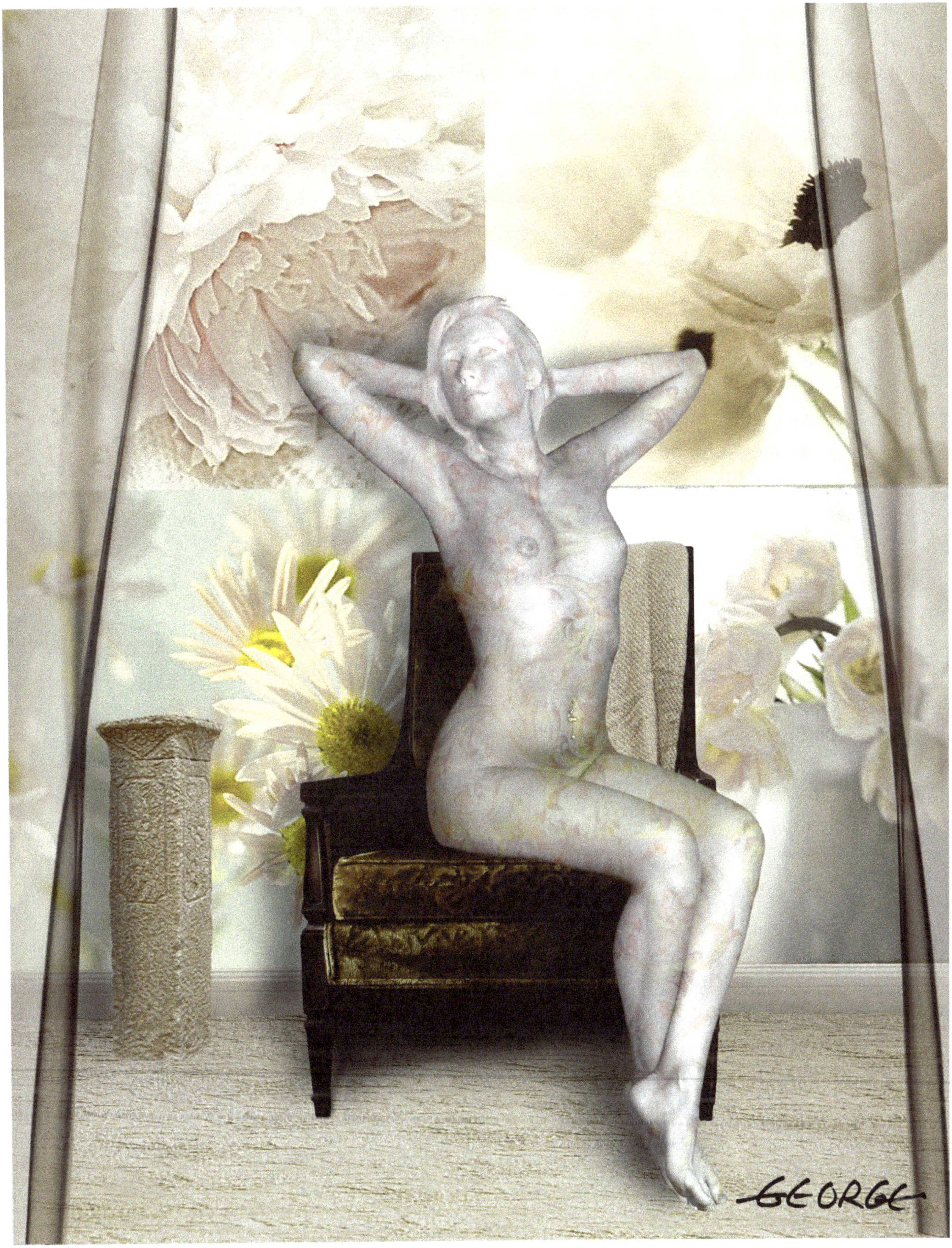
GEORGE

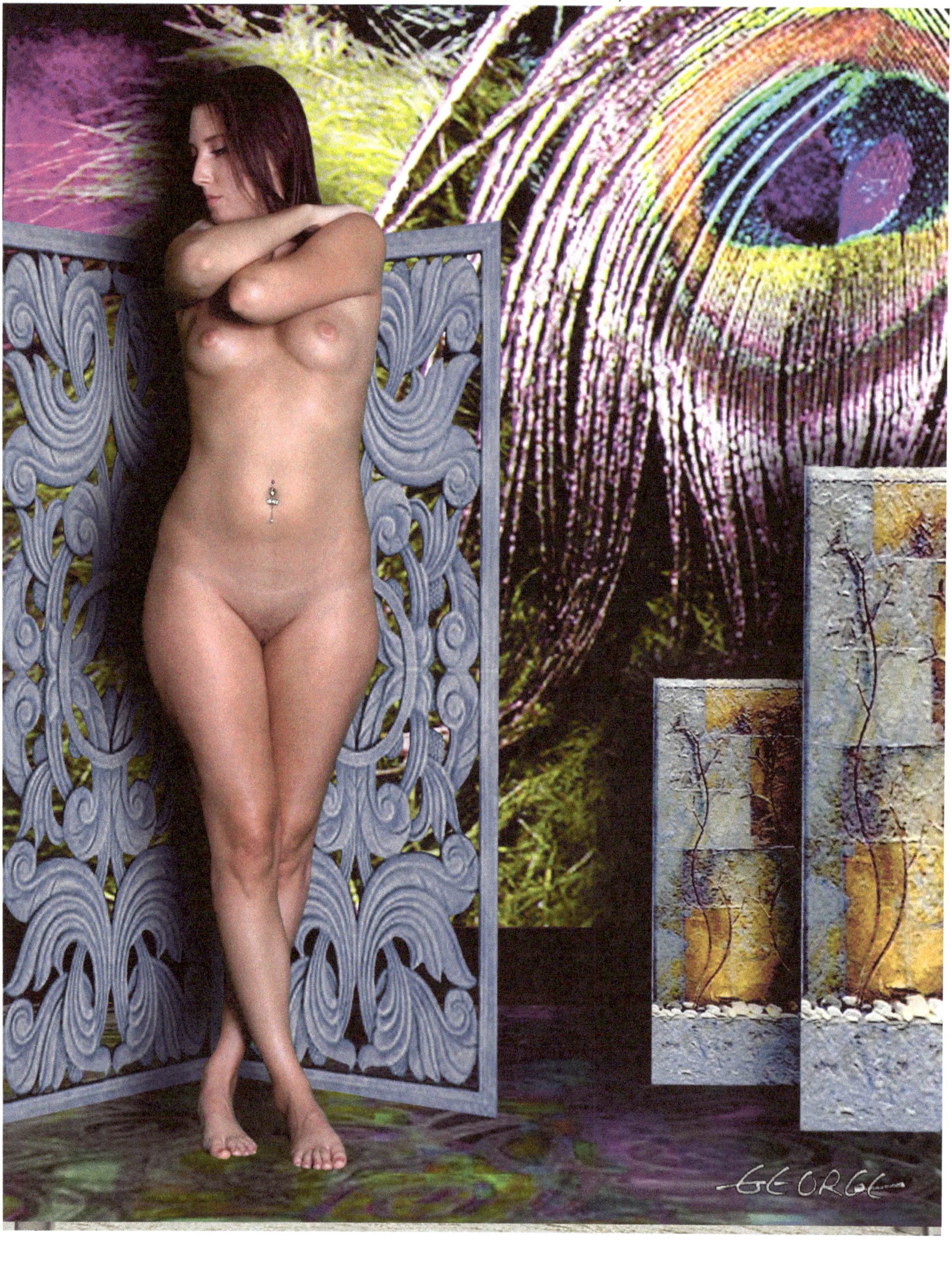
GEORGE

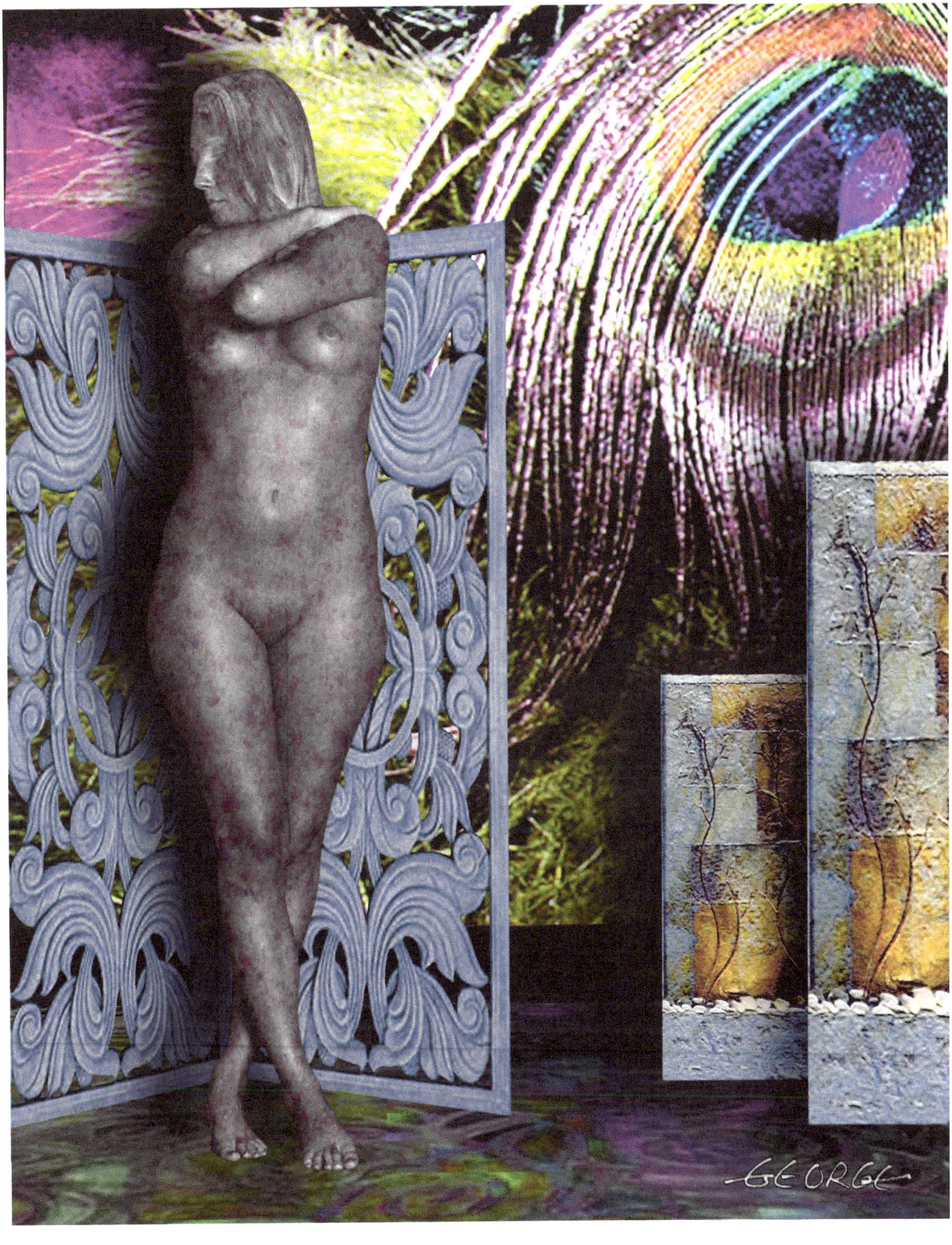
GEORGE

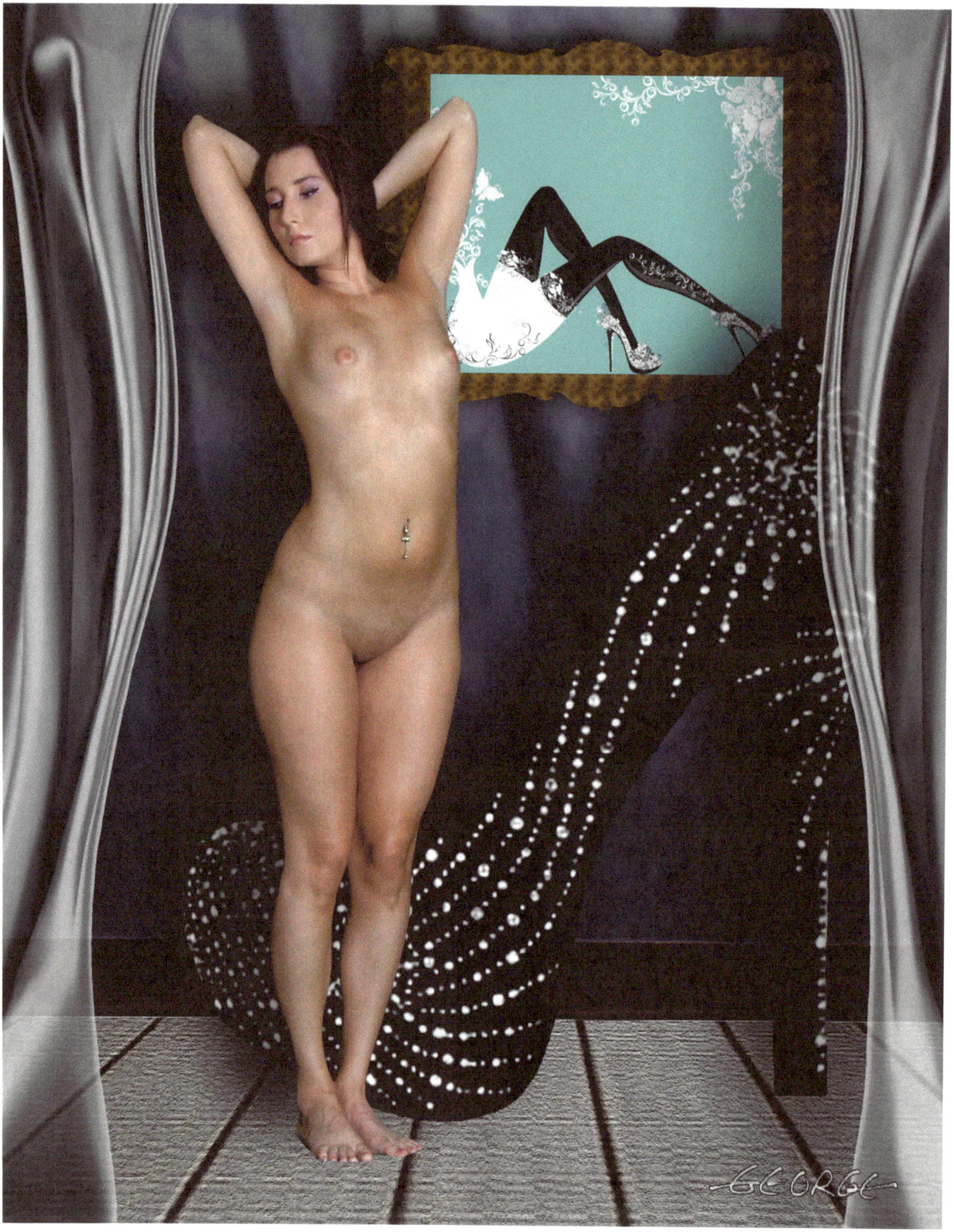
GEORGE

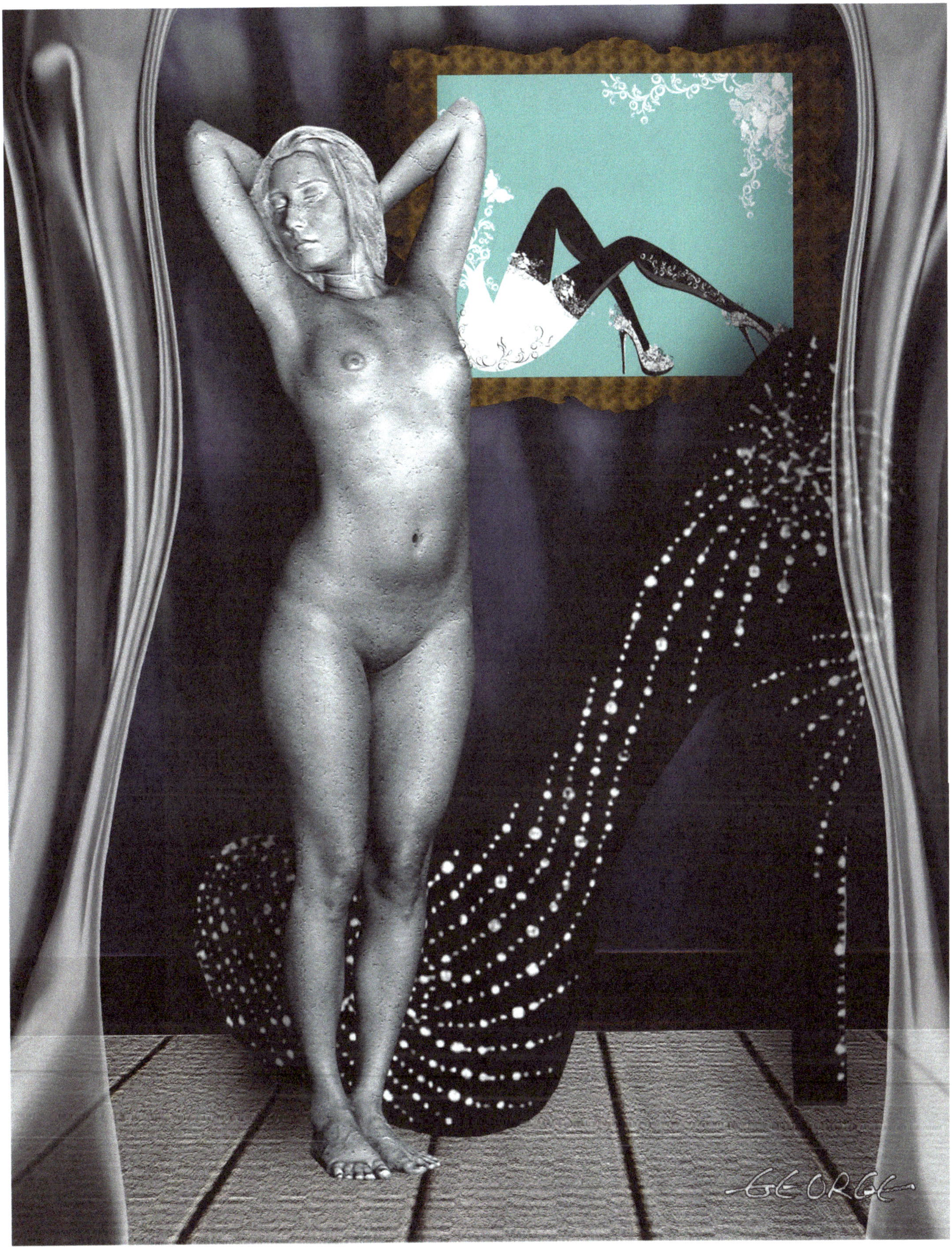
GEORGE

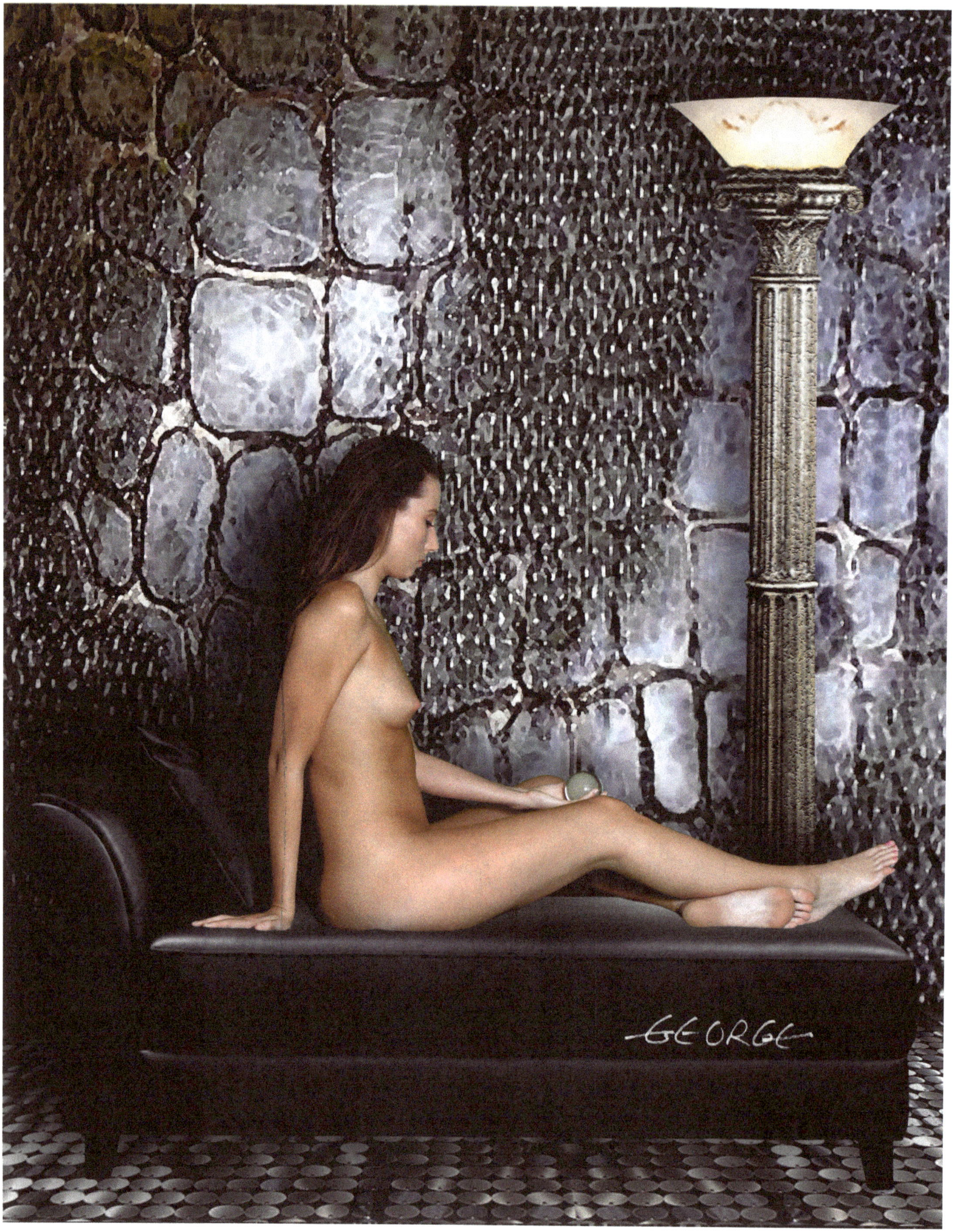
GEORGE

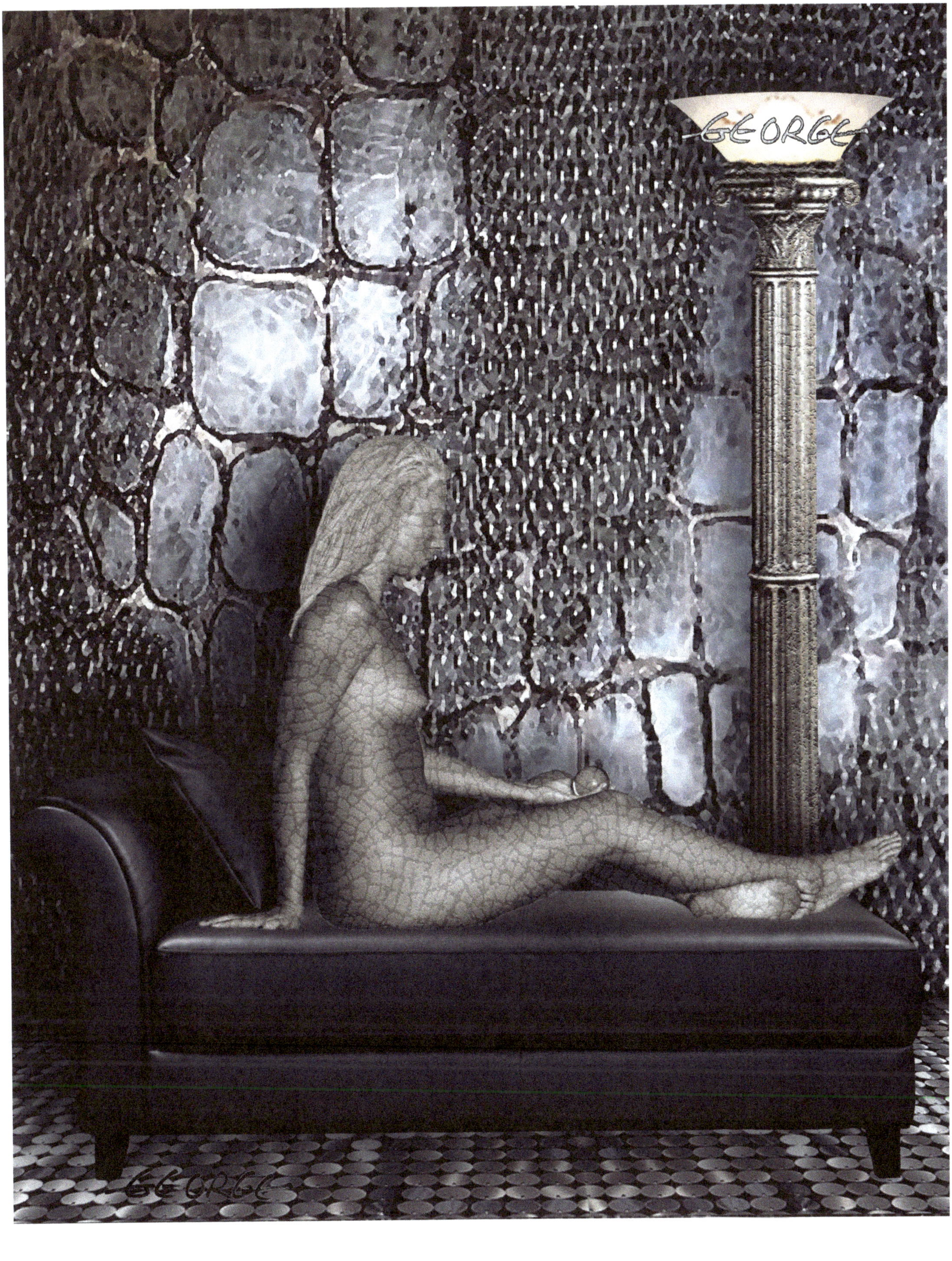
GEORGE
GEORGE

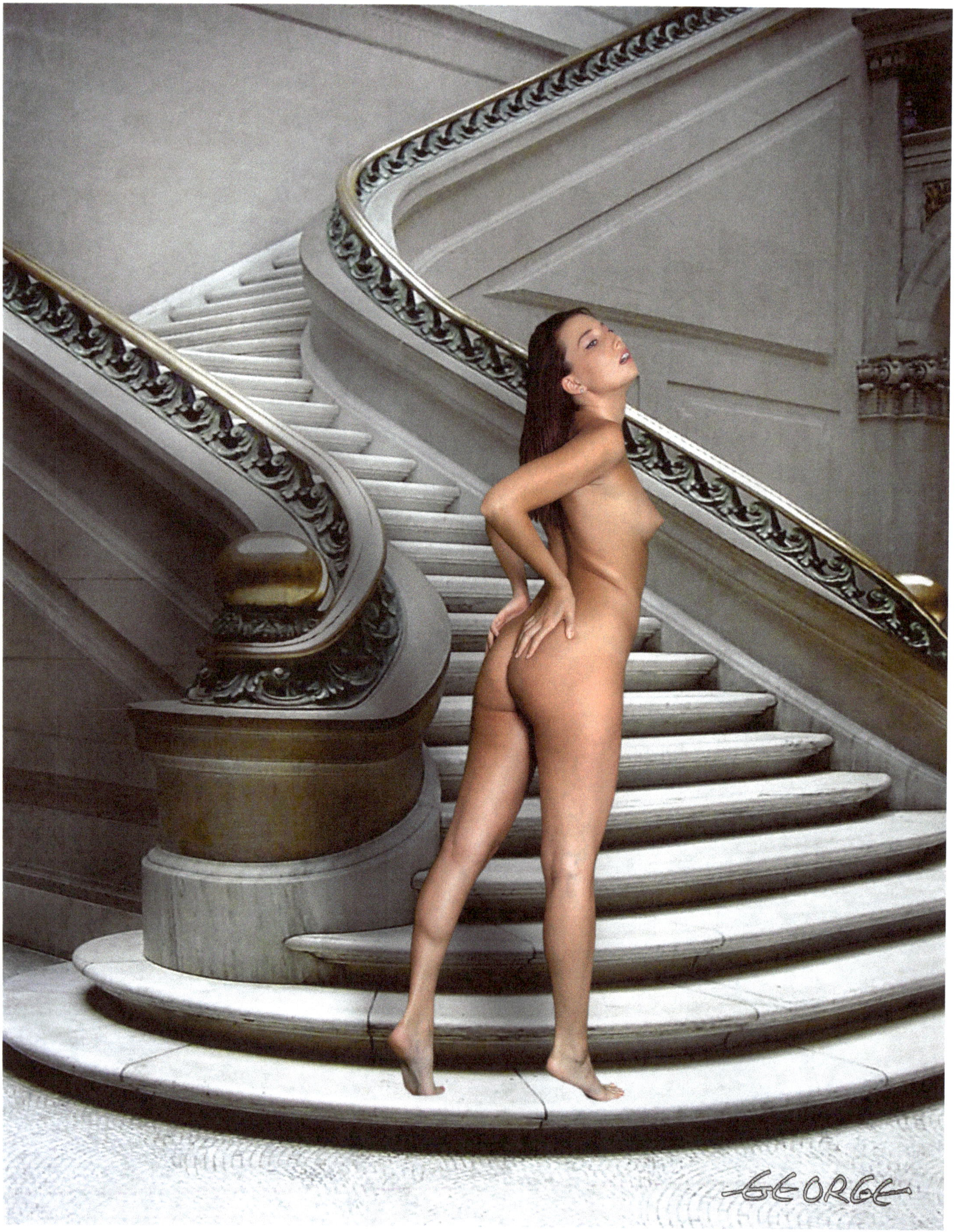
GEORGE

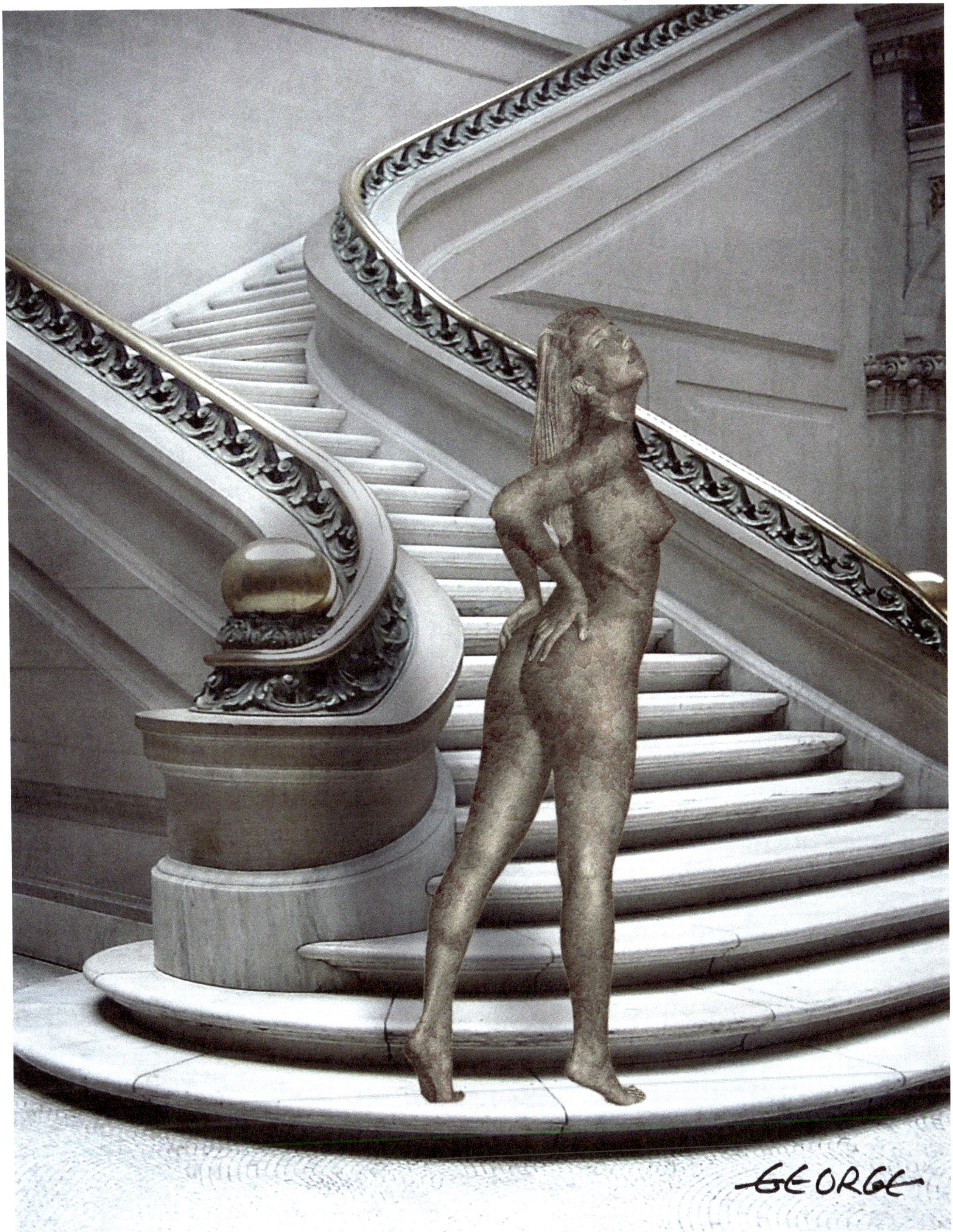
GEORGE

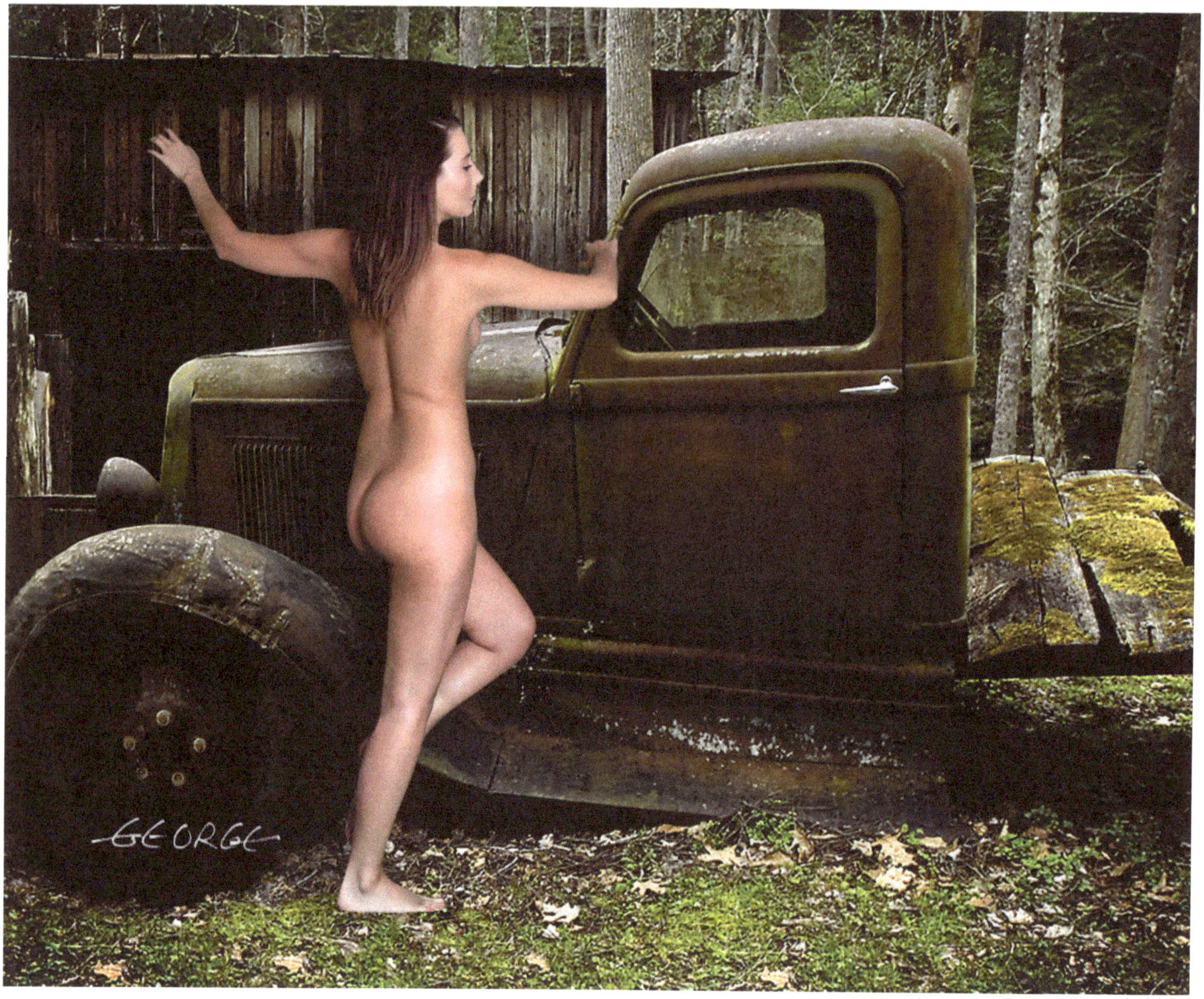
GEORGE

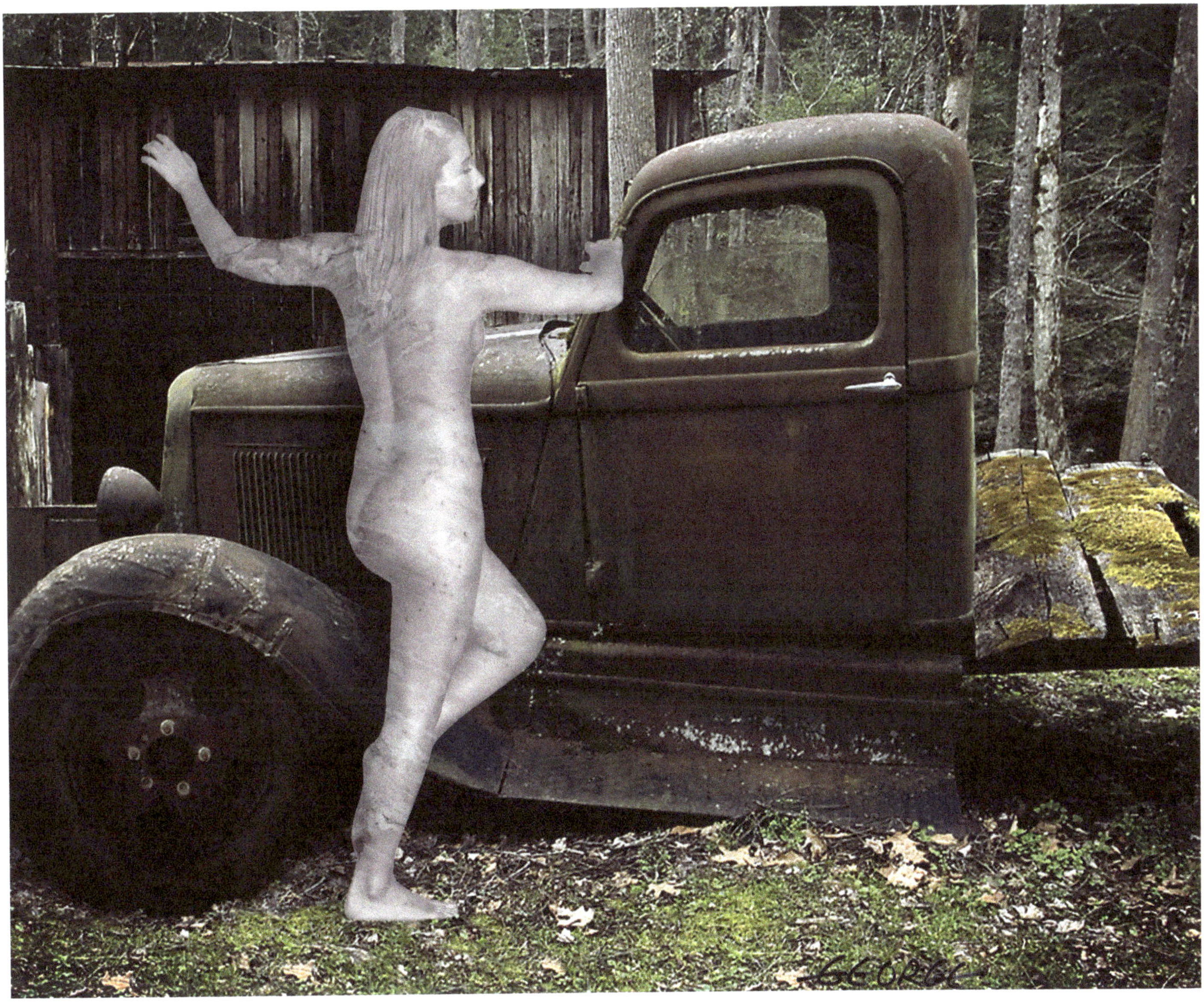
GEORGE

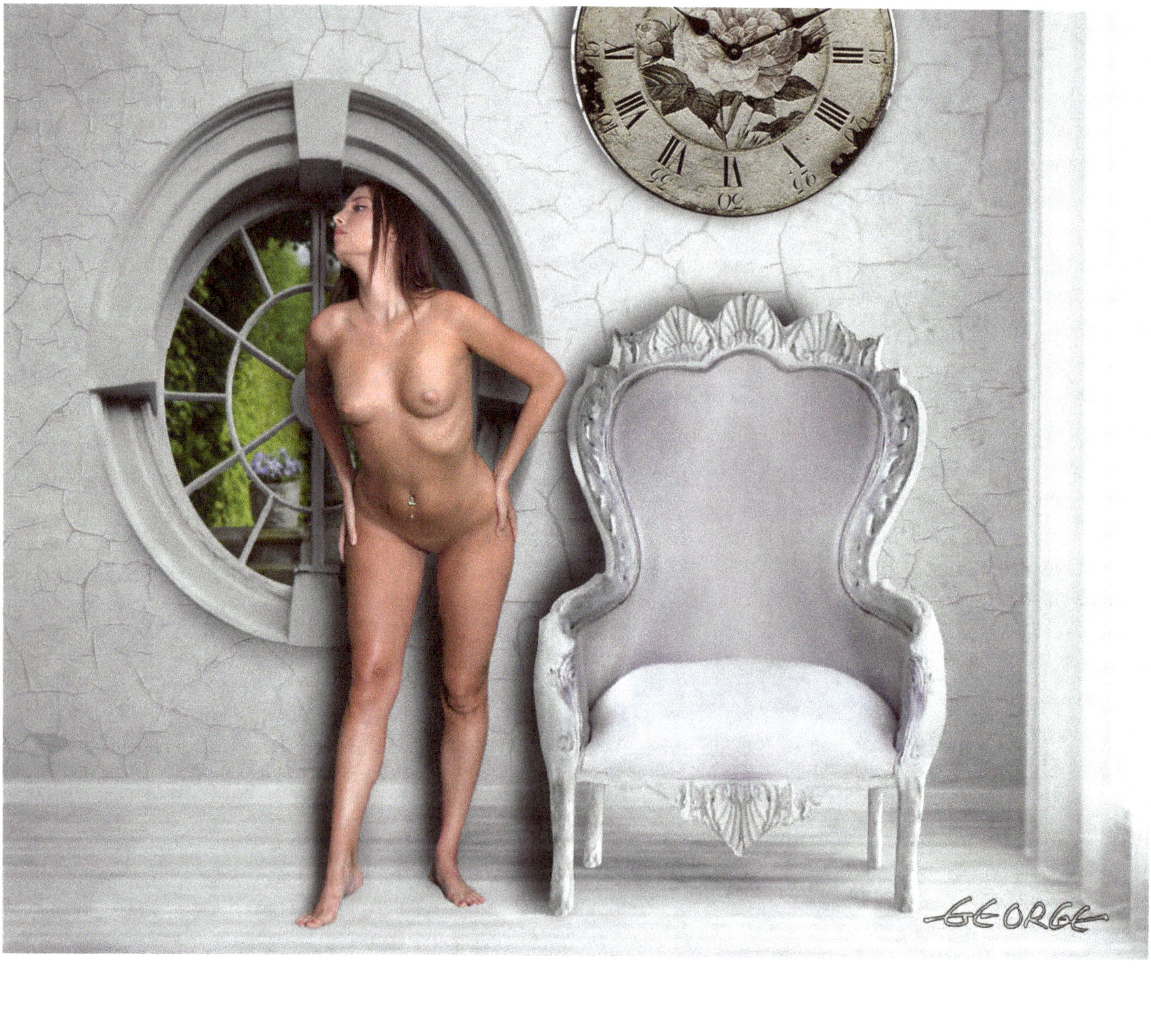
GEORGE

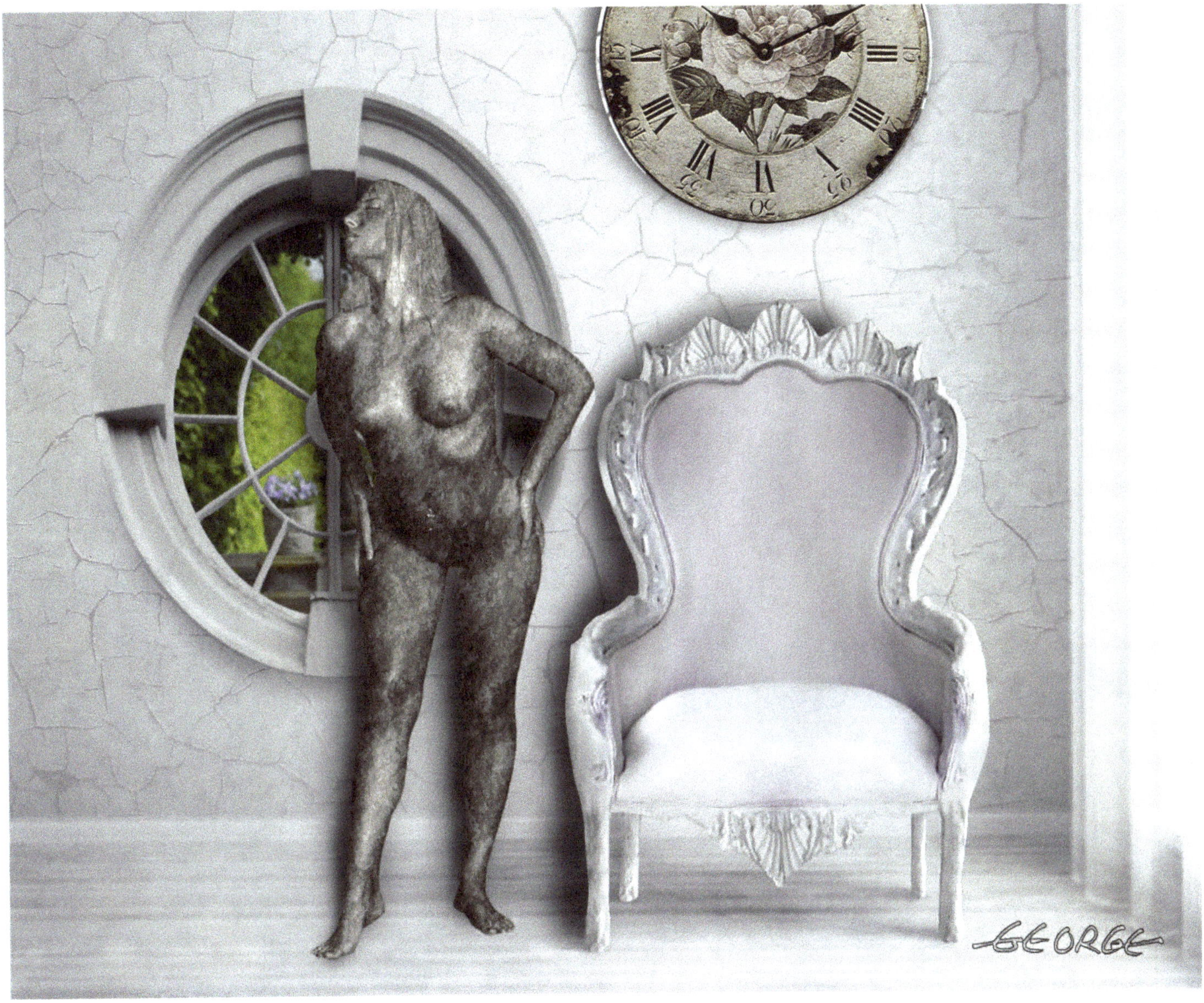
GEORGE

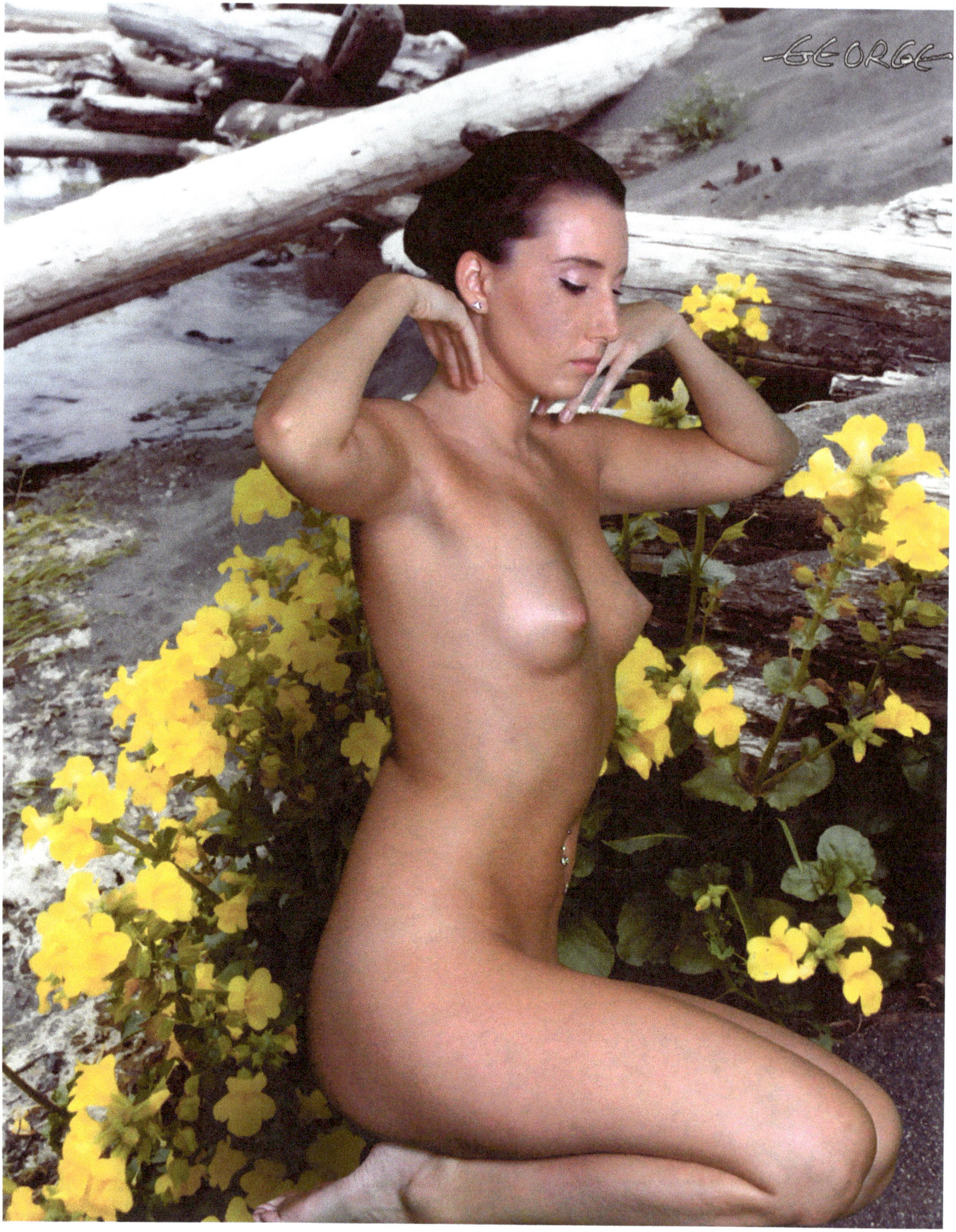
GEORGE

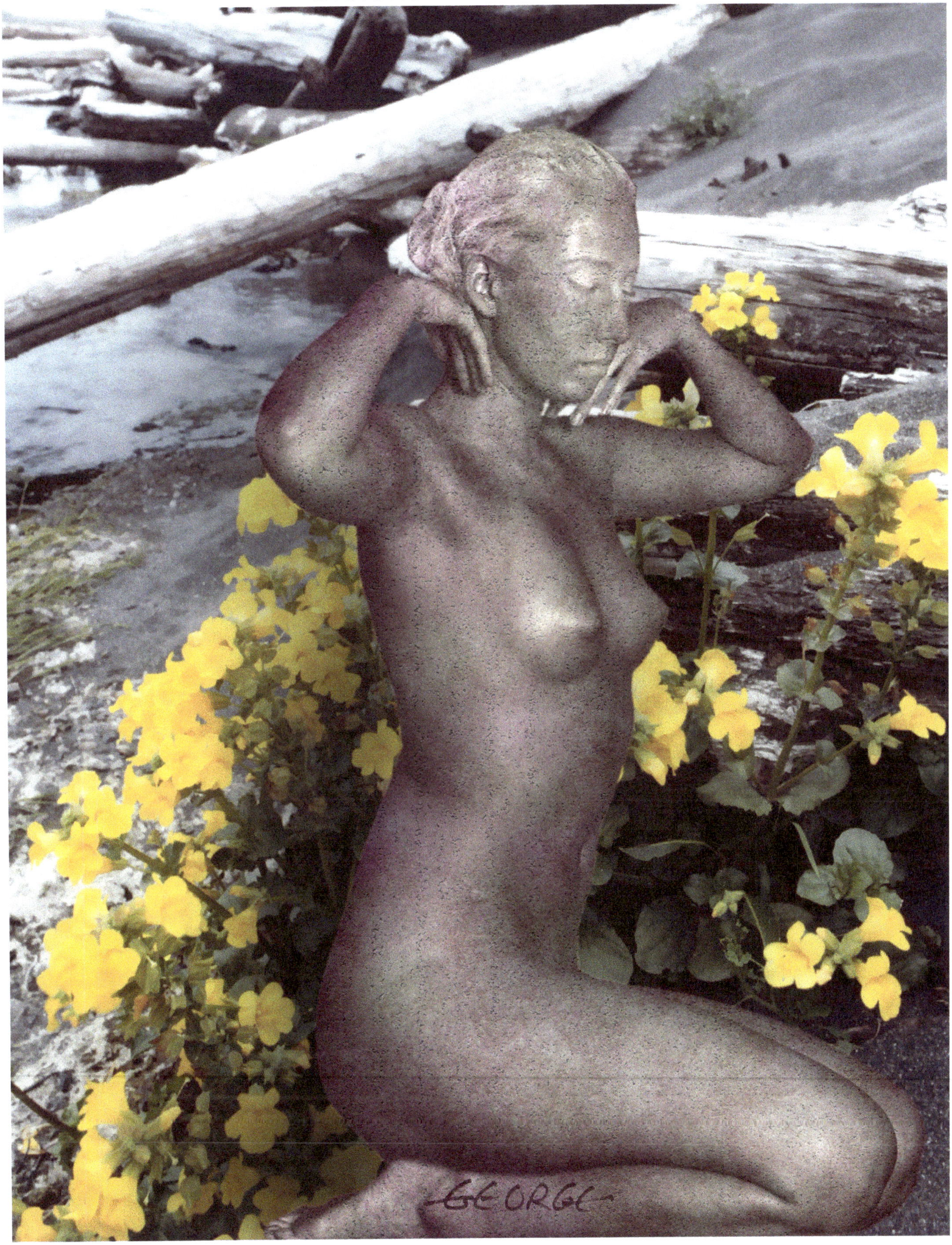
GEORGE

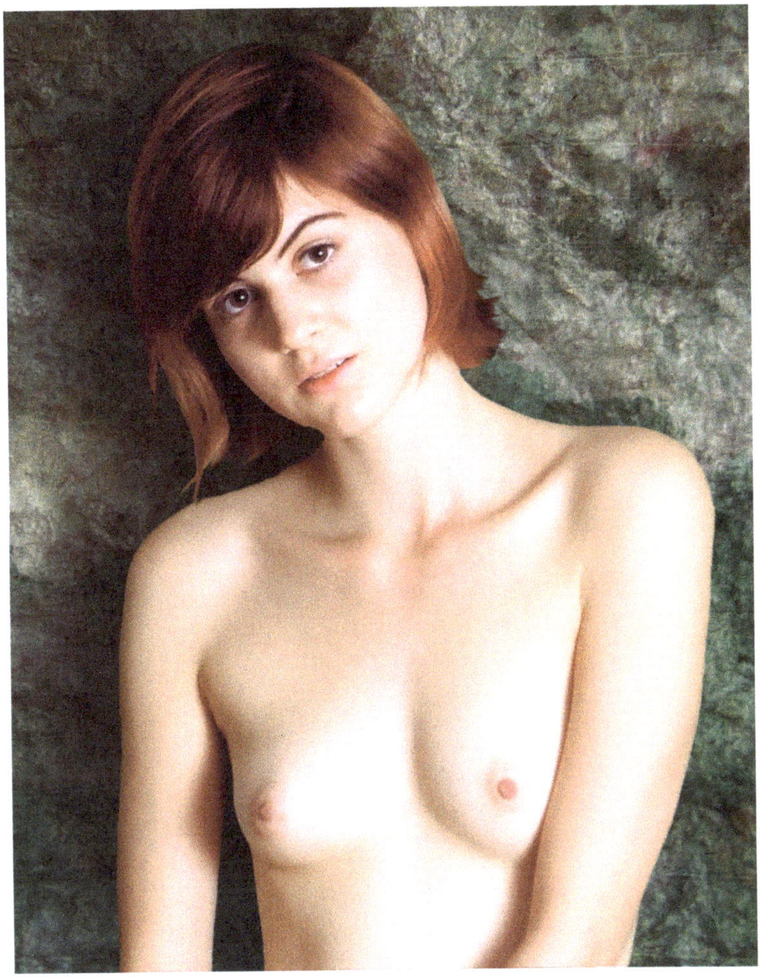

MELLOW

Height 5'4" Weight 103 lbs Bust 32" Waist 24" Hips 35" Cup B

I am flexible, elegant, macabre, creative, and fearless. My muses are death, religion, myths, madness, and surrealism. I have three tattoos: a phoenix on my back, the words "always twirl the kaleidoscopic" on my hip, and a fiddlehead heart on my left wrist.

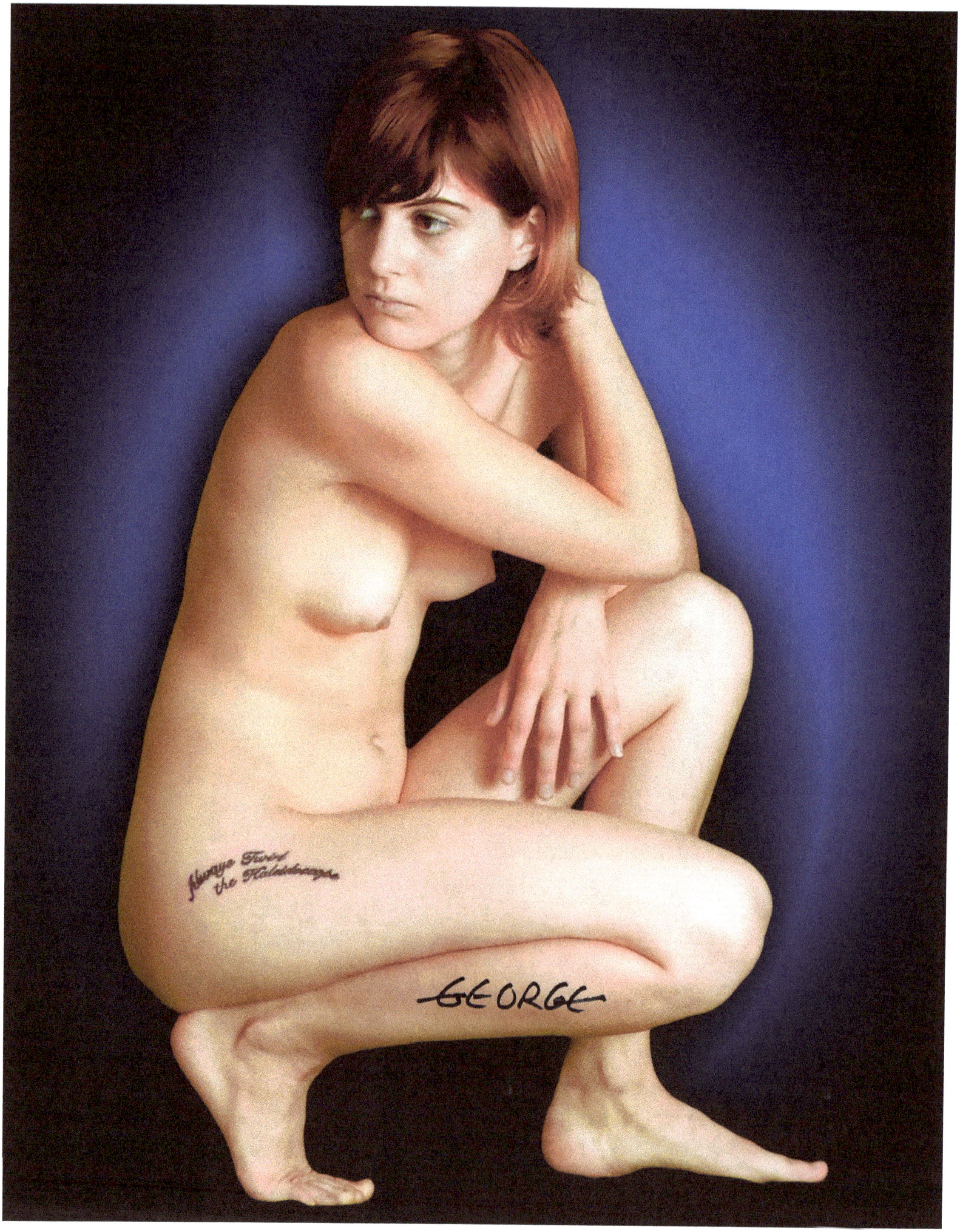
GEORGE

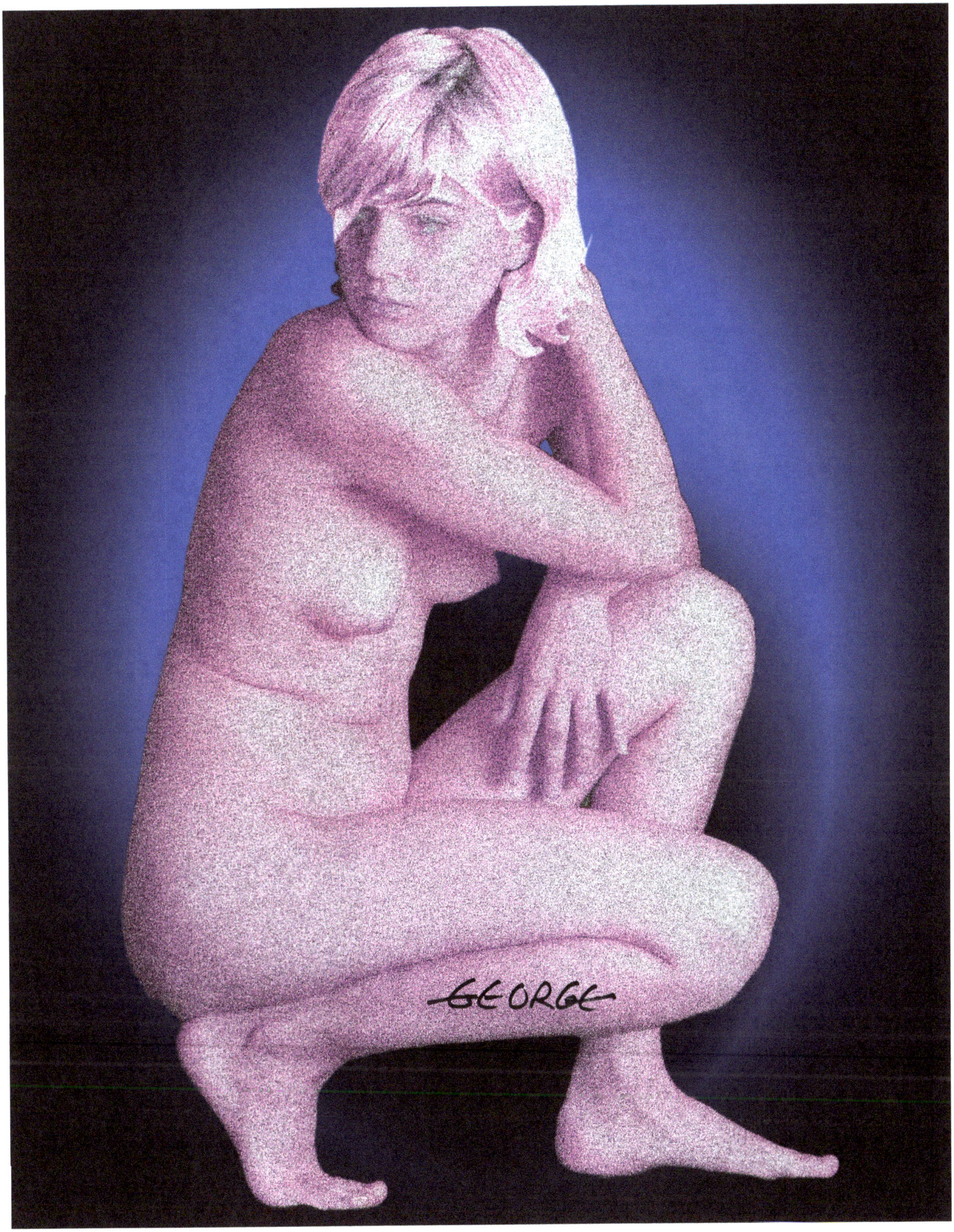
GEORGE

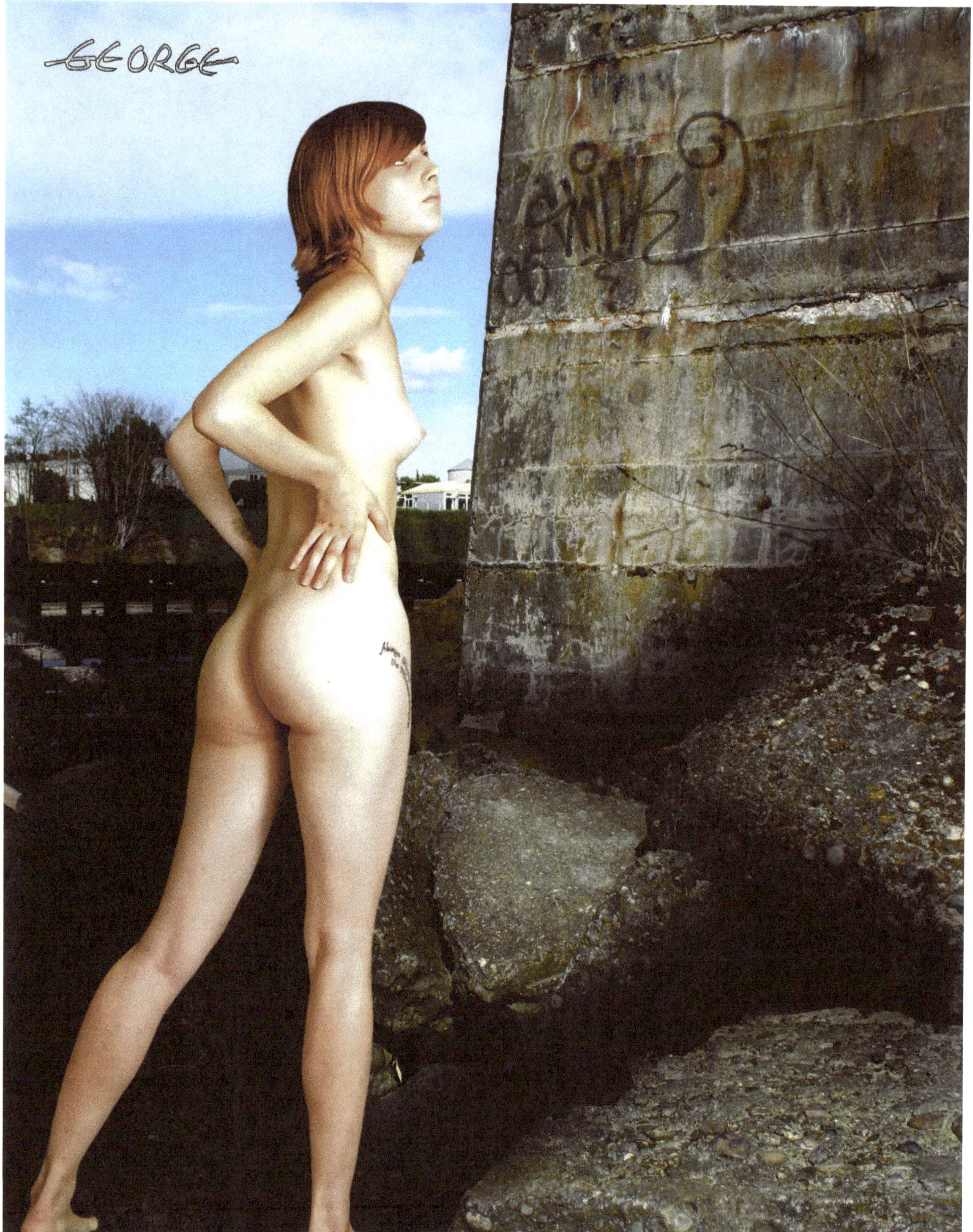
GEORGE

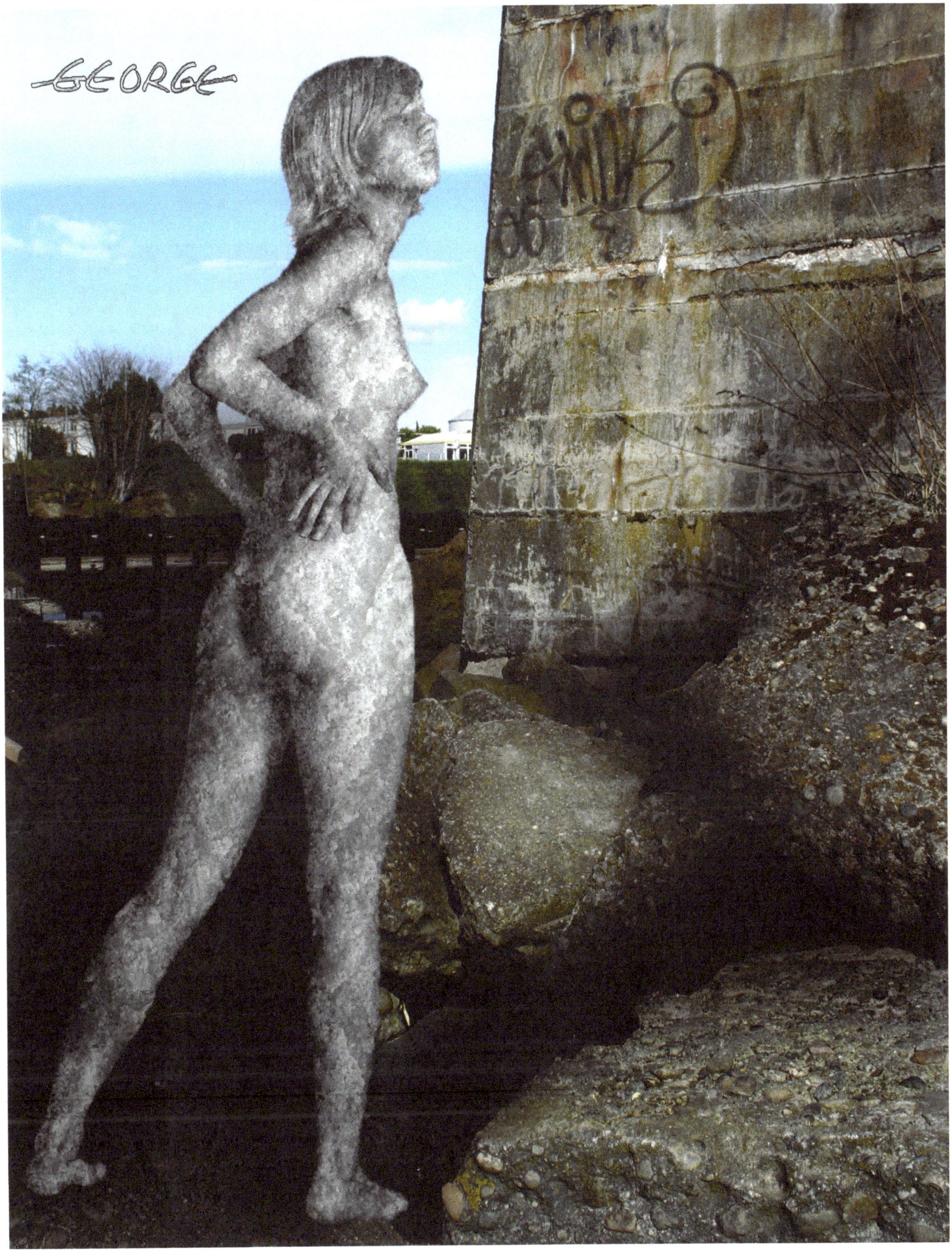
GEORGE

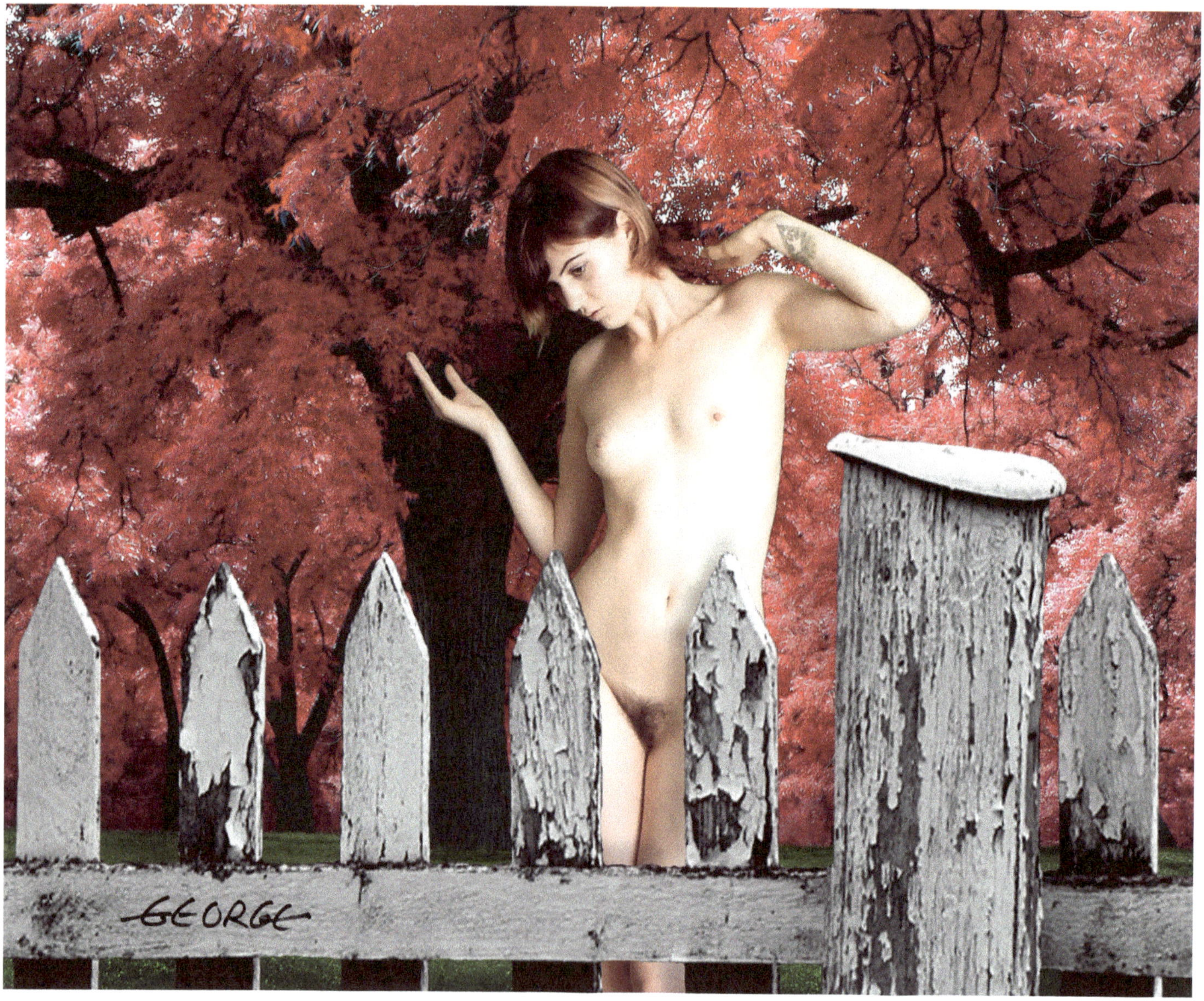
GEORGE

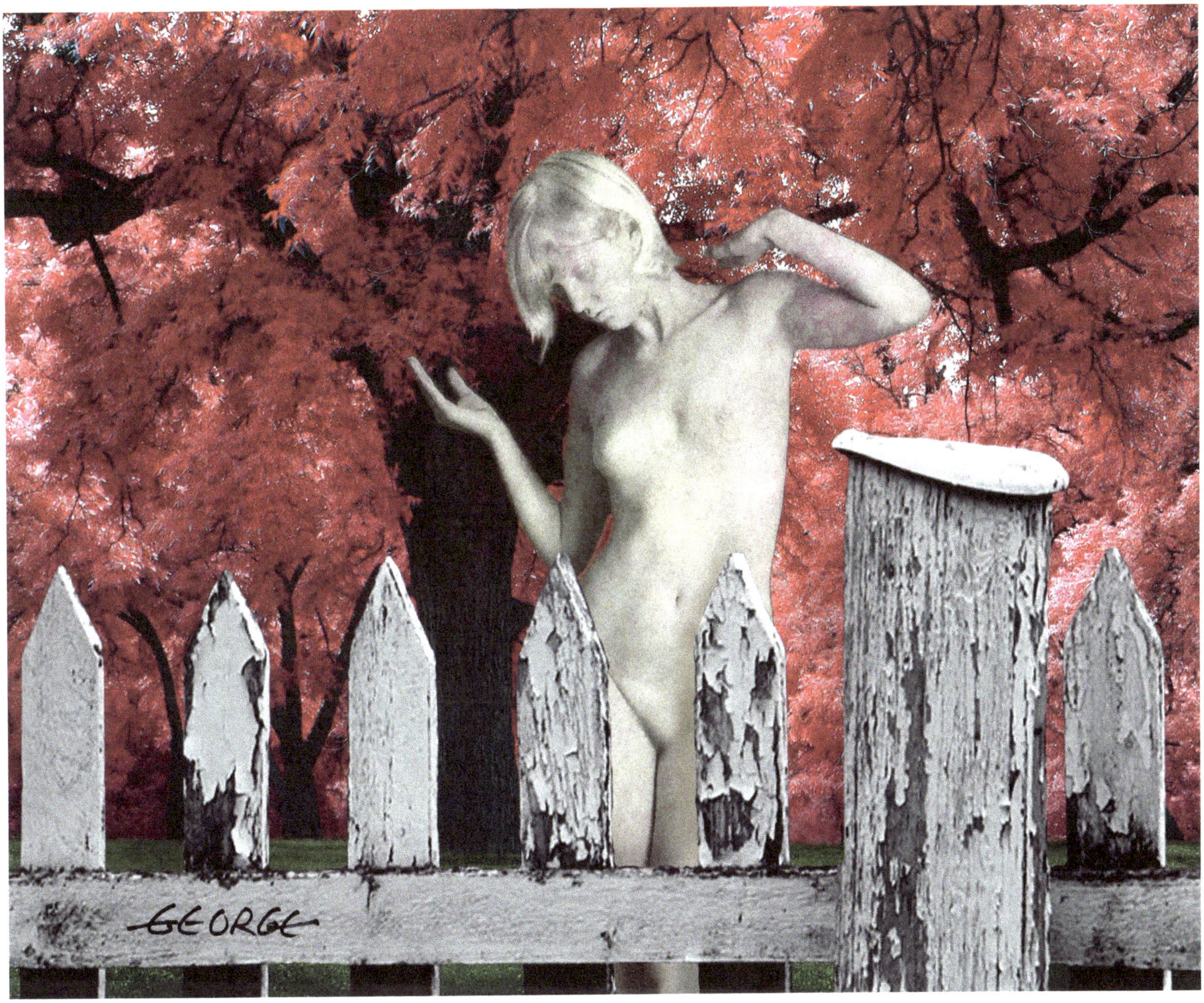
GEORGE

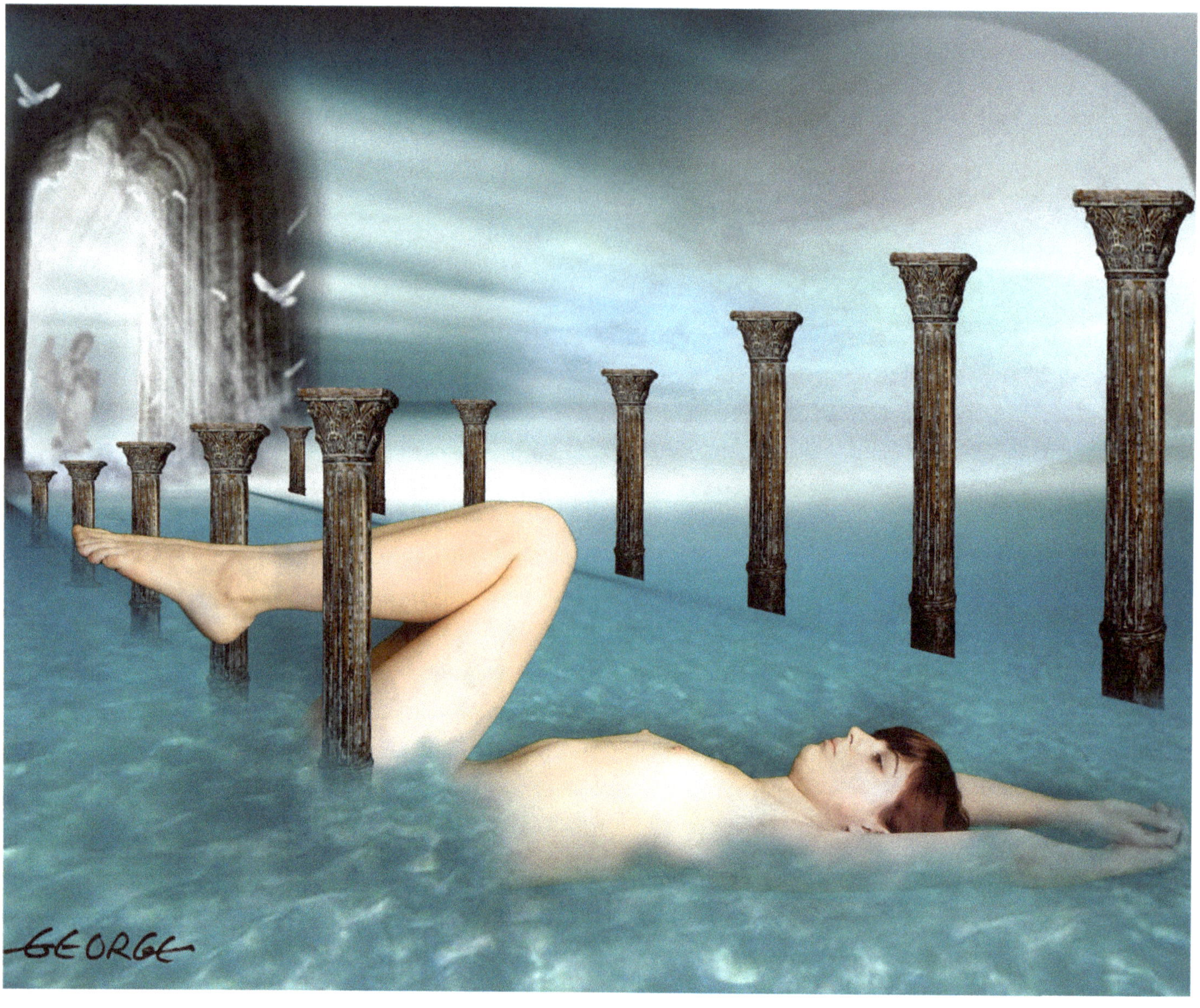
GEORGE

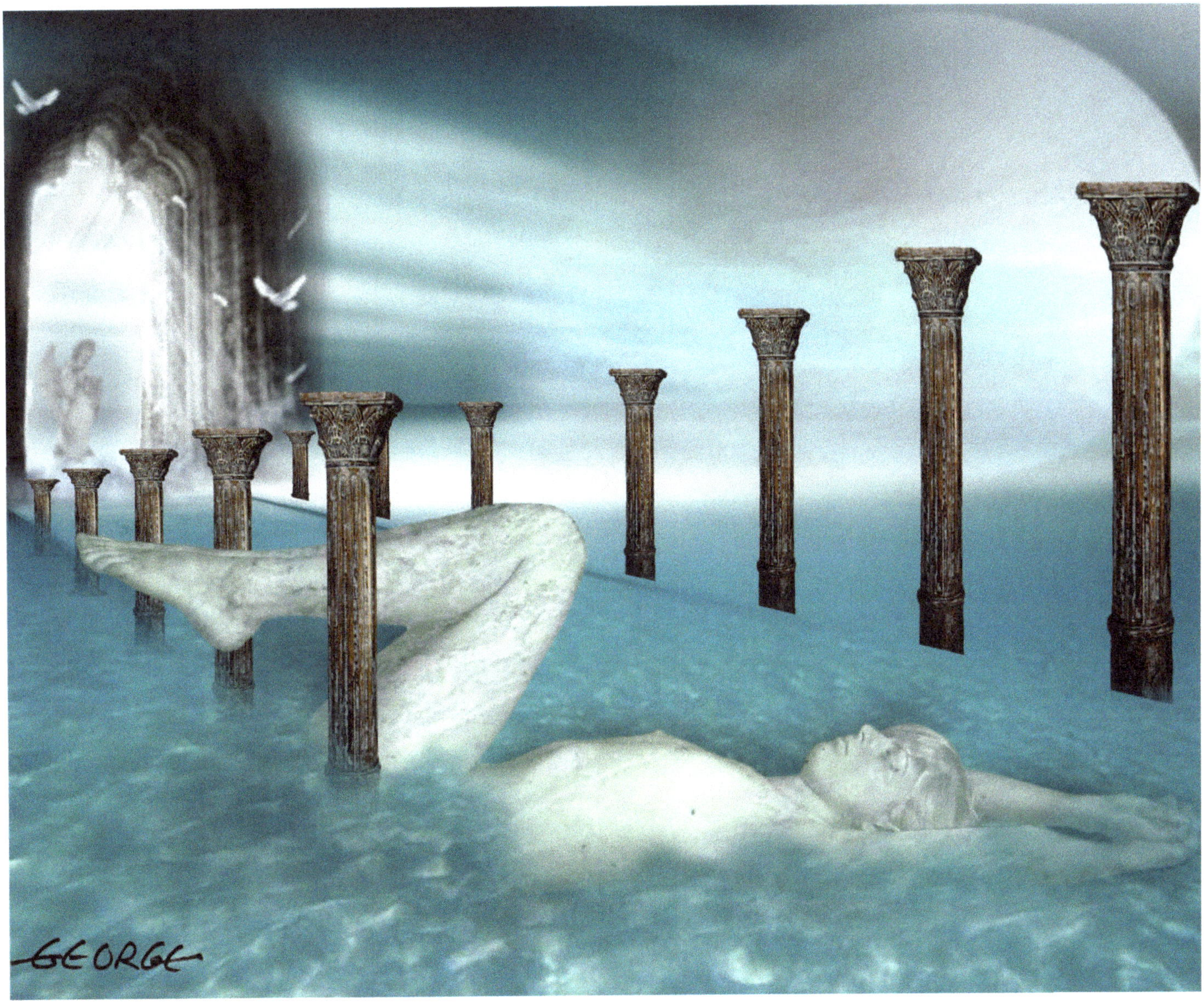
GEORGE

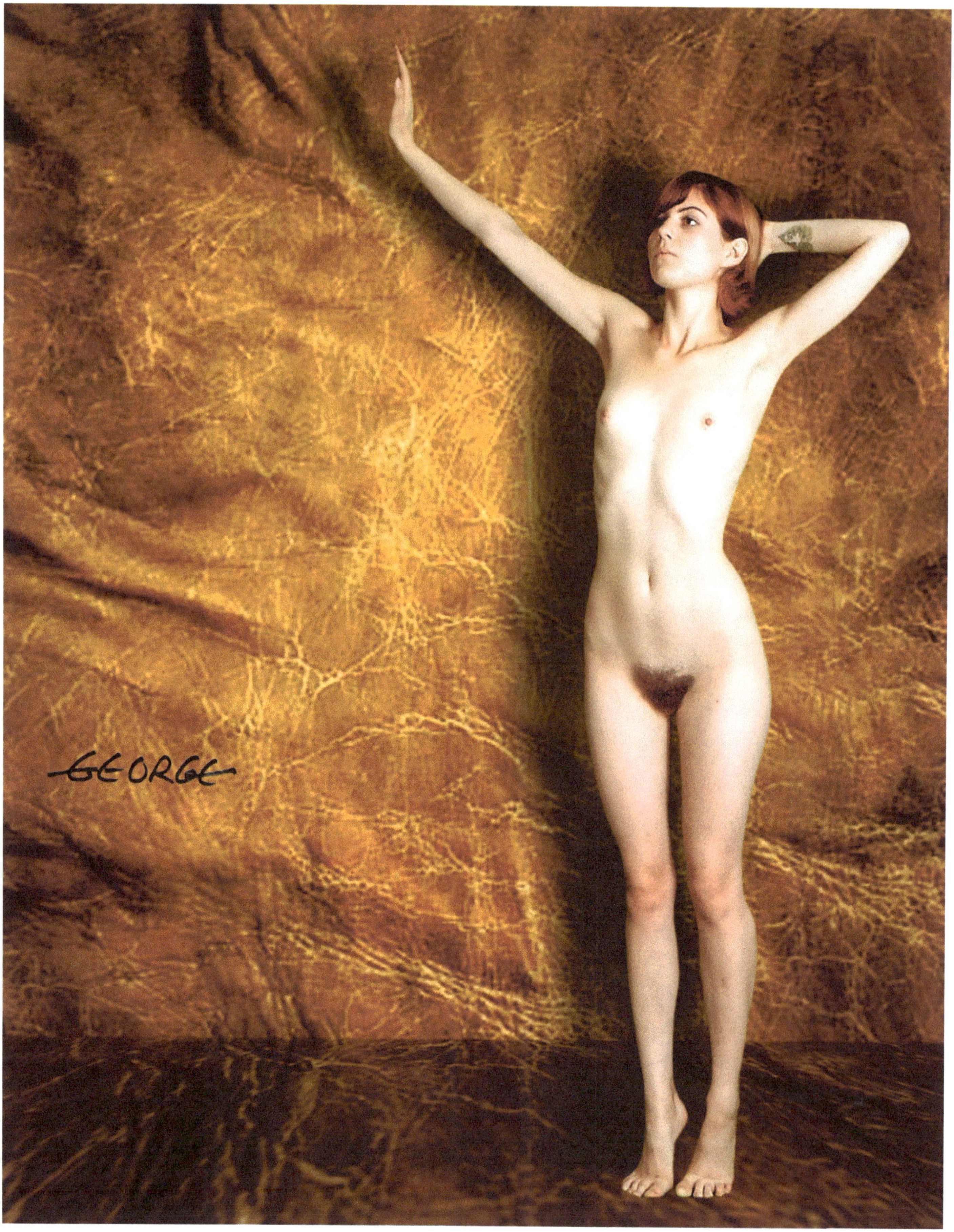
GEORGE

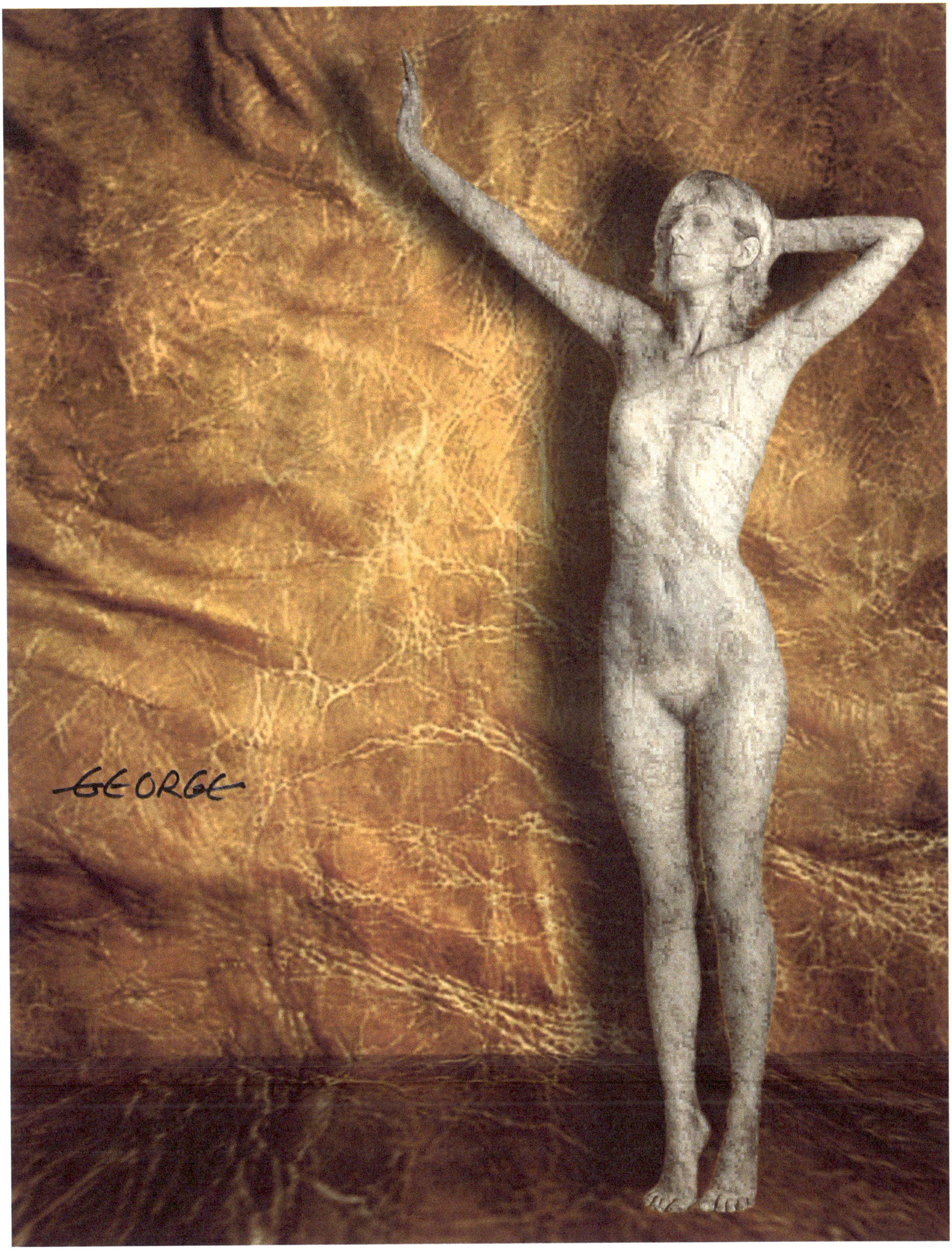
GEORGE

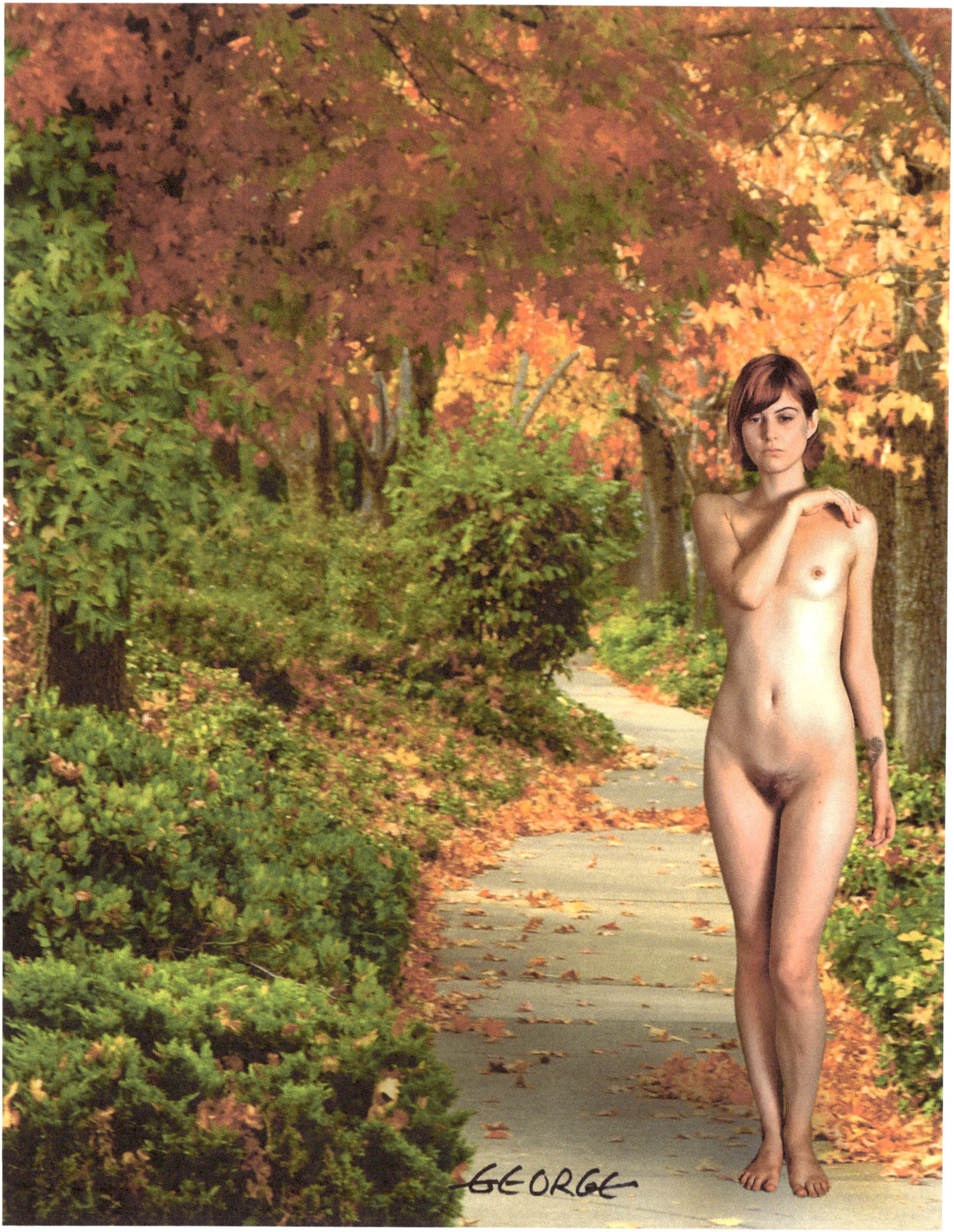

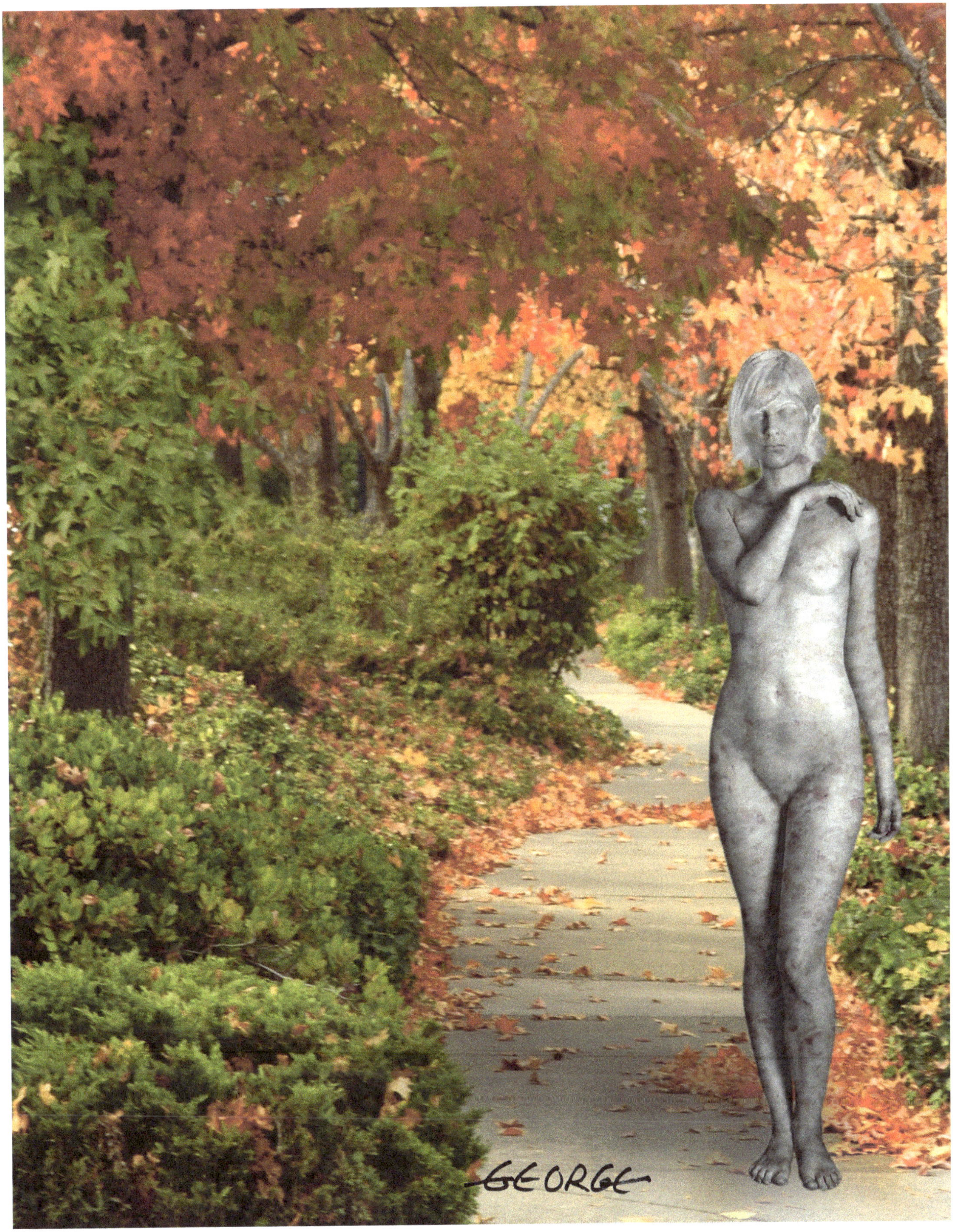
GEORGE

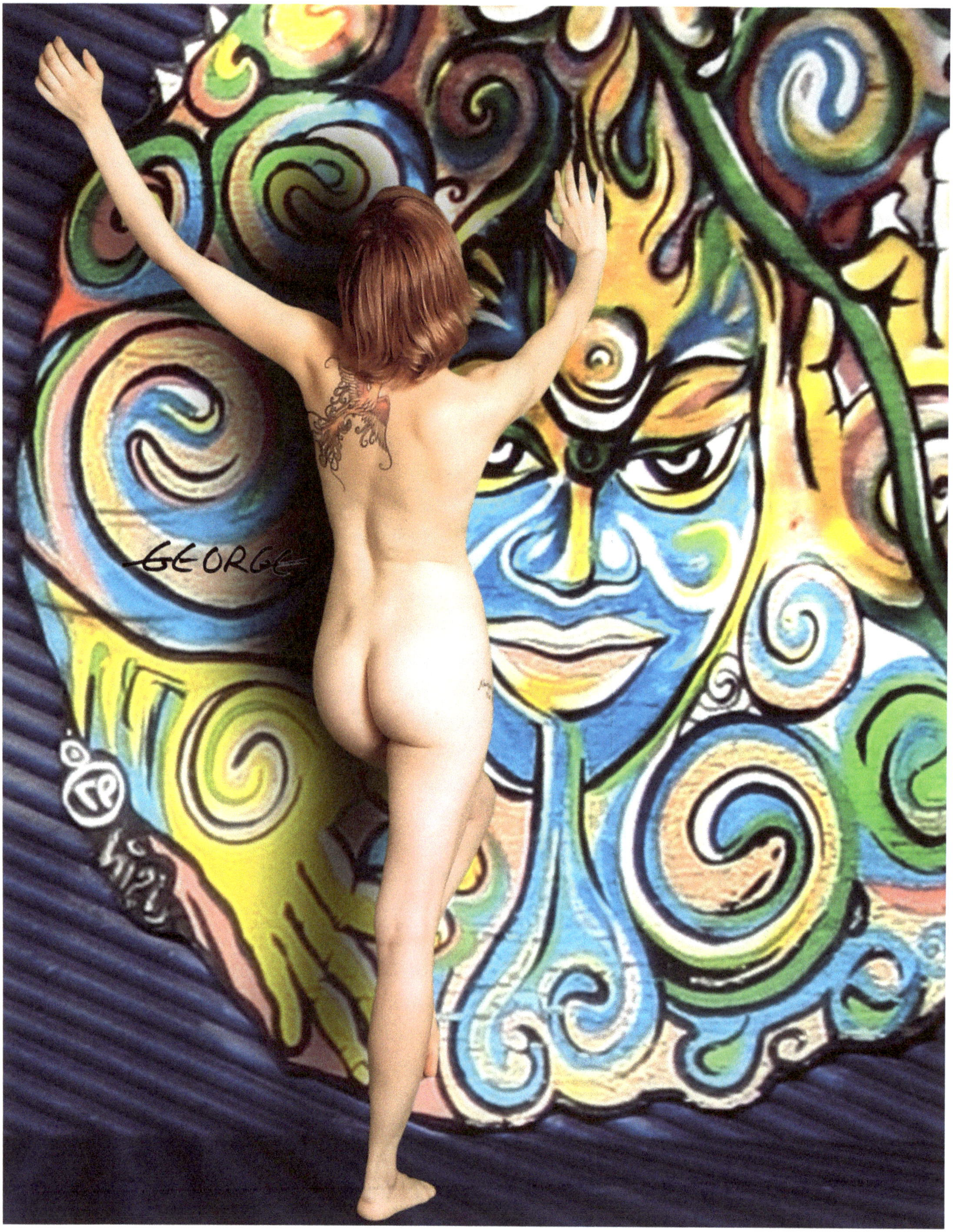
GEORGE

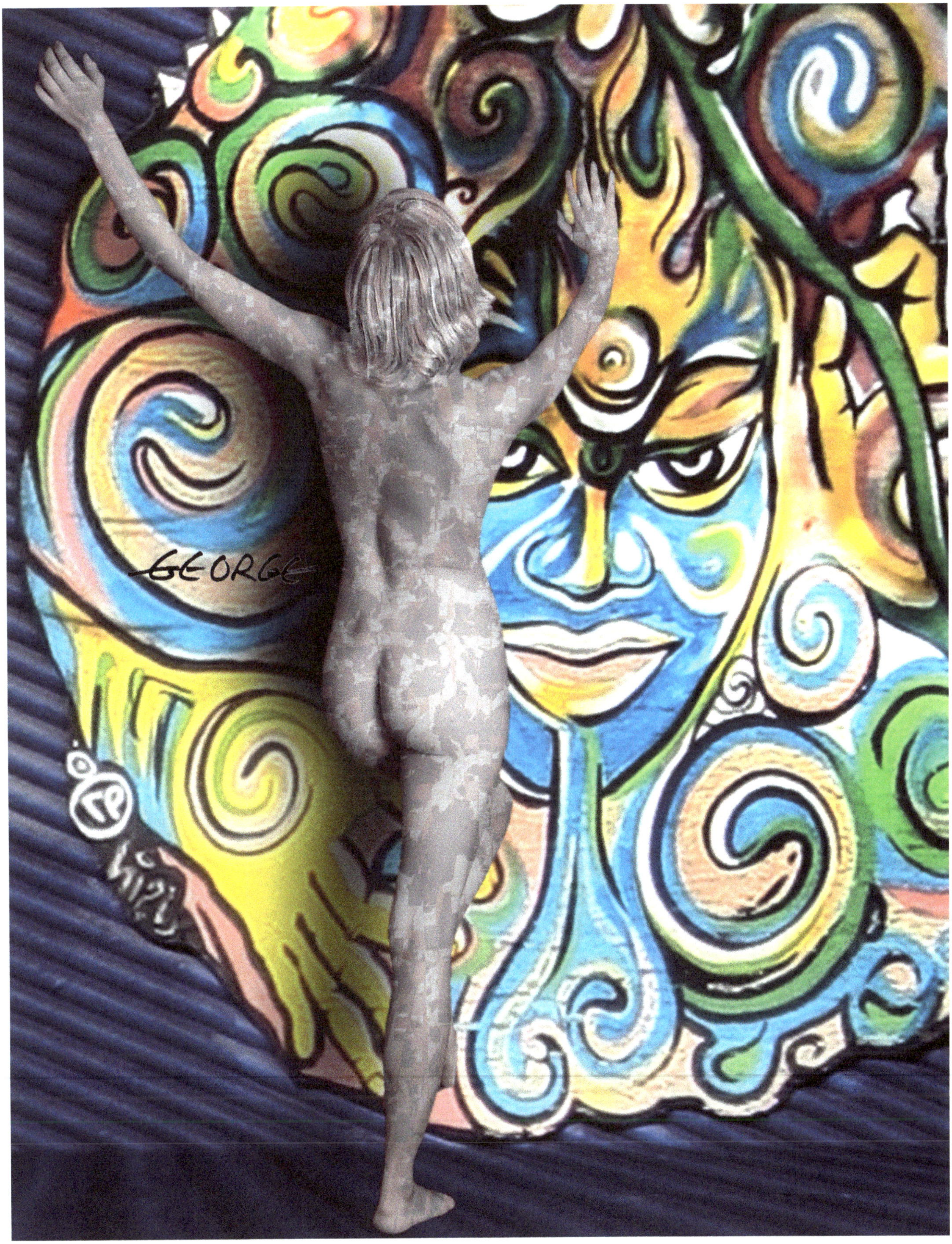
GEORGE

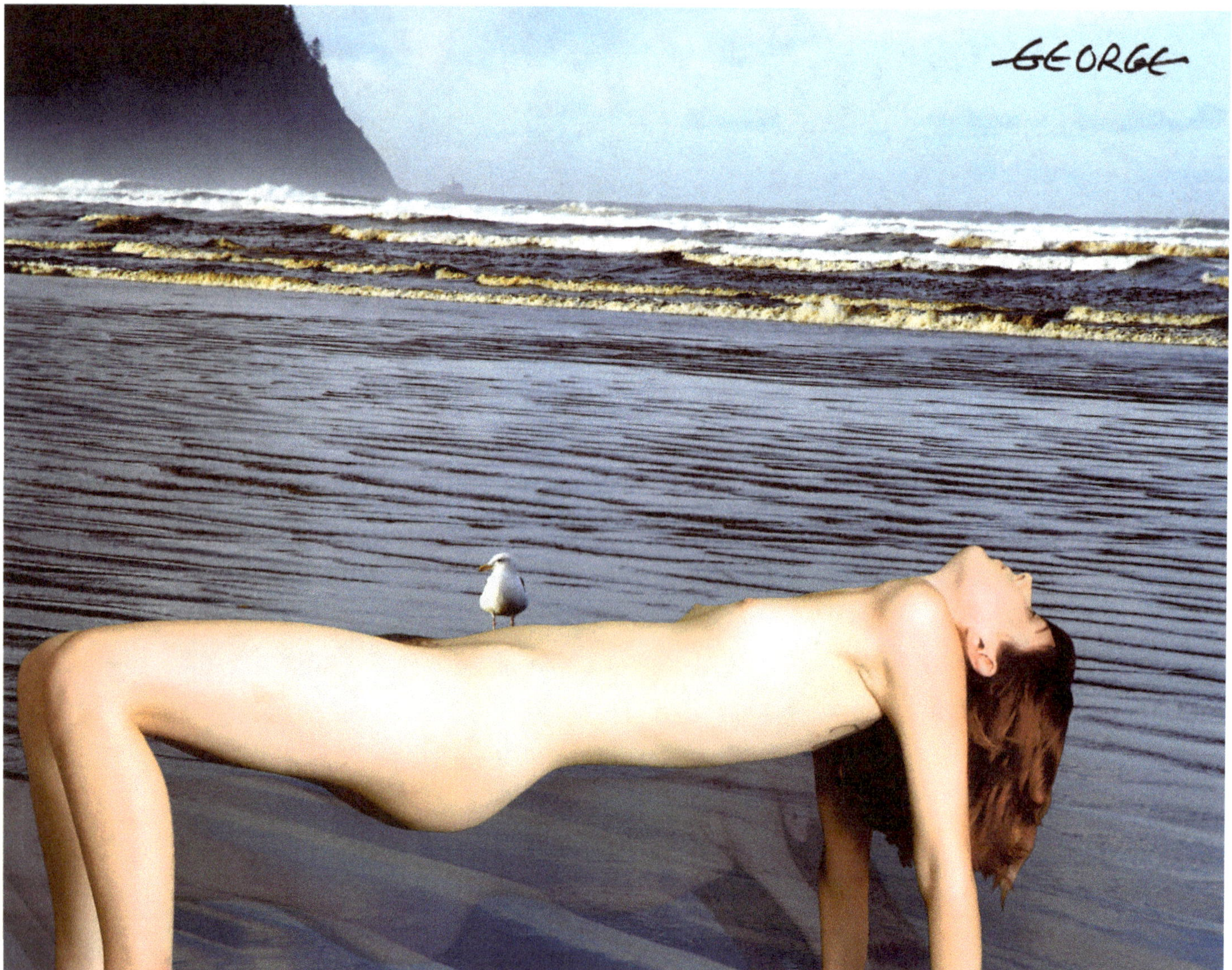
GEORGE

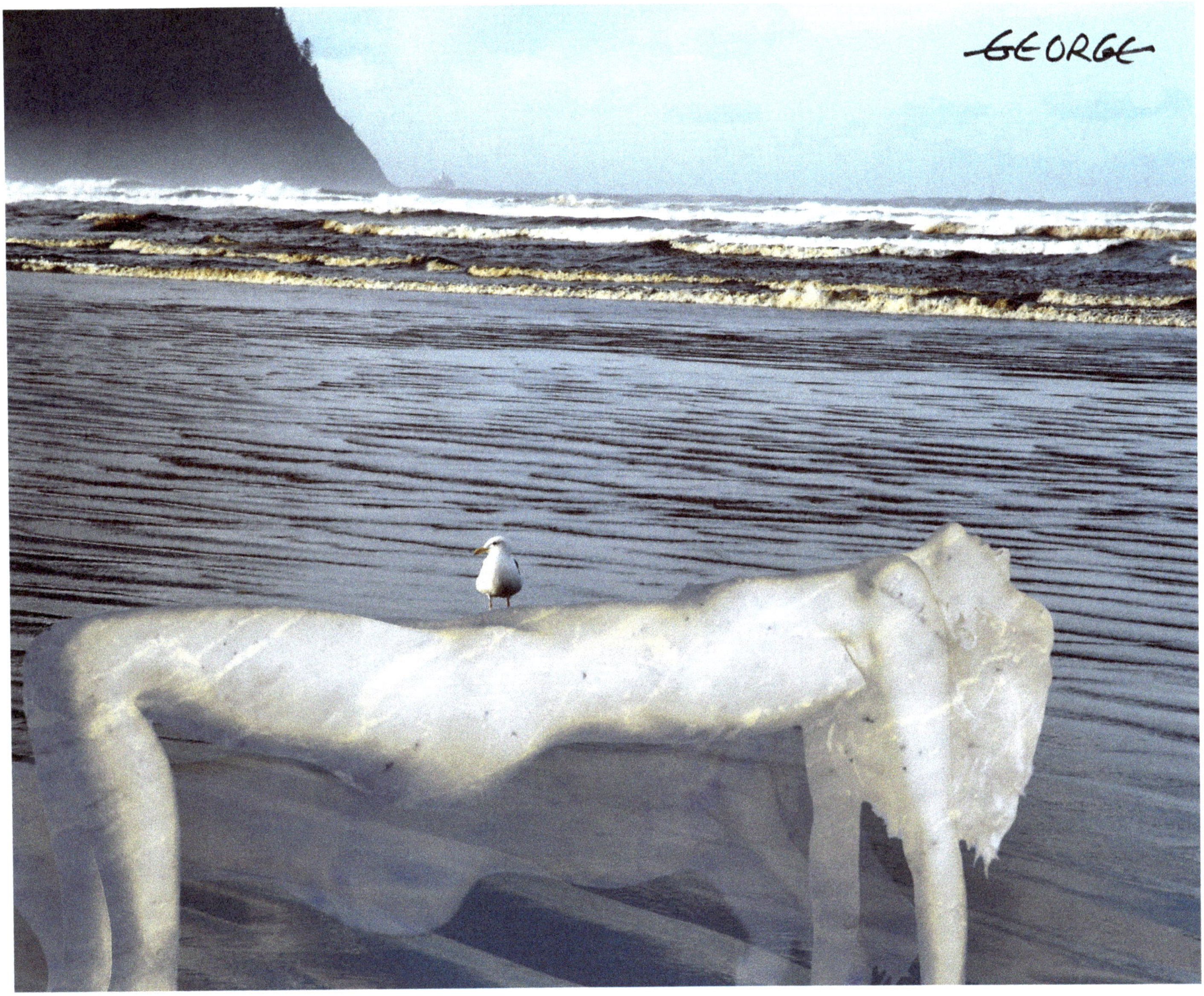
GEORGE

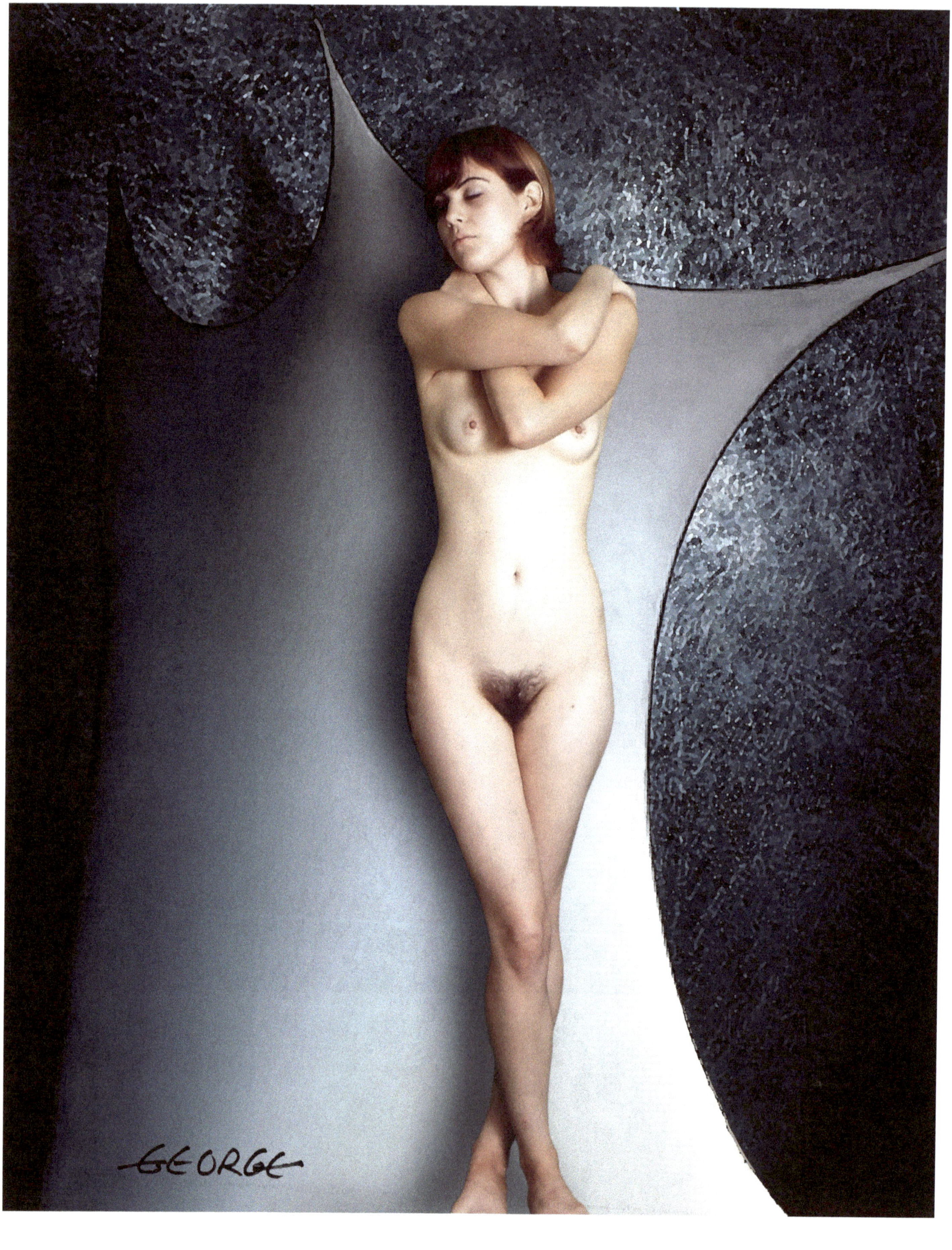
GEORGE

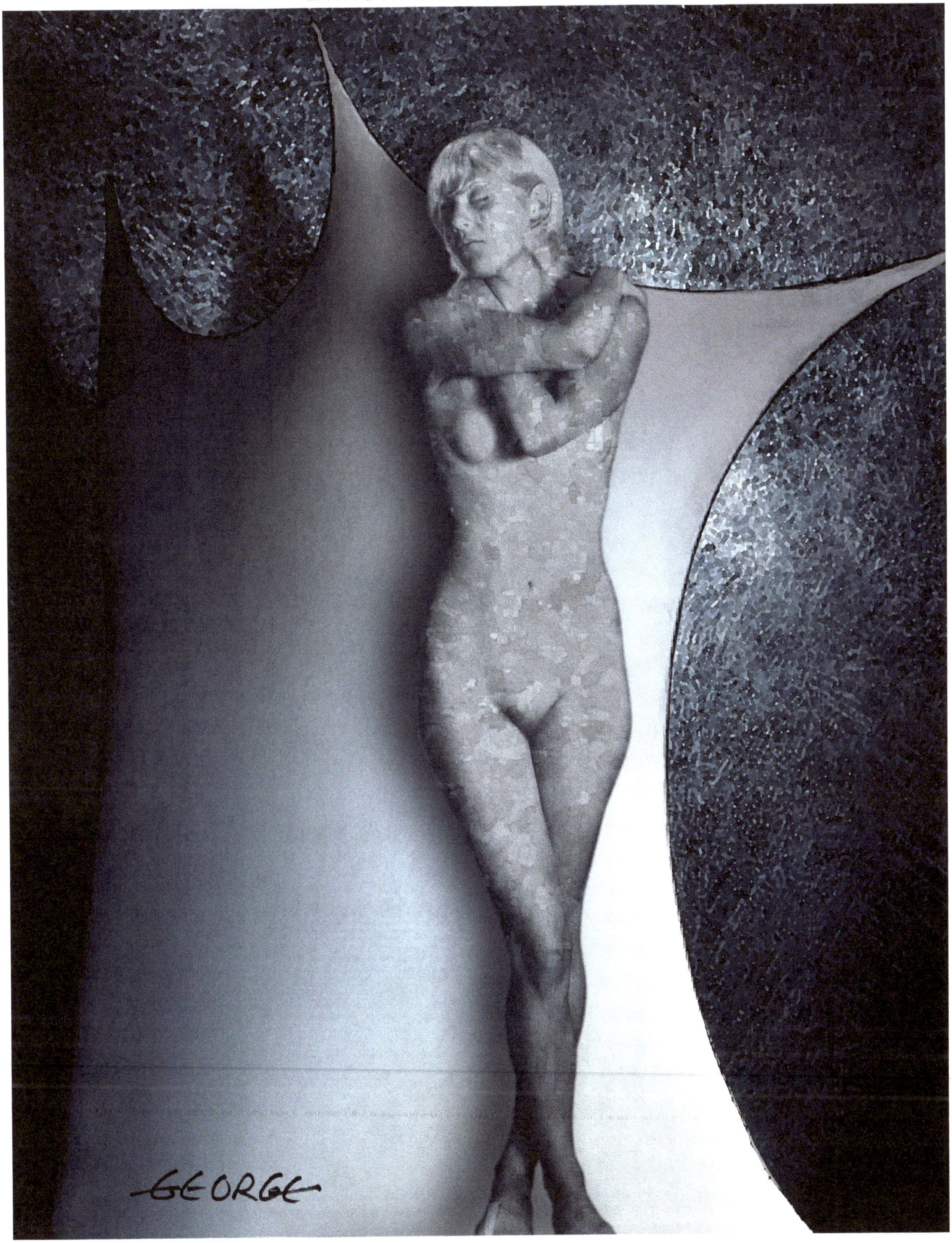
GEORGE

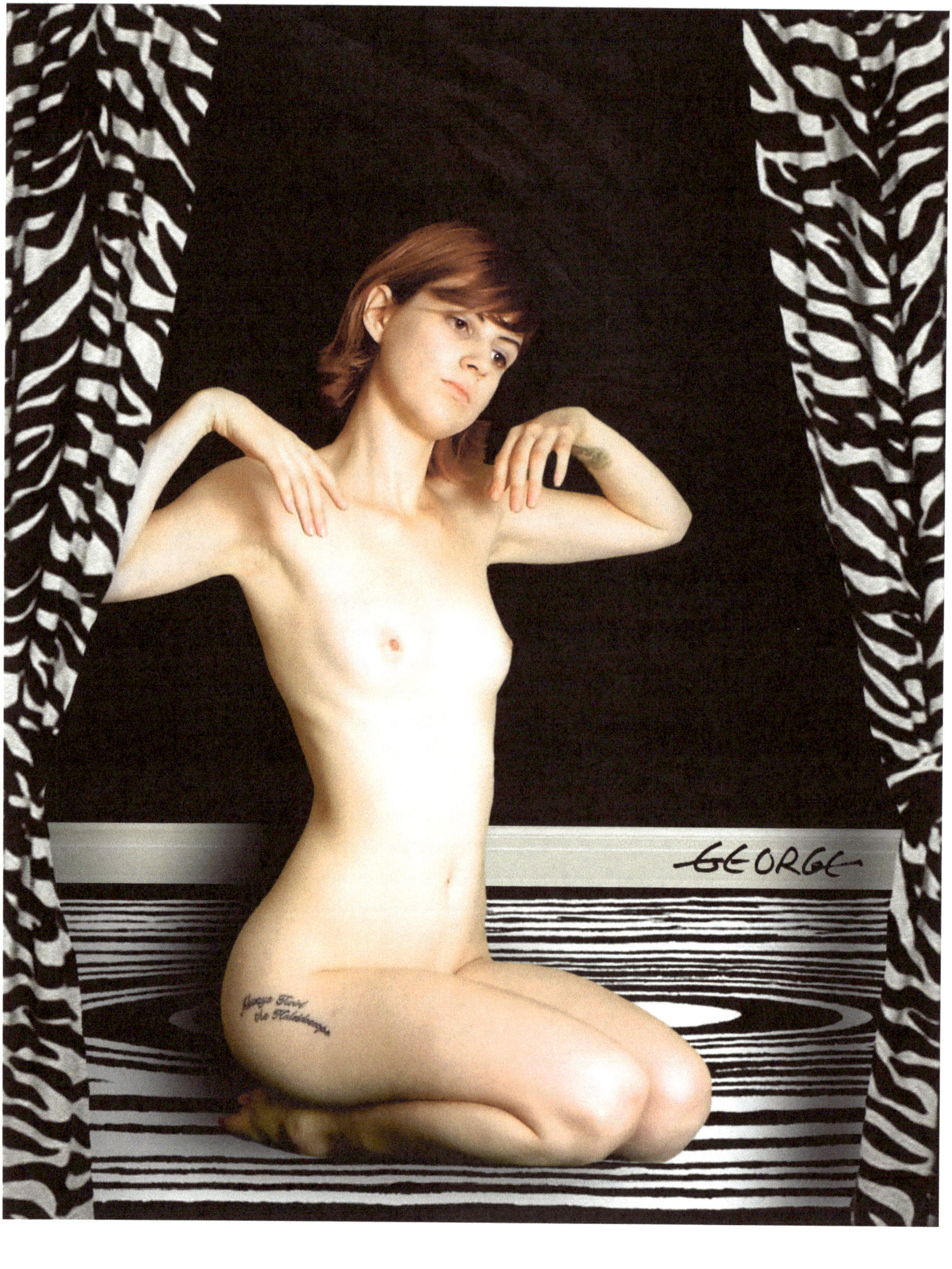
GEORGE

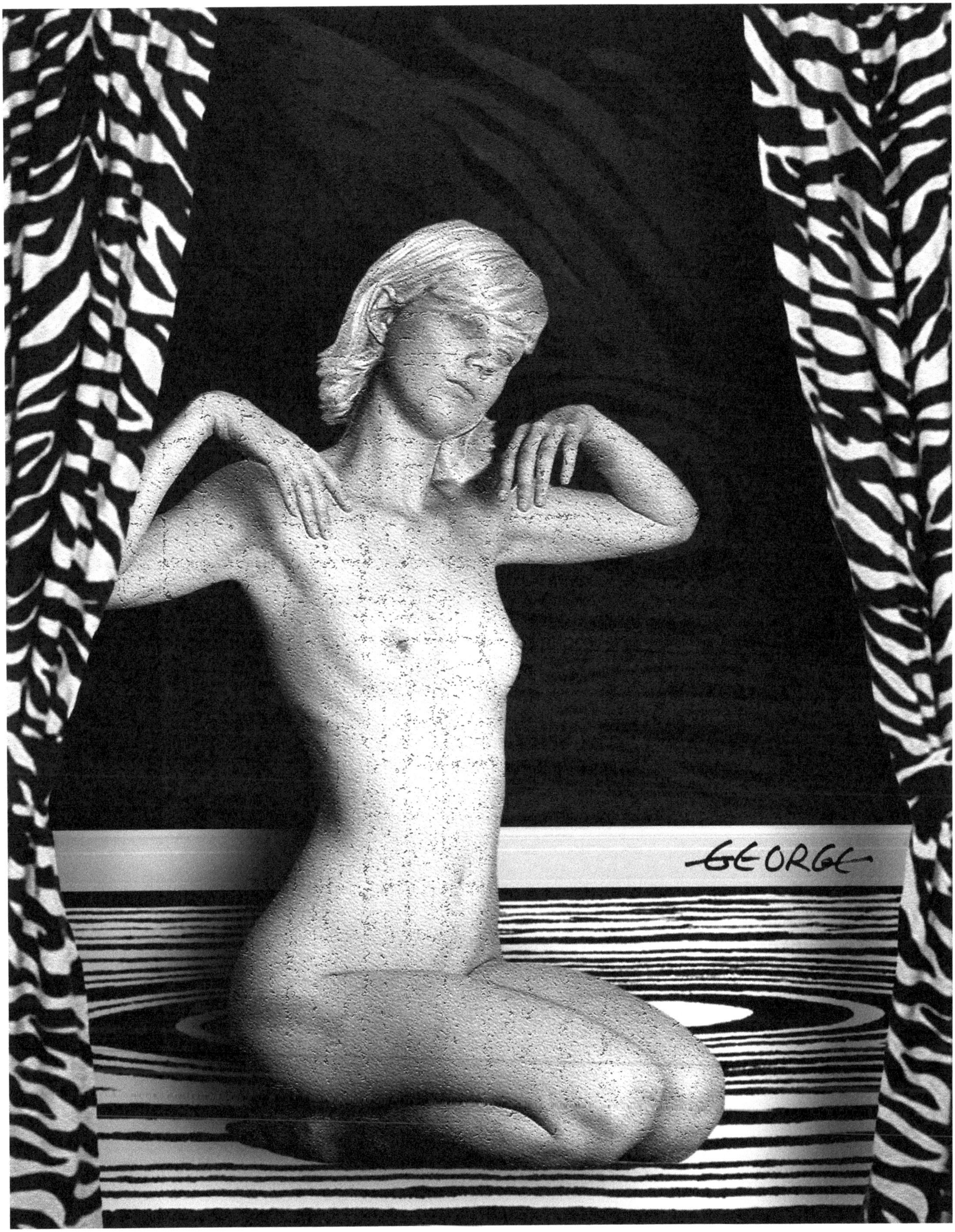
GEORGE

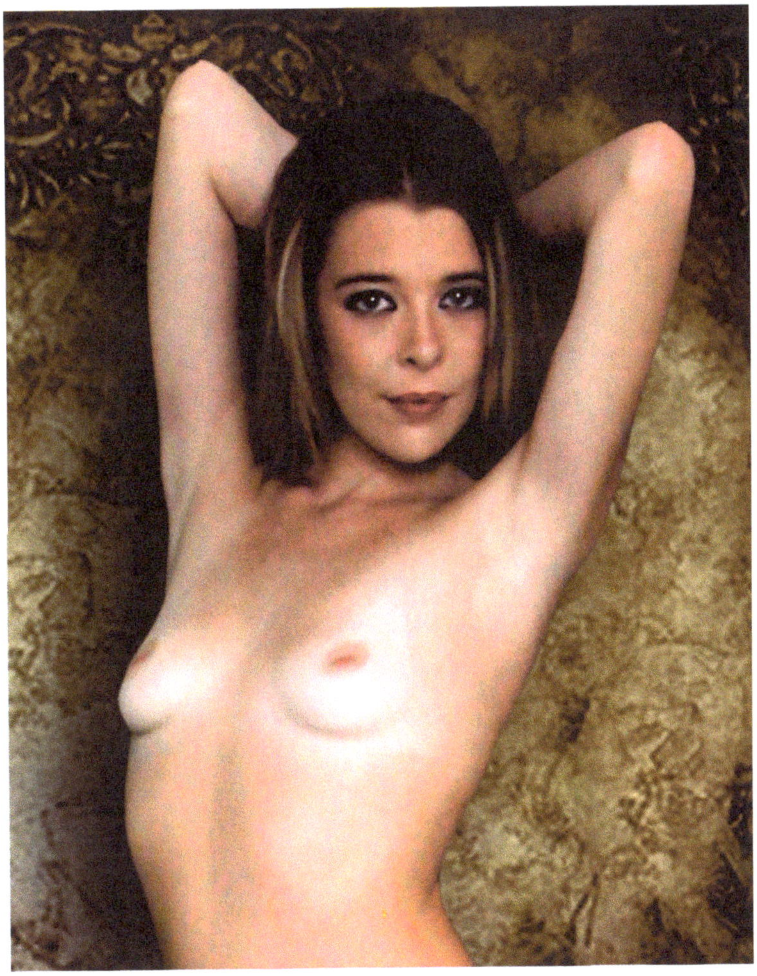

NOLEY C RYAN

Height 5'7" Weight 110 lbs Bust 32" Waist 24" Hips 31" Cup A

I am the current spokes model for Tasty Brands in Phoenix and I also have shot my first magazine spread for Bikini Magazine! I am a spokes model for Affinis Apparel and have done Raw Artist runway shows with them. I am also in Dames, Trains and Automobiles, just released.

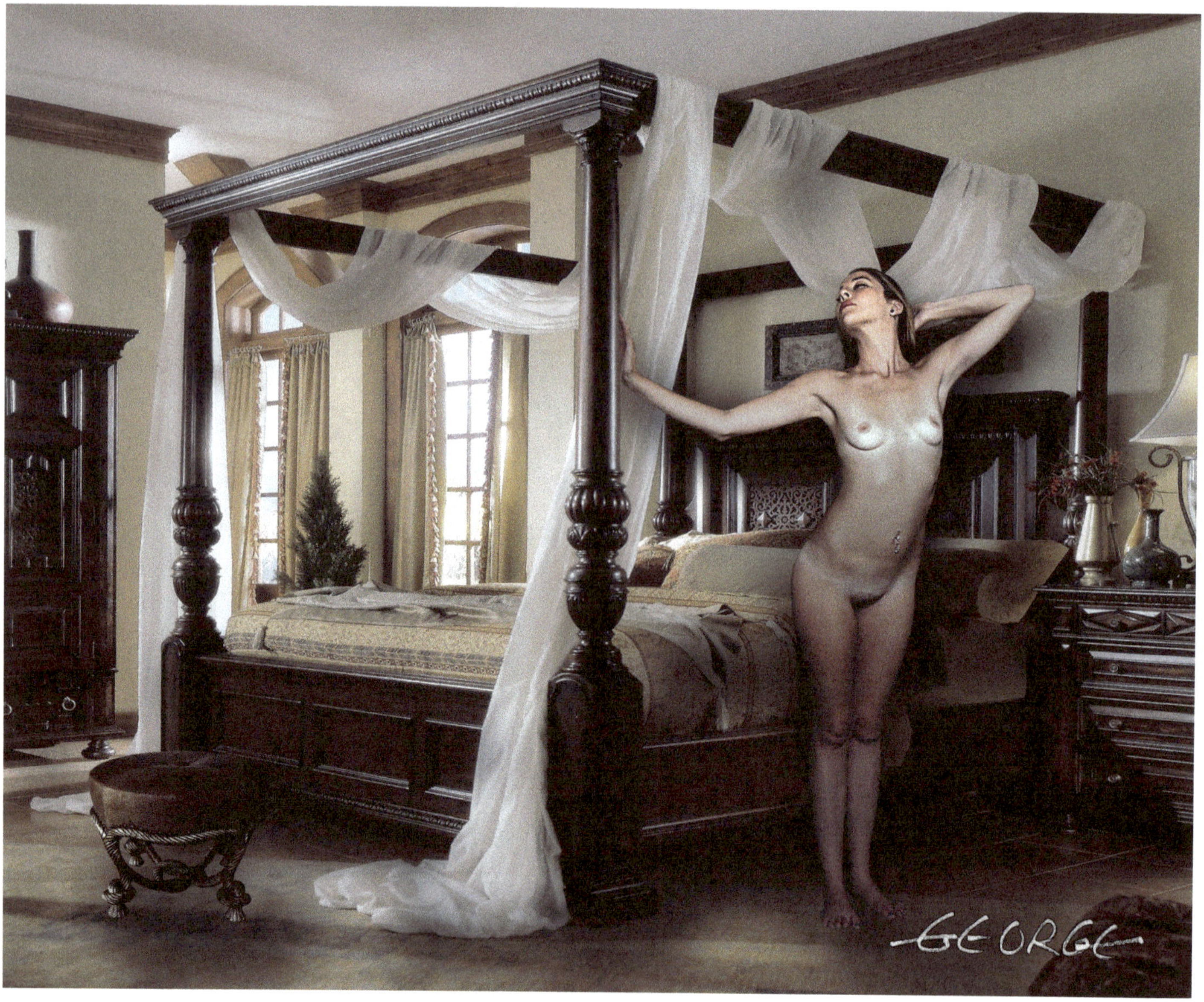
GEORGE

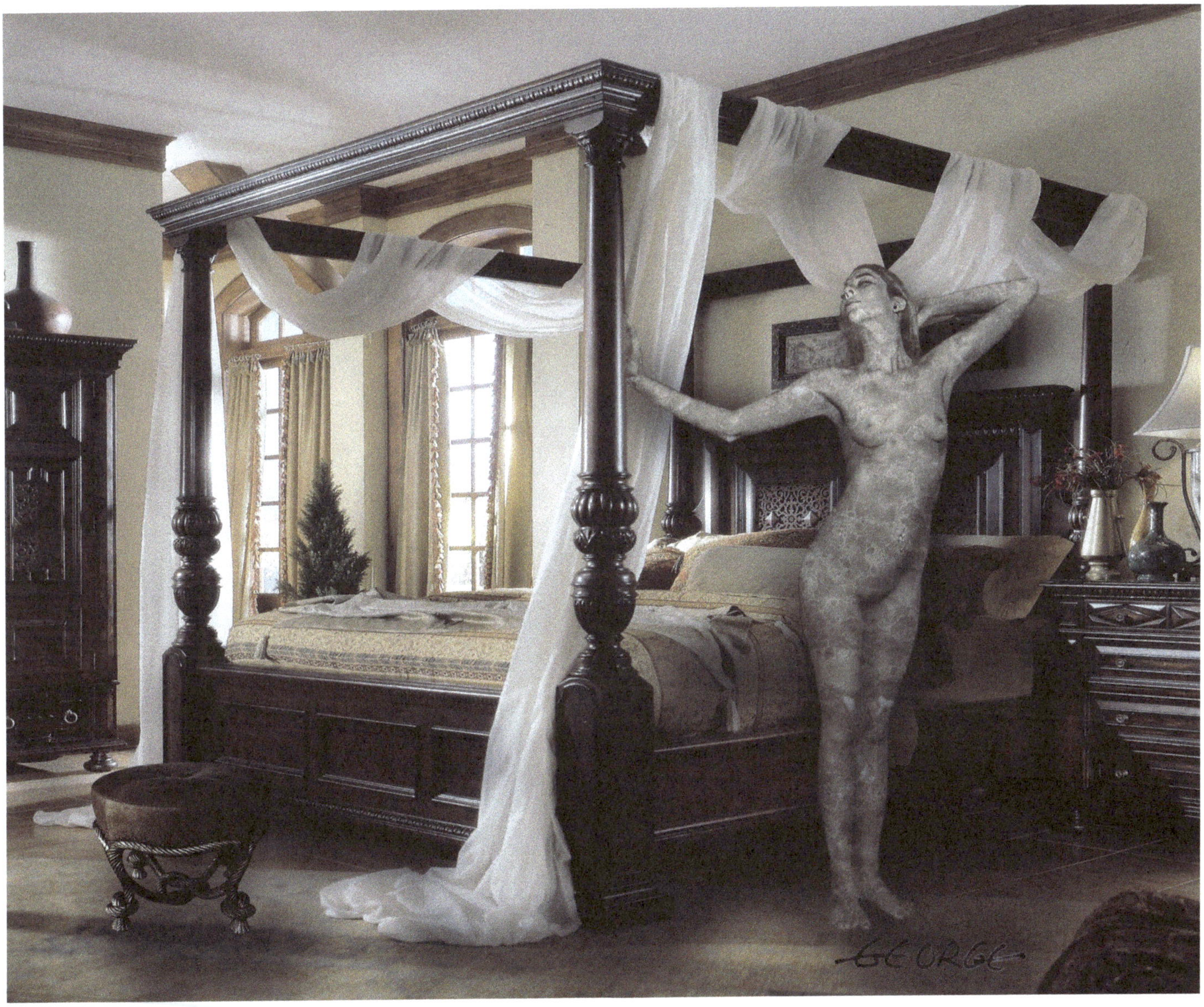
GEORGE

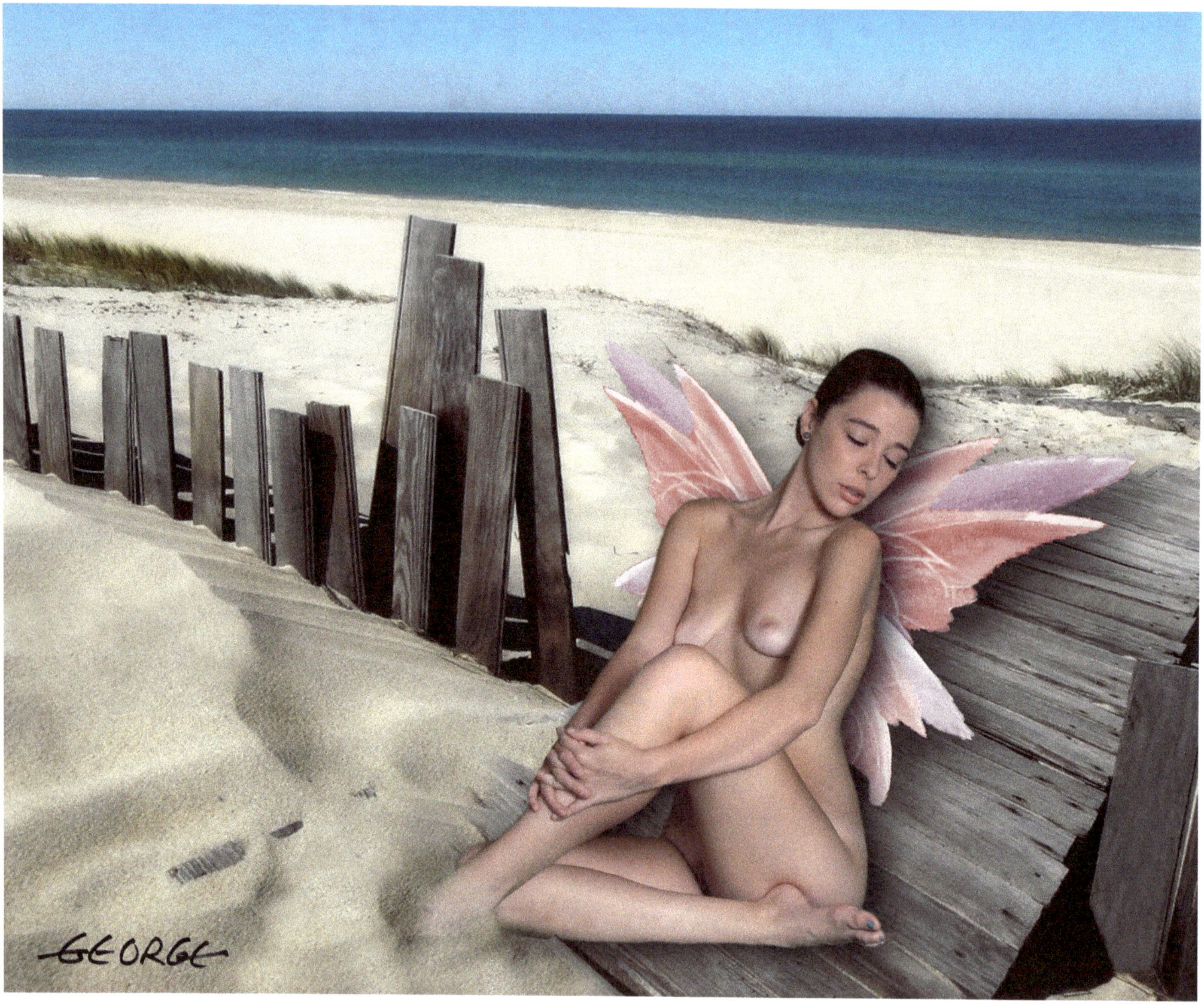
GEORGE

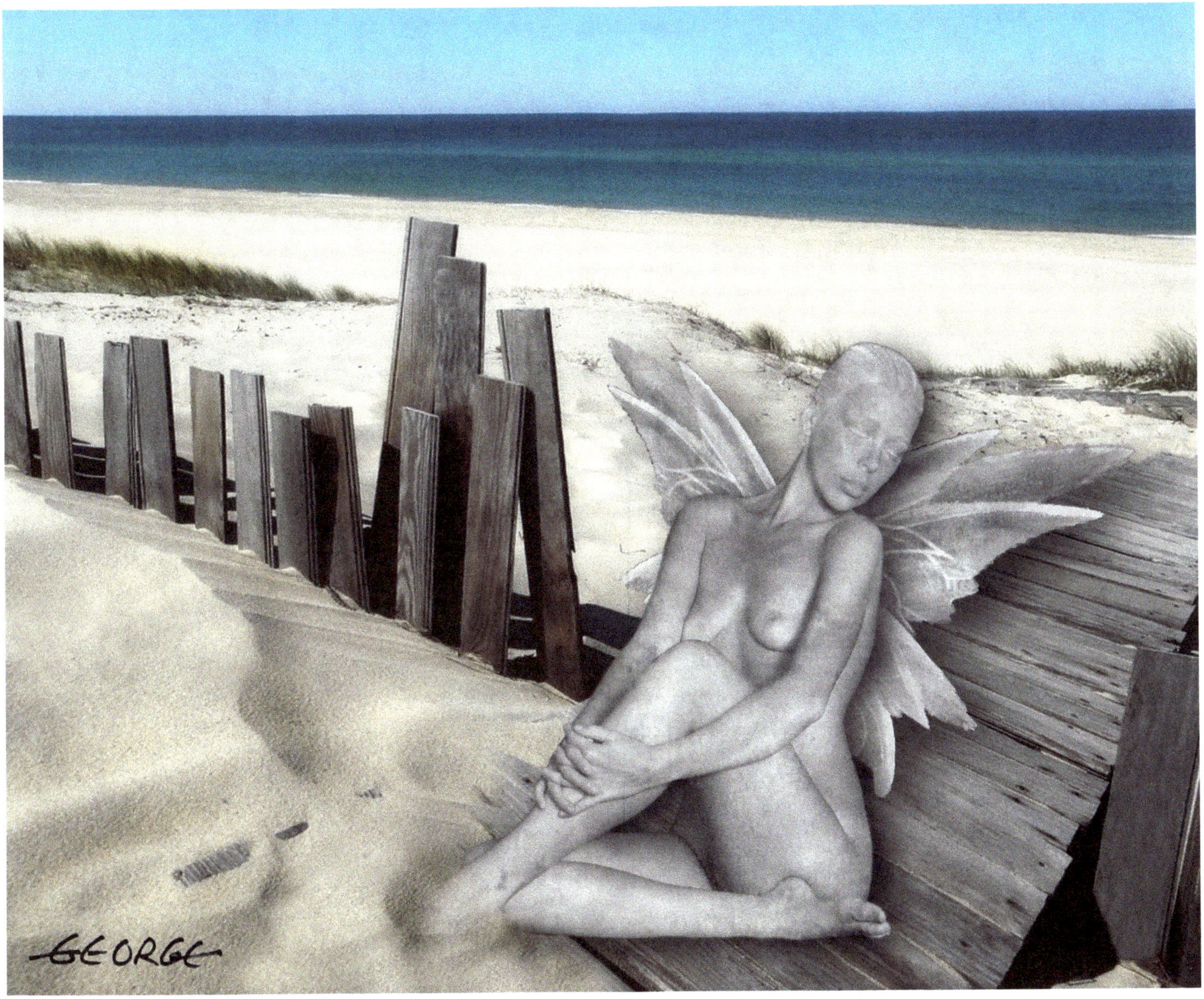
GEORGE

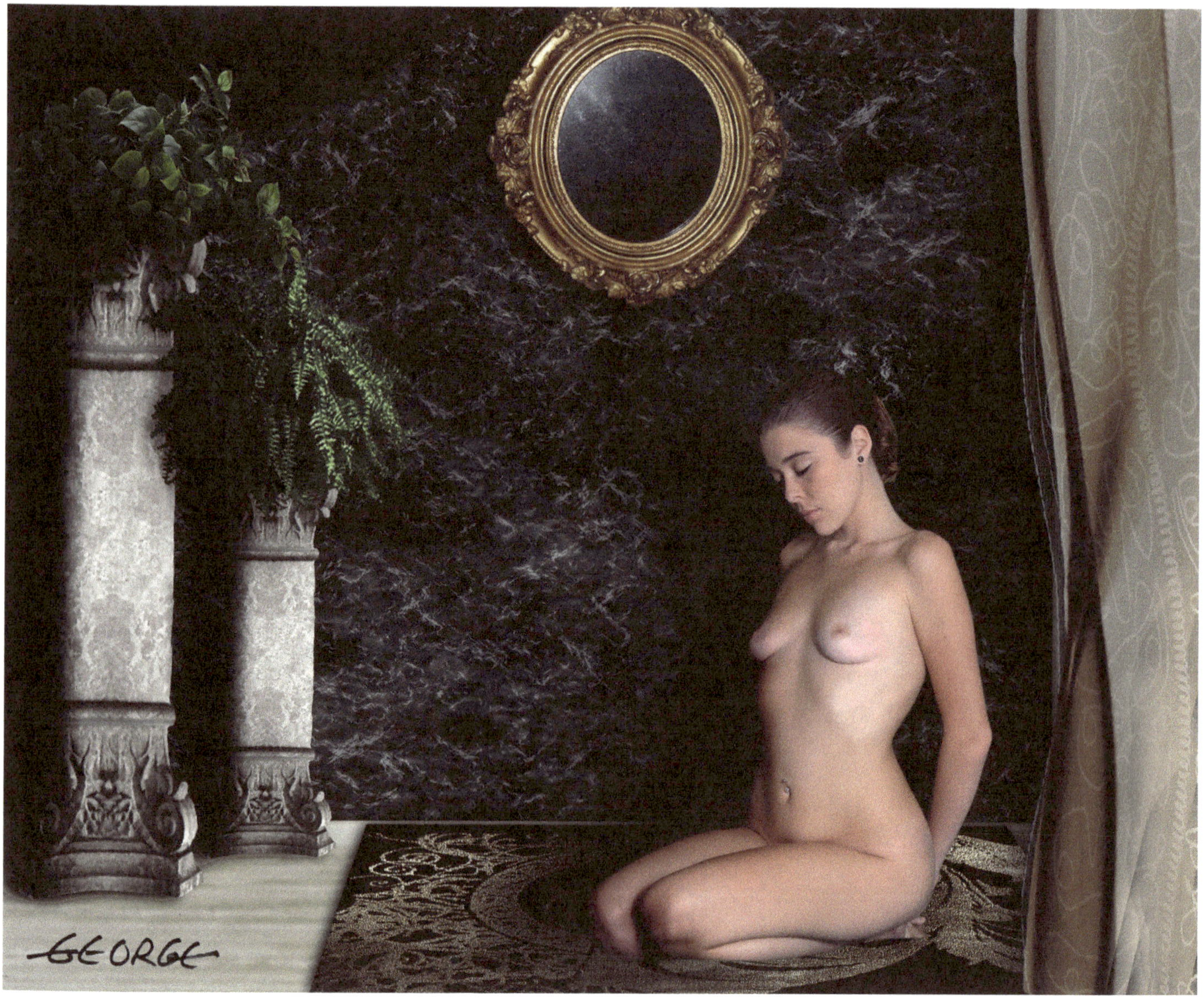
GEORGE

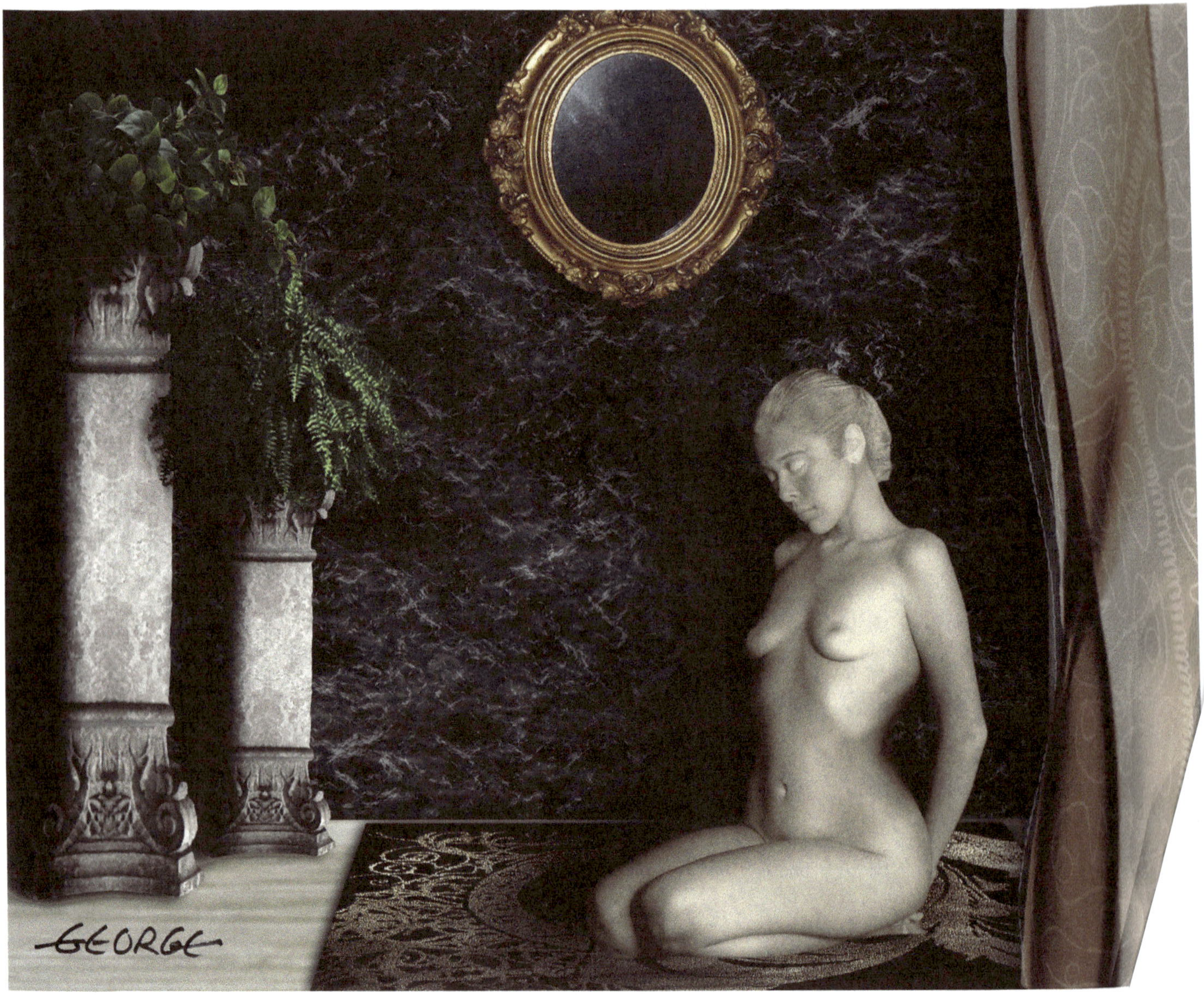
GEORGE

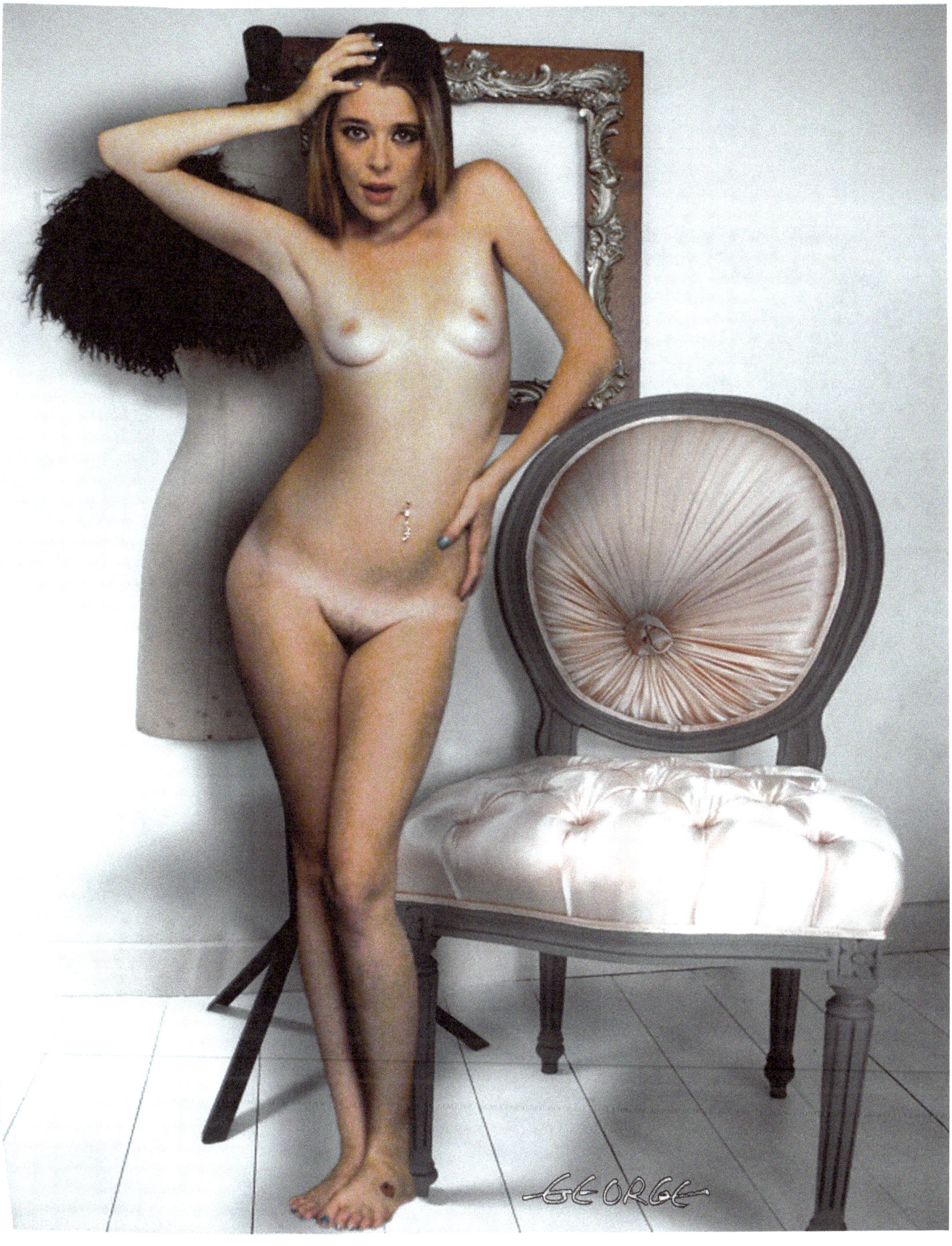
GEORGE

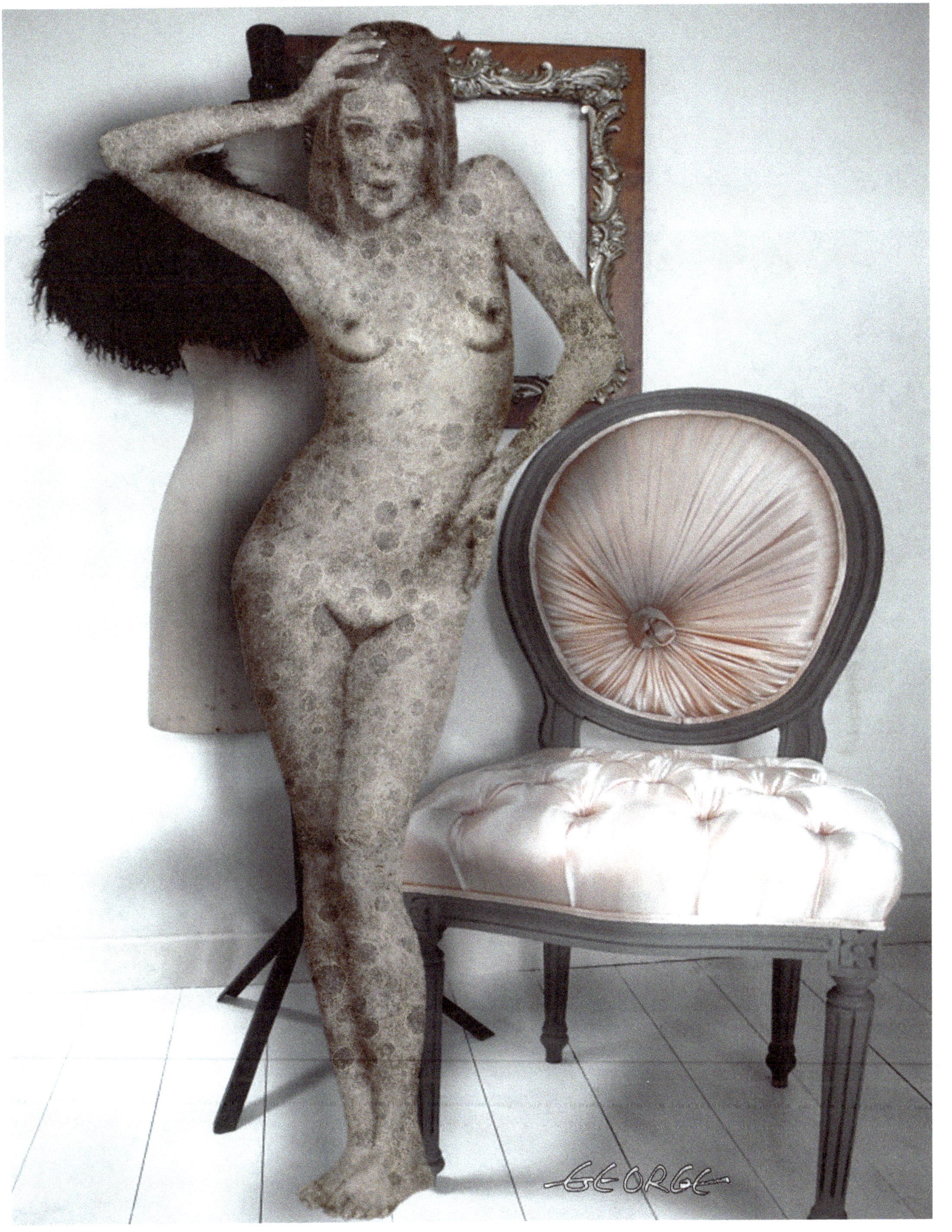
GEORGE

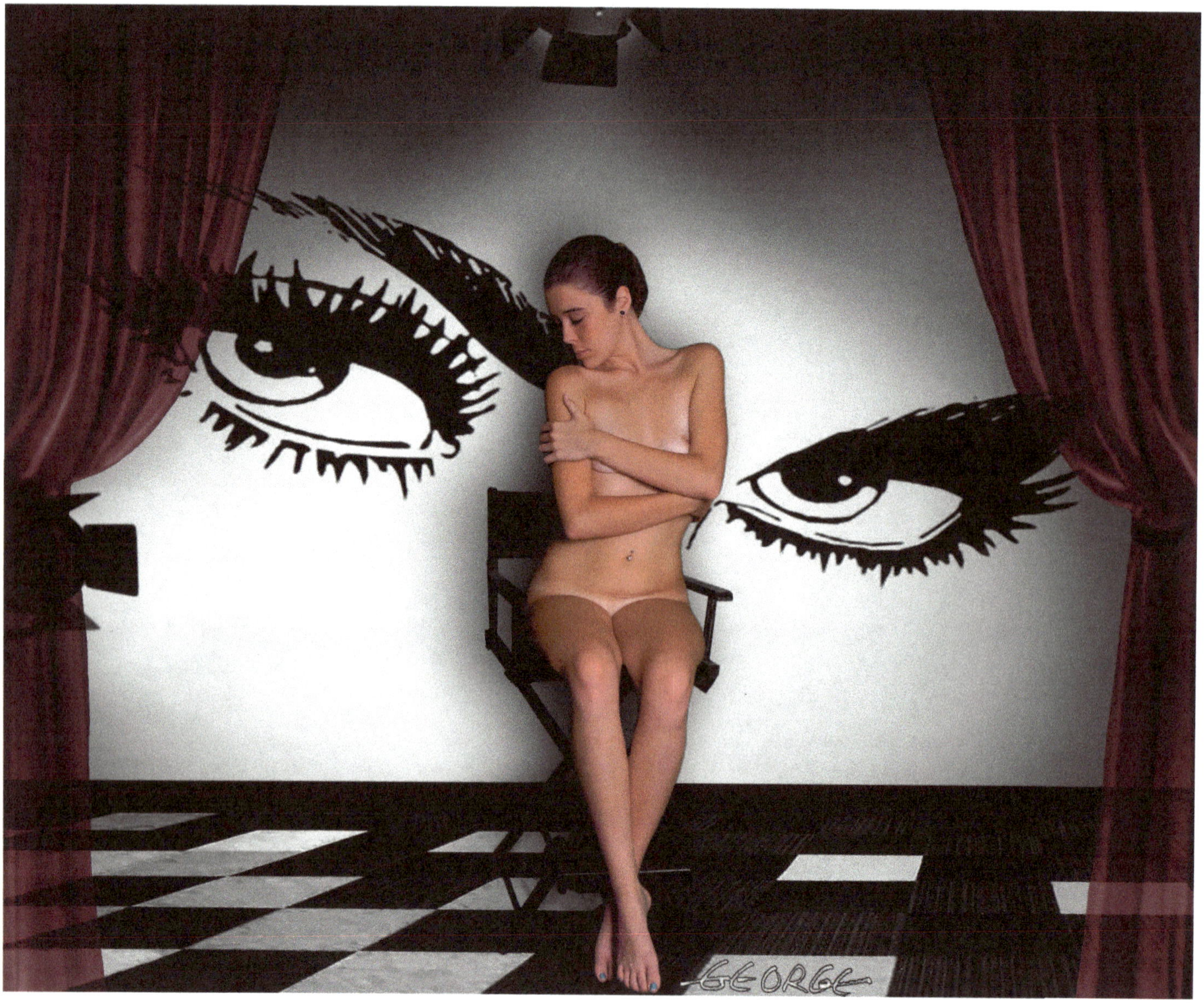
GEORGE

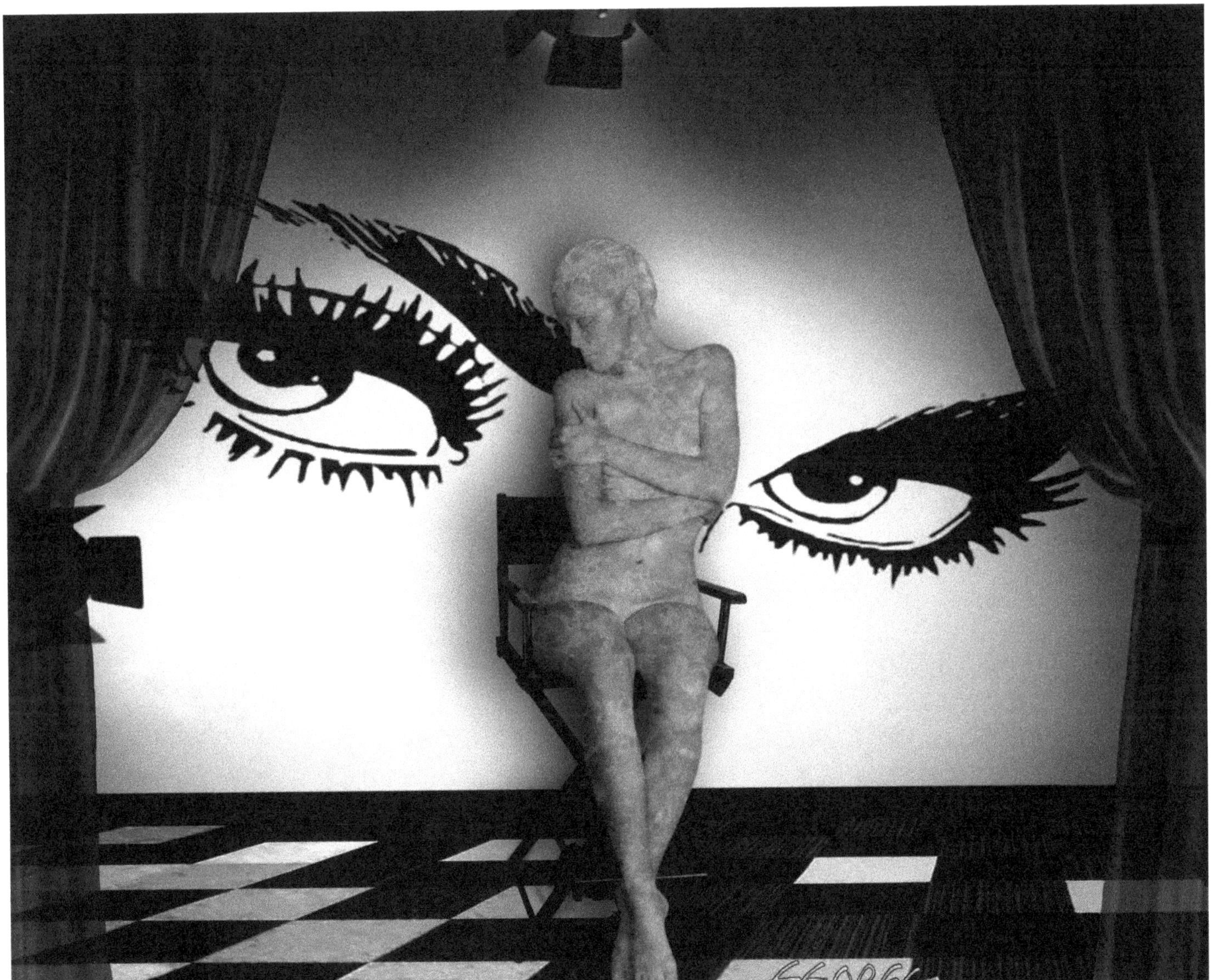
GEORGE

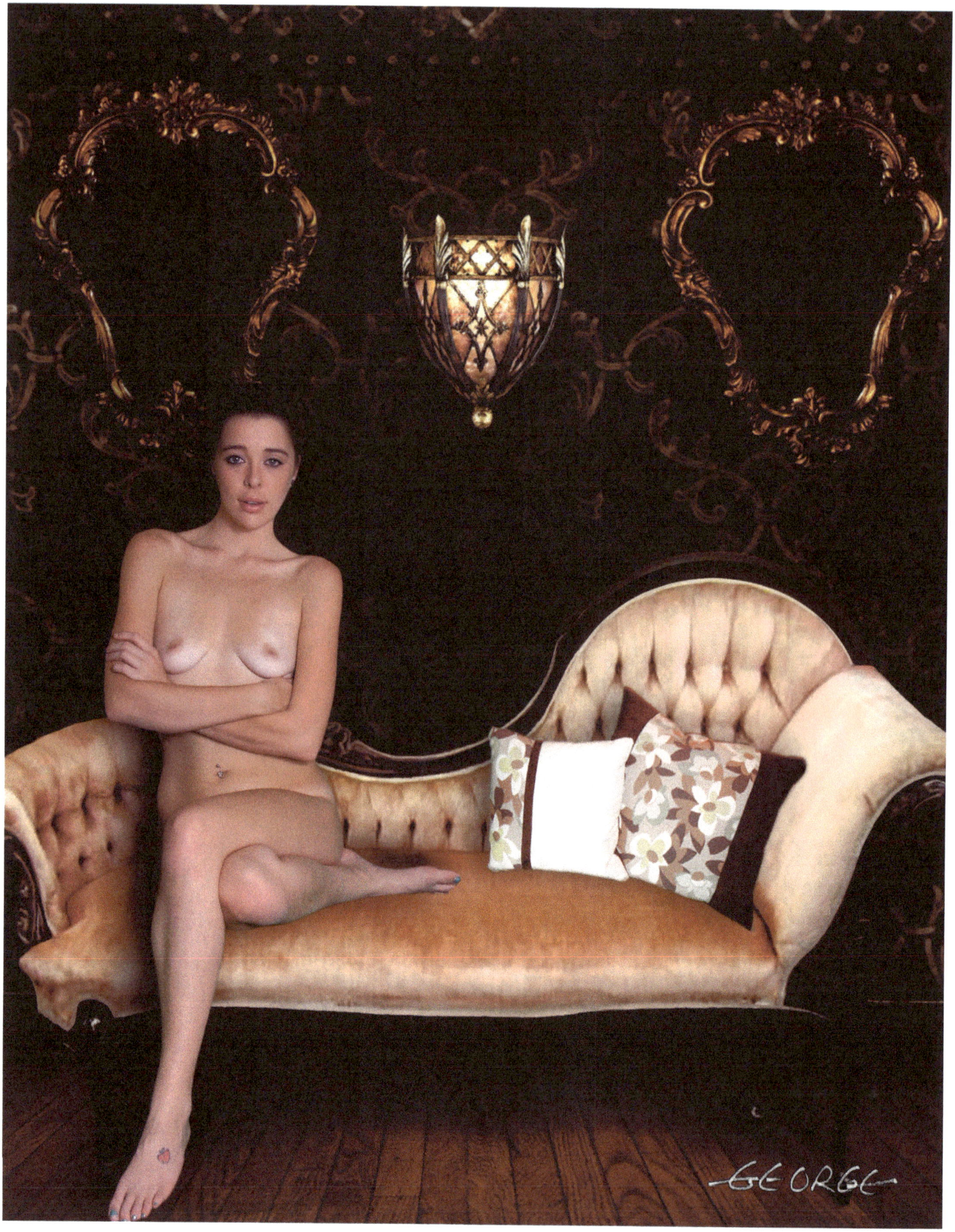
GEORGE

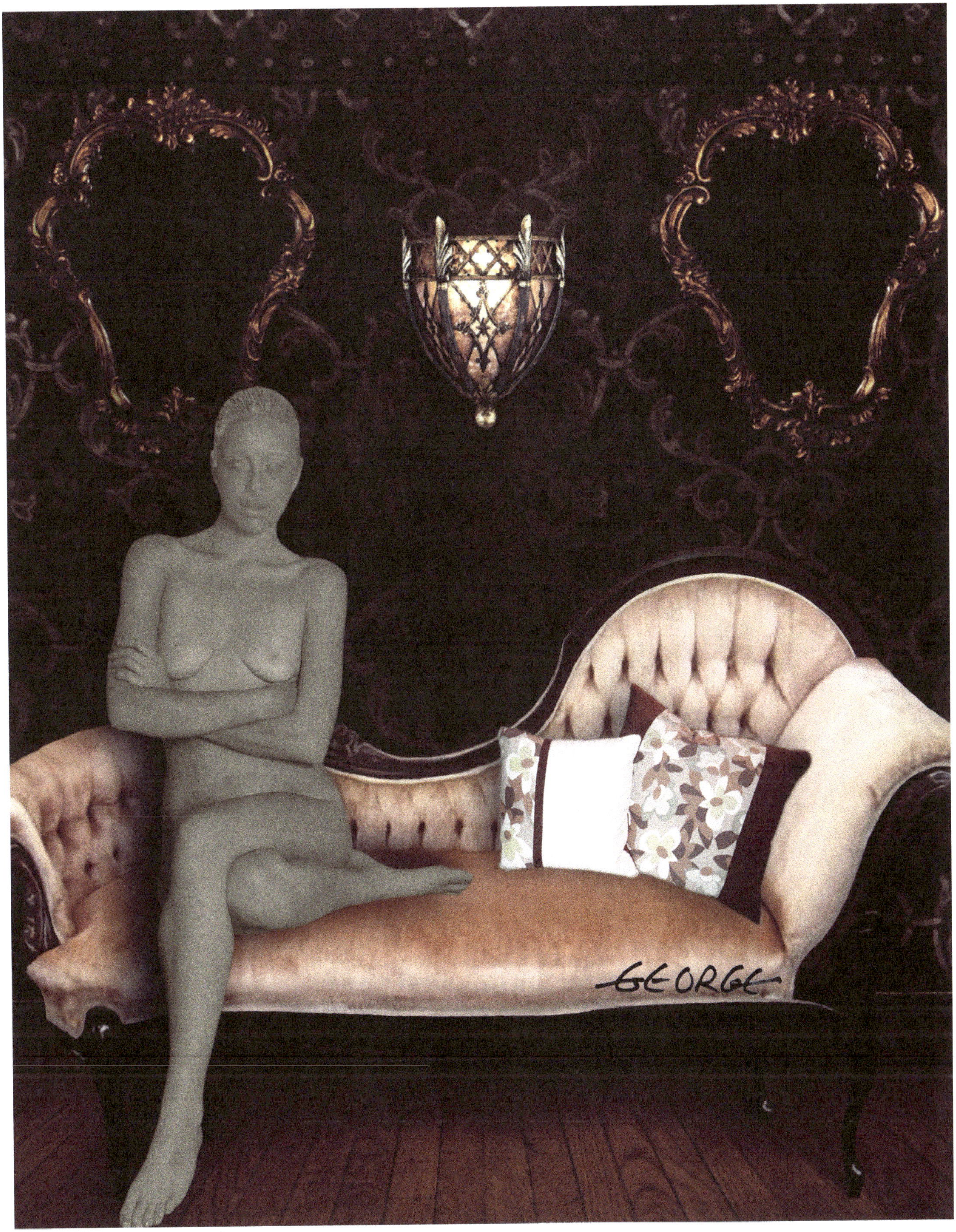
GEORGE

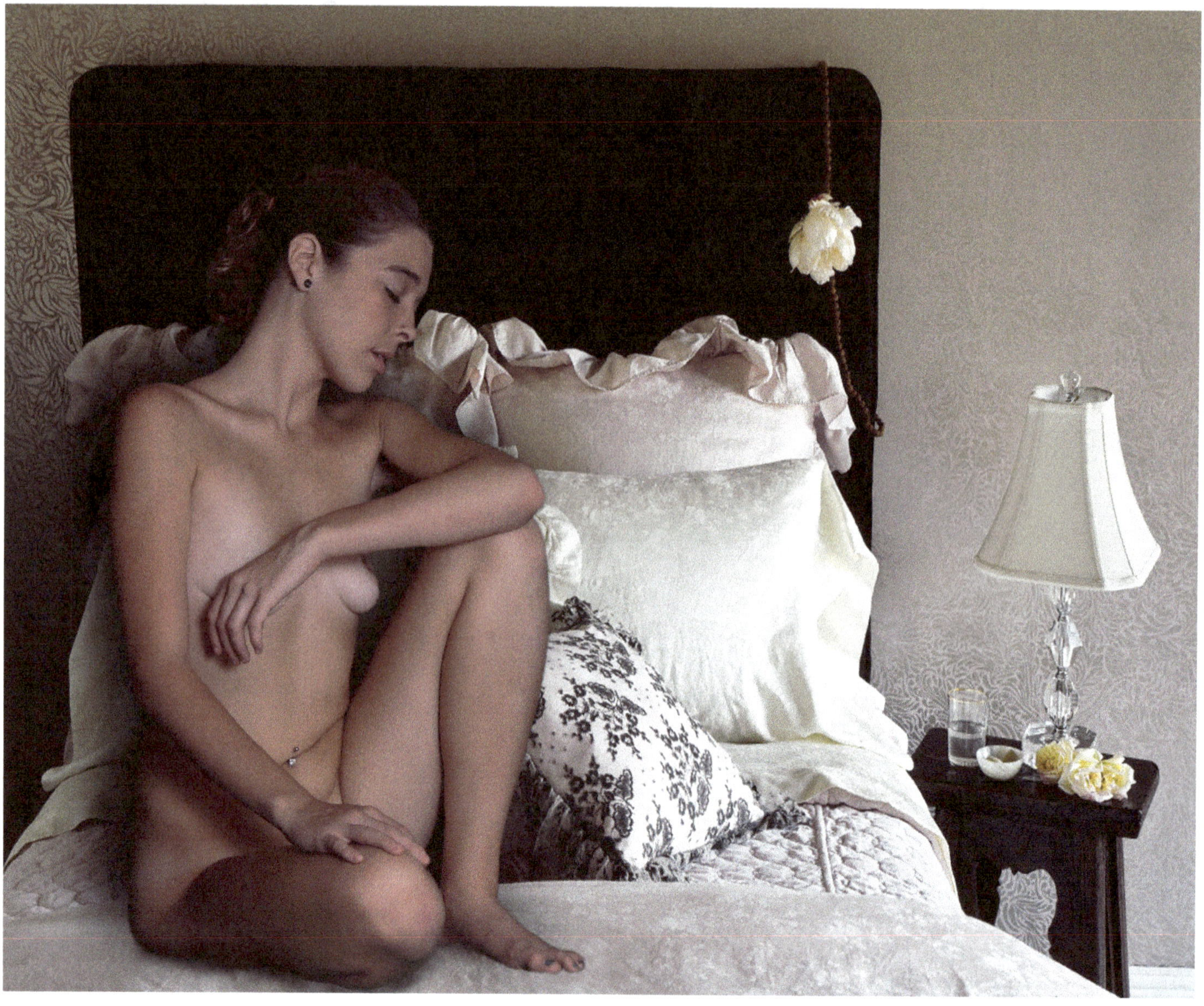

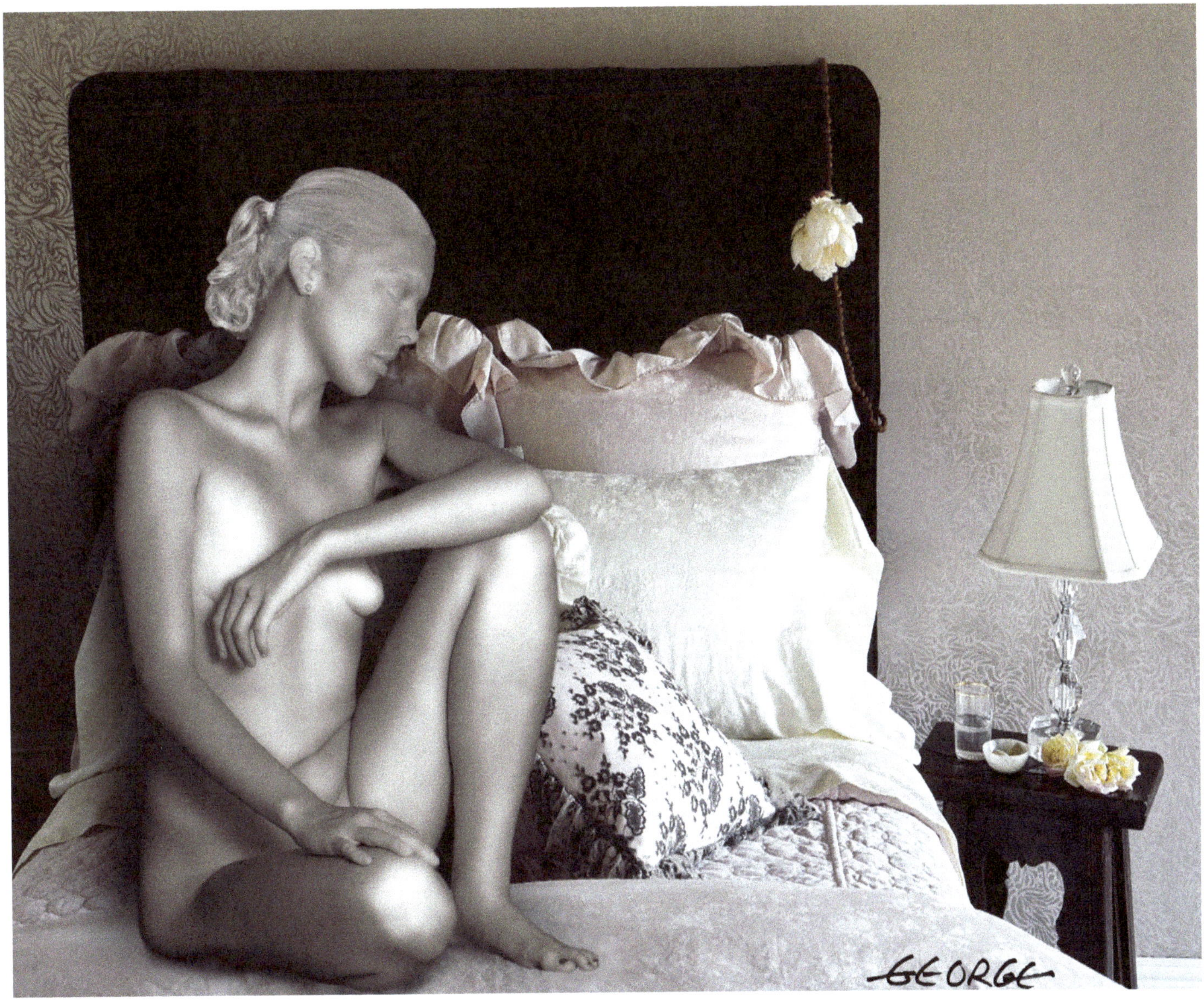
GEORGE

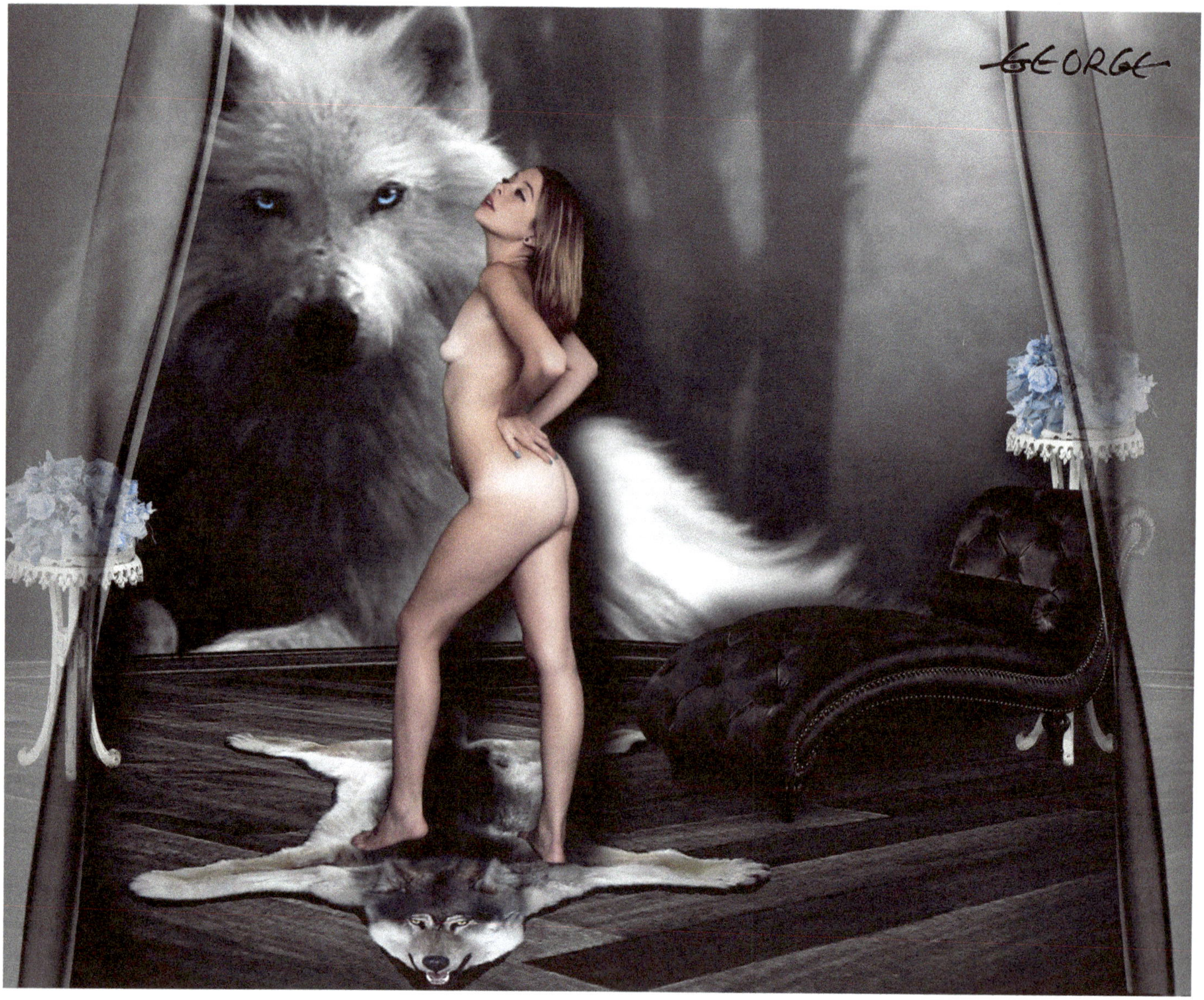
GEORGE

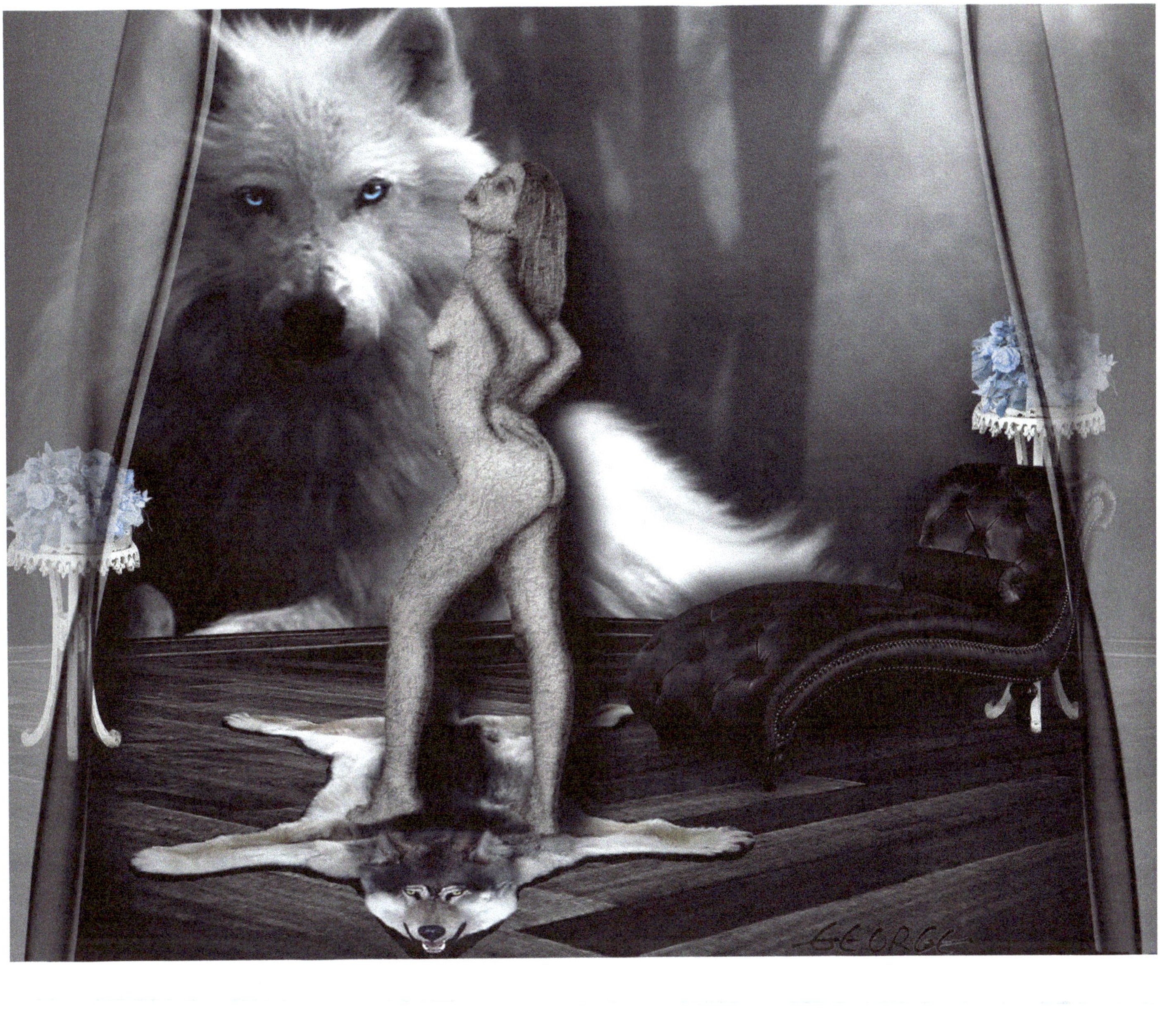
GEORGE

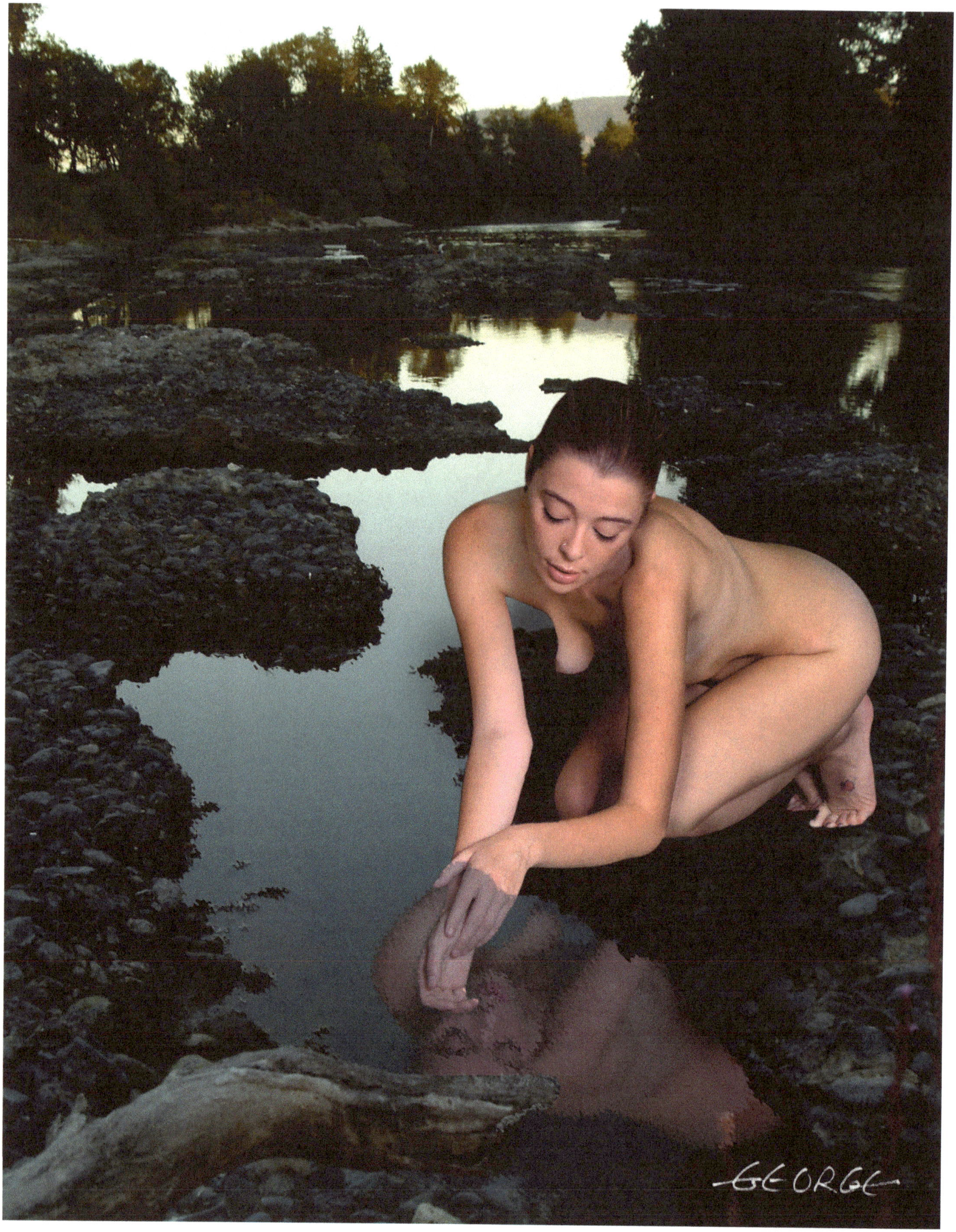
GEORGE

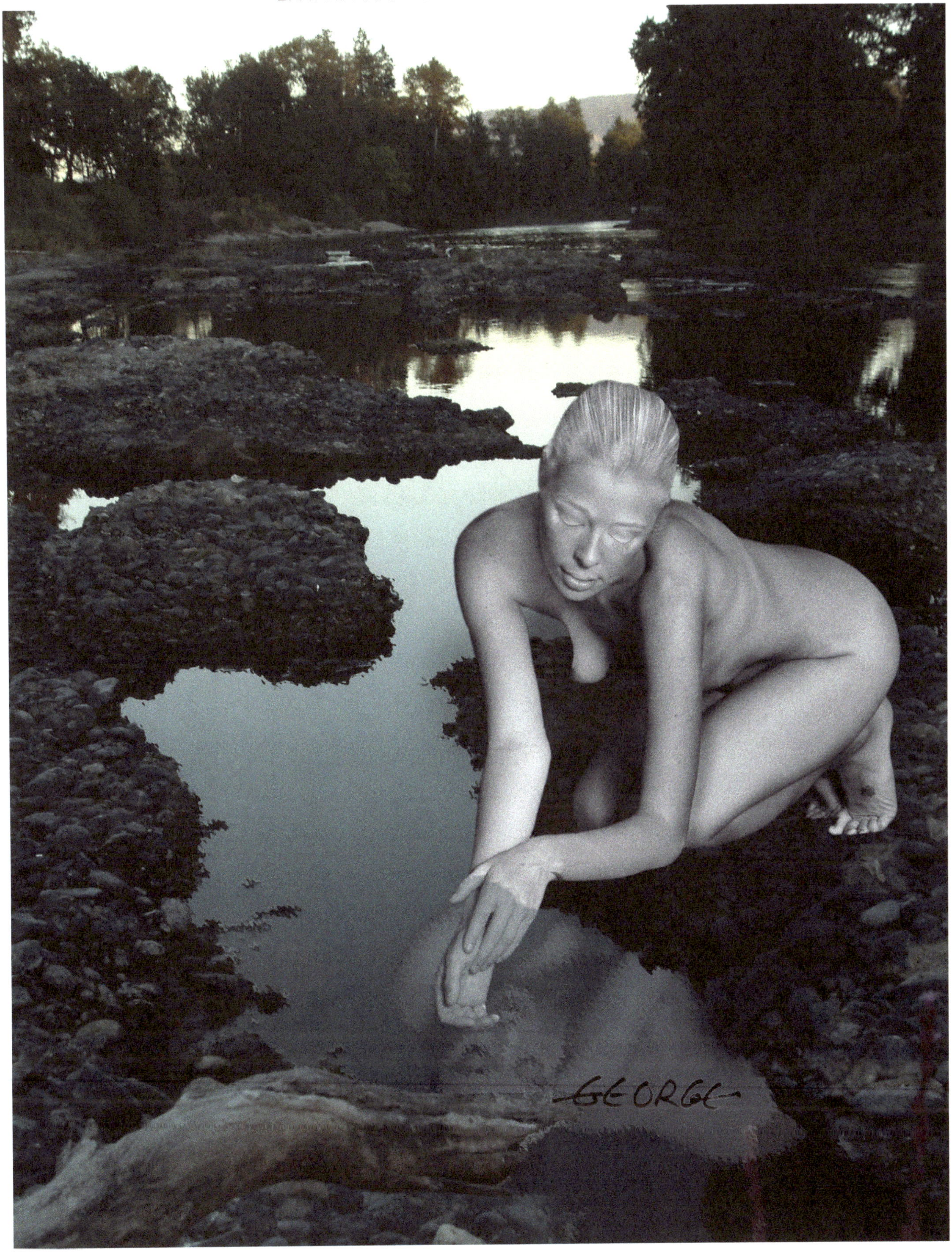
GEORGE

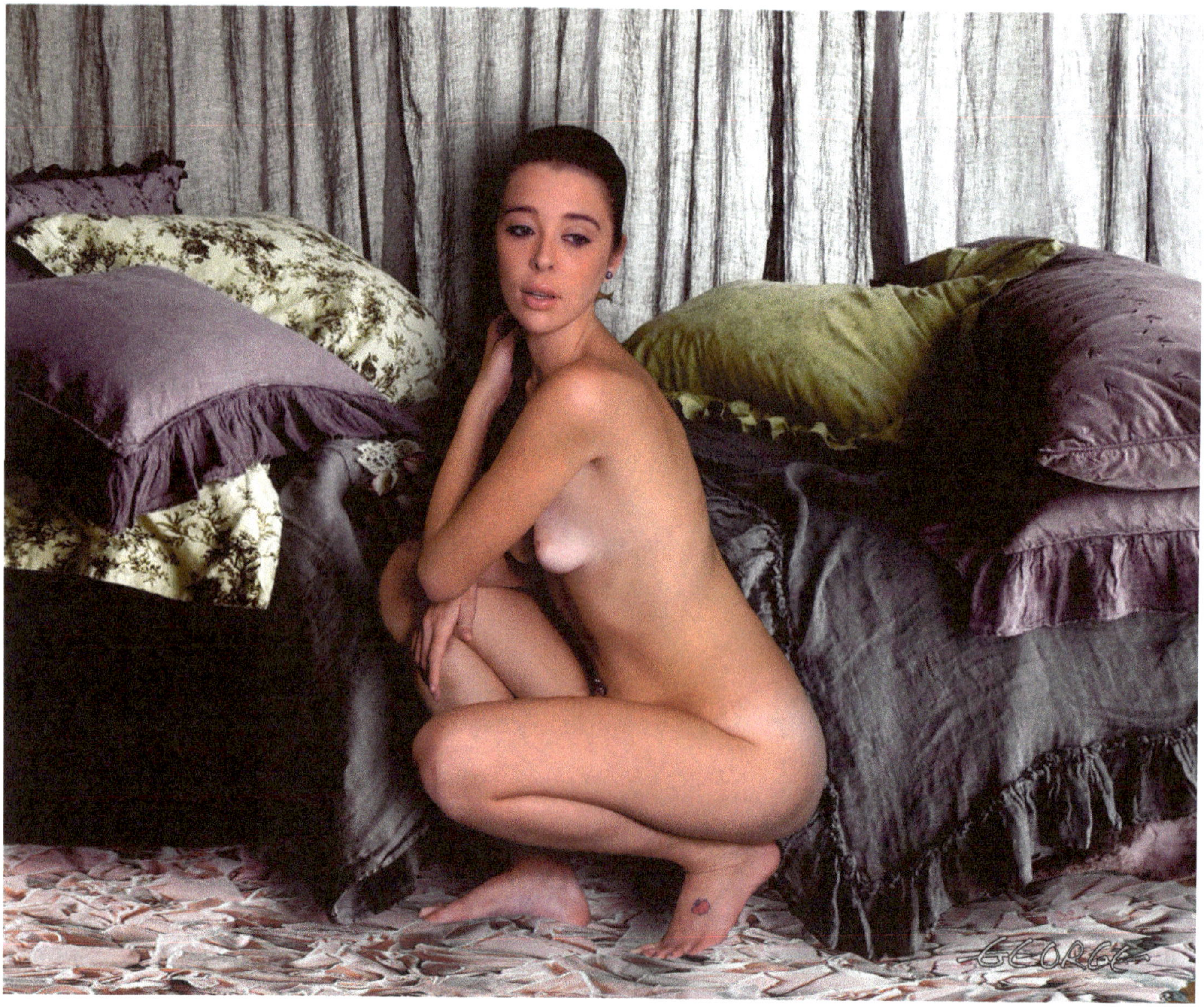

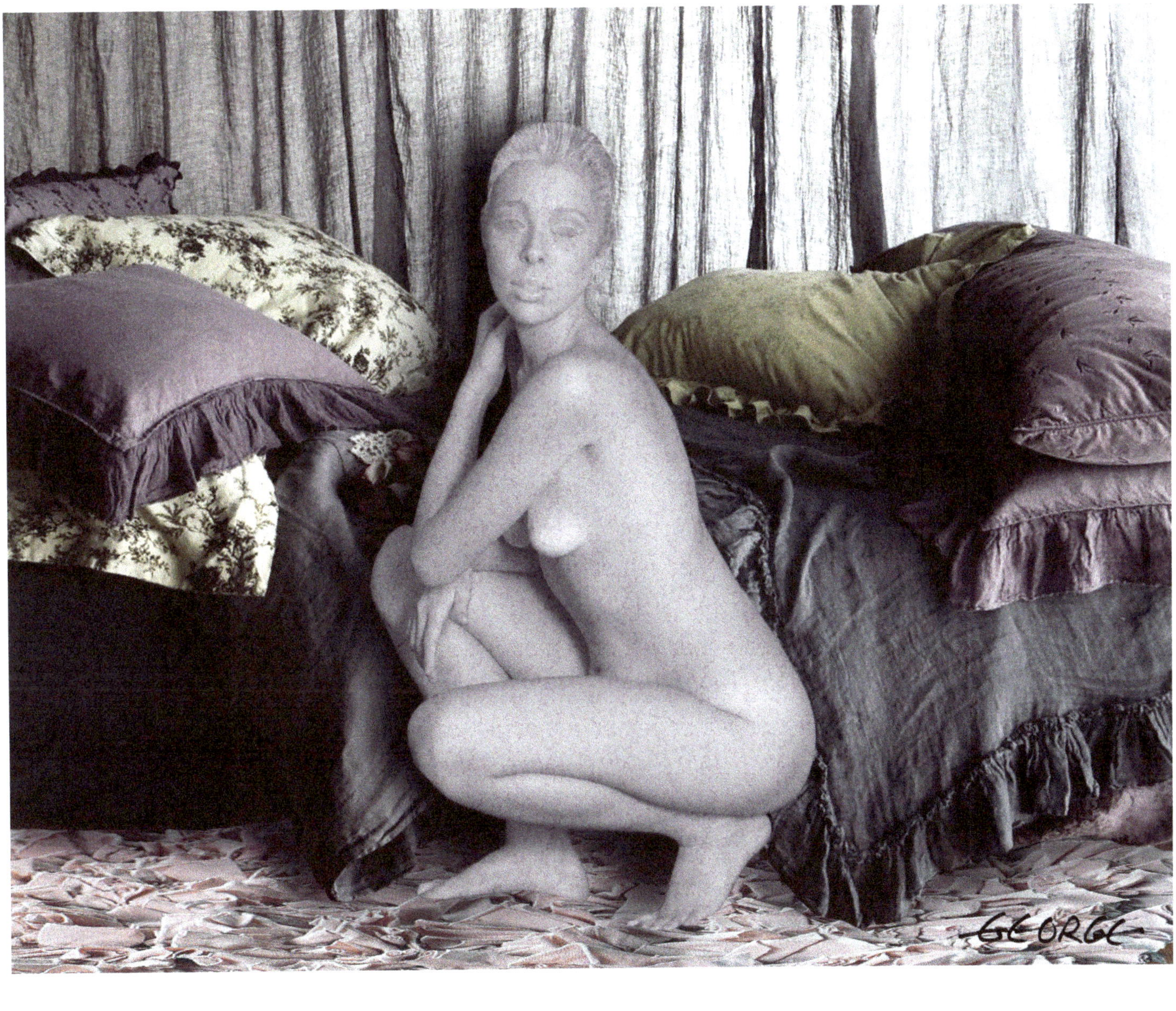
GEORGE

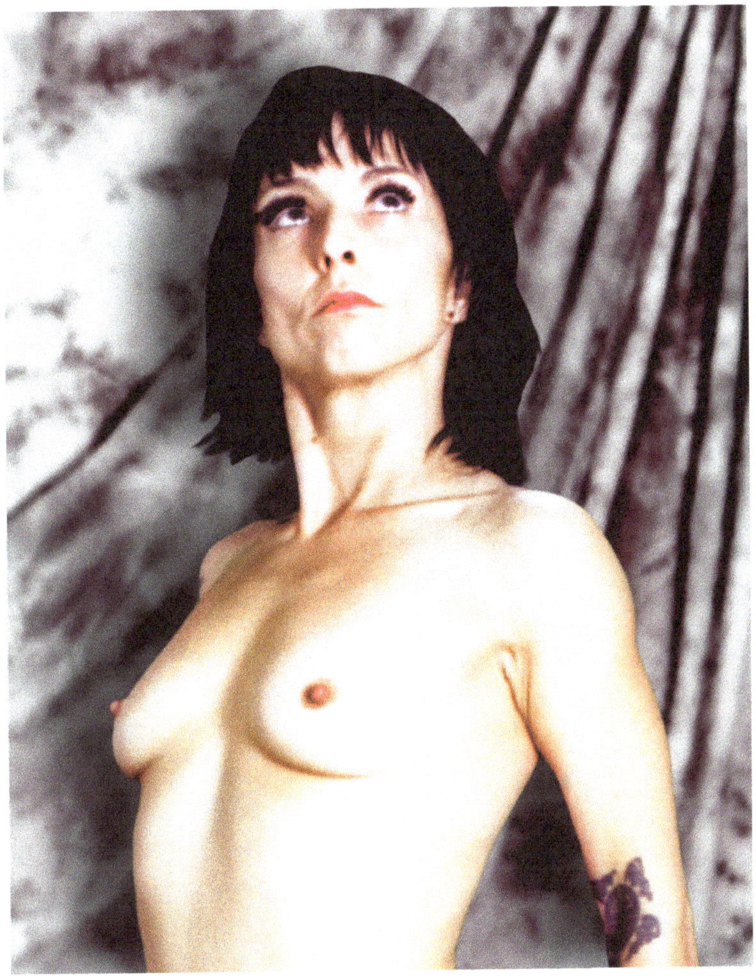

PAIJE DOLZA

Height 5'2" Weight 101 lbs Bust 34" Waist 24" Hips 34" Cup C

I am a classy native San Francisco lady. I like to have fun, work hard and enjoy life. I have modeled with my mom since I was able to put clothes on and remove them. I am an artist and a jack-of-all-trades. I love to orchestrate creating beautiful sets and ladies.

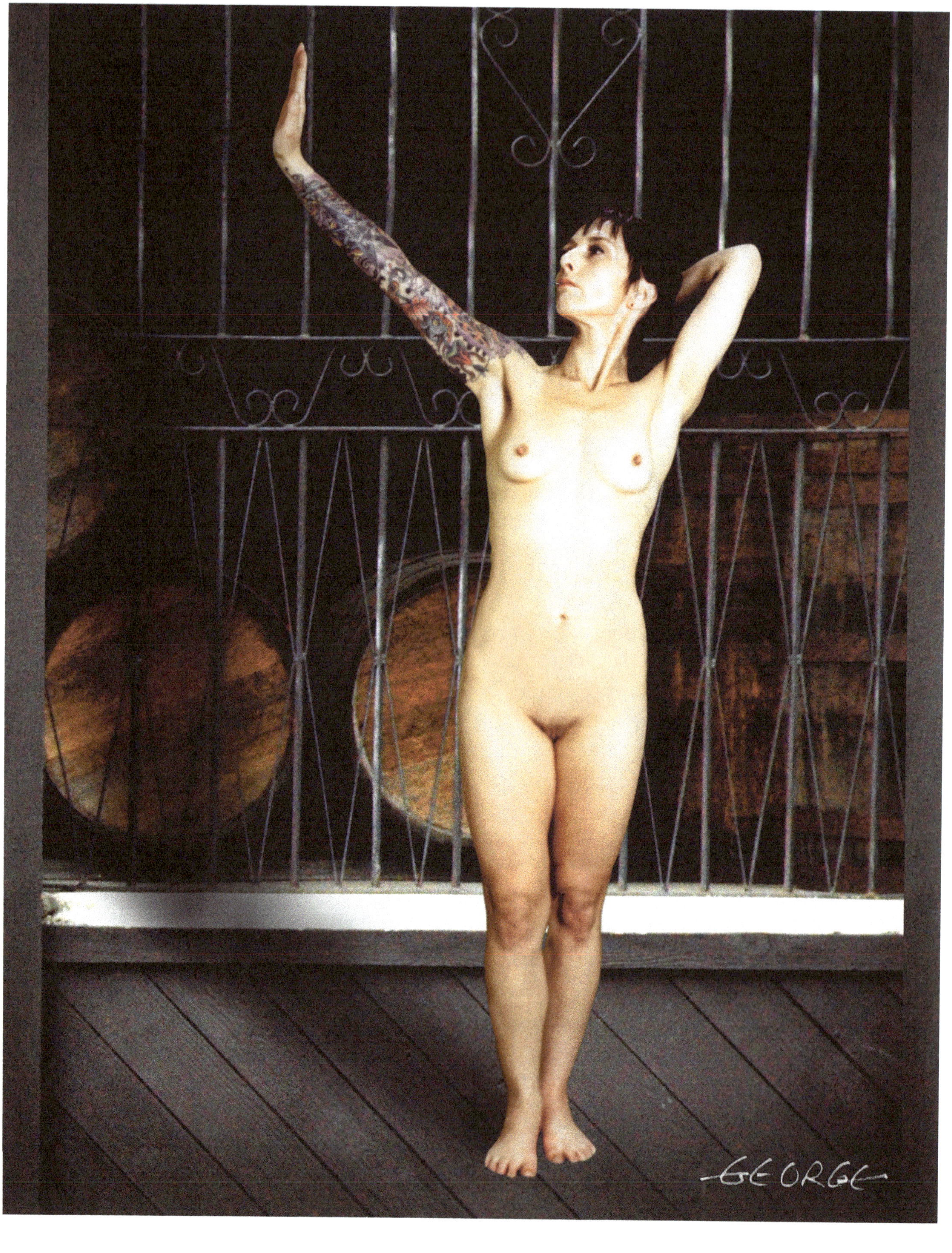
GEORGE

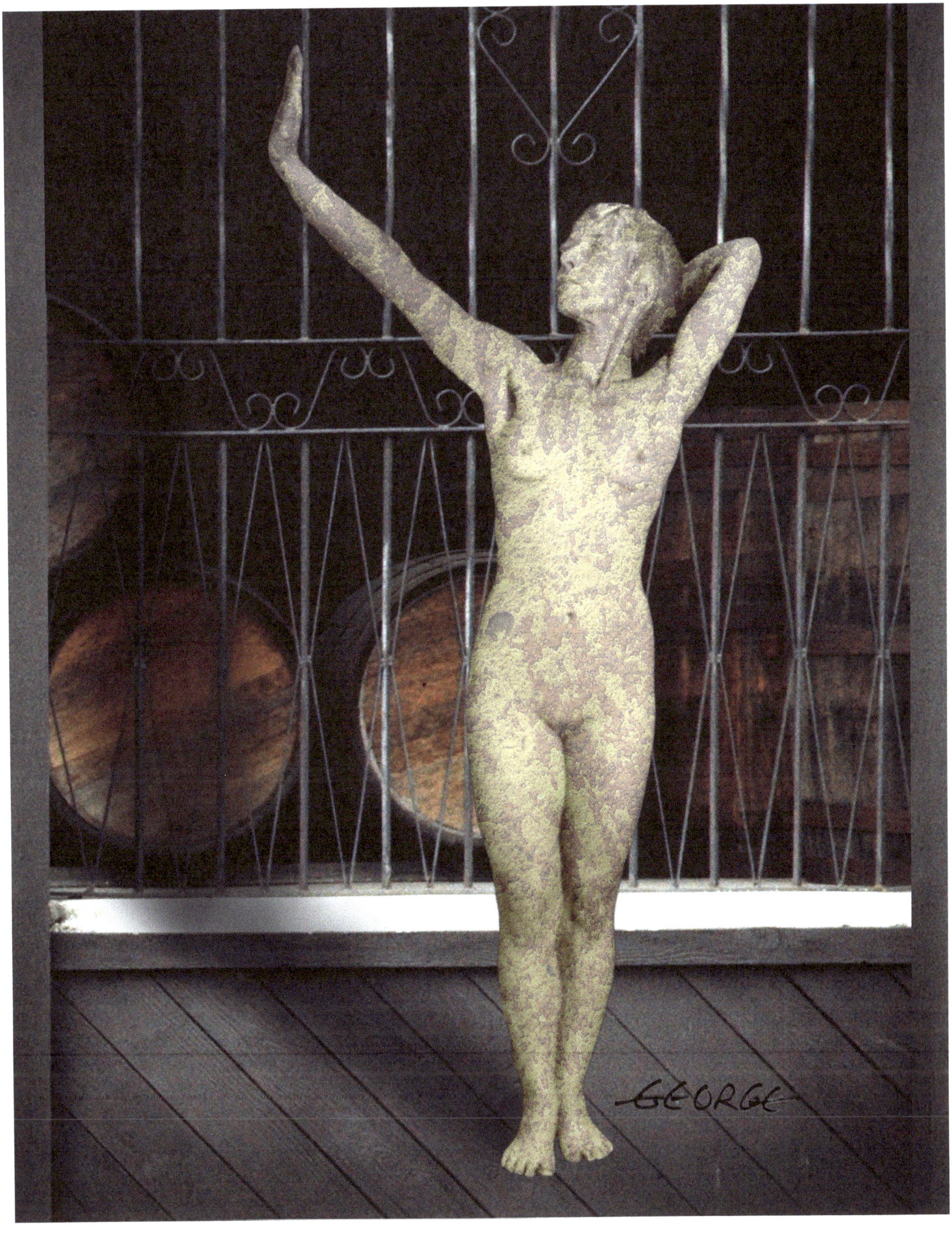
GEORGE

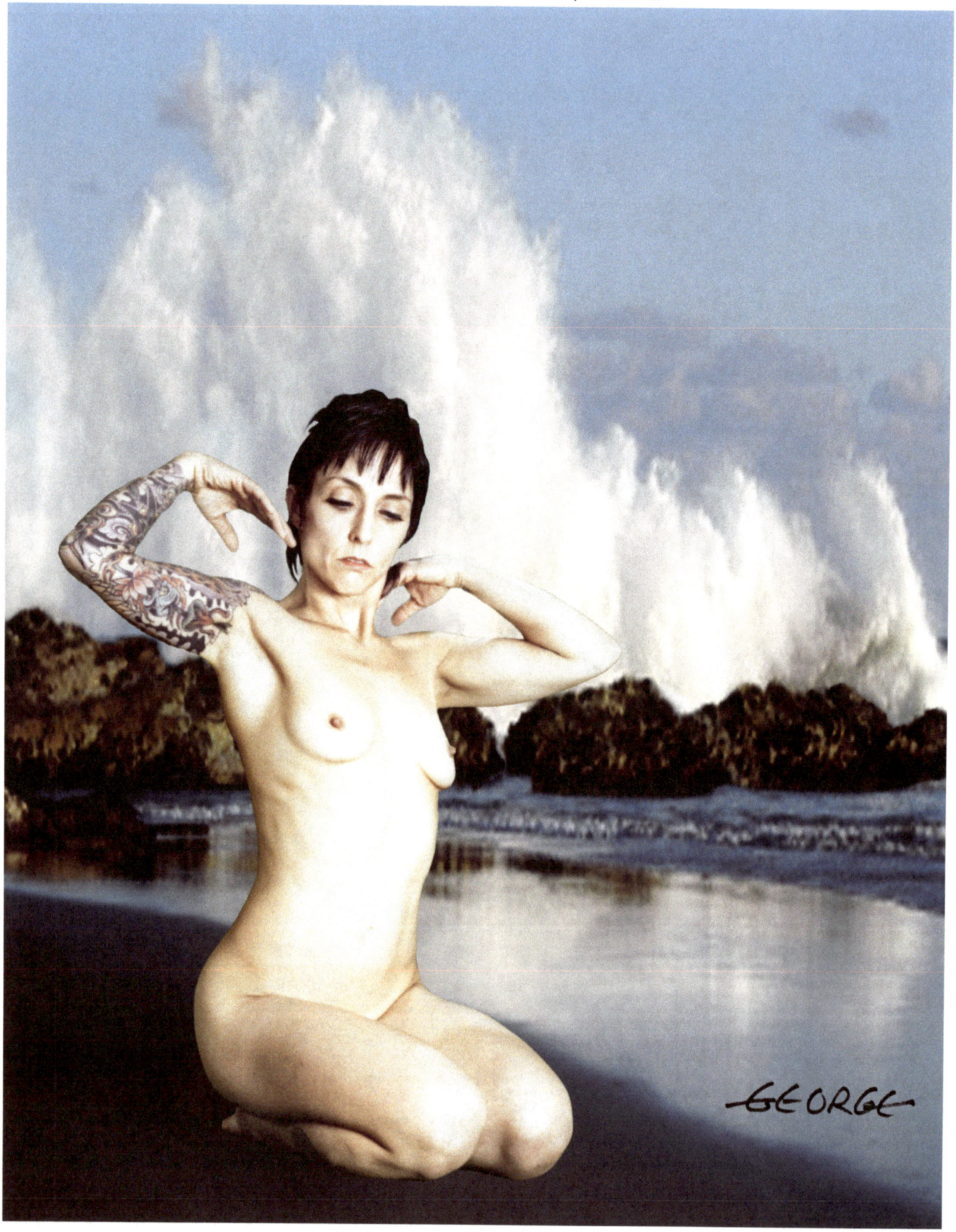
GEORGE

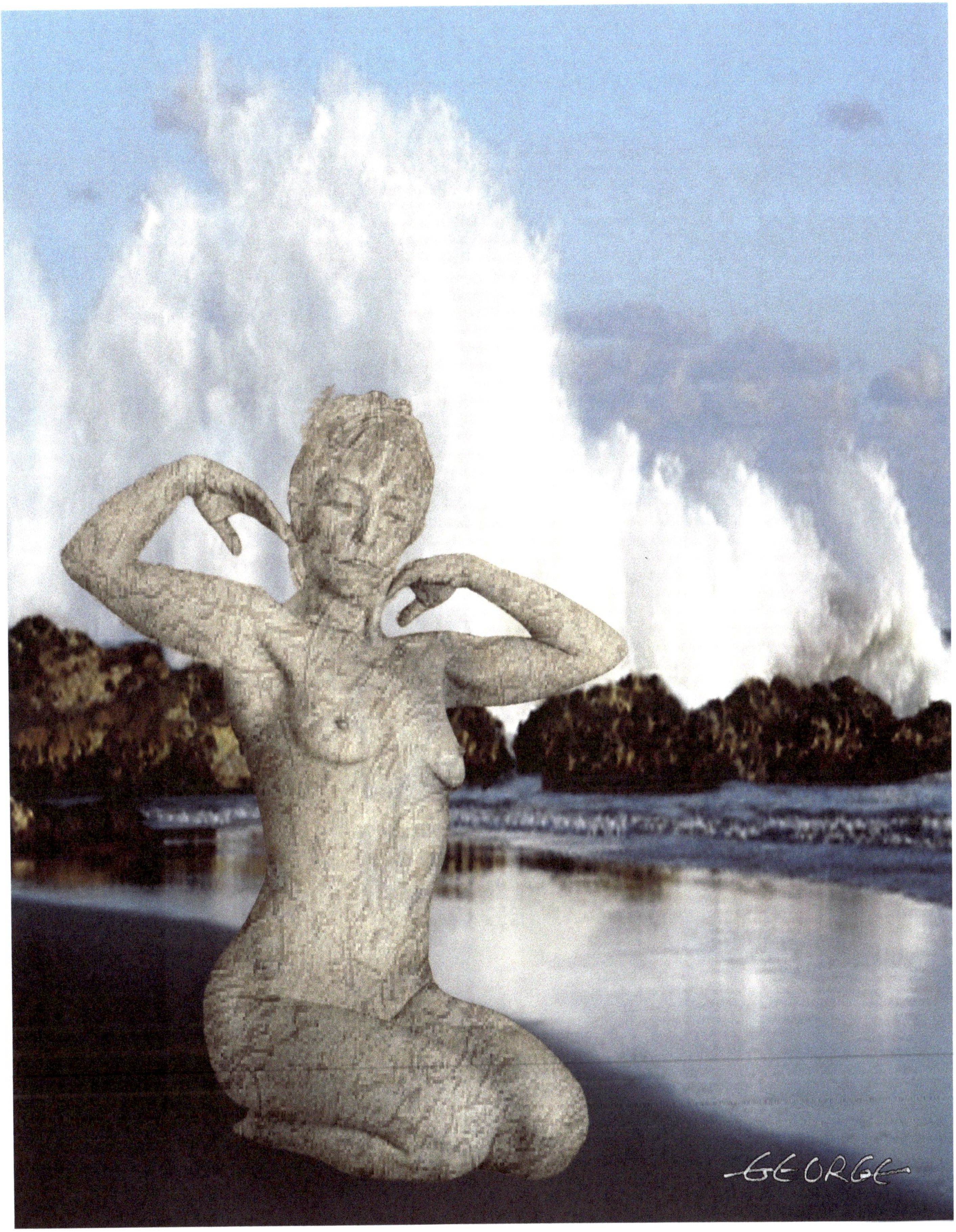
GEORGE

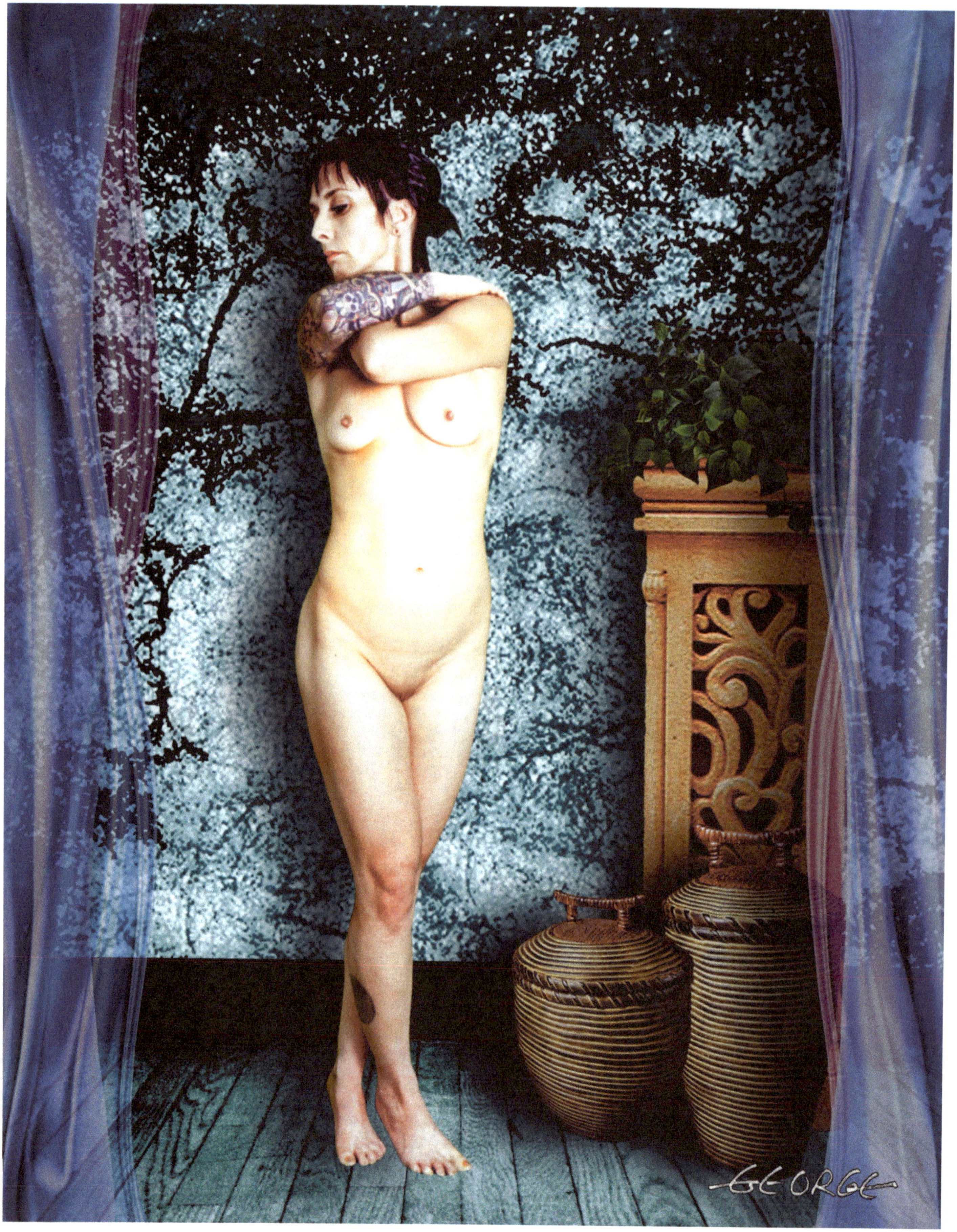
GEORGE

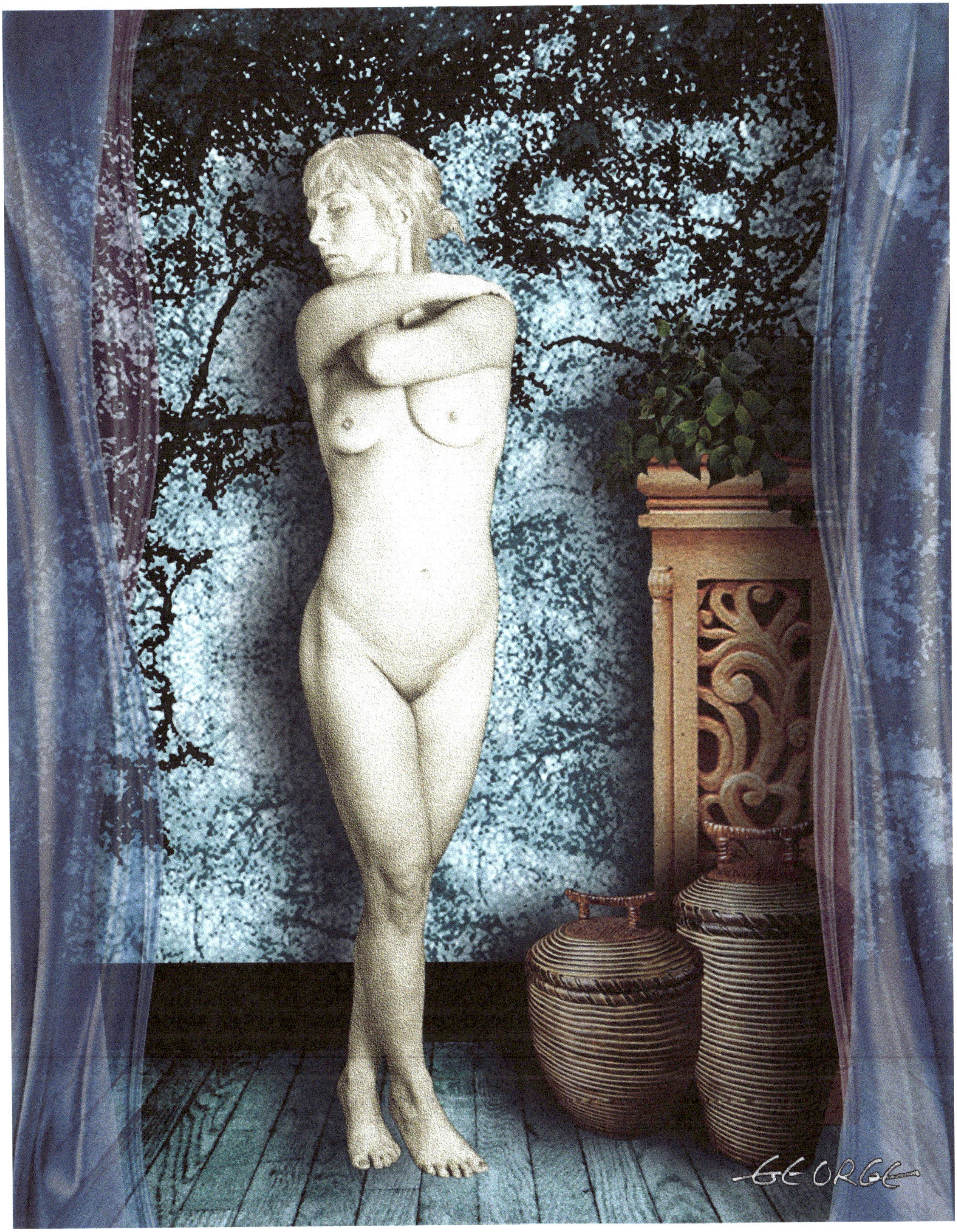
GEORGE

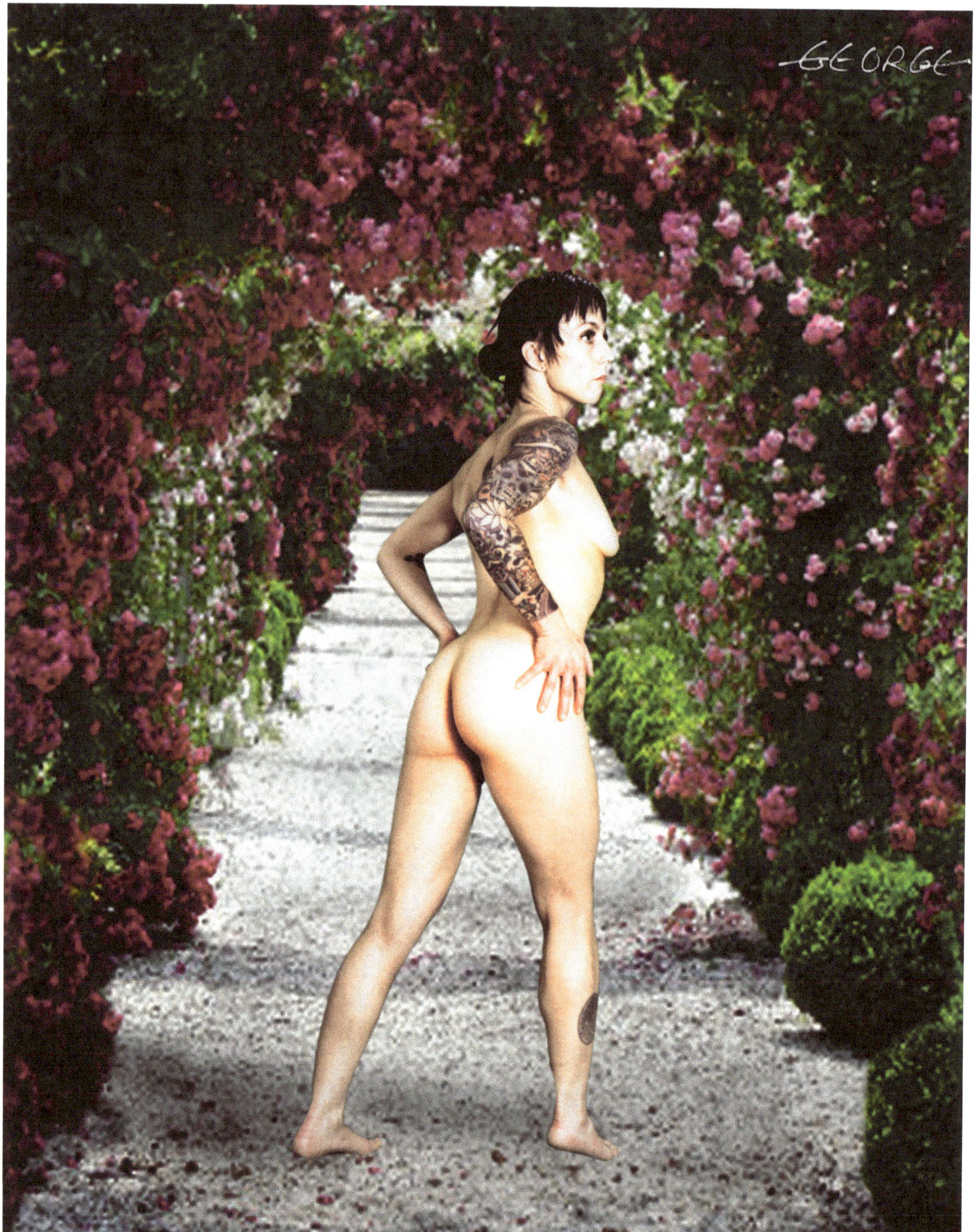
GEORGE

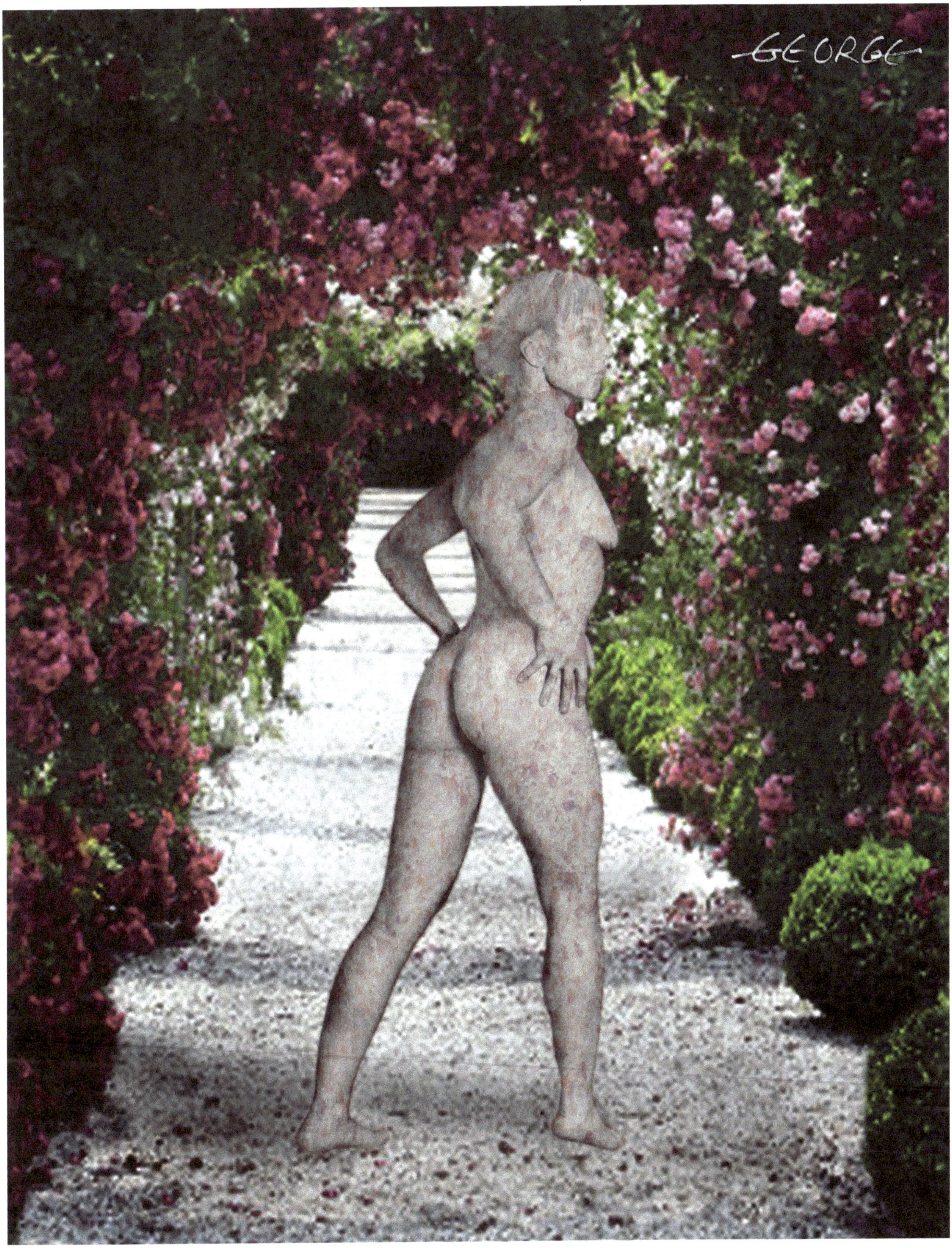
GEORGE

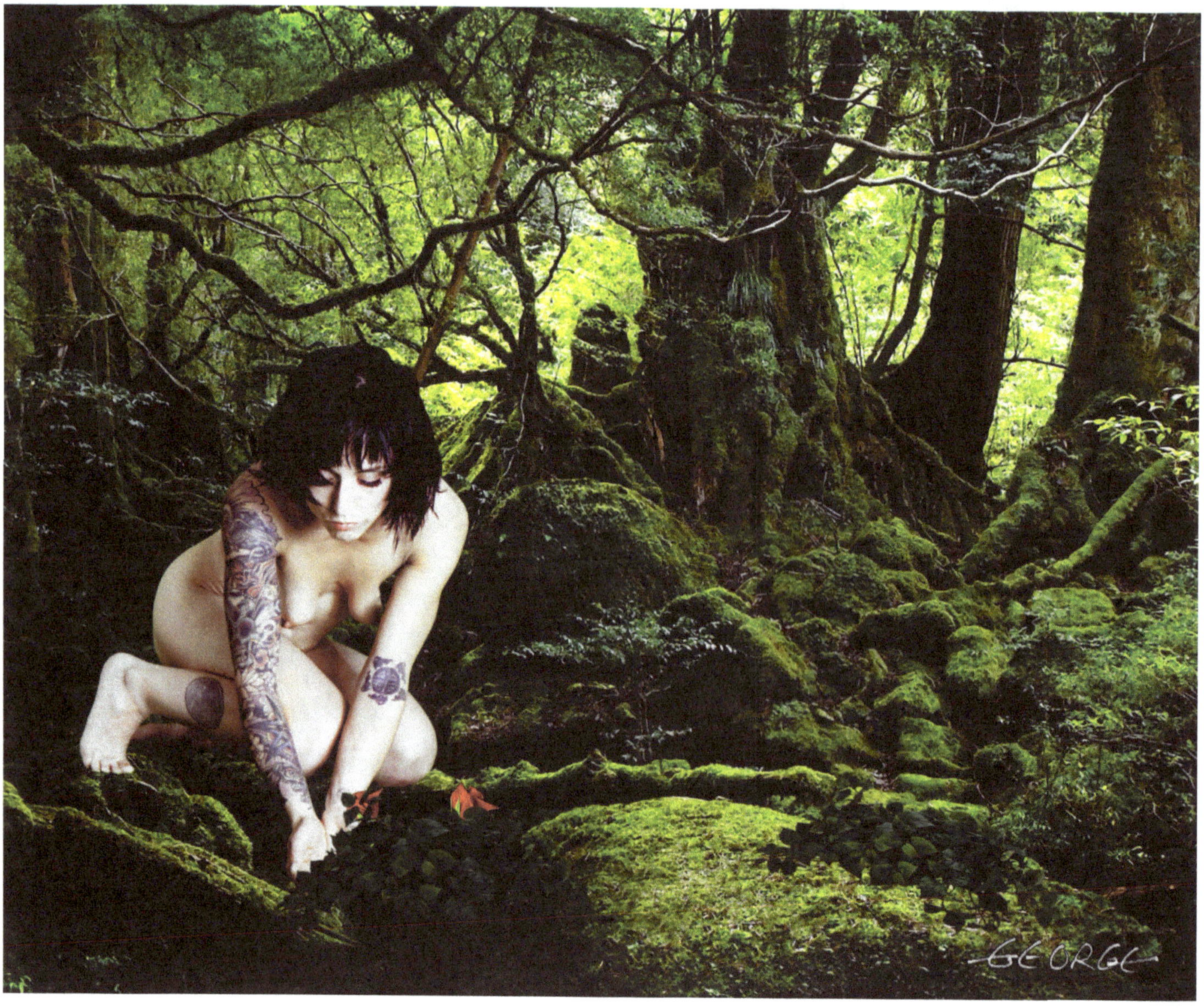
GEORGE

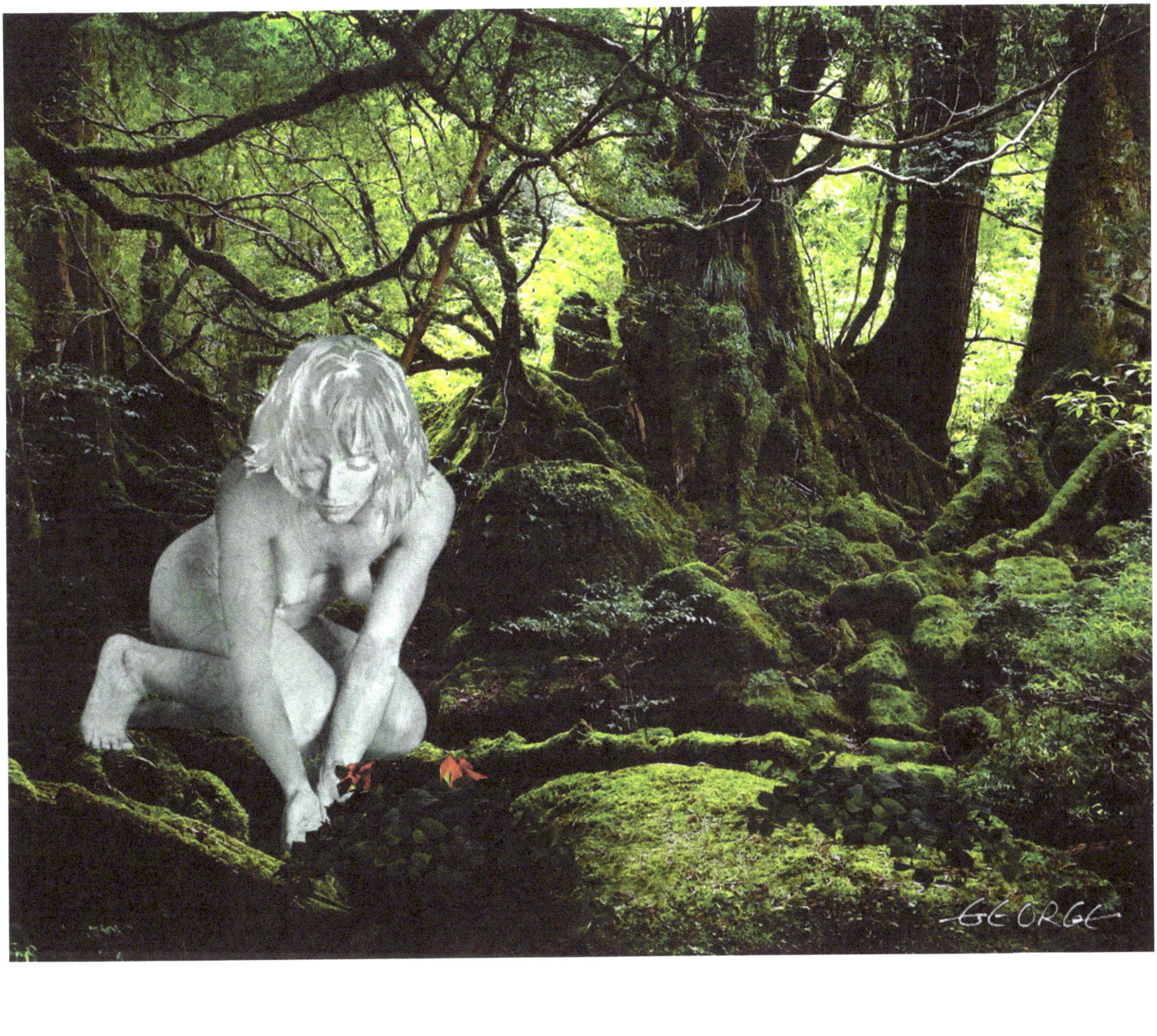
GEORGE

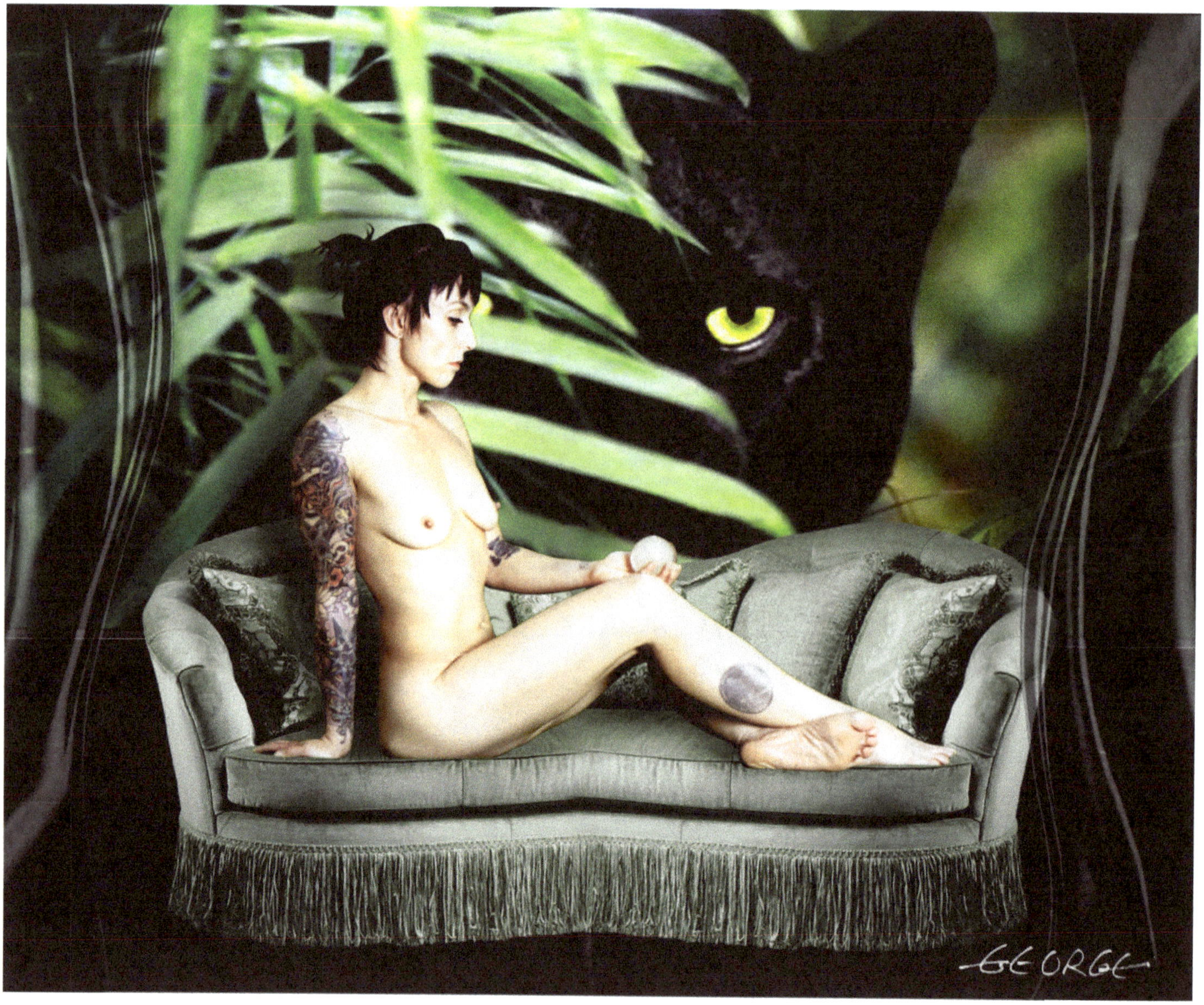
GEORGE

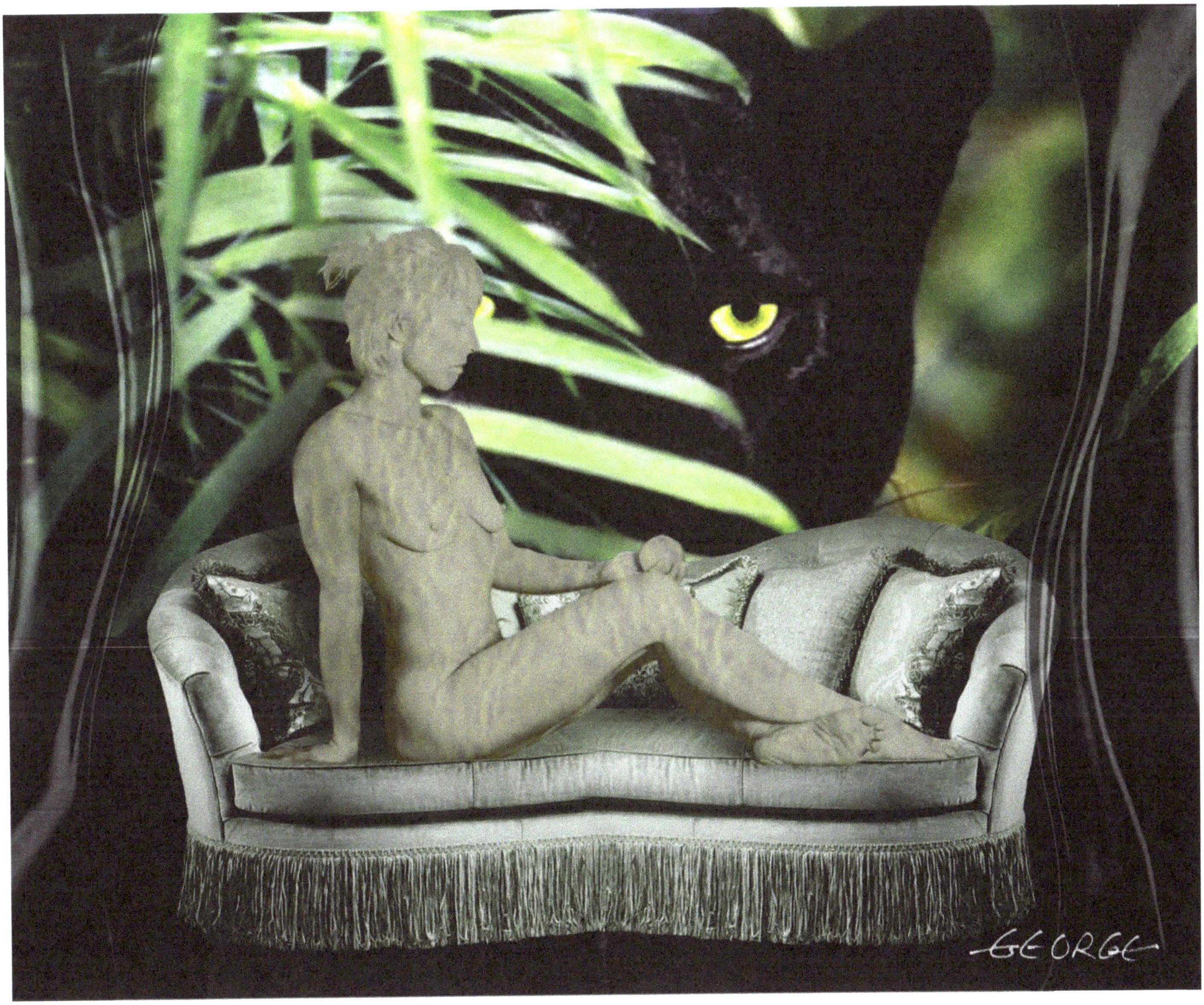
GEORGE

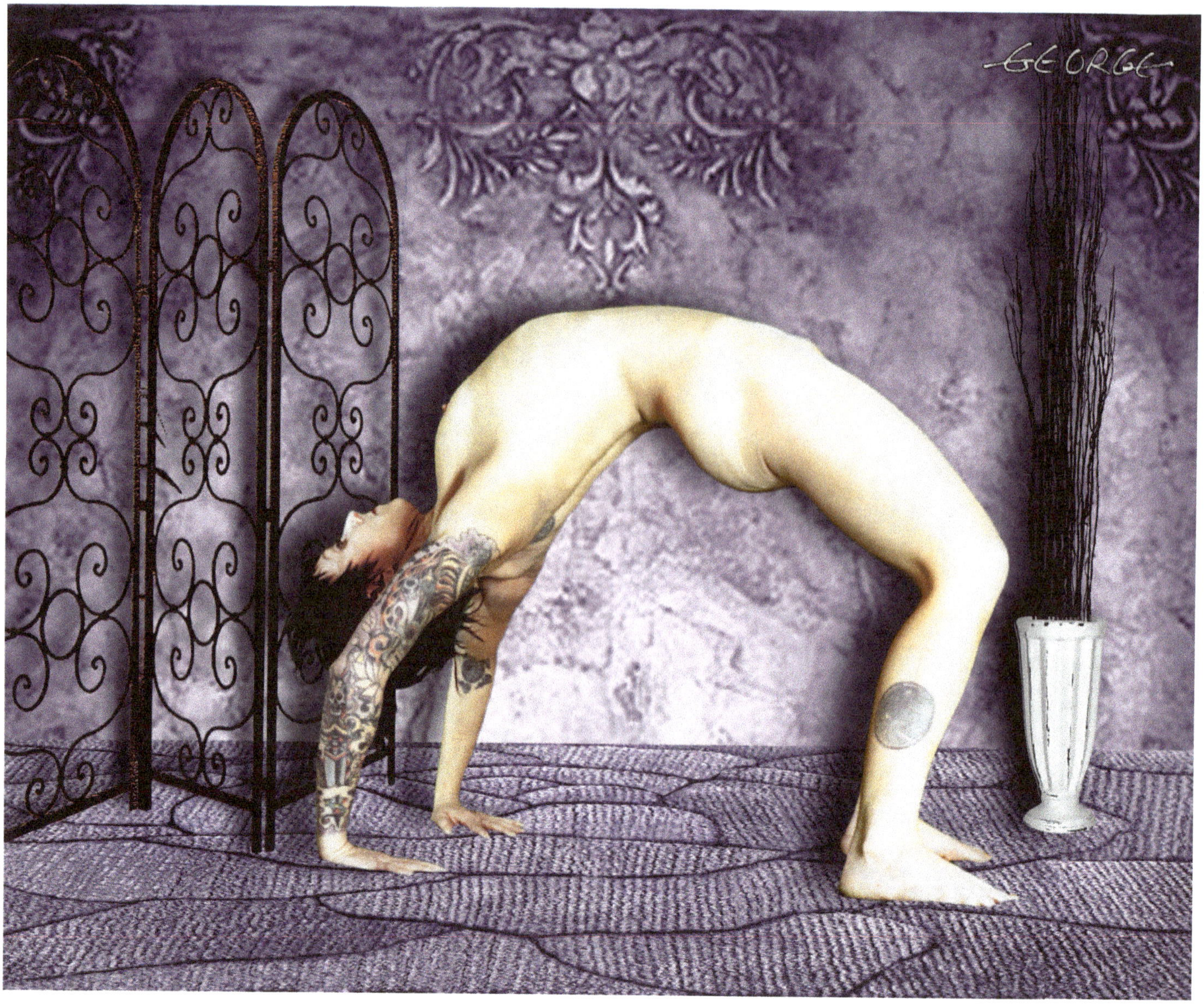
GEORGE

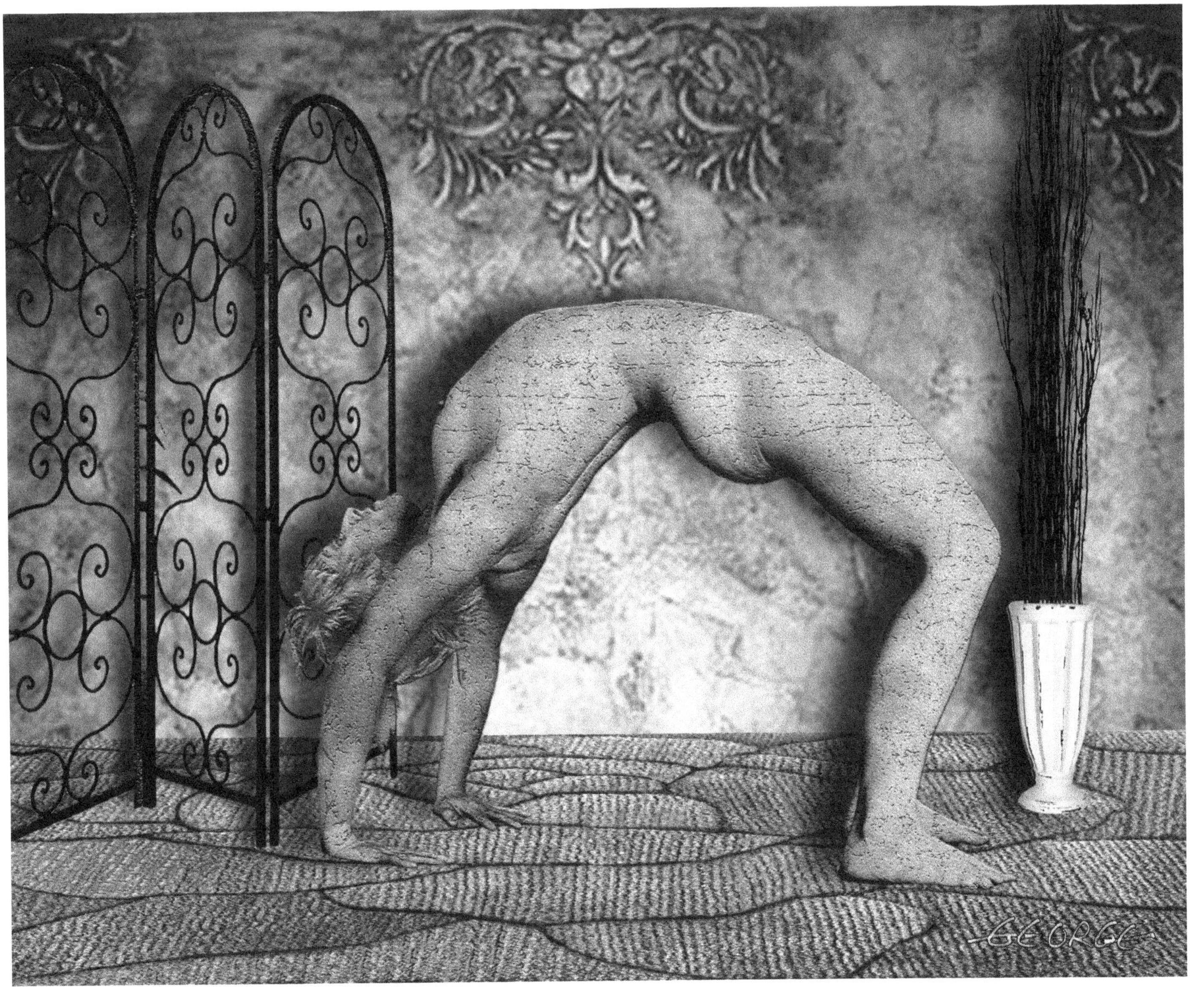
GEORGE

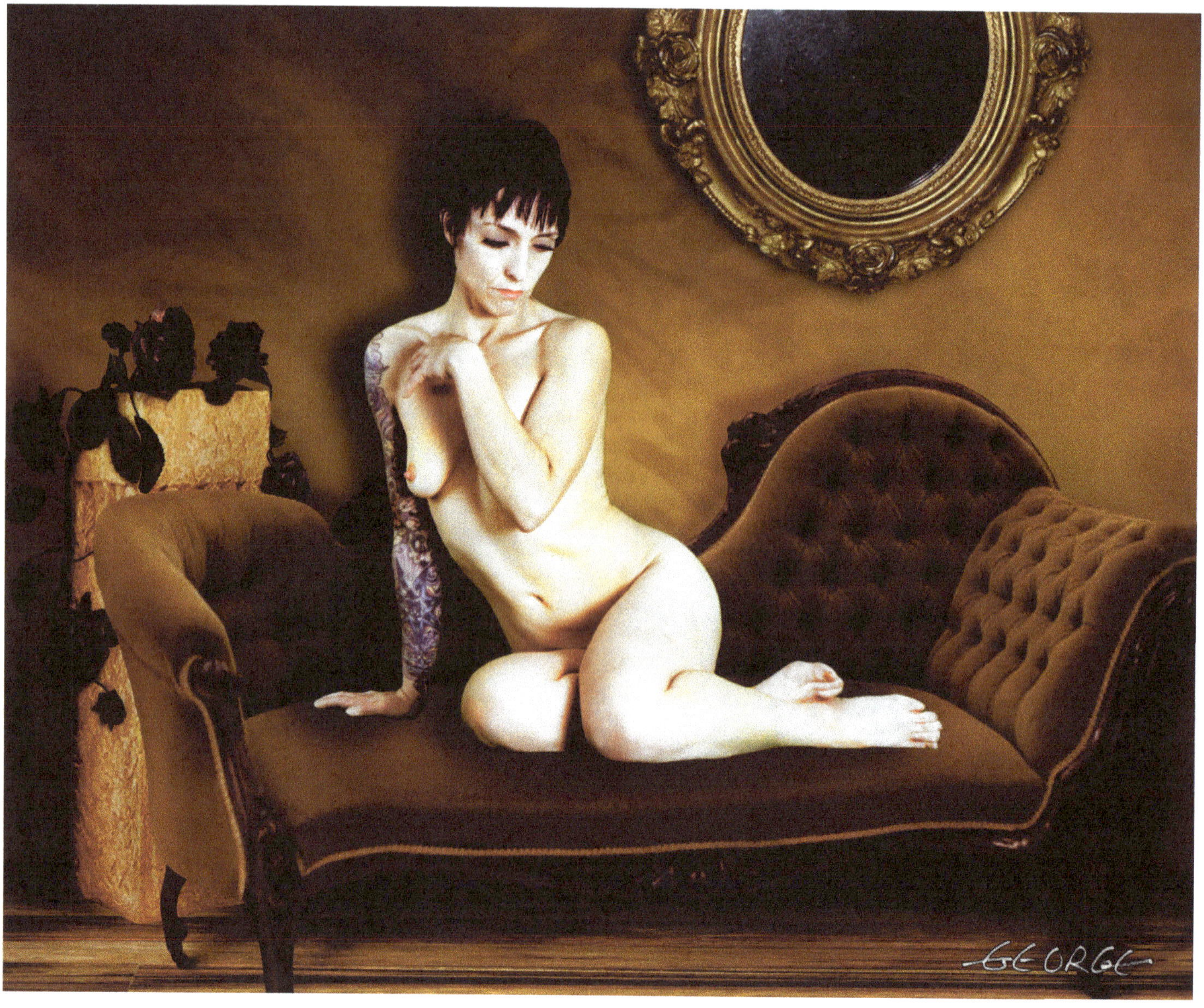
GEORGE

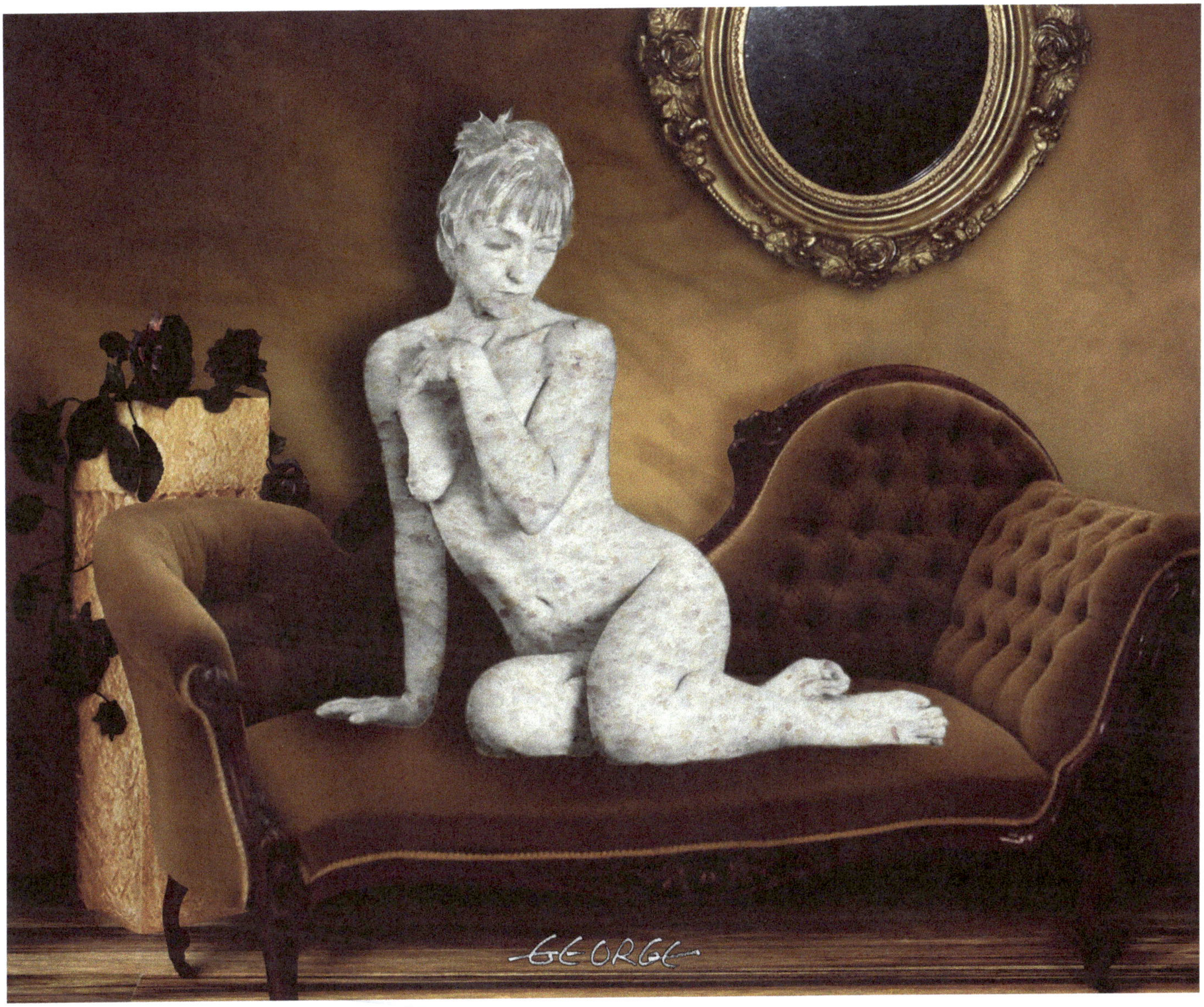
GEORGE

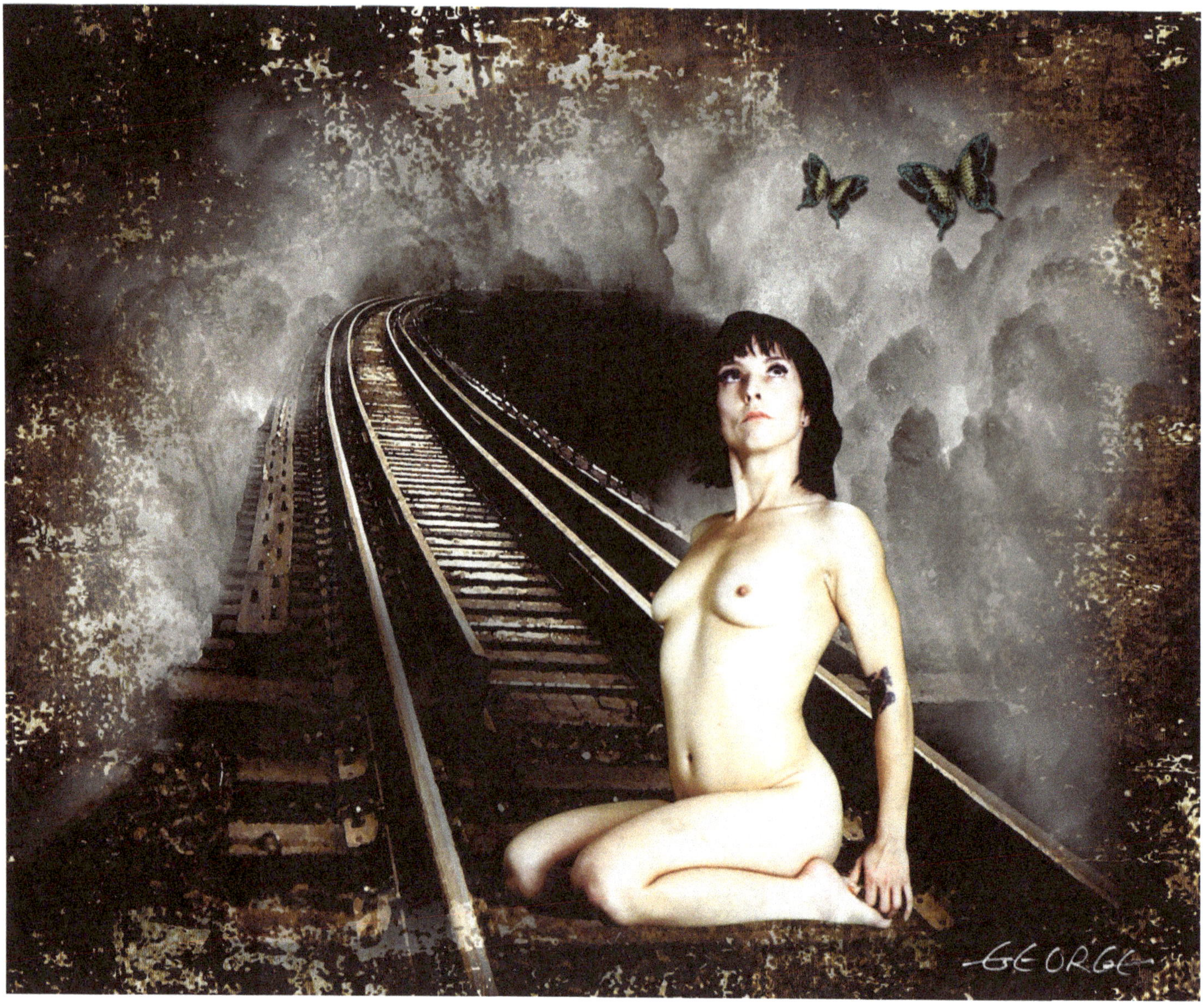
GEORGE

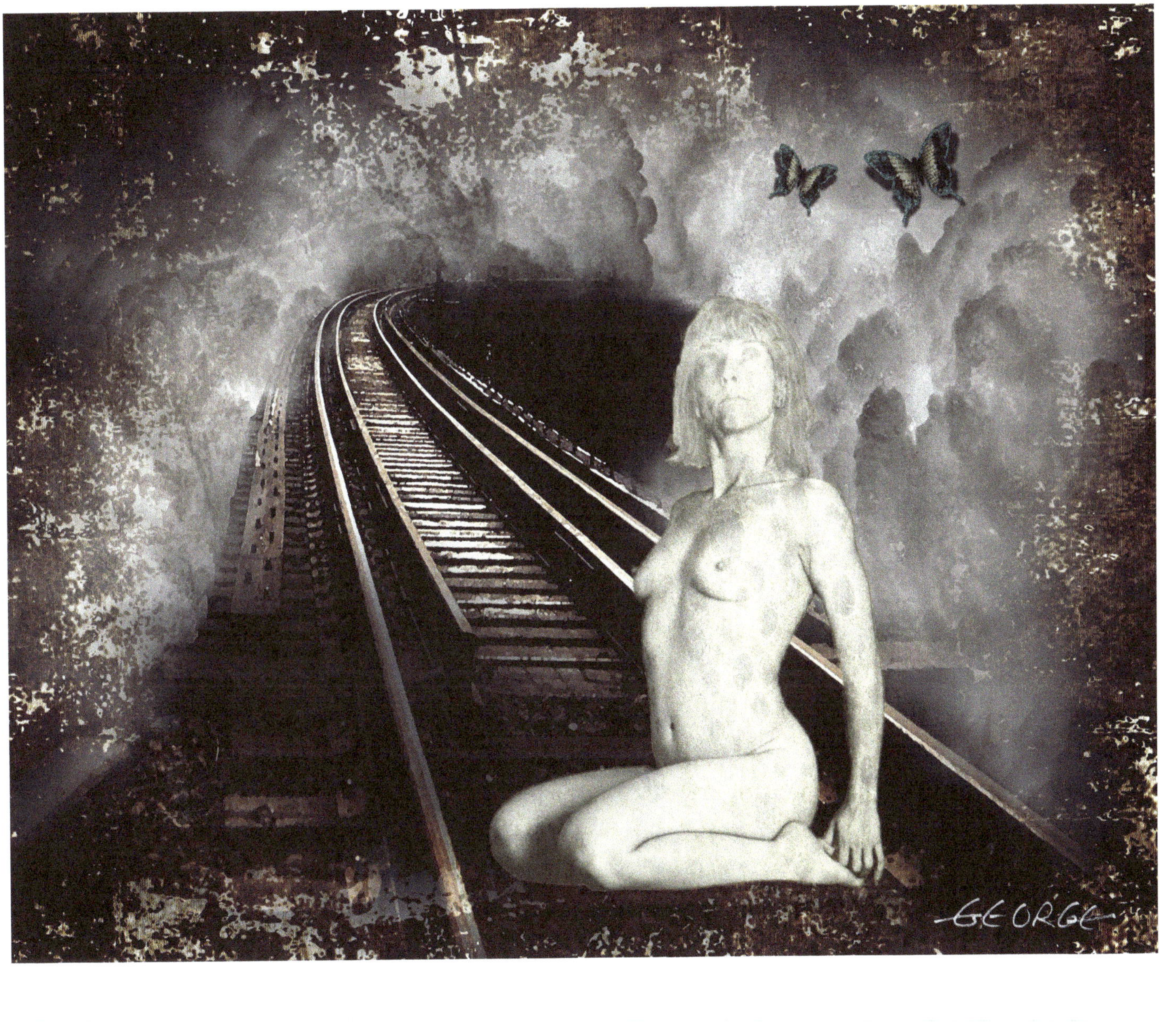
GEORGE

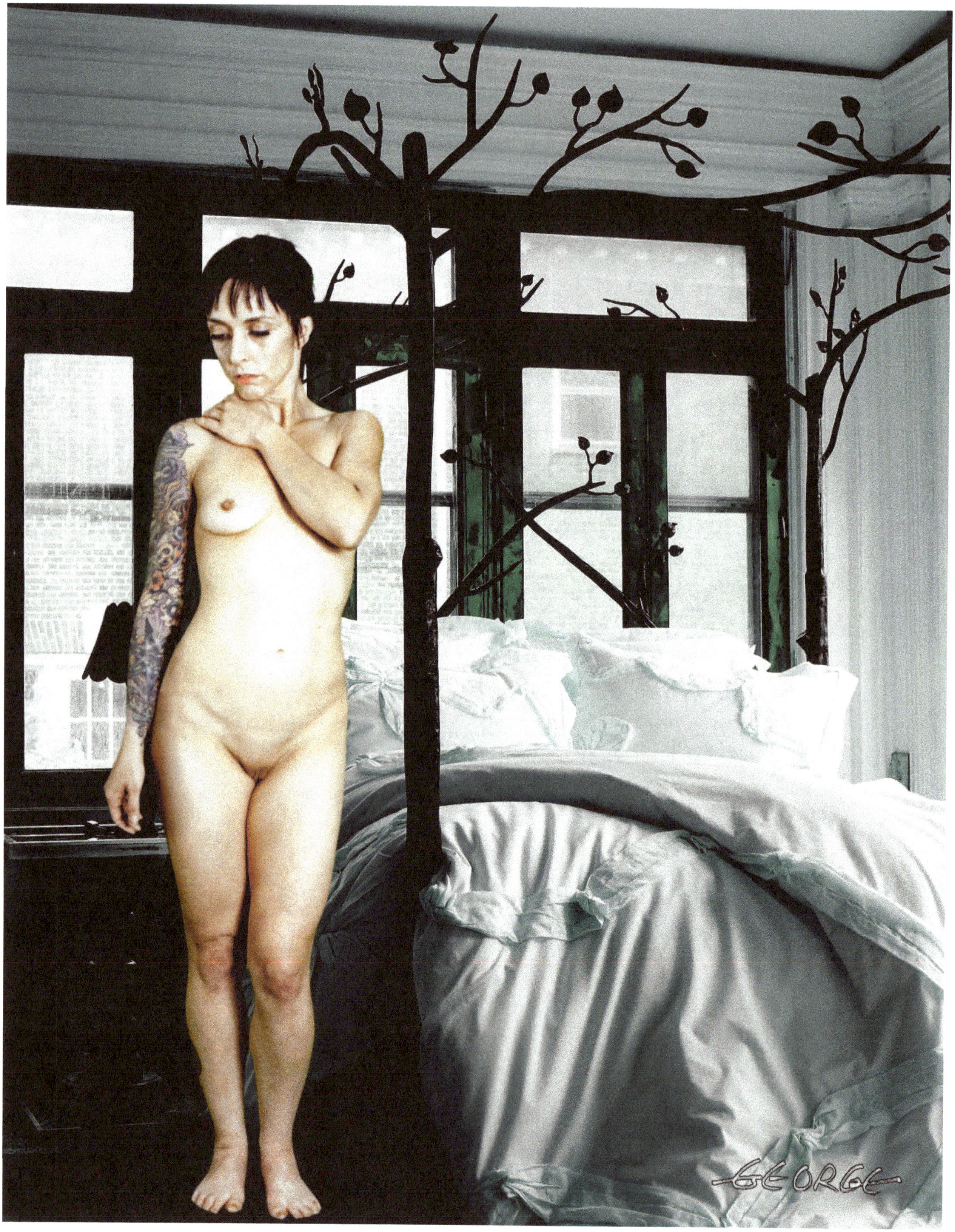
GEORGE

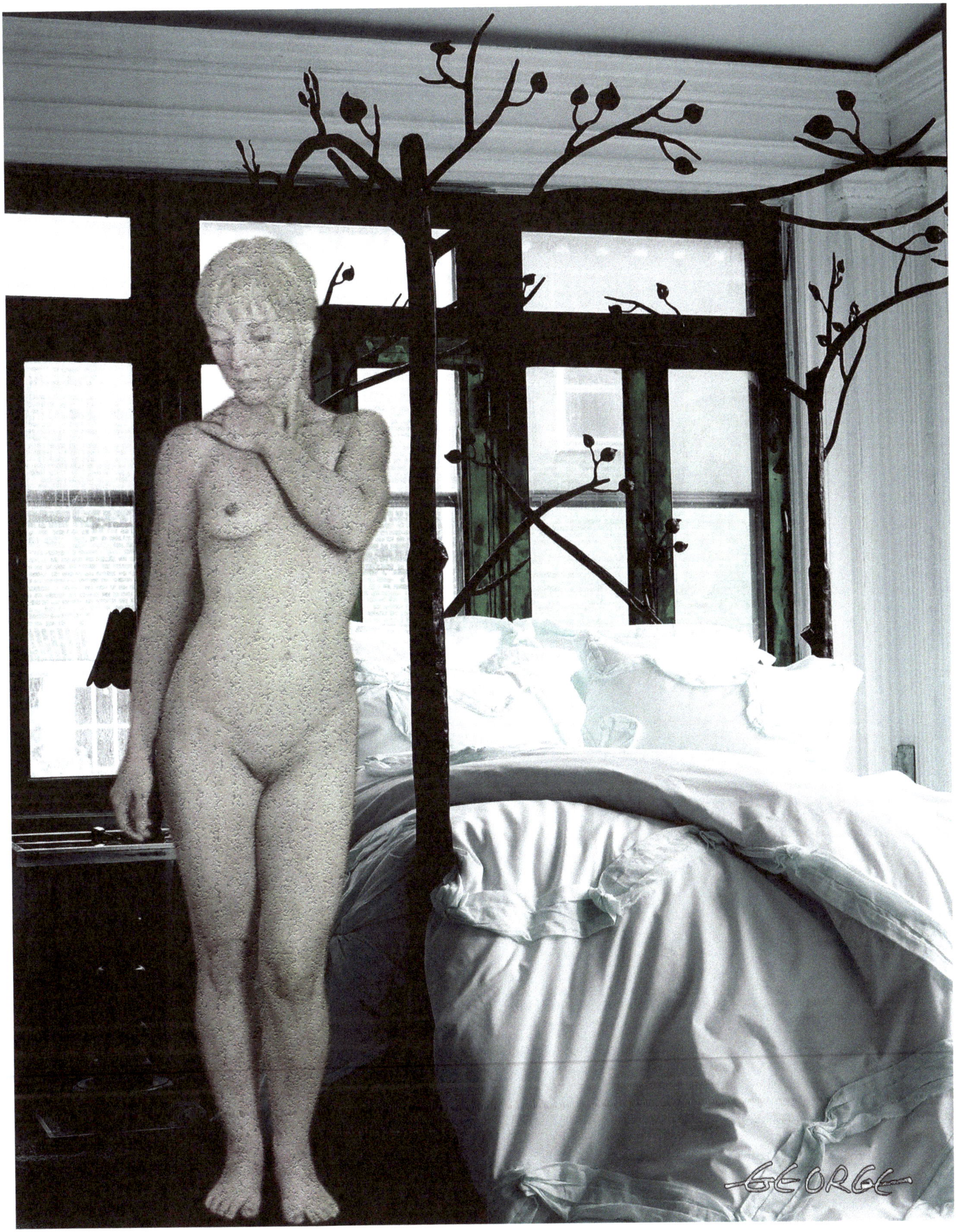
GEORGE

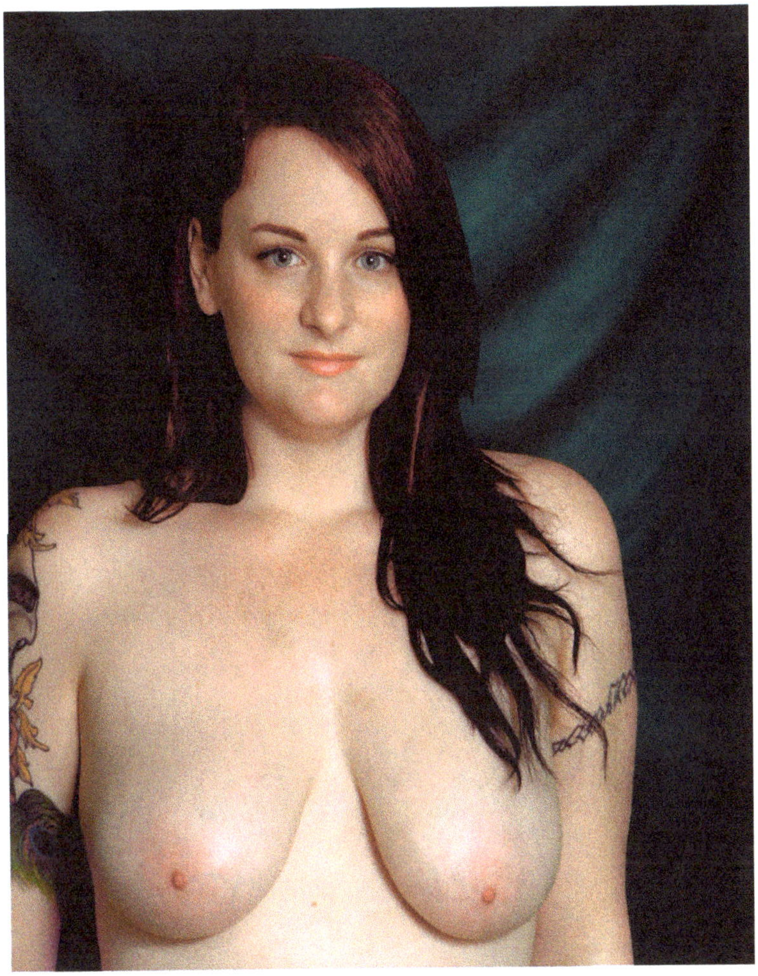

SCARLETT BLUE

Height 5'5" Weight 147 lbs Bust 36" Waist 32: Hips 39" Cup DDD

I am a curvy girl and I know how to make my curves work for me. I started with pin-up since I always had a vintage look. I grew up in the military, which had a big influence on wanting to do pin up. I'm always willing to do any kind of patriotic shoot or anything military related.

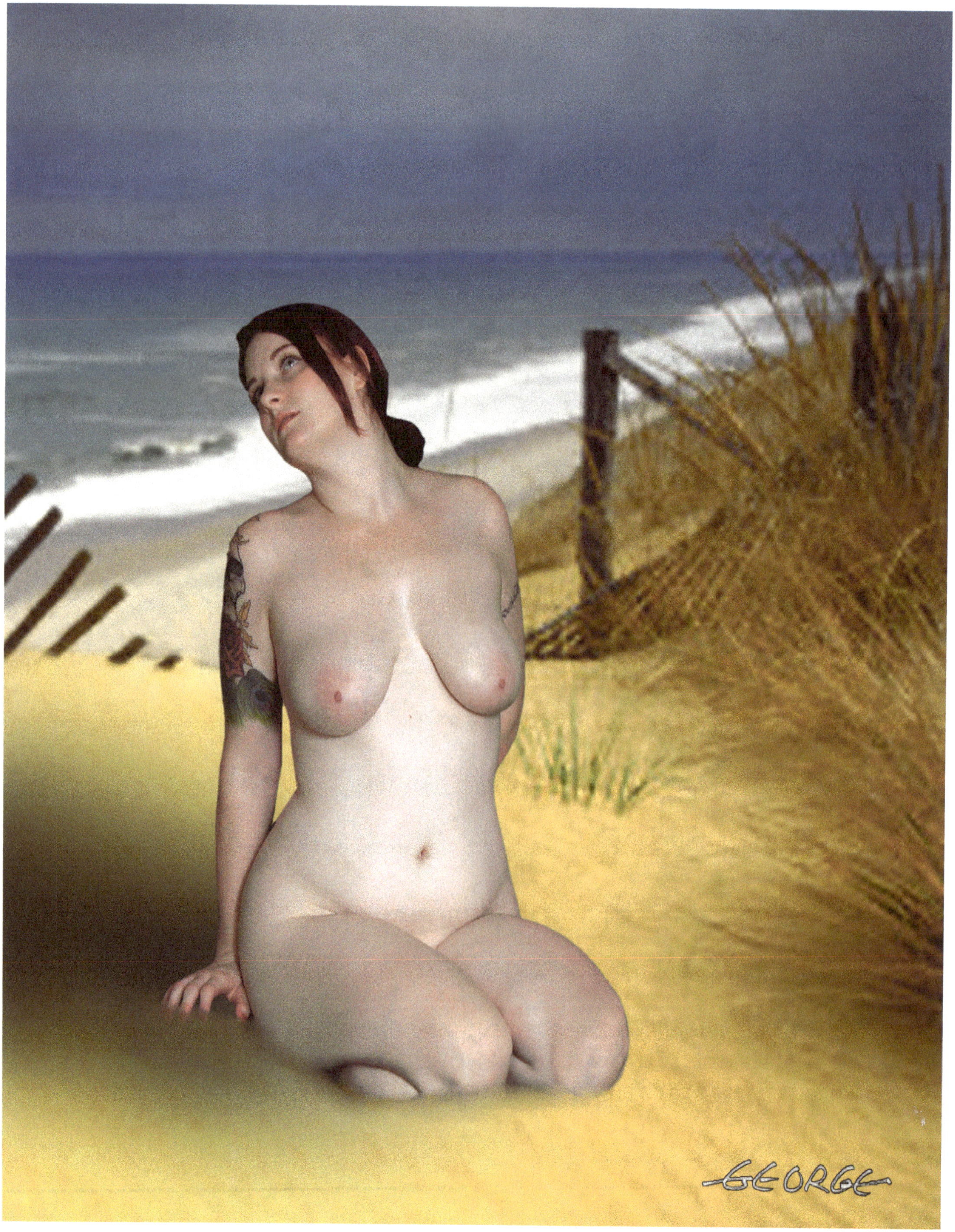
GEORGE

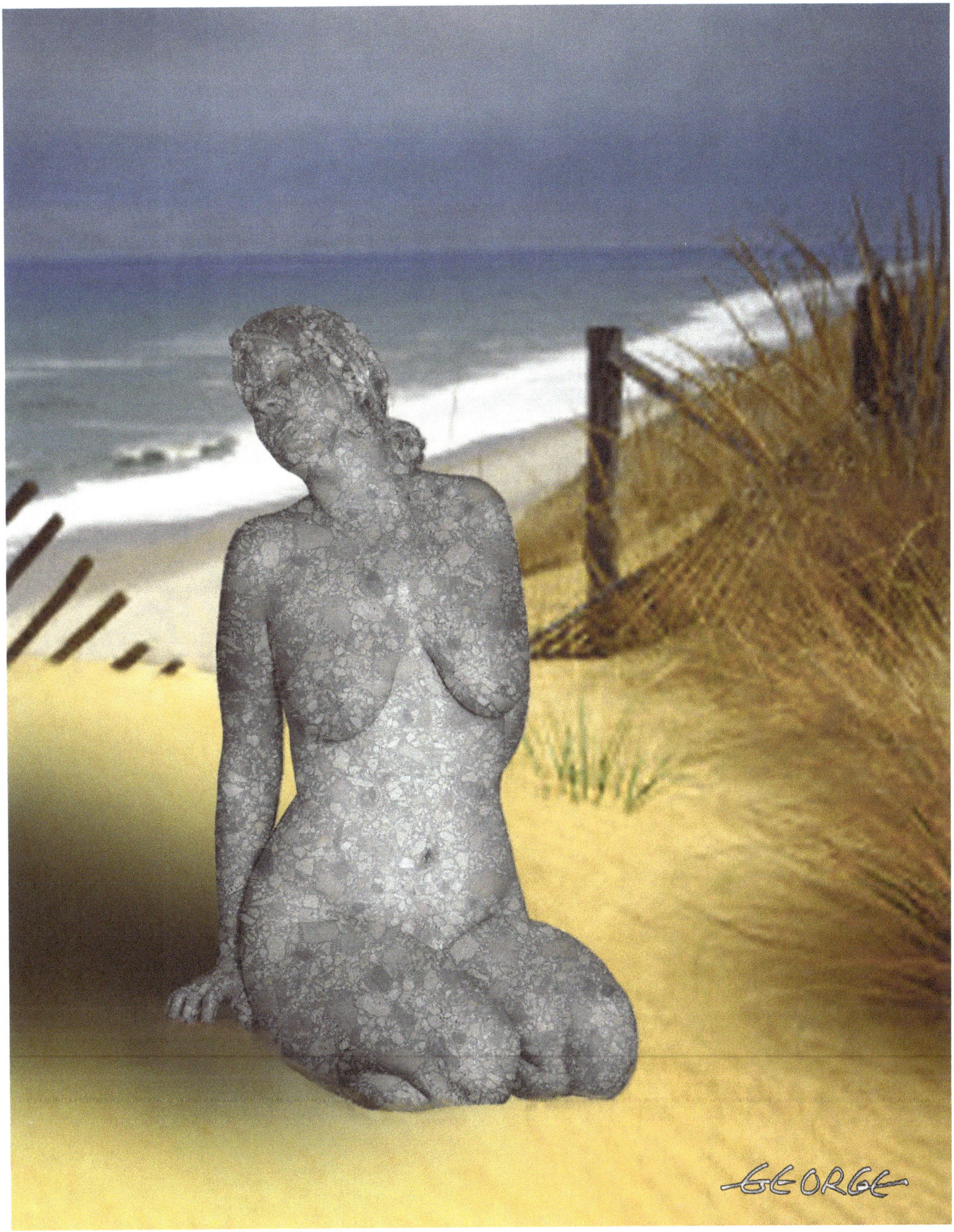
GEORGE

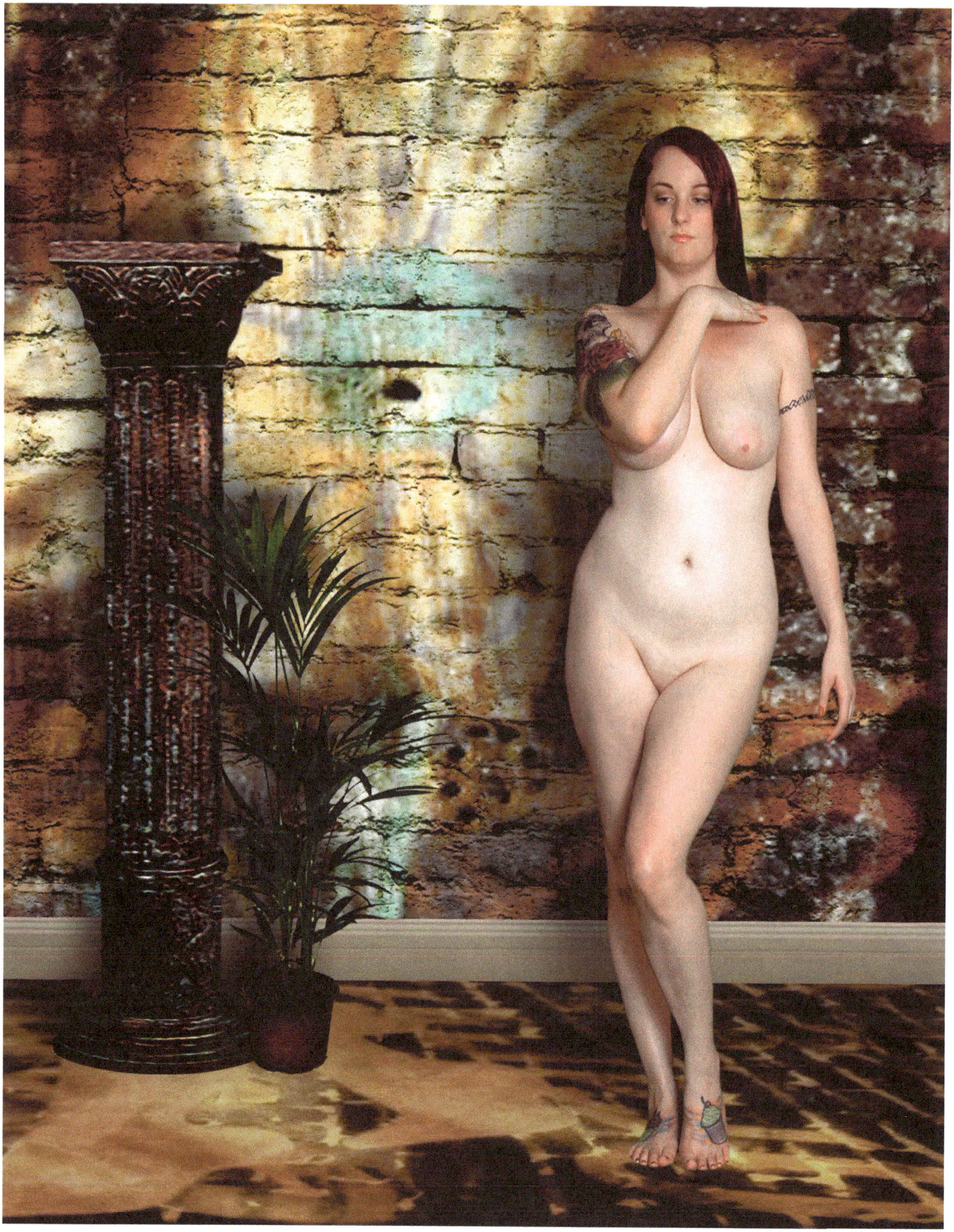

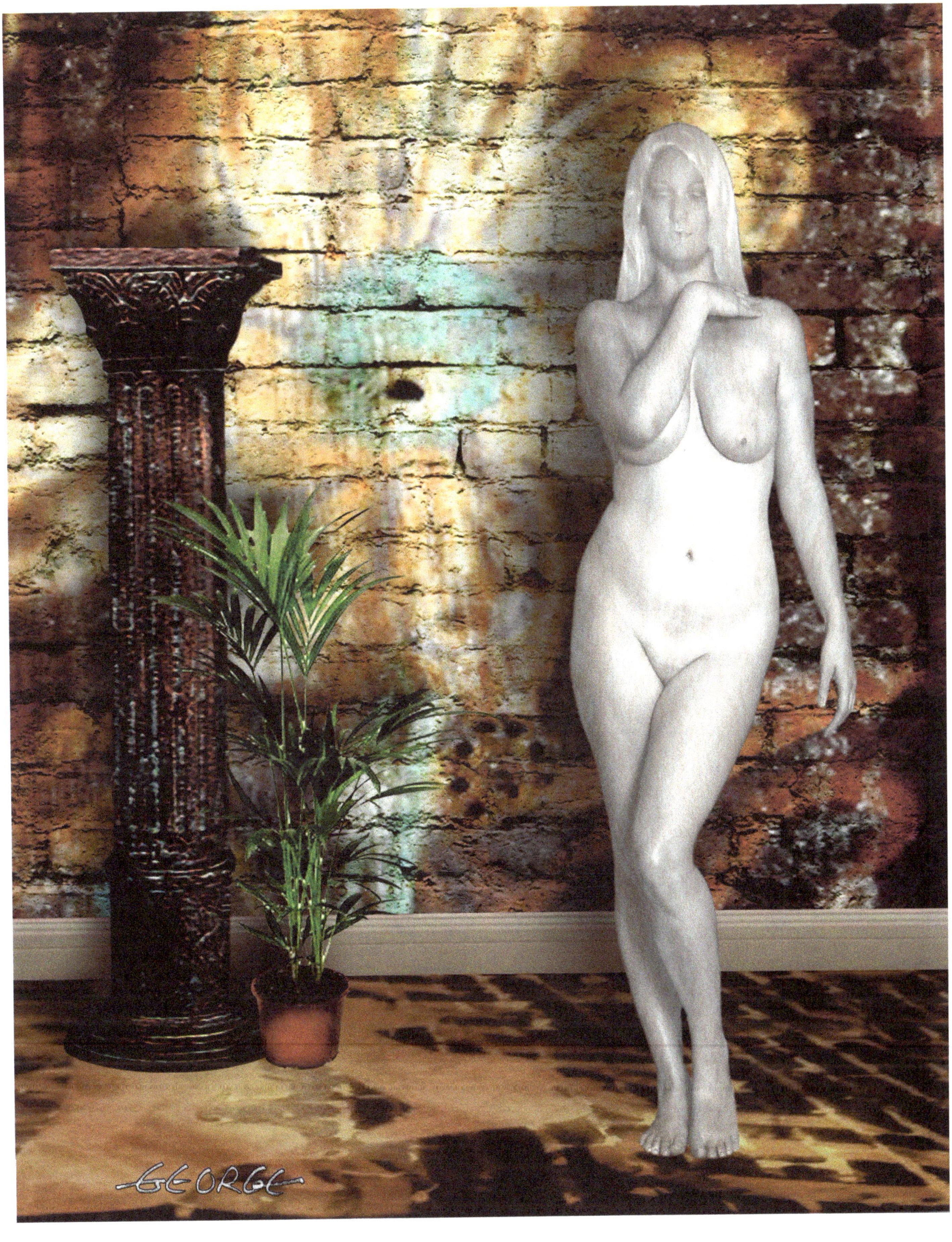
GEORGE

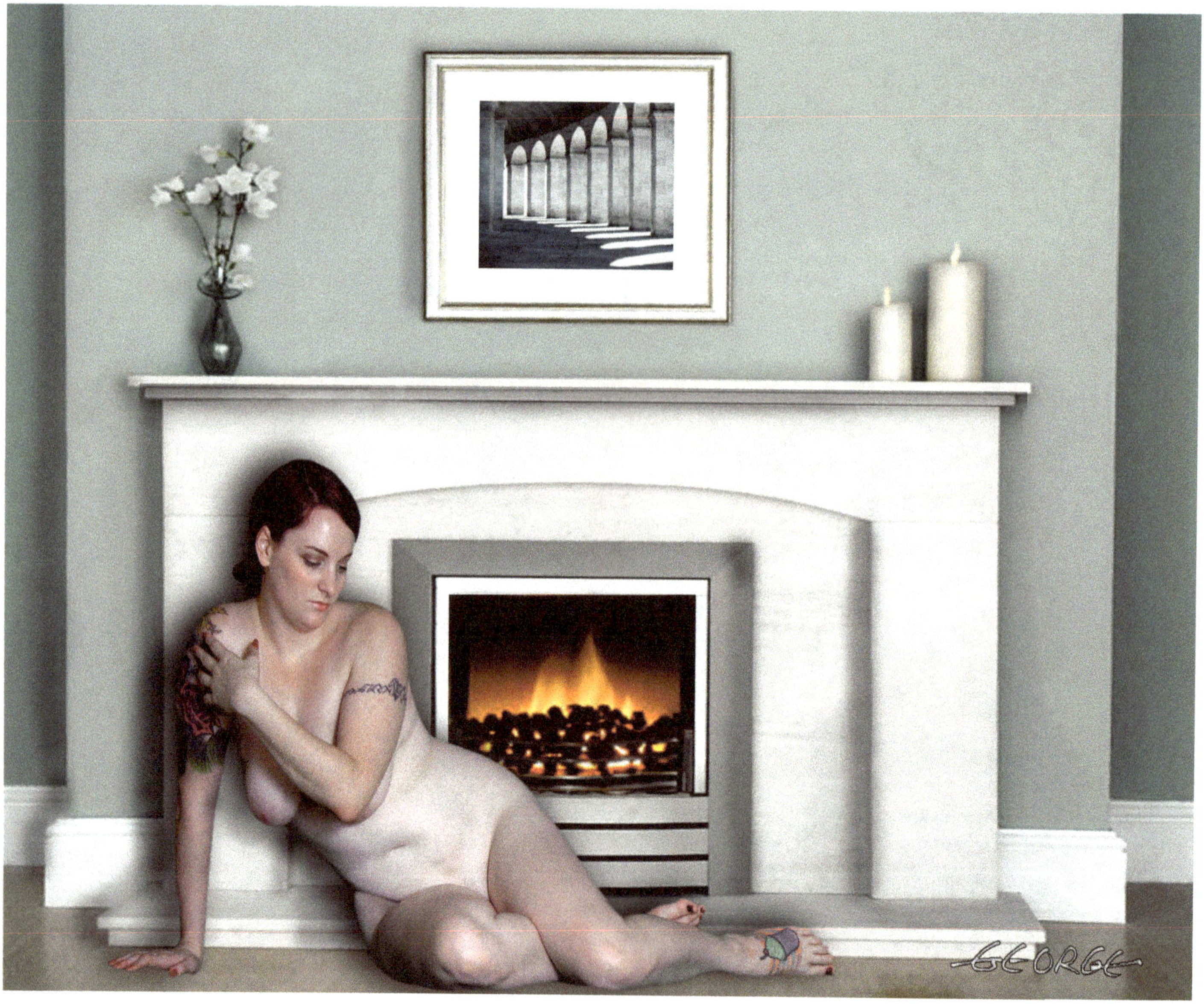
GEORGE

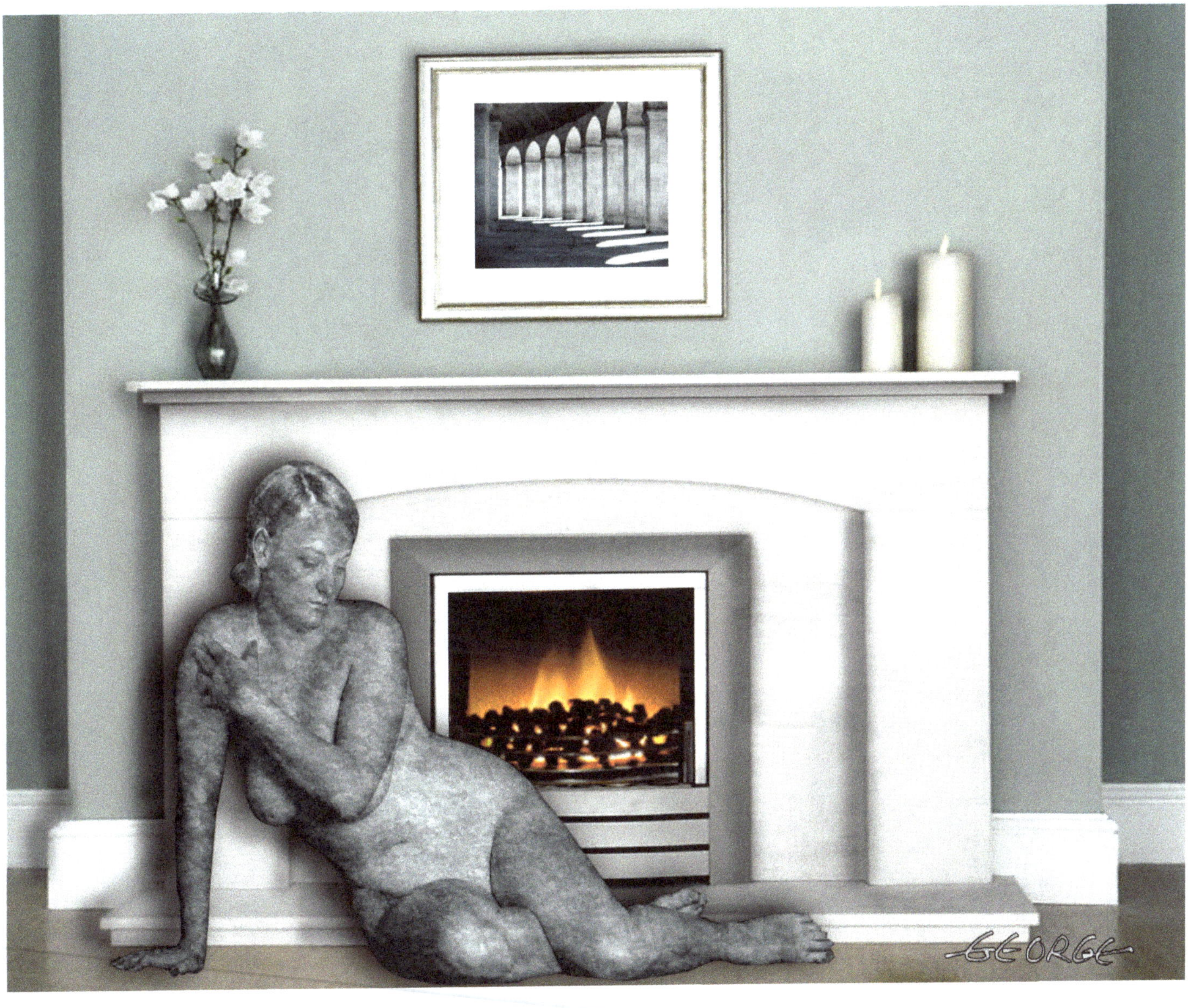
GEORGE

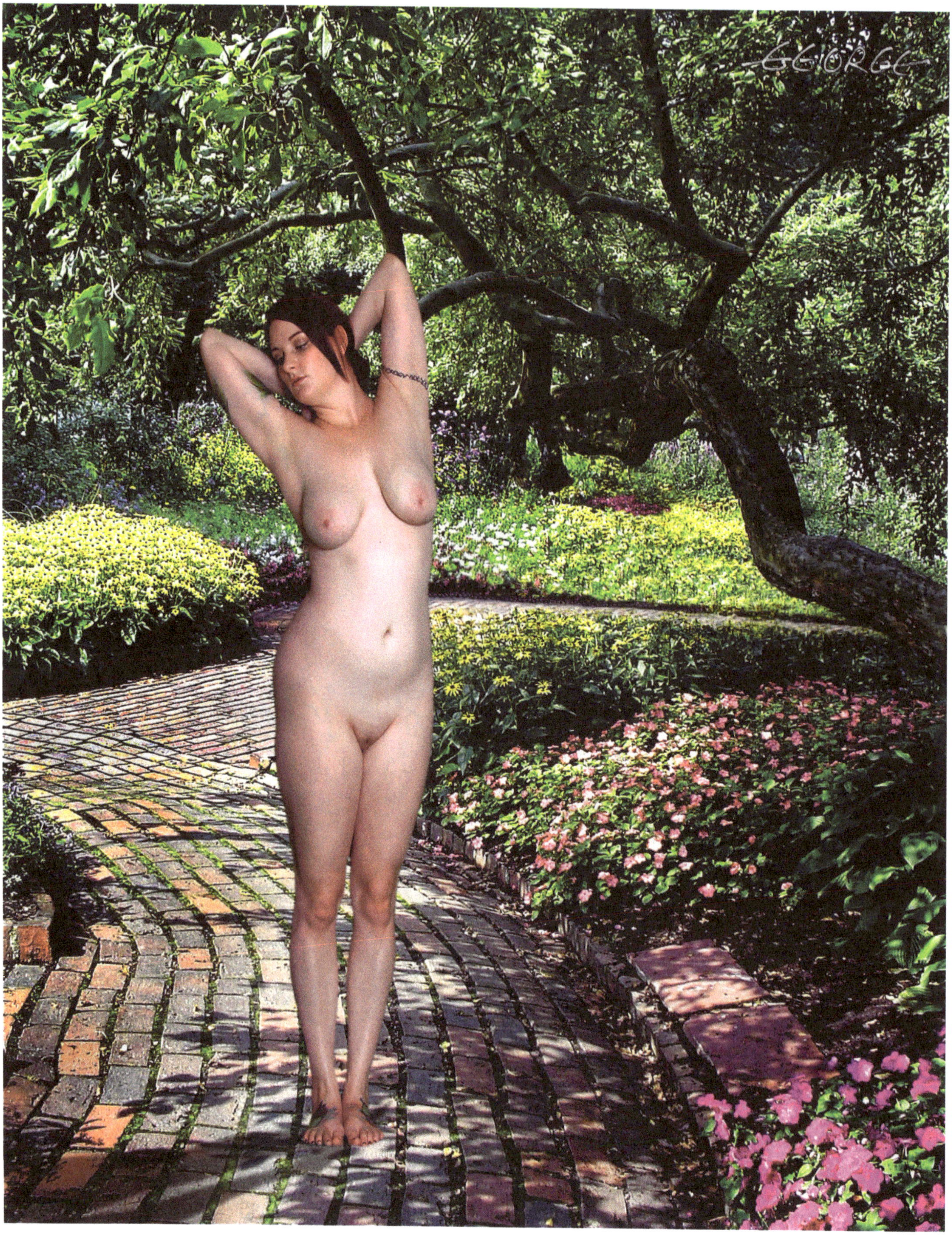
GEORGE

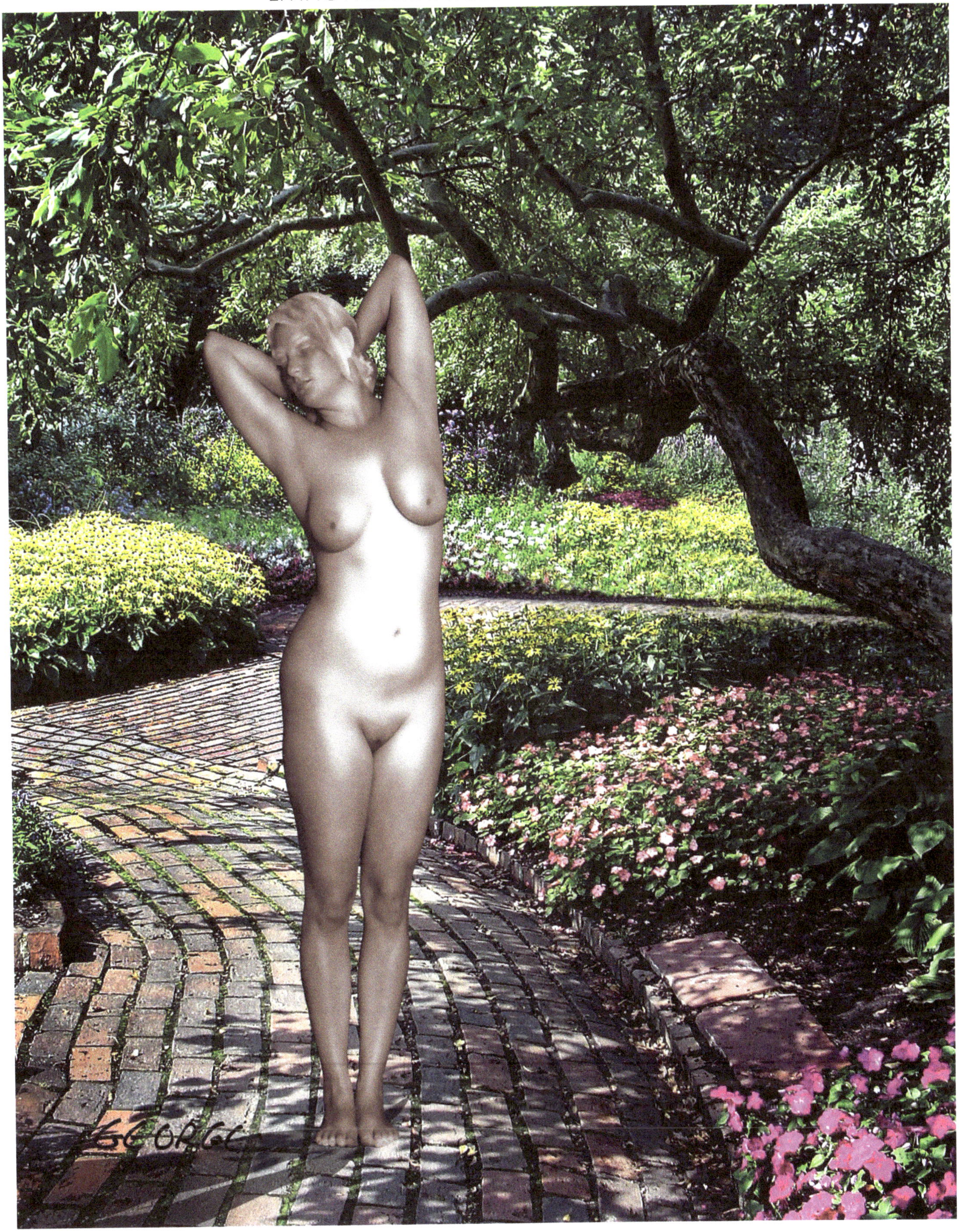
GEORGE

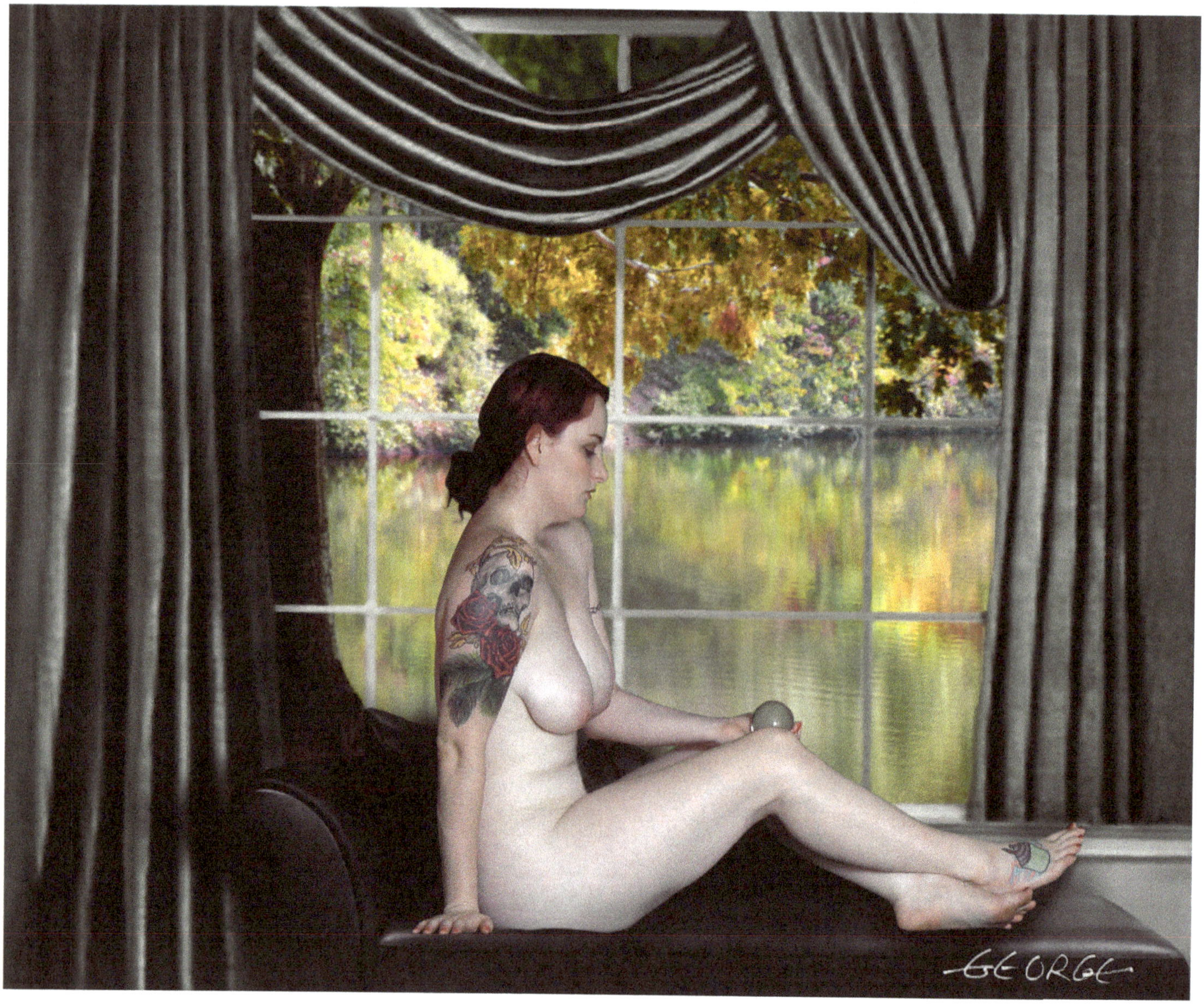
GEORGE

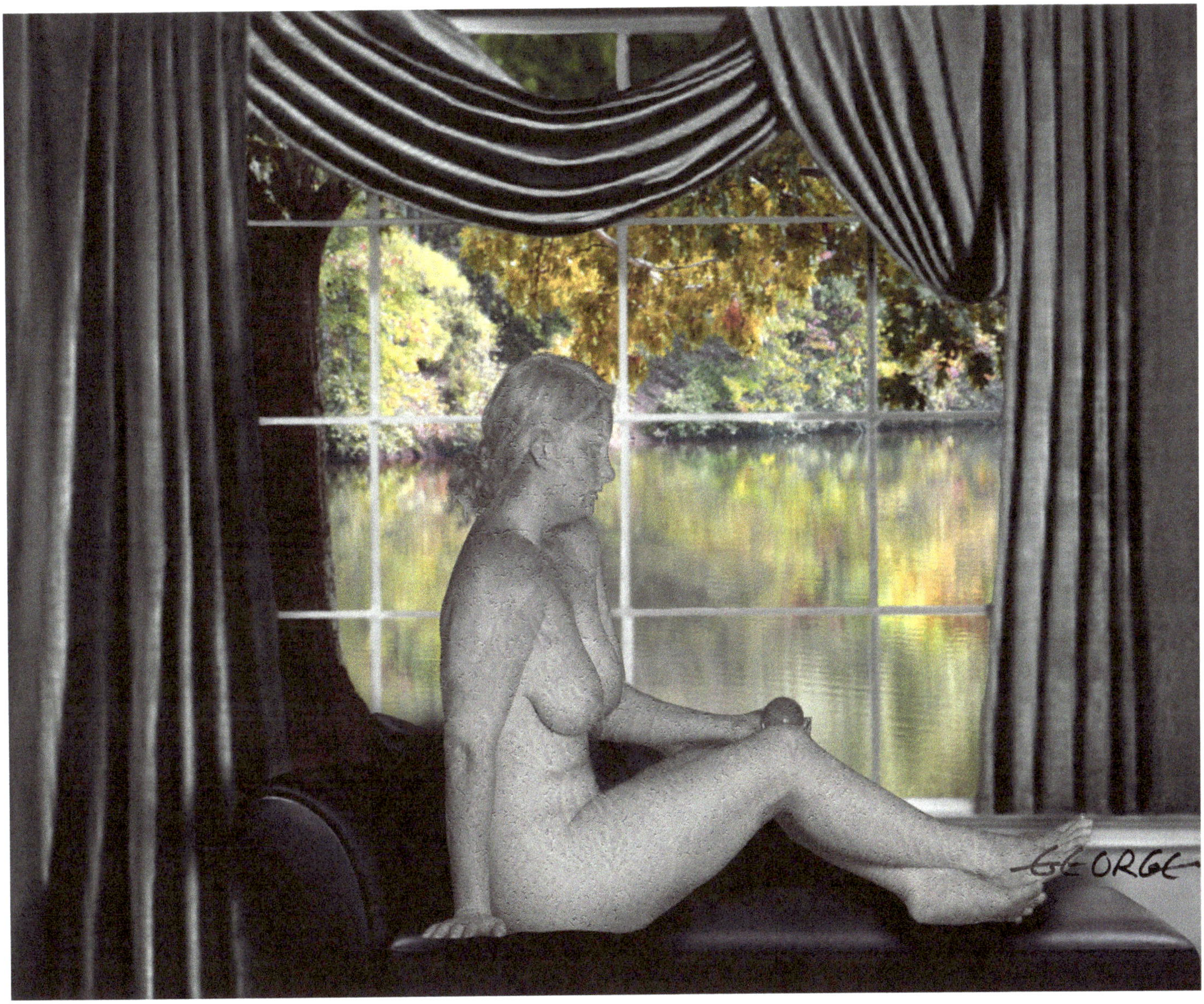
GEORGE

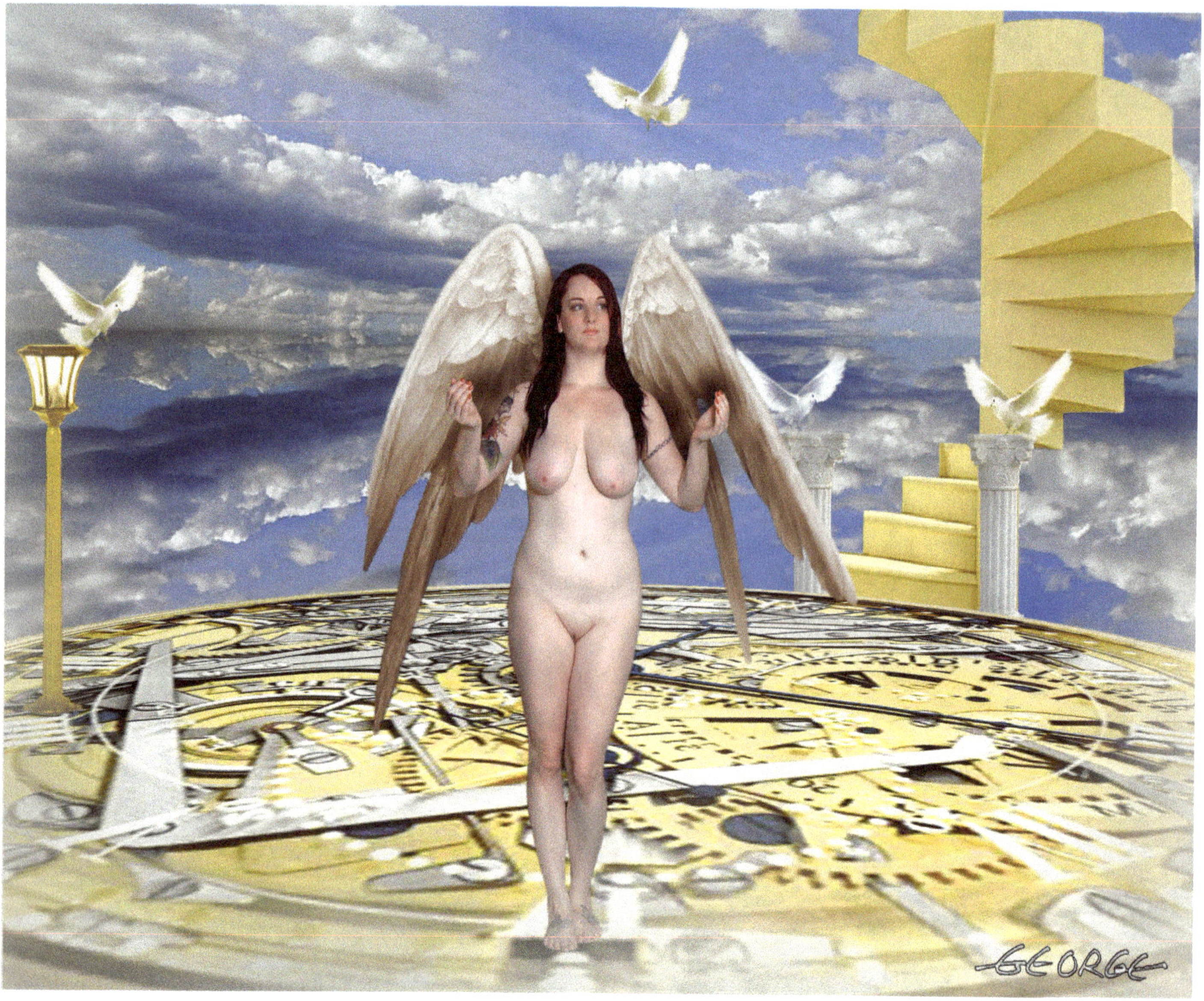
GEORGE

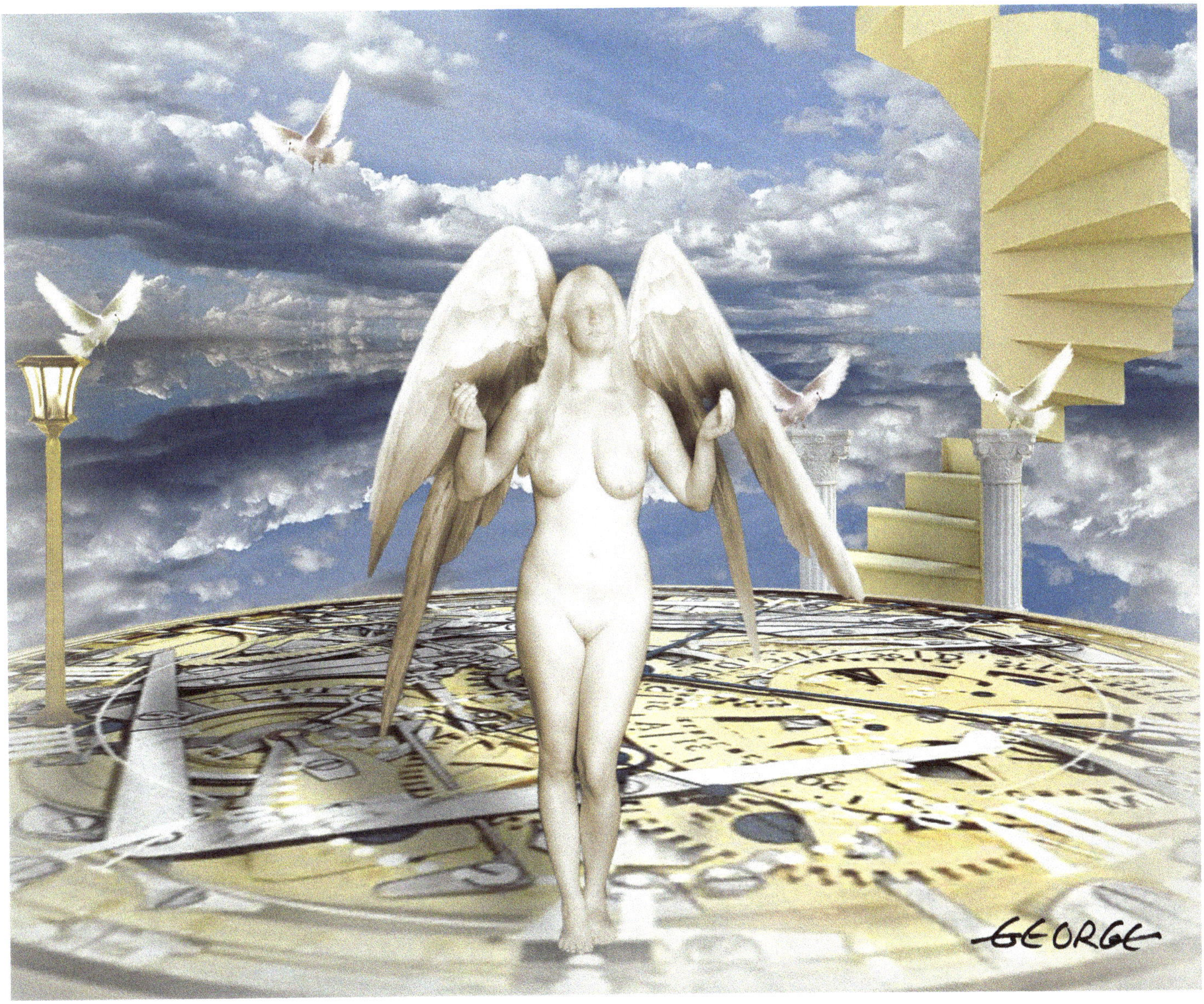
GEORGE

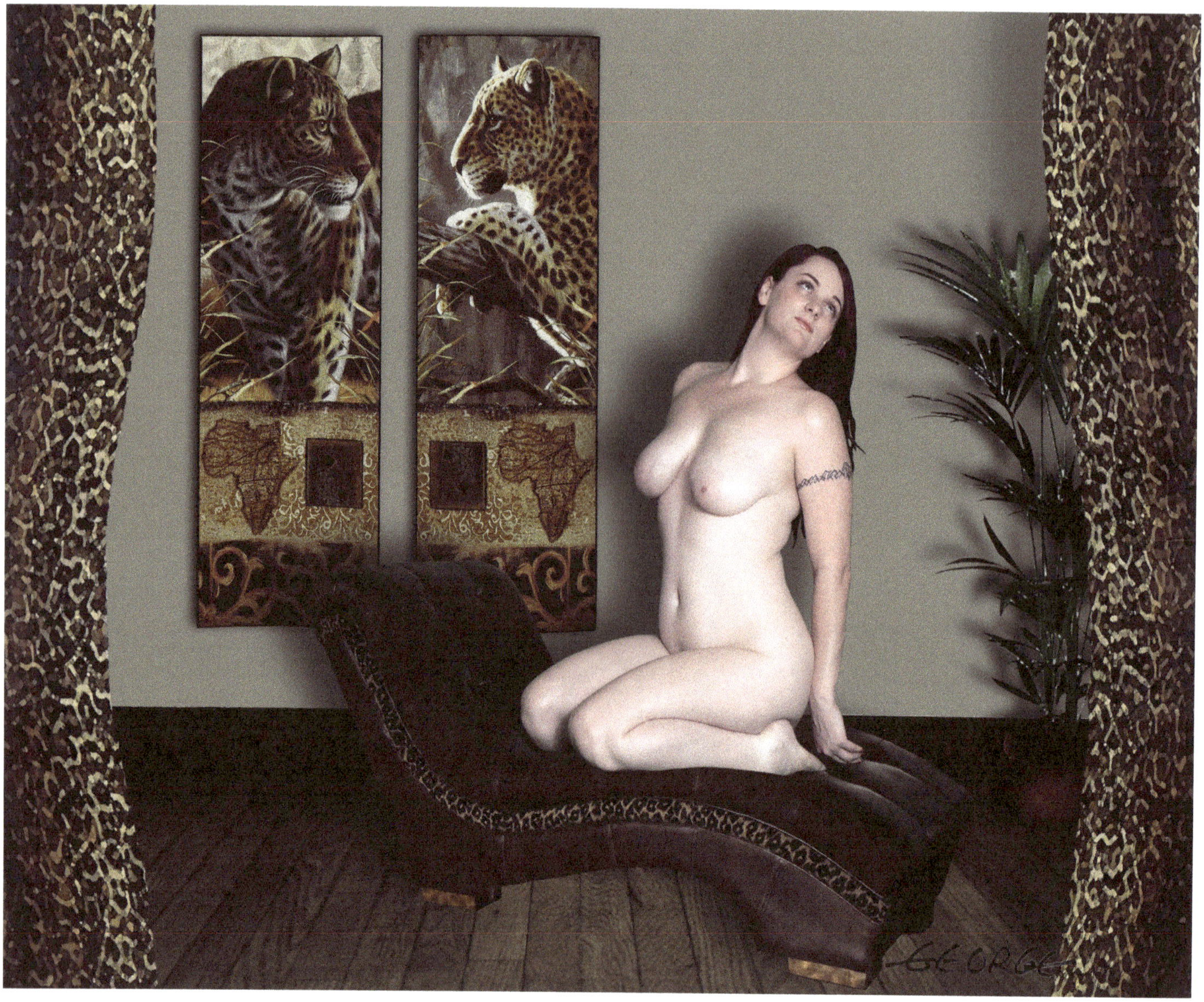
GEORGE

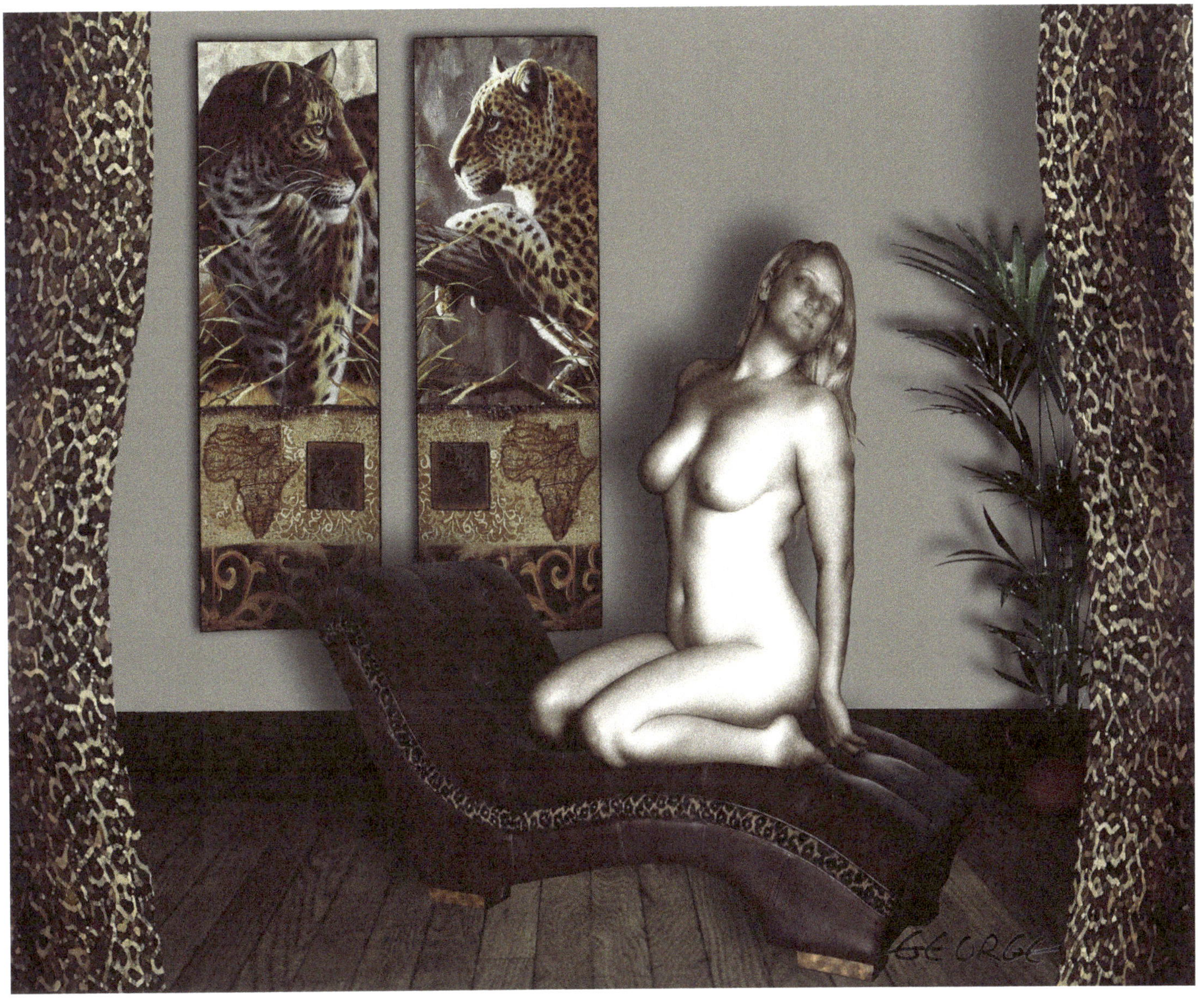
GEORGE

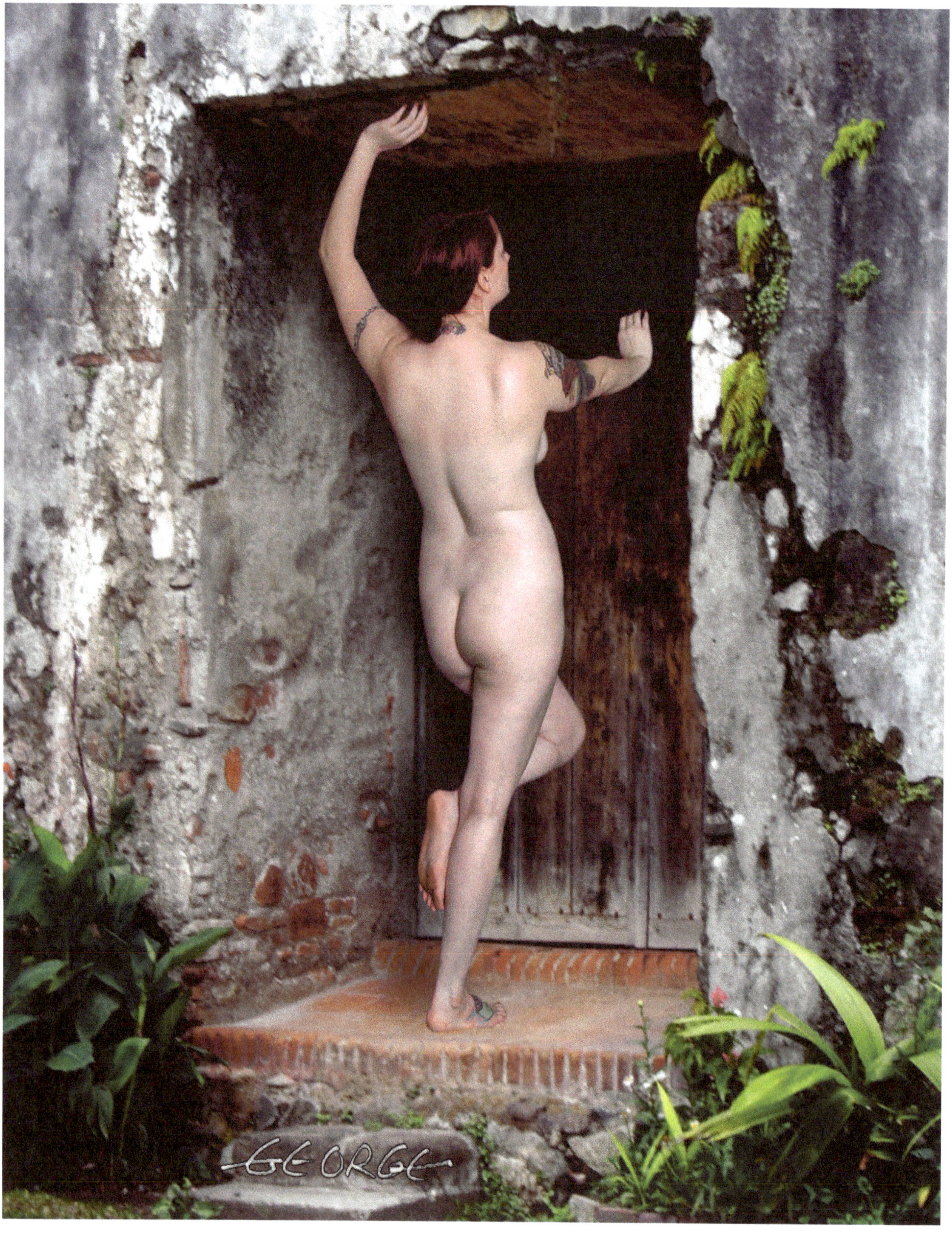
GEORGE

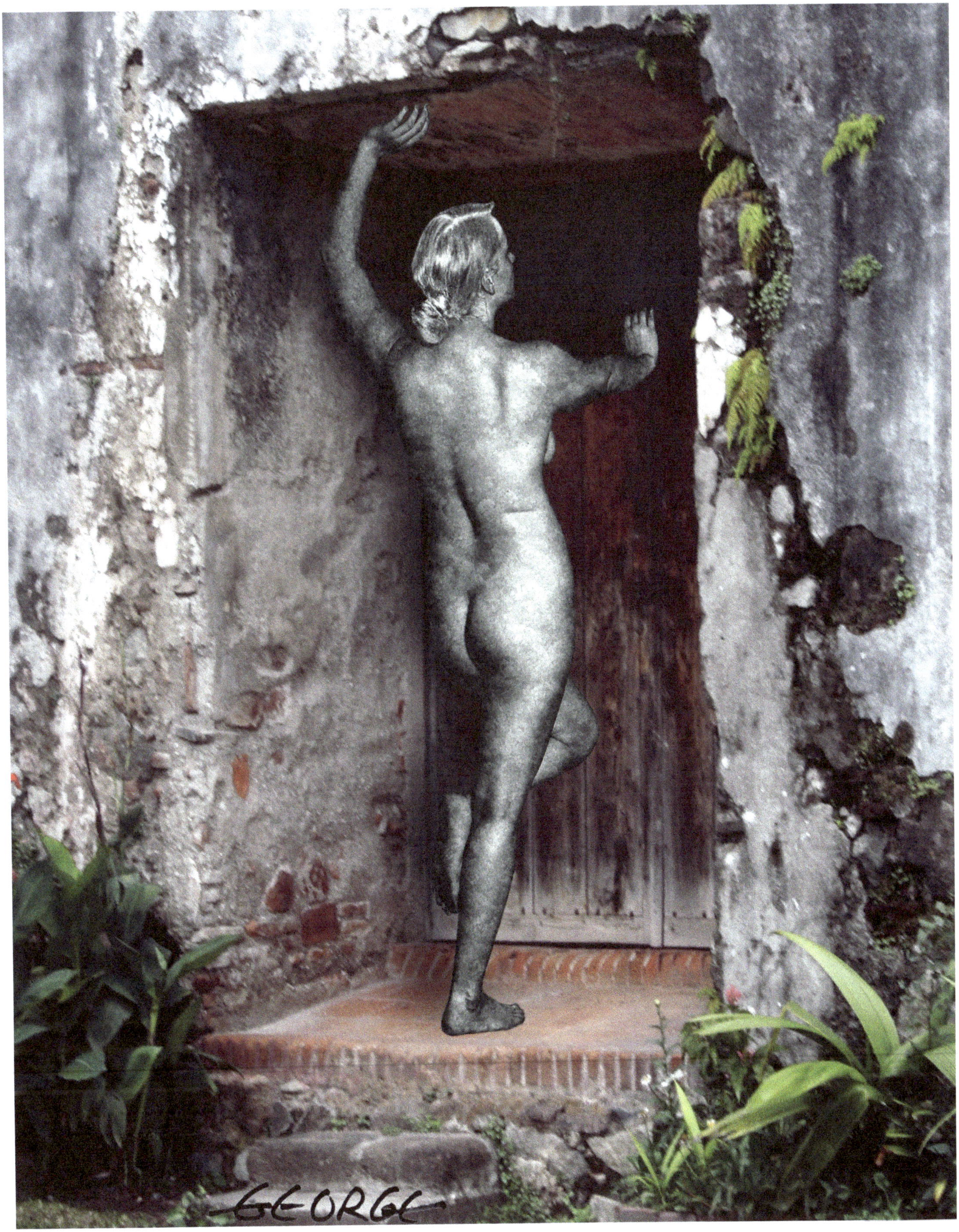
GEORGE

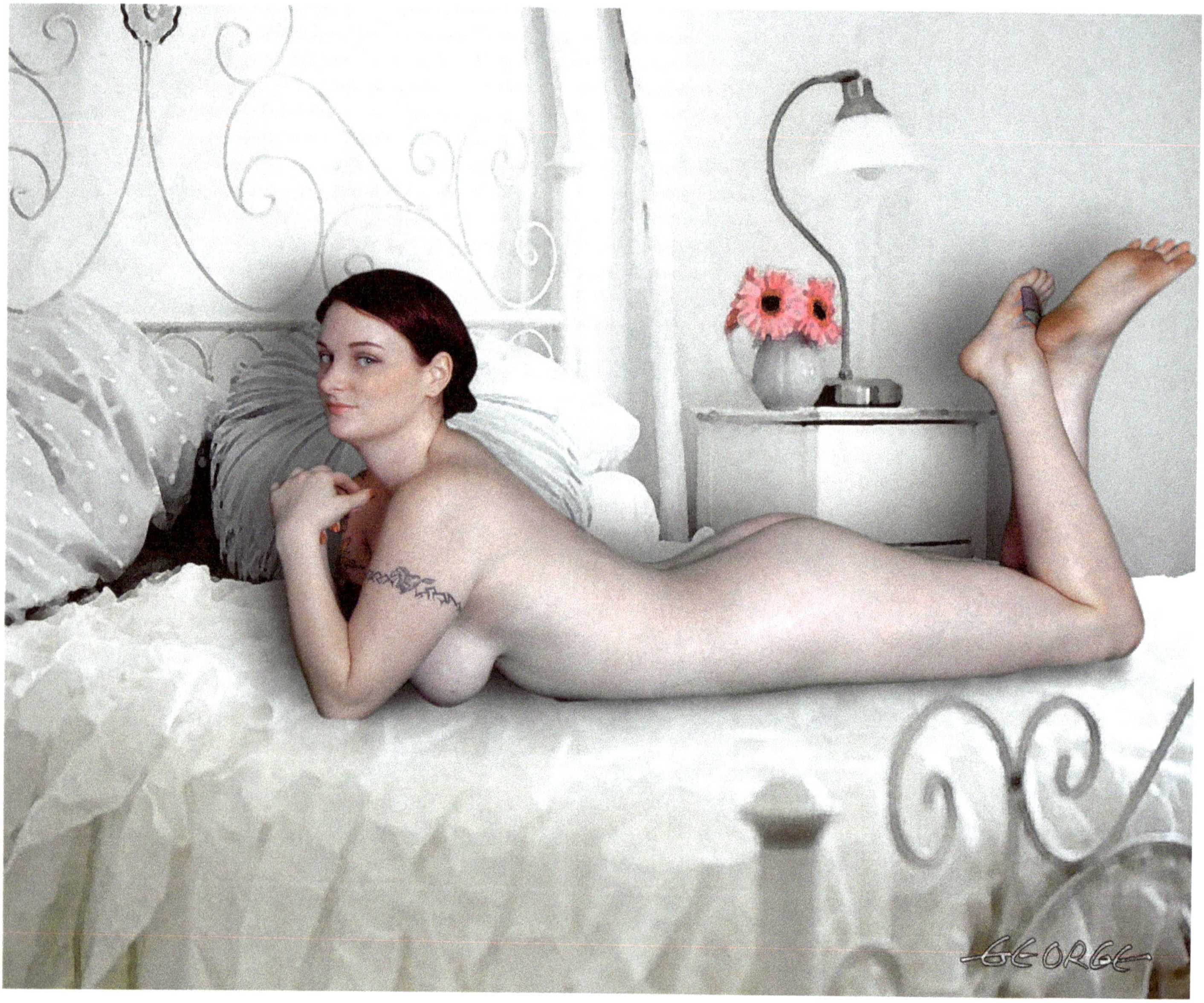
GEORGE

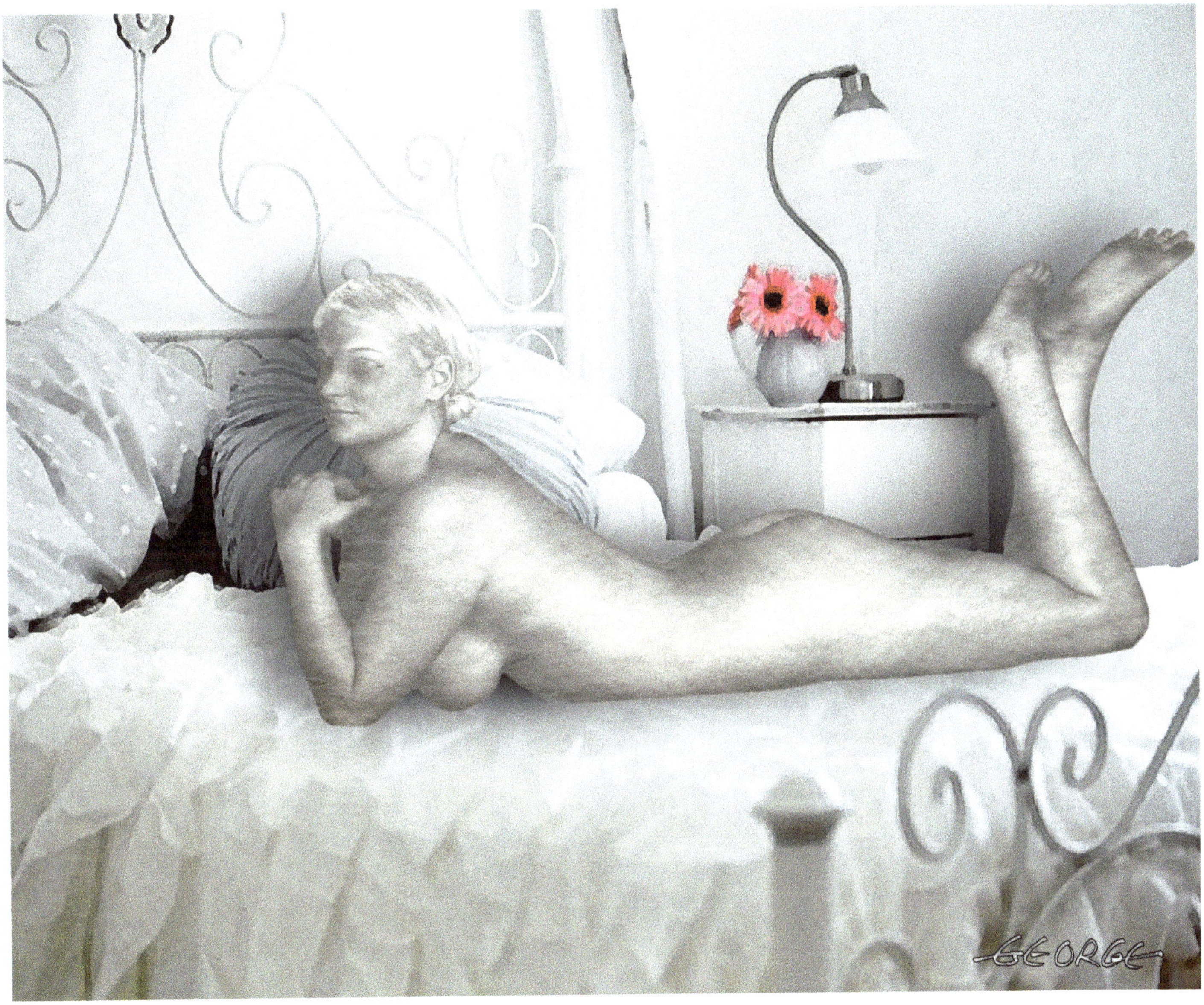
GEORGE

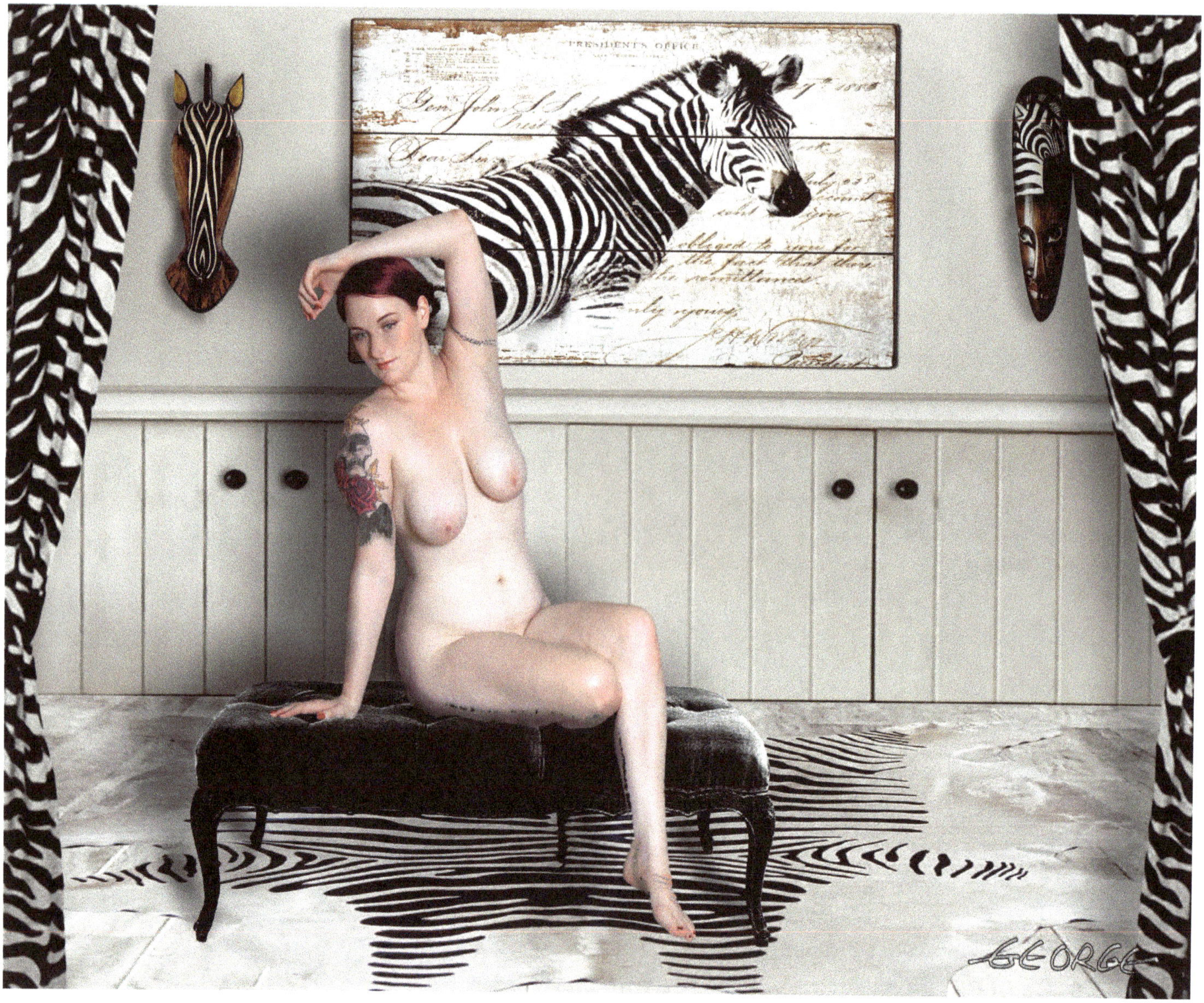
GEORGE

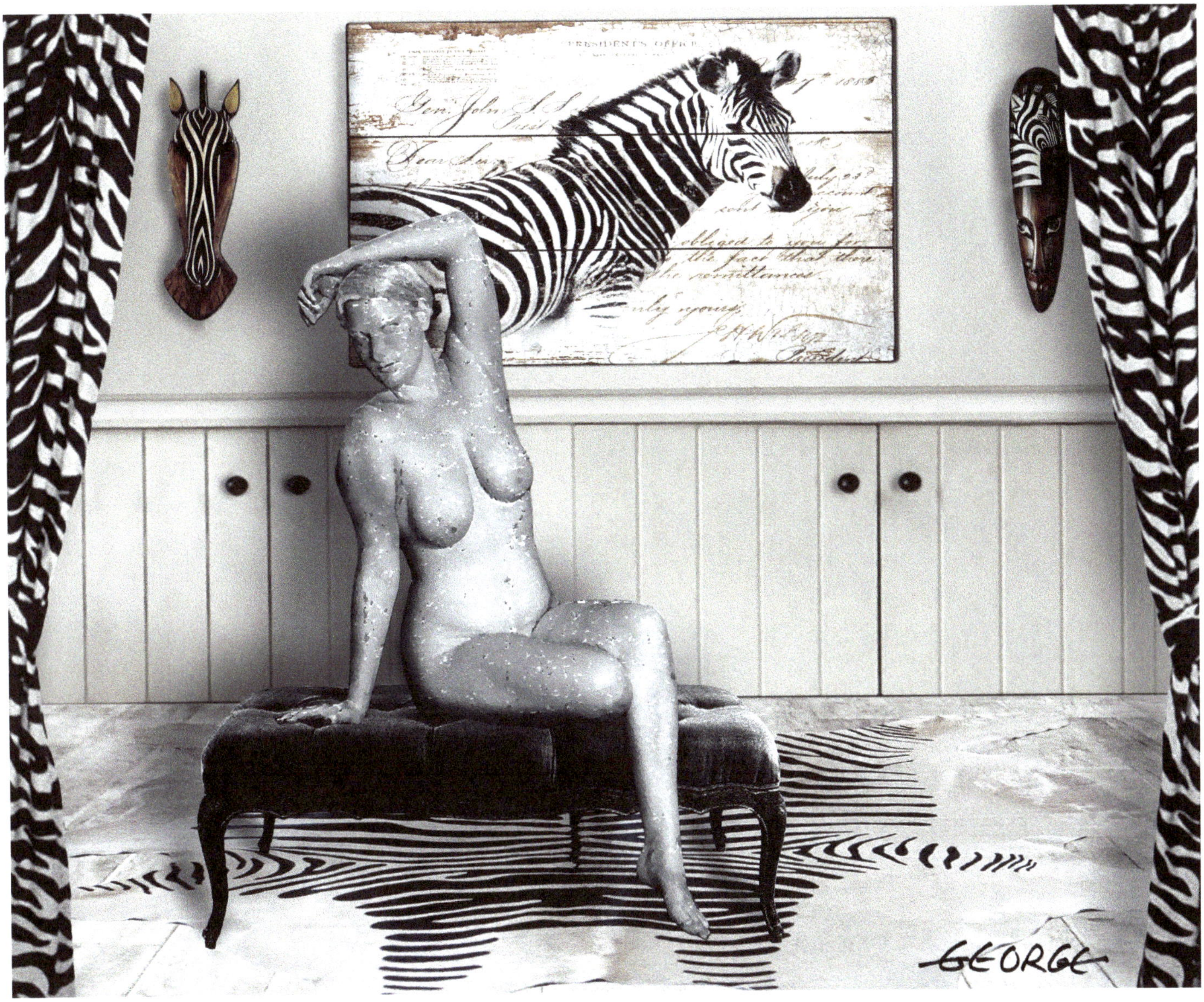
GEORGE

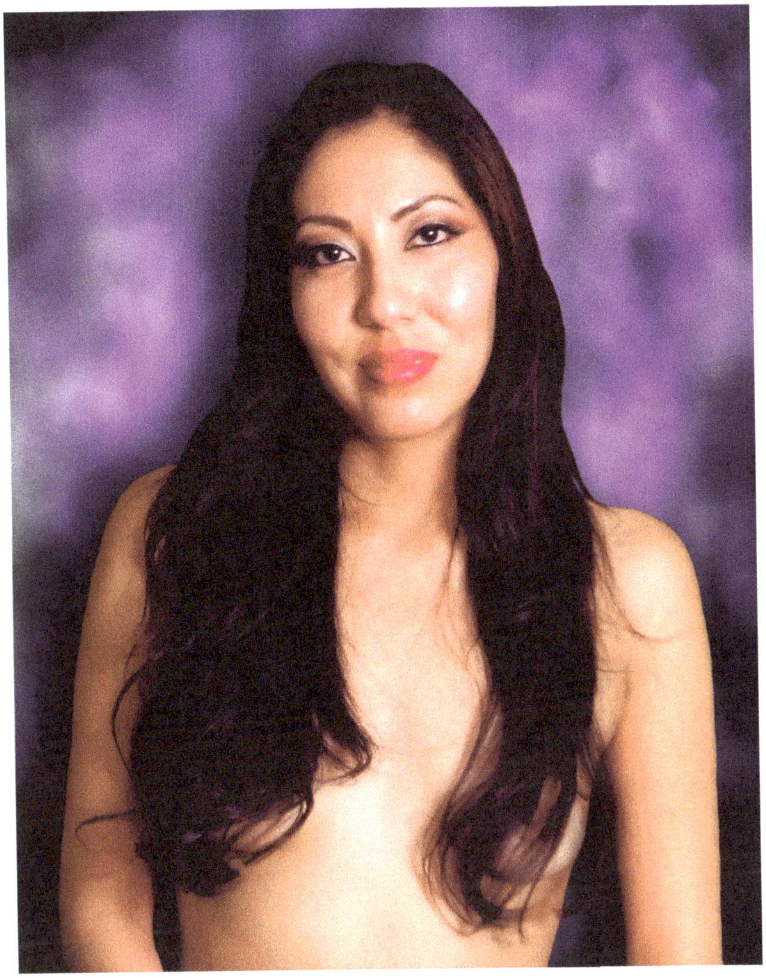

SHORTY GUTHERIE

Height 5'4" Weight 110 lbs Bust 34" Waist 27" Hips 0?" Cup B

I am full-blooded Native American, half Navajo and half White Mountain Apache. I am a mother, writer and copy editor; and for a few years now, a part-time model--a passion of mine. I love creating something beautiful and collaborating to achieve a great shot.

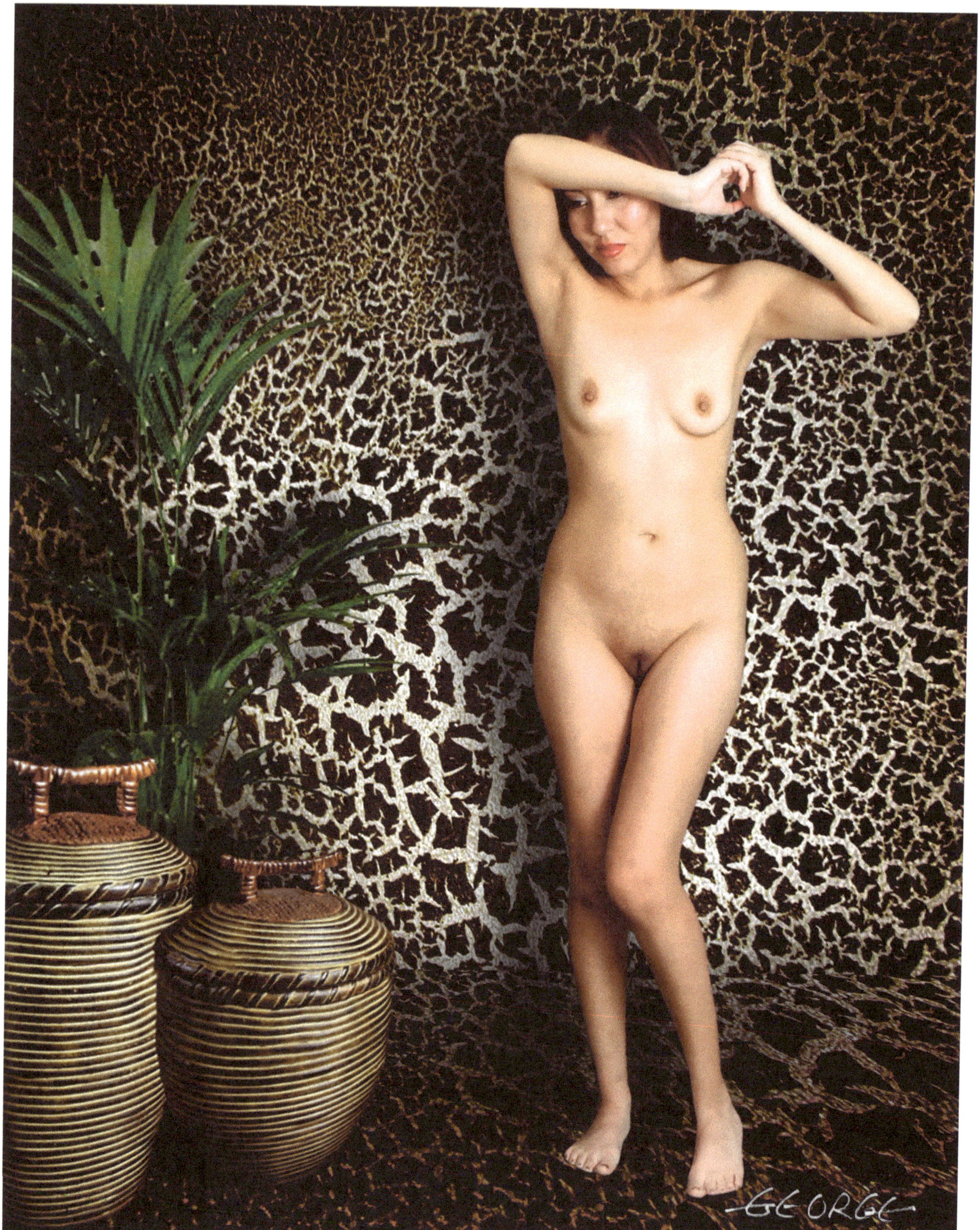
GEORGE

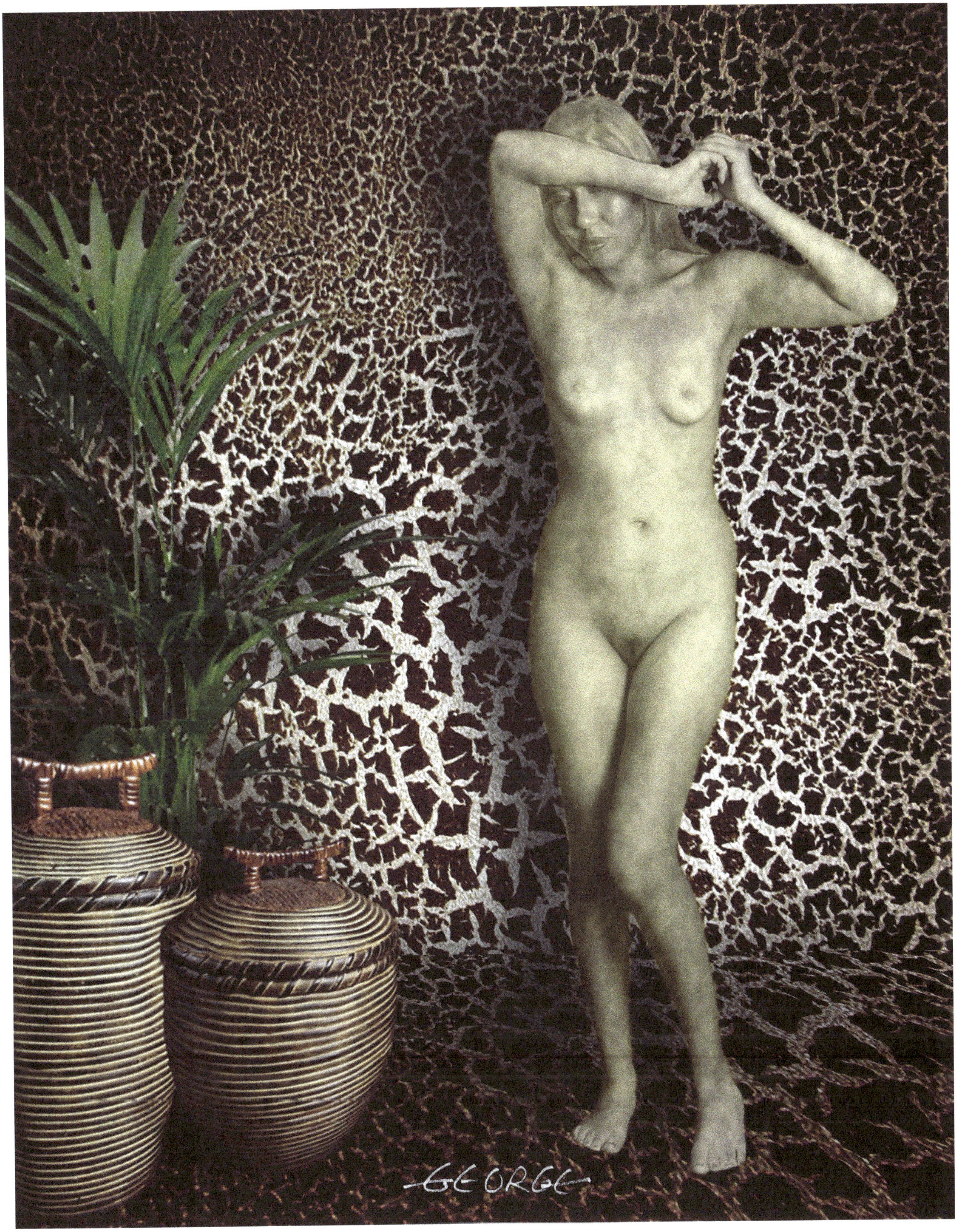
GEORGE

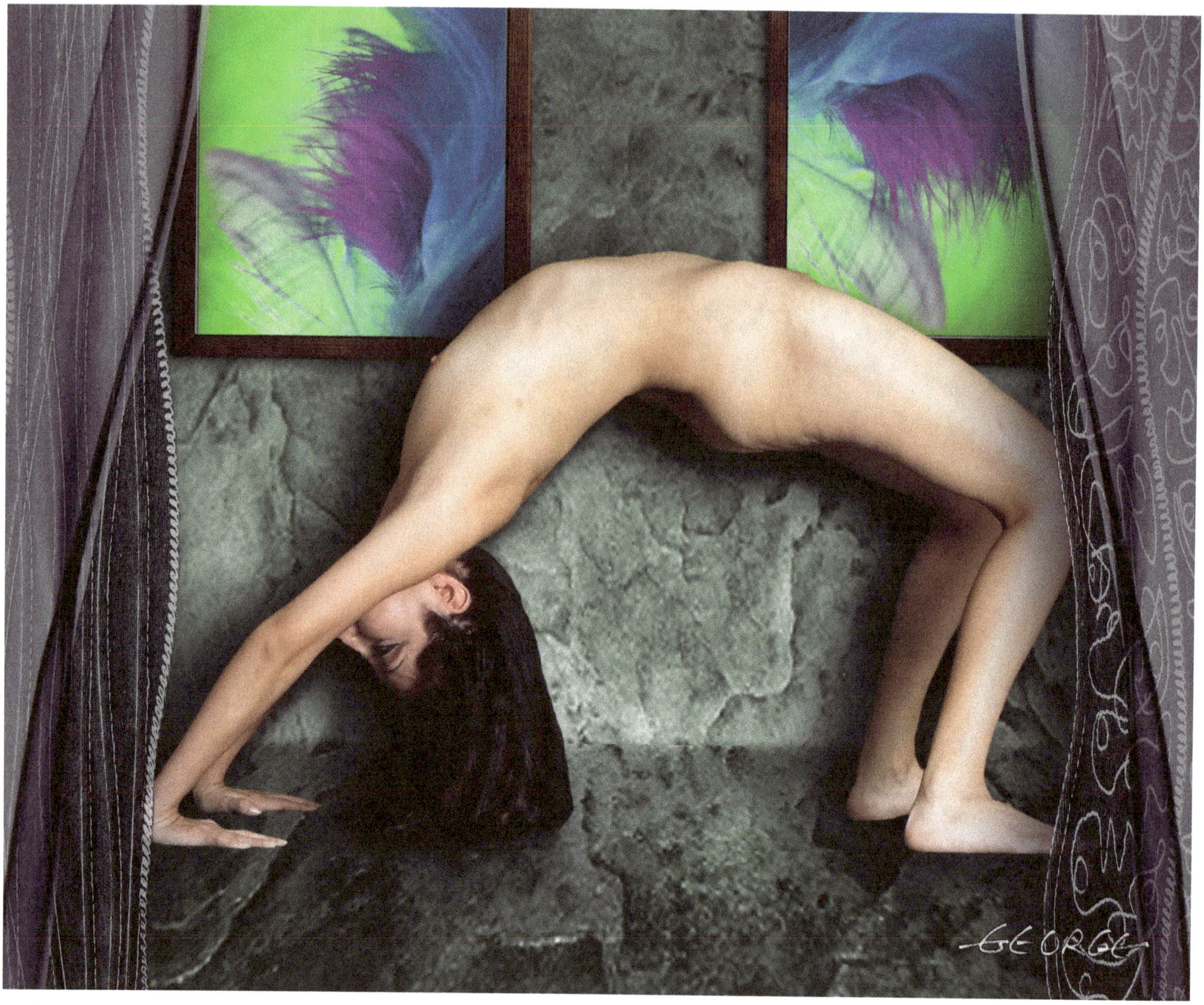
GEORGE

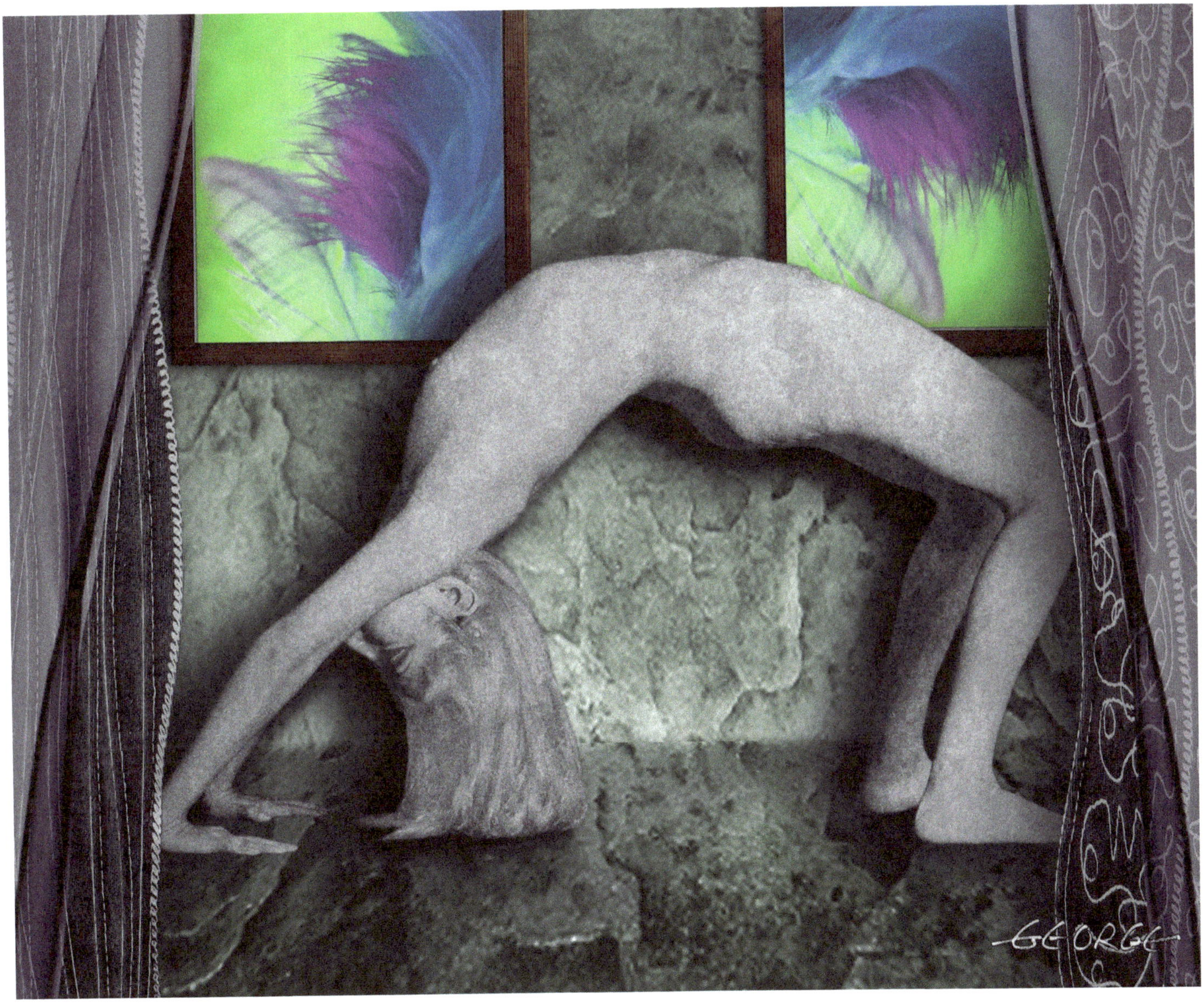
GEORGE

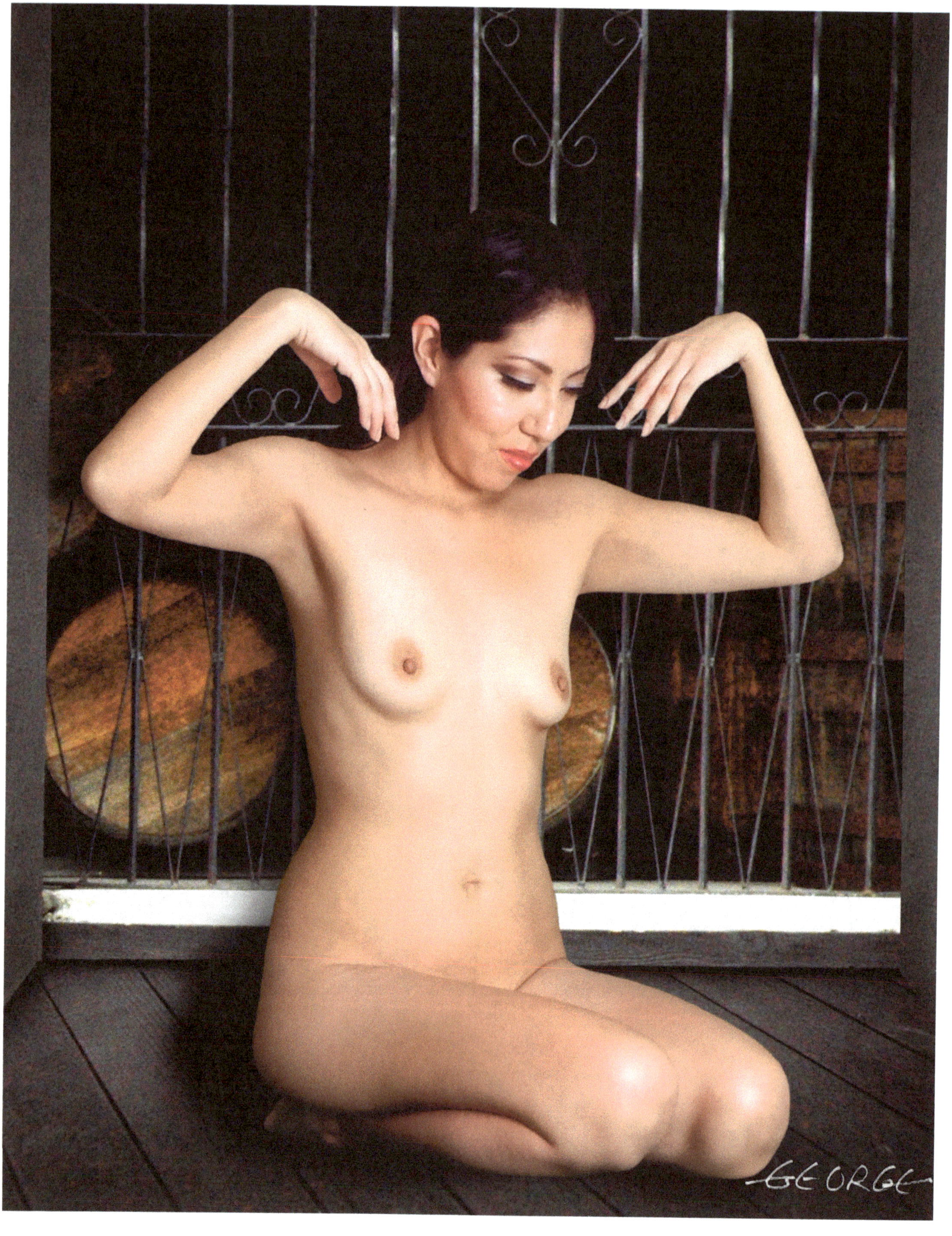
GEORGE

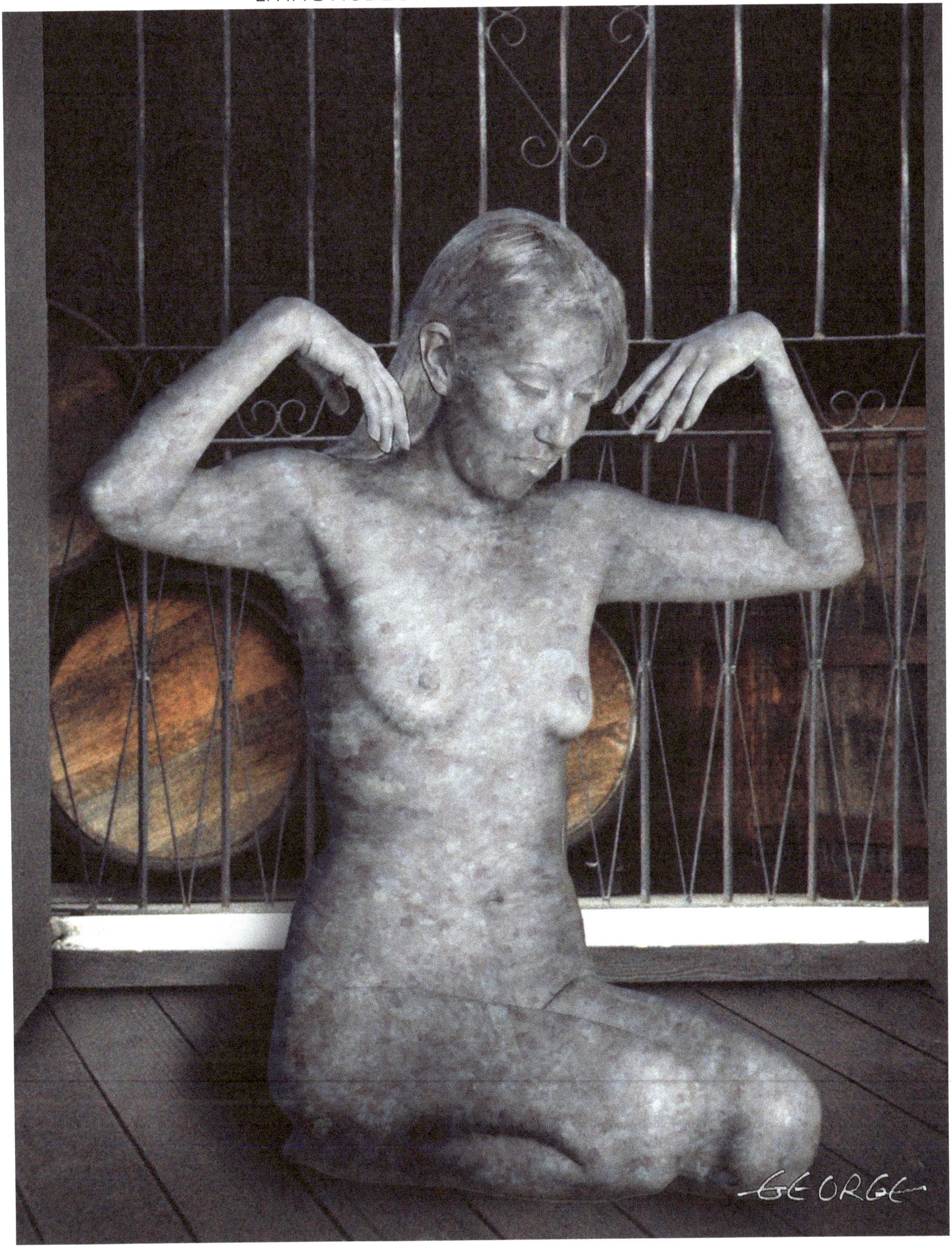
GEORGE

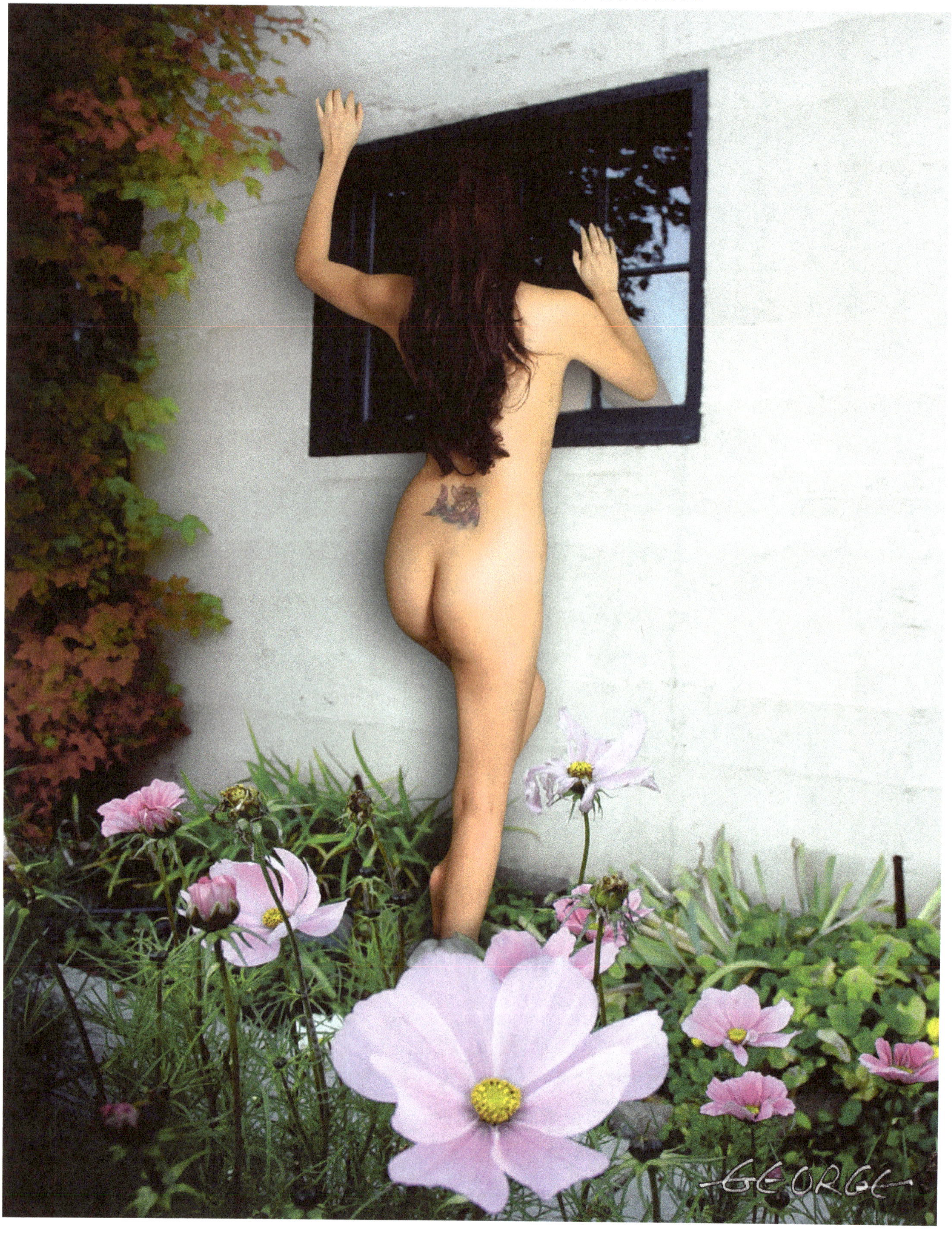
GEORGE

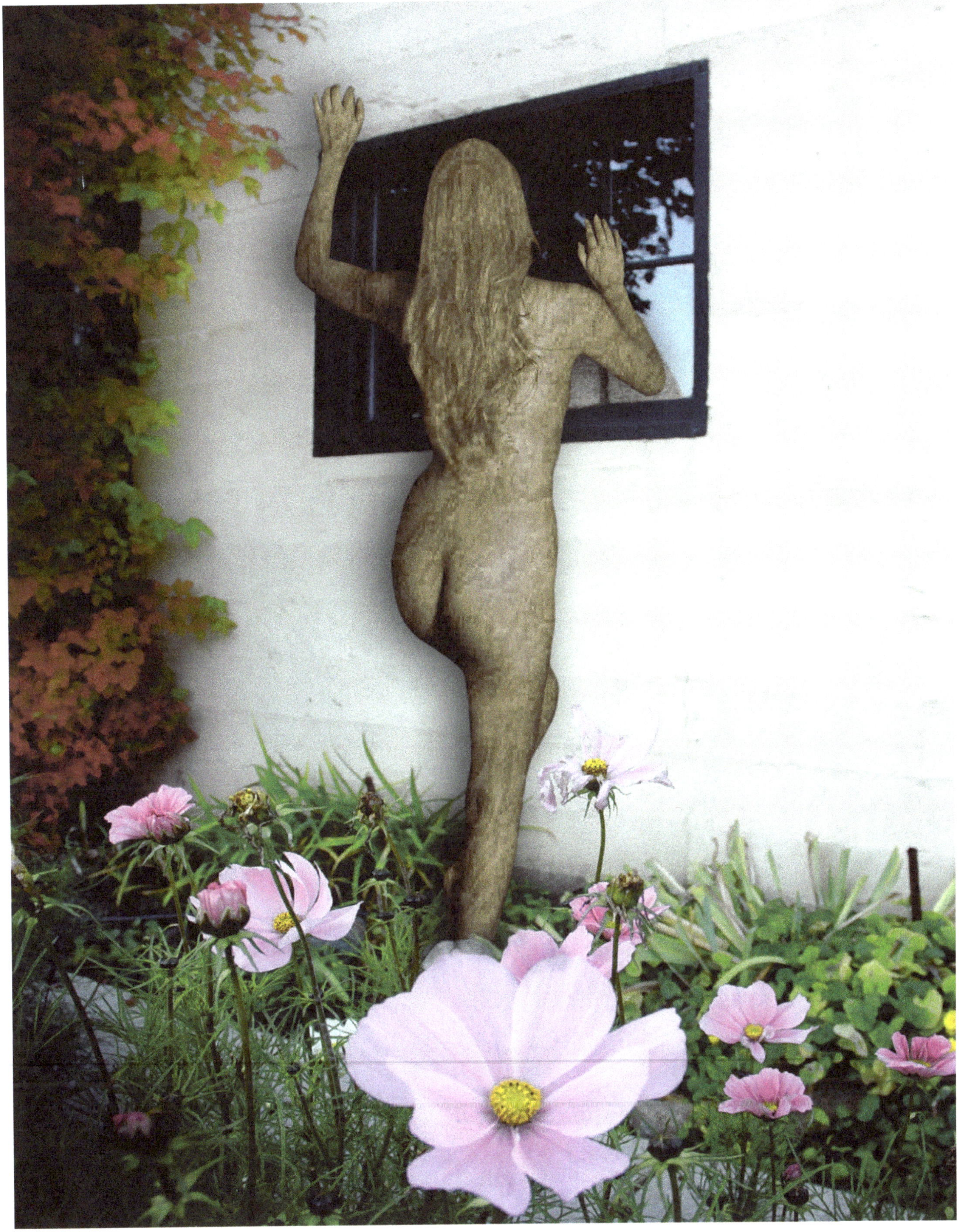

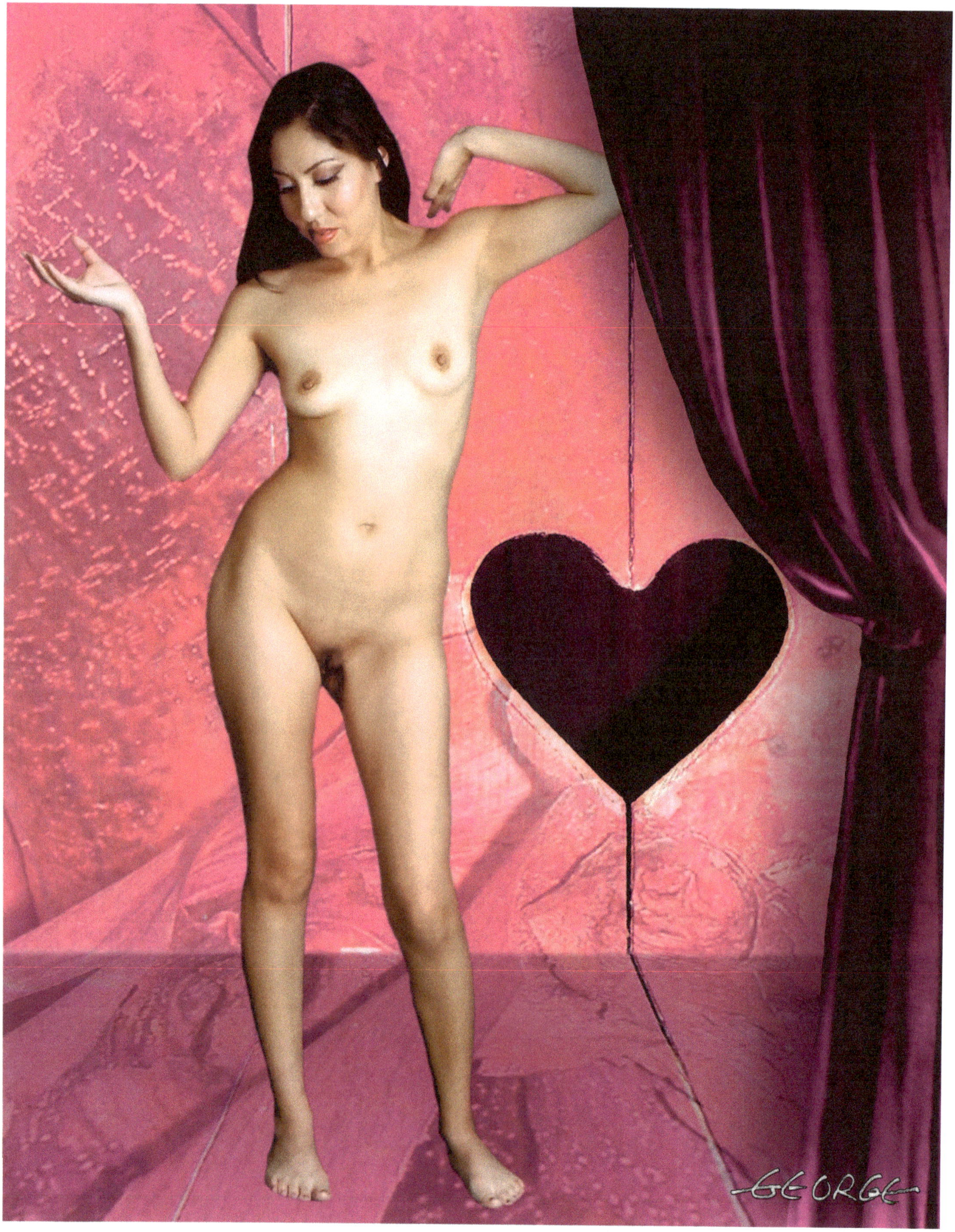
GEORGE

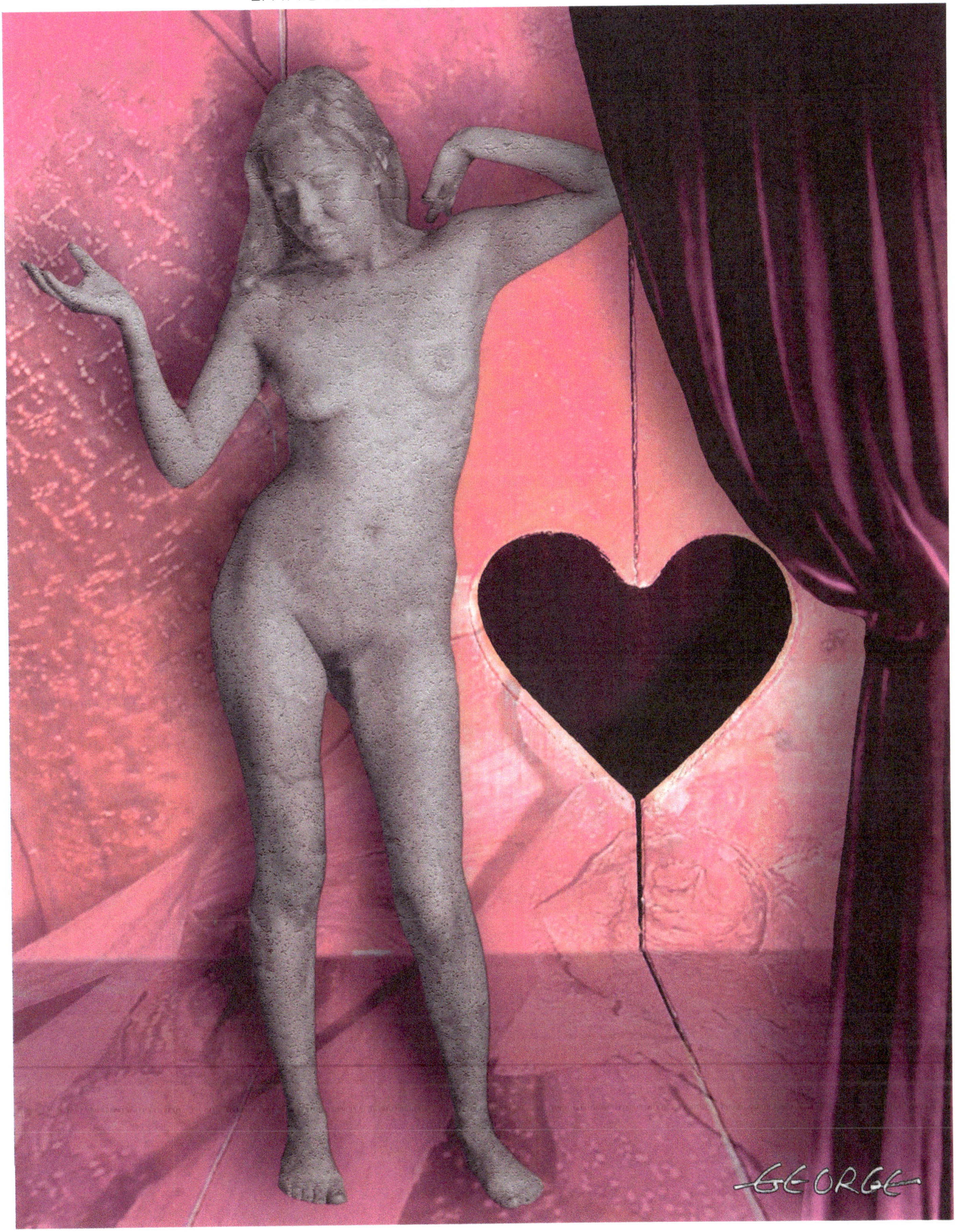
GEORGE

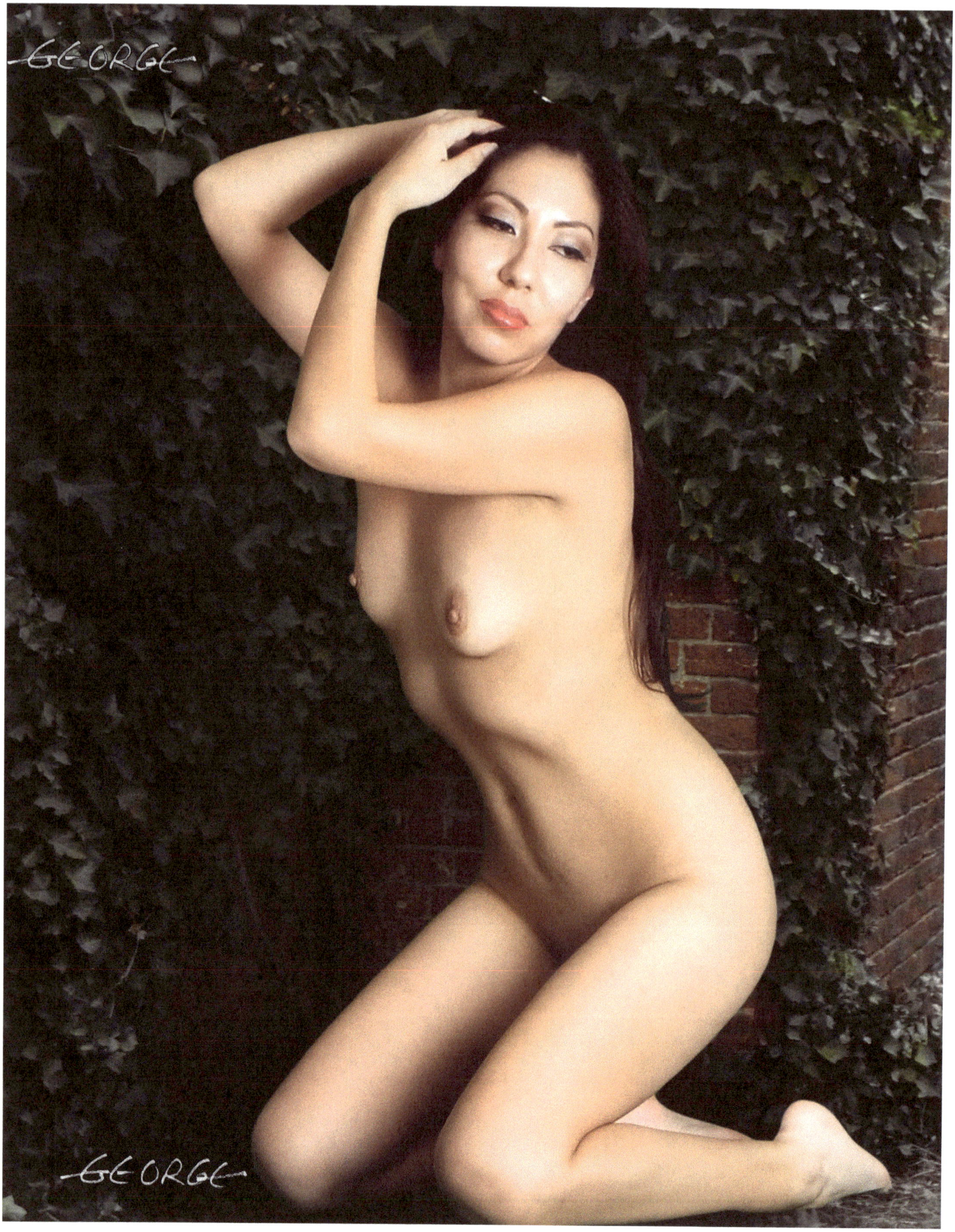
GEORGE
GEORGE

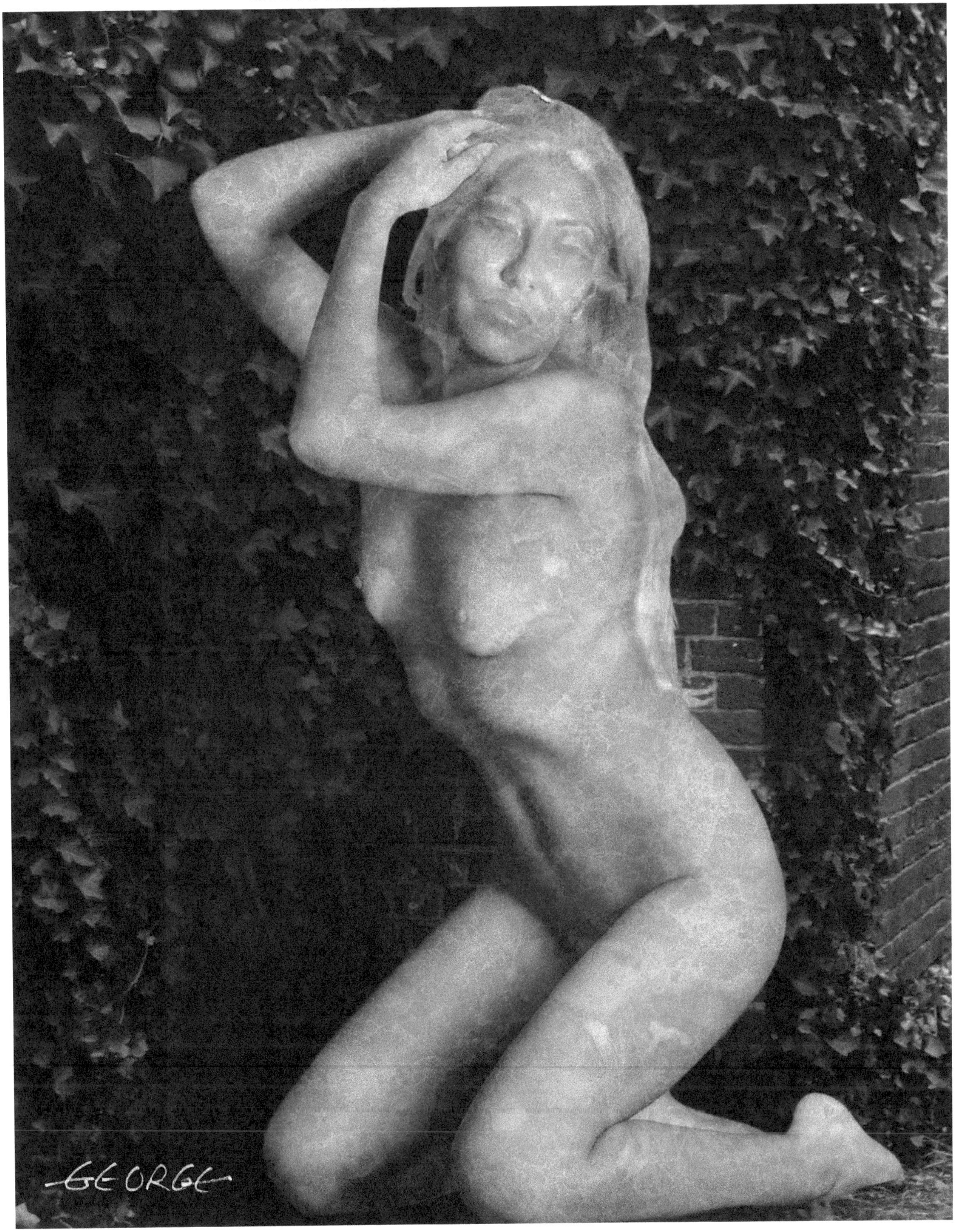
GEORGE

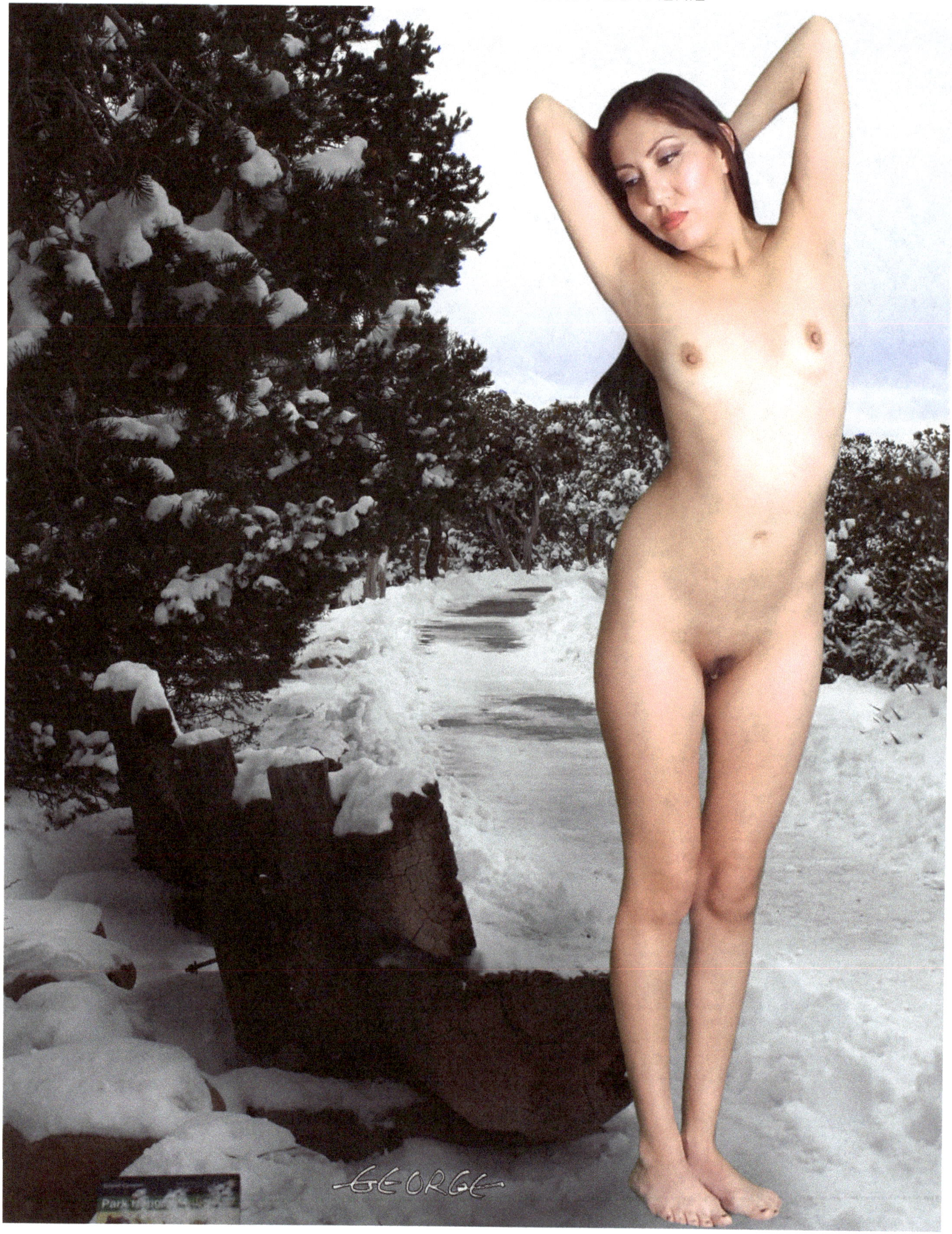
GEORGE

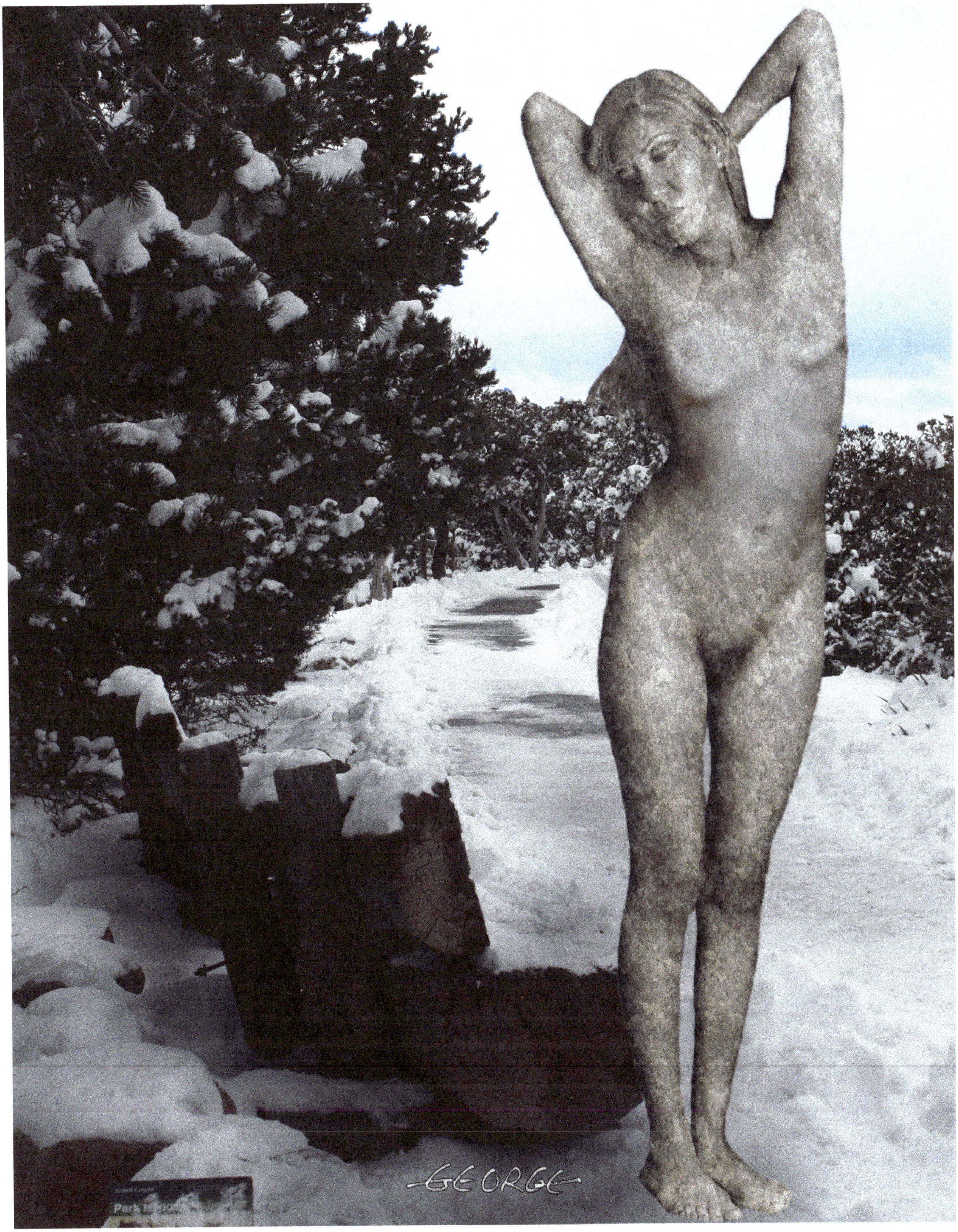
GEORGE

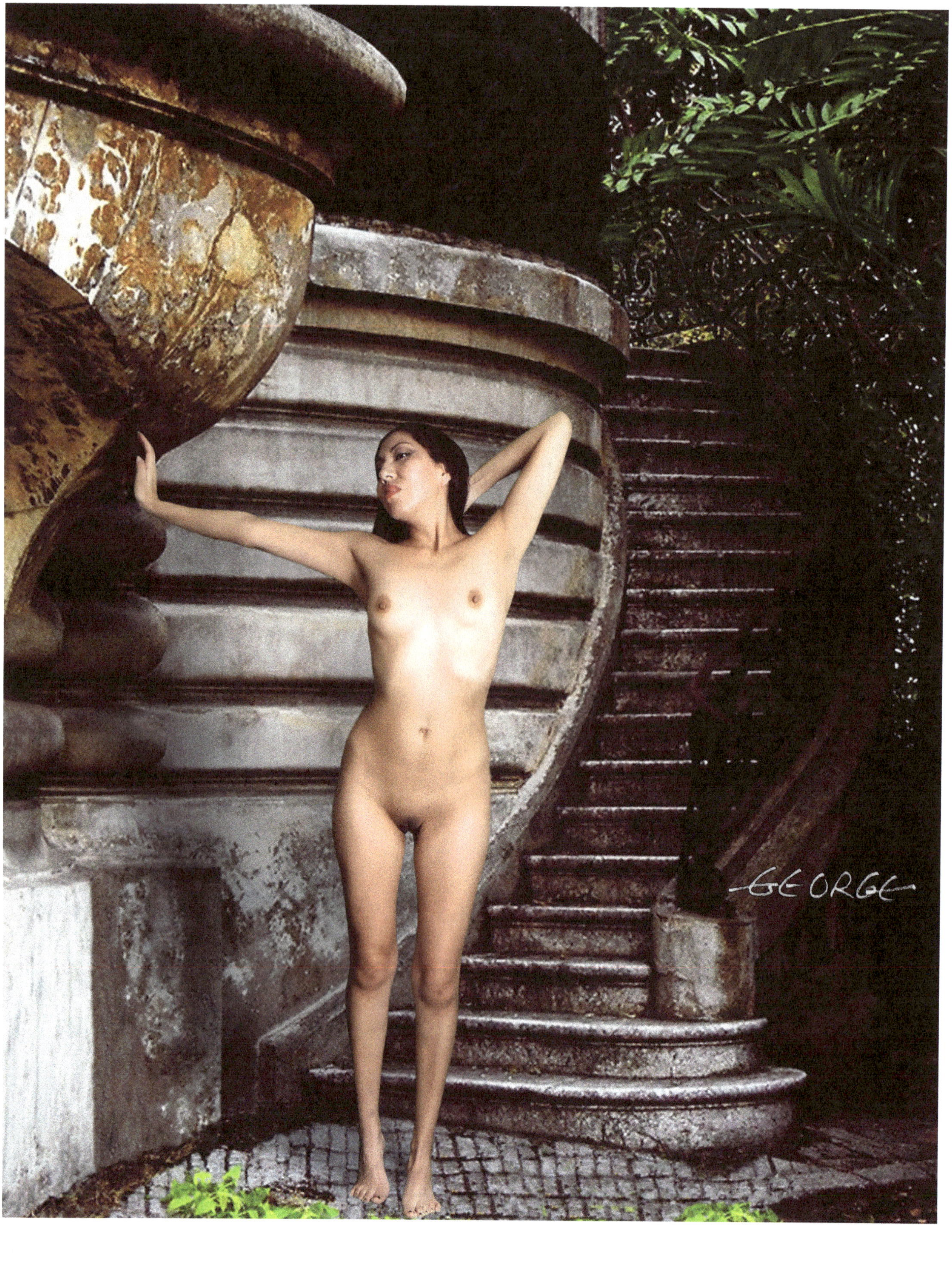
GEORGE

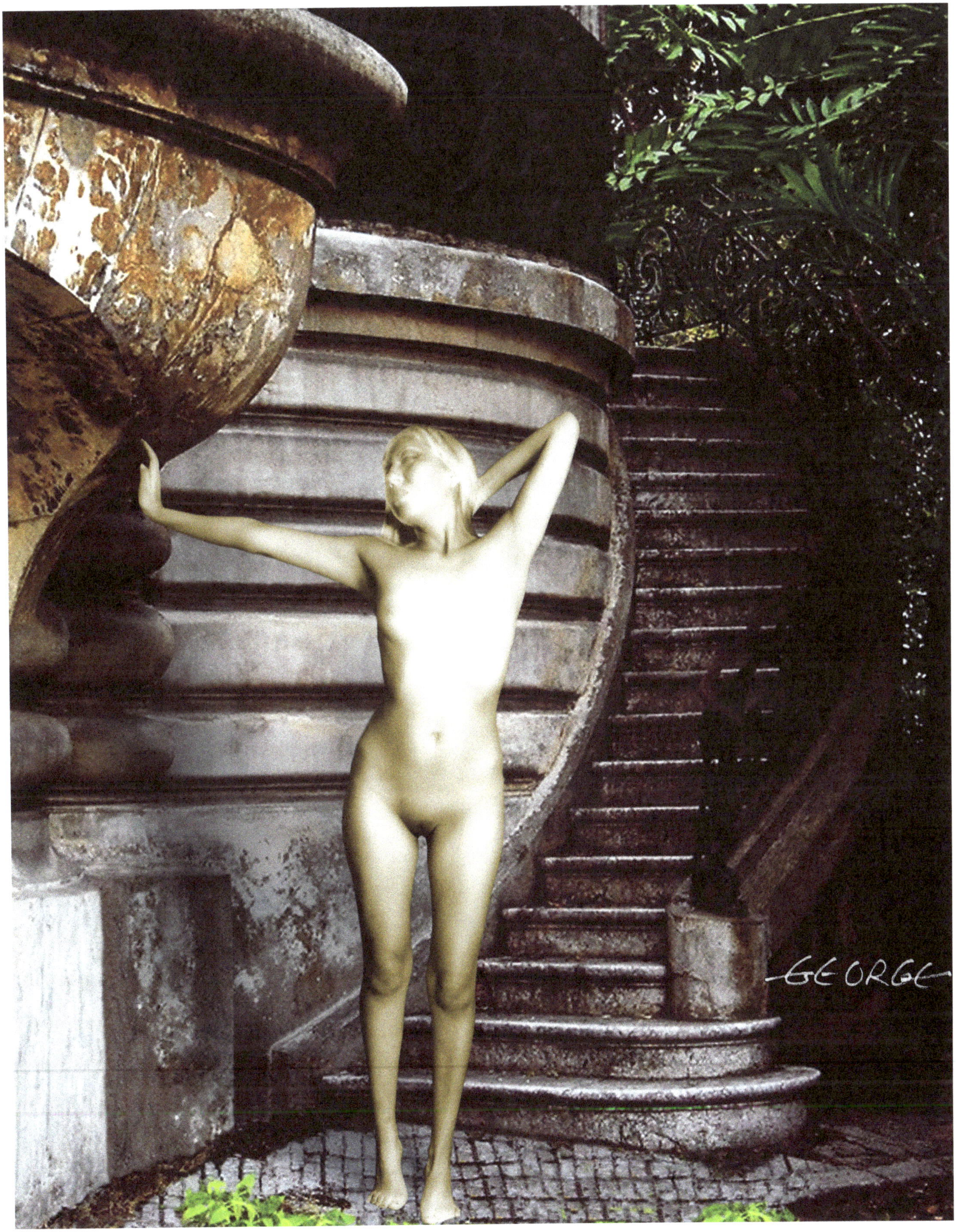
GEORGE

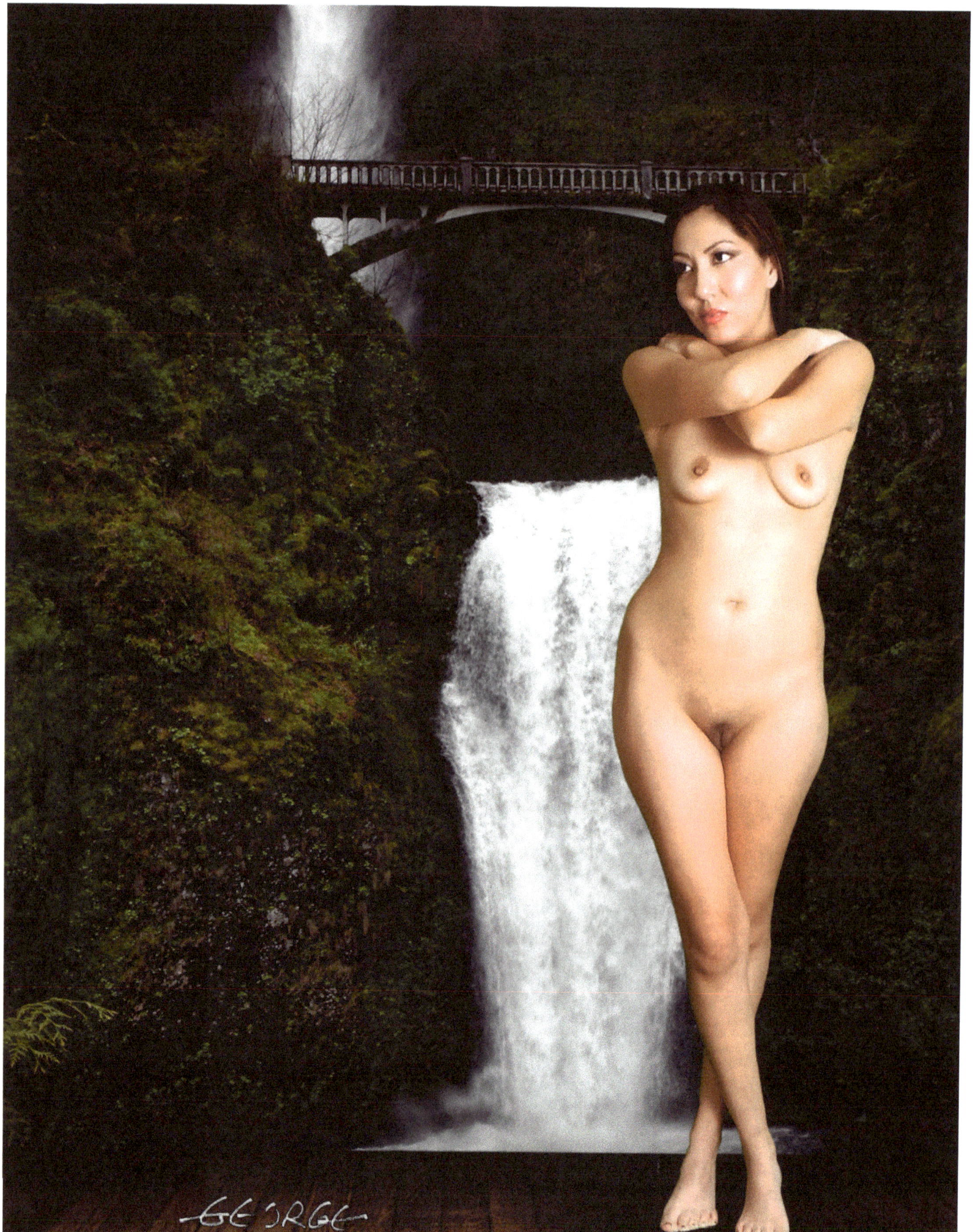
GEORGE

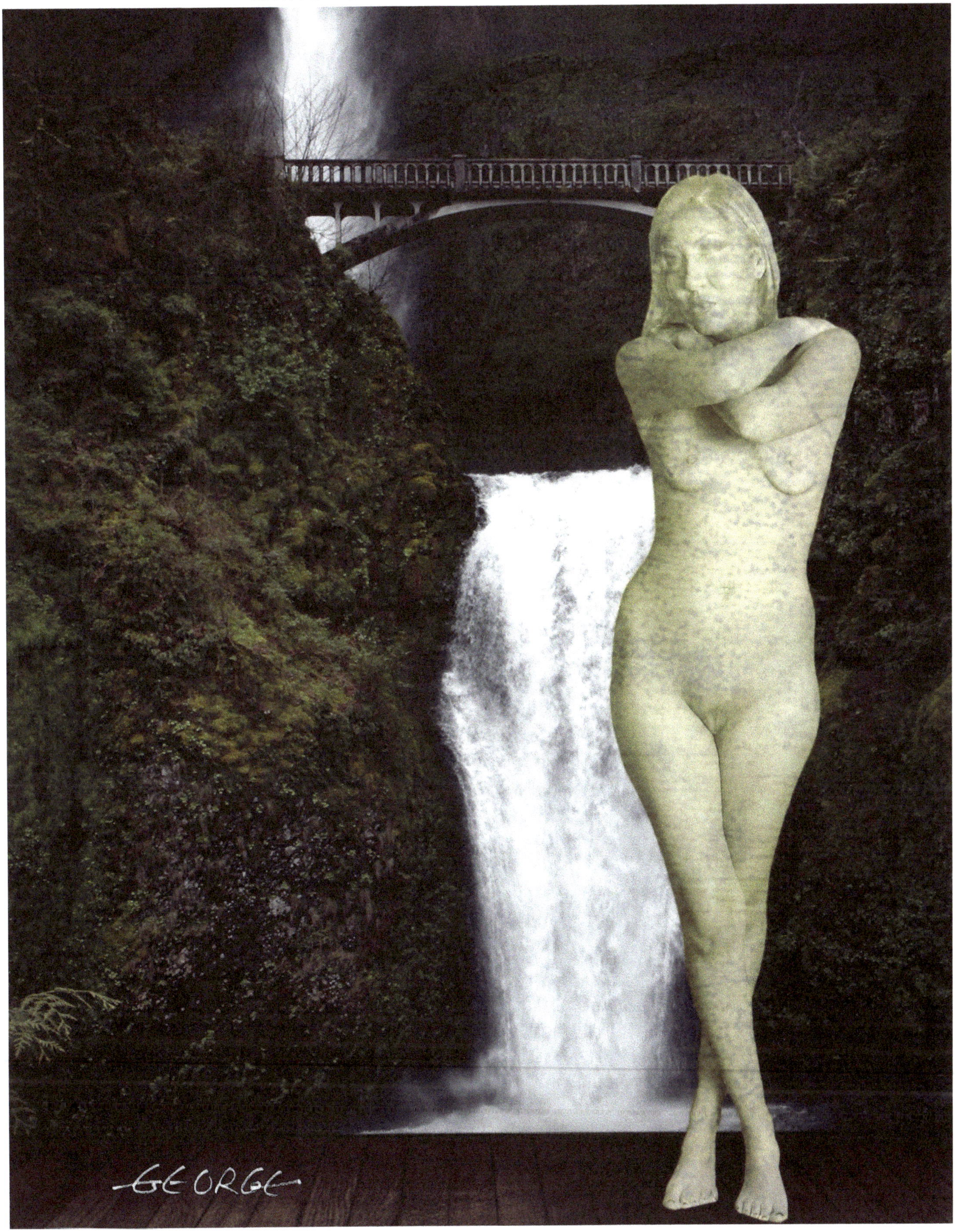
GEORGE

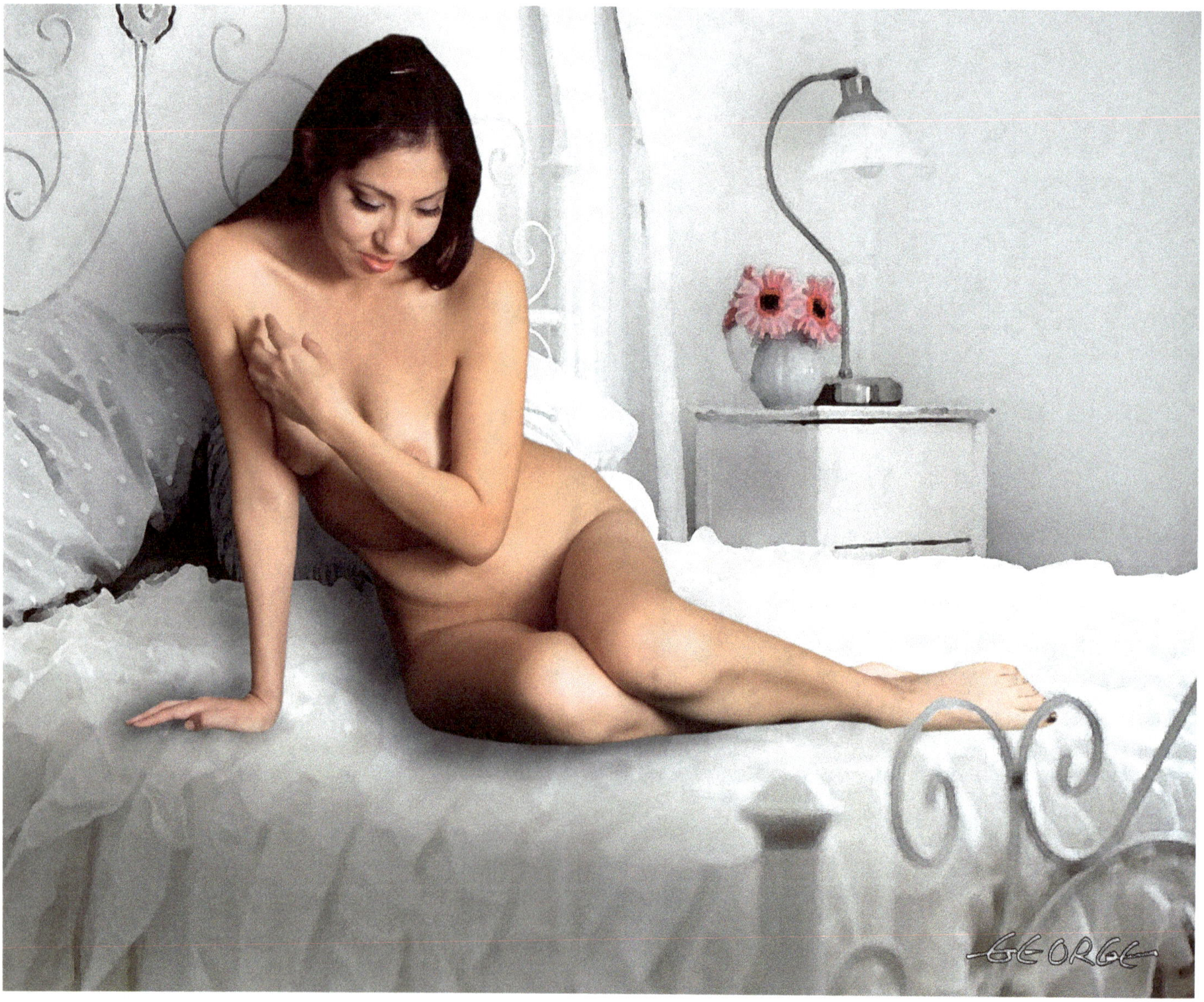
GEORGE

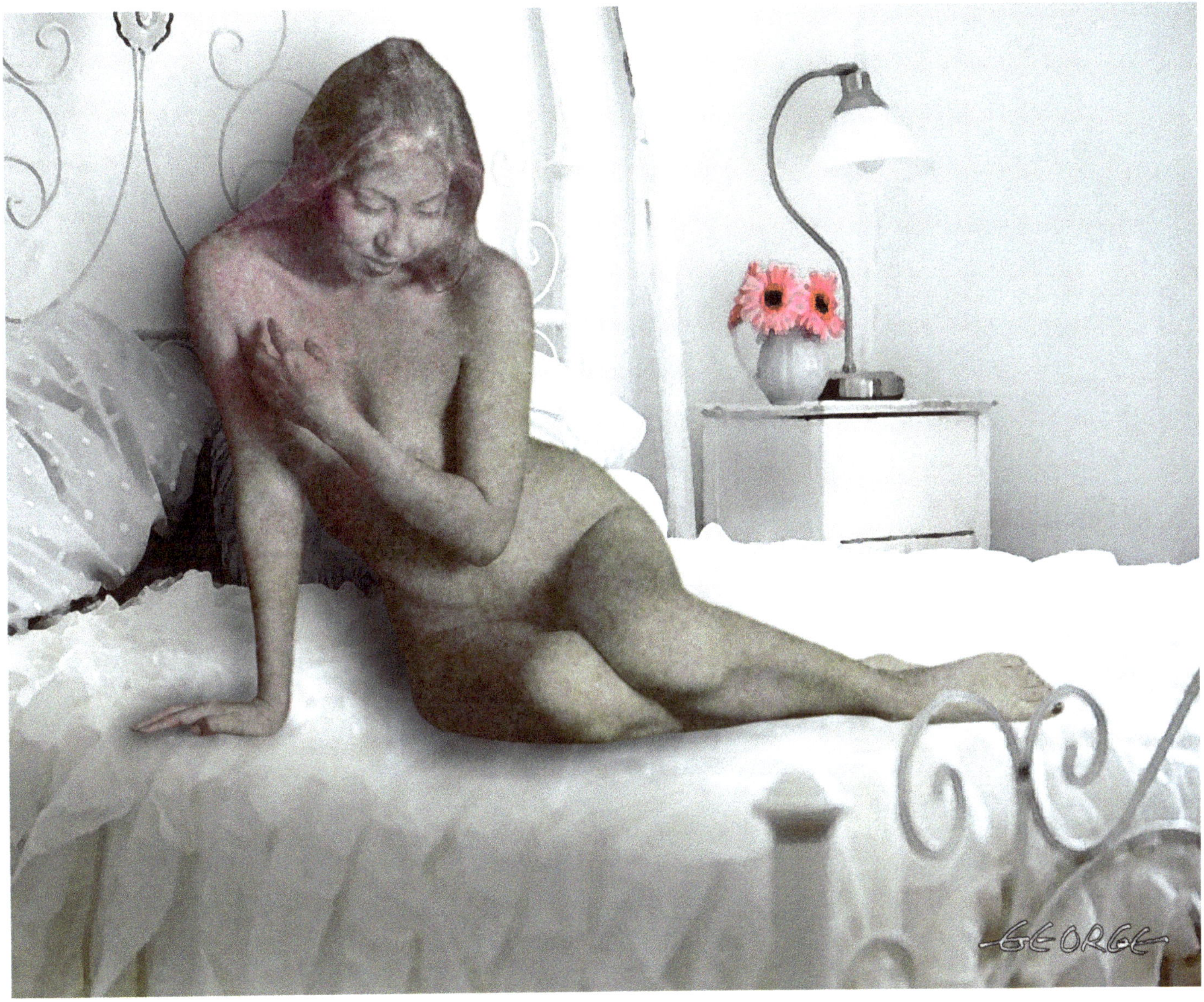
GEORGE